Explorations
in the Teaching
of English

Explorations in the Teaching of English

SECOND EDITION

Stephen N. Judy

MICHIGAN STATE UNIVERSITY

HARPER & ROW, PUBLISHERS, New York
Cambridge, Philadelphia, San Francisco,
London, Mexico City, São Paulo, Sydney

Sponsoring Editor: George A. Middendorf
Project Editor: Eleanor Castellano
Production Manager: Jeanie Berke
Compositor: TriStar Graphics

Art Studio: Vantage Art Inc.

This work was originally published under the title *Explorations in the Teaching of Secondary English: A Source Book for Experimental Teaching.*

Explorations in the Teaching of English, Second Edition

Library of Congress Cataloging in Publication Data

Judy, Stephen N
    Explorations in the teaching of English.

    Previous ed. published under title: Explorations in
the teaching of secondary English.
    Bibliography: p.
    Includes index.
    1. English language—Study and teaching. I. Title.
PE1065.J8 1981   428′.007′1073   80–23880
ISBN 0-06-043445-7

For Wallace Douglas
Teacher, Advisor, Mentor, and Friend

Contents

9
The Process of Composing 185

10
Writing for the Here and Now 208

11
Exploring Language 228

12
The Spoken Language 247

13
Classroom Drama 261

Preface

The English teacher today faces an incredibly complex task. Attached to the simple title "Teacher of English" are responsibilities that can tax the capabilities of a dozen specialists in diverse fields. It is not enough that the English teacher takes on two-thirds of the 3Rs with less than one-tenth of the school budget. Beyond the teaching of fundamentals of literacy, many other assignments remain. The English teacher must be reading consultant and diagnostician, literary critic, writing teacher, librarian, media specialist, linguist, and even psychologist and counselor. These roles are multiplying and becoming more complex in an electronic age of television, telephones, cassette recorders, communications satellites, video tape, information retrieval systems, and popular films.

Adding further complexity, the schools are awash with "innovative" approaches that, it is alleged, will solve the teacher's problems. The teacher must often choose among programs with widely differing aims and philosophies: programmed texts, individualized modules, behavior modification approaches, new grammars and rhetorics, classical rhetorics updated, electronic instructional systems, and, as always, the possibility of trying to return to the good old days when students supposedly *learned* their lessons and did what they were told.

Given the complexity of the task, it is tempting for teachers to look for the method, a clear-cut, no-nonsense approach to English that will reduce complexity and bring serenity to the teacher and his or her classes, a set of techniques that can be followed with certainty through good times and bad. It is also tempting for the writer of a book on the teaching of English to develop something that passes for the method, a compendium of rules and lesson plans purporting to solve the teacher's dilemma.

However, through my own experience—which includes teaching in elementary schools, in junior and senior high schools, undergraduate and graduate university courses, and in-service courses and summer institutes—I have become thoroughly persuaded that the search for the method, something developed elsewhere to be implemented by the teacher, is misguided. The truly effective method must evolve from within. Through reading, thinking, talking, and experimenting—a process of trial and error—teachers must discover their own strategies and approaches for their own classes. Personal abilities and teaching styles differ; and teachers must learn how their own unique competencies—their knowledge of English, their interests, their ability to work with young people—best combine in the classroom. Unfortunately, when teachers attempt to implement an external model, they lose the sense of their own style, with the result, as often as not, that the method proves to be a failure.

What teachers need, I think, is not a set program for teaching but a clear set of values and the self-confidence and self-knowledge that are required to operate in the classroom from one's own strengths. This is not to suggest that "anything goes" in the classroom, that a teacher can justify any bizarre thing on the grounds, "This seems to work for me" or "I like to do it this way." Obviously there are good and bad values in teaching, sound practices and unsound. The teacher's personal behavior needs to draw on external information as well as native abilities.

Thus *Explorations in the Teaching of English* is a source book for experimental teaching designed for those who want to engage in the personal search for their own method. It is a starting point for individual experimentation, not a program to be followed literally. Although it includes numerous practical examples and many teaching ideas, these are intended to encourage the teacher to develop original ideas, not to serve as a set of academically approved and tested recipes.

Each chapter focuses on a single issue or problem, practical or theoretical, that English teachers face today. An introductory essay on each topic surveys the dimensions of the problem and suggests some approaches to it. However, these essays are not simply surveys or reviews of research; they also represent my belief that personal growth or experience-centered approaches offer an important direction for English.

The heart of this book is a series of Explorations—some things to think about, talk over, and do—that appear at the close of each chapter. These activities are not mere discussion questions or homework assignments; they are open-ended problems that both prospective and experienced teachers can explore as a way of seeking information and ideas about themselves, their students, and the teaching of English.

Despite its many rewards, experimental teaching is sometimes difficult, painful, lonely work. It can cause stomach aches and headaches and occasional sleepless nights. The failures of an experimental teacher are more obvious to everyone than are the systematic failures of a dull, conventional teacher. *Explorations in the Teaching of English* supports the experimental teacher both by providing ideas and by sharing with the reader some of the classroom successes, failures, and struggles I have experienced. But I also encourage the reader to find another person with whom to work, talk, and share results.

Indeed, I have long felt that people engaged in experimental teaching should apply for a grant to establish a special kind of telephone service. After an especially trying day, one in which failures seem to be outnumbering successes, the teacher could call a toll free number and pour out all the problems of the day. After listening patiently, the person at the other end would say in a most reassuring way, "Listen, you think you've got troubles? Let me tell you about what happened to me fourth period today. . . ."

A NOTE ON THE SECOND EDITION

A great deal has happened in language education since the first edition of *Explorations* six years ago. Most notably, in the mid-1970s, following the announcement of score declines in college entrance examinations, the public, the media, and even many teachers themselves became convinced that a "crisis" in literacy existed and that, by and large, something called "the new education" was to blame. Actually, as the historical overview in Chapter 1 demonstrates, dissatisfaction with English instruction has been around as long as have the schools themselves. Still, there has been a retreat from many of the English teaching advancements of the late 1960s and early 1970s, perhaps best illustrated by the offerings of educational publishers, whose school books are more conservative and pedagogically less sound that were those of a decade ago.

I do not wish to debate the myths and realities of the "back to basics" movement of the mid- and late 1970s; nor do I want to comment upon the obvious advantages that the current interest in literacy gives to English teachers. But it is clear that the climate into which this edition of *Explorations* will be introduced is far different than that of 1974.

It is tempting for an author to adapt to the more conservative times to promote sales. I want to assure readers and users of the first edition that the changes in this book represent expansion and clarification of the philosophy and methods I presented initially, not a change in values. The reader will not find a section on "grammar drill" tucked away in corner as a safeguard or a precaution, either for the teacher or the author. Experience-based English teaching of the kind recommended by this book does, of course, make ample provision for students to learn "the basics," but it does so by engaging students in experiences with their language, not by promoting workbooks or drill. *Explorations* is based on the belief that teachers must find a consistent philosophy from which to work. This second edition will not waffle on that commitment.

Indeed, despite the current unfavorable climate, it seems to me that the time is right for a resurgence of interest in experimental, exploratory teaching. The late 1960s and early 1970s gave us the "new" education, which opened up exciting new possibilities for the teaching of English; the late 1970s countered with "back to basics." The opportunity of the 1980s, I believe, is that of a kind of Hegelian synthesis, with the possibility that English teachers can think seriously about the claims of both the traditional and the new English, reject what has been faddish or trendy about the new, and blend it sensibly with the workable parts of the old. Such a synthesis will happen only in individual classrooms as good teachers explore, test, probe, and reexamine their aims and basic approaches. It is to aid these teachers—both new and experienced—that this edition of *Explorations in the Teaching of English* has been prepared.

Stephen Judy

Explorations in the Teaching of English

1

A Documentary History of the Teaching of English

Good Boys at their Books.

HE who ne'er learns his A,B,C,
　　Forever will a Blockhead be;
But he who to his Book's inclin'd,
Will foon a golden Treafure find.

The New England Primer, 1785–1790

With this little poem, one of the earliest recorded efforts of a teacher to motivate a child to study, the history of English teaching in America begins, over three hundred years ago. *The New England Primer, or an easy and pleasant Guide to the Art of Reading, Adorn'd with Cuts. To which are added, The Assembly of Divines and Mr. Cotton's CATECHISM* was a complete curriculum in English. Following its motivational opening, the primer presented the alphabet, and following in sequence, "Words of one Syllable," "Words of two Syllables," up through "Words of five Syllables"—a course of instruction that ranged from "fire" to "fornication" (pronounced with five syllables). After the students had mastered spelling and vocabulary, they read "The Lord's Prayer," "The Dutiful Child's Promises," "Lessons for Youth," biblical excerpts, and the catechism, or "Spiritual Milk For American Babes, Drawn out of the Breasts of both Testaments, for their Souls Nourishment" (Figure 1.1). For many years instruction in the schools centered on books like *The New England Primer*, and the primer constituted the whole of instruction in the mother tongue. Few children received more than rudimentary instruction in English spelling and reading, and the academies and colleges in the country concentrated their language teaching on Latin and Greek.

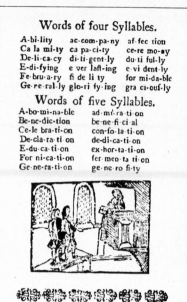

Words of four Syllables.

A·bi·li·ty	ac·com·pa·ny	af·fec·tion
Ca·la·mi·ty	ca·pa·ci·ty	ce·re·mo·ny
De·li·ca·cy	di·li·gent·ly	du·ti·ful·ly
E·di·fy·ing	e·ver·laft·ing	e·vi·dent·ly
Fe·bru·a·ry	fi·de·li·ty	for·mi·da·ble
Ge·re·ral·ly	glo·ri·fy·ing	gra·ci·ouf·ly

Words of five Syllables.

A·bo·mi·na·ble	ad·mi·ra·ti·on
Be·ne·dic·tion	be·ne·fi·ci·al
Ce·le·bra·ti·on	con·fo·la·ti·on
De·cla·ra·ti·on	de·di·ca·ti·on
E·du·ca·ti·on	ex·hor·ta·ti·on
For·ni·ca·ti·on	fer·men·ta·ti·on
Ge·ne·ra·ti·on	ge·ne·ro·fi·ty

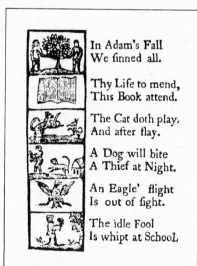

In Adam's Fall
We finned all.

Thy Life to mend,
This Book attend.

The Cat doth play,
And after flay.

A Dog will bite
A Thief at Night.

An Eagle' flight
Is out of fight.

The idle Fool
Is whipt at SchooL

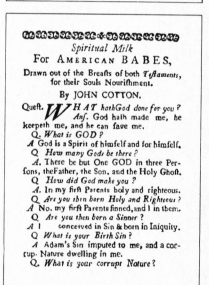

Spiritual Milk
For AMERICAN BABES,
Drawn out of the Breafts of both *Teftaments*,
for their Souls Nourifhment.
By JOHN COTTON.

Queft. *WHAT* hathGod done for you ?
  Anf. God hath made me, he
keepeth me, and he can fave me.
  Q. What is GOD ?
  A God is a Spirit of himfelf and for himfelf.
  Q How many Gods be there ?
  A. There be but One GOD in three Per-
fons, theFather, the Son, and the Holy Ghoft.
  Q How did God make you ?
  A. In my firft Parents body and righteous.
  Q Are you thin born Holy and Righteous ?
  A No, my firft Parents finned, and I in them.
  Q Are you then born a Sinner ?
  A I   conceived in Sin & born in Iniquity.
  Q What is your Birth Sin ?
  A Adam's Sin imputed to me, and a cor-
rup· Nature dwelling in me.
  Q. What is your corrupt Nature ?

Figure 1.1   (From *The New England Primer*, edition of 1785–1790.)

    In the early years of American education, much schooling took place
in the home. The Colonial "dame" schools, for instance, were conducted in
the home of a community member who took on the task of teaching hers
and her neighbors' children to read and write. Thus many books were

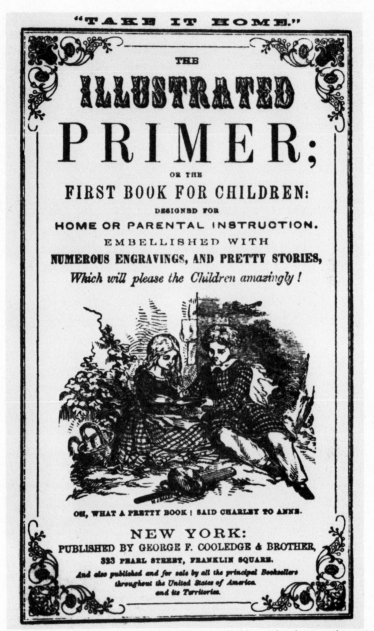

Figure 1.2   A primer for home instruction, probably early nineteenth century.

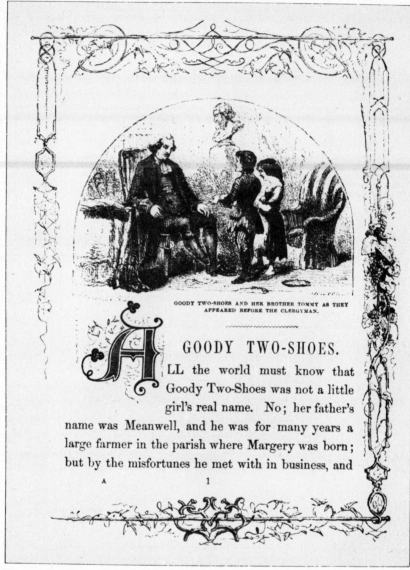

GOODY TWO-SHOES AND HER BROTHER TOMMY AS THEY
APPEARED BEFORE THE CLERGYMAN.

GOODY TWO-SHOES.

ALL the world must know that Goody Two-Shoes was not a little girl's real name. No; her father's name was Meanwell, and he was for many years a large farmer in the parish where Margery was born; but by the misfortunes he met with in business, and

A   1

Figure 1.3 (From *Goody Two-Shoes,* by H. W. Hewit [circa 1855].)

designed for home instruction (Figure 1.2). Interest in outside-of-school teaching is evident in the following passage from an early nineteenth-century book, *Goody Two-Shoes,* about a very, very good little girl and her equally good brother. Goody's real name was Margery Meanwell. She received her nickname after expressing great joy over a new pair of shoes given to her by a clergyman who provided shelter to her and her brother during hard times (Figure 1.3):

Little Margery saw how good and how wise Mr. Smith [the clergyman] was and concluded that this was owing to his great learning; therefore she wanted, of all things, to learn to read. For this purpose, she used to meet the little boys and girls as they came from school, borrow their books, and sit down and read till they returned. By this means she soon got more learning than any of her playmates, and laid the following plan for instructing those who were more ignorant than herself. She found that only twenty-six letters were required to spell all the words; but as some of these letters are large, and some small, she with her knife cut out of several pieces of wood ten sets of each. And having got an old spelling-book she made her companions set up the words they wanted to spell.

. . . every morning she used to go round to teach the children. I once went her rounds with her, and was highly diverted. . . . [One place we visited] was Farmer Simpson's. "Bow, wow, wow!" says the dog at the door. "Sirrah!" says his mistress, "why do you bark at little Two-Shoes? Come in, Madge; here's Sally wants you sadly; she has learned all her lesson." "Yes, that's what I have," replied the little one, in the country manner; and immediately taking the letters, she set up these syllables:

ba be bi bo bu
da de di do du
ma me mi mo mu
sa se si so su

and gave them their exact sounds as she composed them; after which she set up many more, and pronounced them likewise.

After this, little Two-Shoes taught Sally to spell words of one syllable, and she soon set up pear, plum, top, ball, pin, puss, dog, hog, doe, lamb, sheep, ram, cow, cock, bull, hen, and many more. . . .

Since *Goody Two-Shoes* was probably meant to be read aloud to children, parents were given a basic course in "methods of teaching reading" simply by following the stages used by the precocious Goody in her teaching.

American education has always grown toward democratization, extending educational opportunities to more and more people, and instruction in literacy has generally been at the center of that expansion. Home instruction was never seen as entirely satisfactory and was gradually replaced by required formal schooling. In the early days of the new country, the extension of education to older children was promoted by no less a person than Benjamin Franklin. His "Proposals for an Academy" included recommendations for increased attention to the teaching of English, and his own academy in Philadelphia followed the proposal and emphasized English instruction for young men about to enter commercial life.

Early educators perceived English as practical, so that many academies and free public high schools in the nineteenth century spoke of instruction in the "English" branches, which were placed in opposition to the

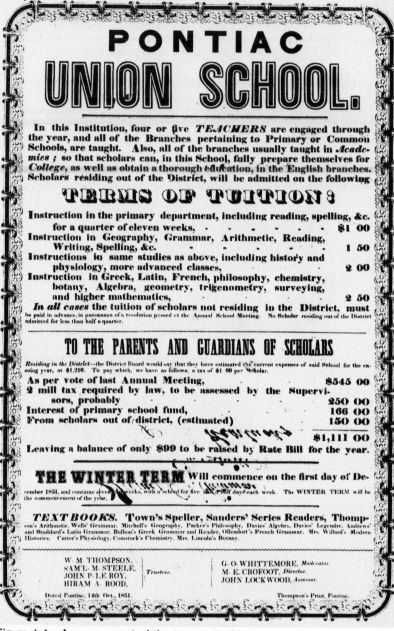

Figure 1.4 Announcement of the terms of tuition and taxation for an early public secondary school, 1851 (Michigan History Collection).

more traditional education in Latin and Greek (Figure 1.4). However, the English branches also covered such school subjects as geography, arithmetic, history, and physiology.

From their earliest days, the secondary schools taught English "Grammatickally," through the study of grammar textbooks. Often this meant examination of one of the grammars of Lindley Murray, published around the beginning of the nineteenth century. Murray's grammar was "traditional," emphasizing mastery of parts of speech and syntactic analysis, and his main pedagogical tool was "parsing," a form of sentence analysis that, it was held, would discipline the mind, while teaching students to speak and write "with propriety" (Figure 1.5).

Murray's work emitted a strong moral tone, one that linked the proper use of language to "proper" human conduct. Writing of "Guarding the Innocence: English Textbooks Into the Breach" (*The English Journal*, December 1974), Conrad Geller, an English teacher from Chappaqua, New York, noted as an illustration this passage from a Murray grammar:

> [The author] wishes to promote, in some degree, the cause of virtue, as well as of learning; and with this view, he has been studious, through the whole of the work, not only to avoid every example and illustration, which might have an improper effect on the minds of youth; but also to introduce, on many occasions, such as have moral and religious tendency. His attention to objects of so much importance will, he trusts, meet with the approbation of every well-disposed reader. If they were faithfully regarded in all books of education, they would doubtlessly contribute very materially to the order and happiness of society, by guarding the innocence, and cherishing the virtue, of the rising generation.

"Guarding the innocence" did not end with Murray. Morality has been linked to grammar and language instruction ever since, with English teachers often perceived as defenders of the language against the onslaughts of "barbarians" (including their students).

After Murray, only one component was needed to round out the

"Every heart knows its sorrows."
Every is an adjective pronoun of the distributive kind, agreeing with its substantive "heart" according to Note 3, under RULE VIII which says, &c. *Heart* is a common substantive *(Repeat the gender, person, number, and case.) Knows* is an irregular verb active, agreeing with its nominative case "Heart" according to RULE I which says, &c . . . (p. 218).

Figure 1.5   An Example of Parsing. (From Lindley Murray, *English Grammar, Adapted to Different Classes of Learners,* first published in 1795.) It should be noted that although Murray chose not to write out the rules in his example, he asked his students to write out all rules, genders, numbers, cases, etc., so that a single exercise might run several pages.

grammar curriculum as many of us know it. In 1877, convinced that grammatical parsing as a form of sentence analysis was too time-consuming, Alonzo Reed and Brainerd Kellogg invented a shorthand version: the sentence diagram (Figure 1.6).

Composition followed grammar into the school program. Most nineteenth-century texts on writing look surprisingly familiar to a twentieth-century graduate of American schools. The texts emphasized analysis of structure—including discourse forms (narration, description, exposition, and argumentation), paragraphs (the "topic sentence" is a nineteenth-century invention), and theme organization (complete with outlining skills). Even such familiar activities as "narrowing the topic" emerged at this time, as T. Whiting Bancroft's *A Method of English Composition* (1884) reveals (Figure 1.7).

---

54   THE SENTENCE AND THE PARTS OF SPEECH

Analysis and Parsing

1. Ah! anxious wives, sisters, and mothers wait for the news.

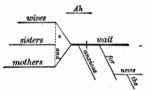

Explanation. The three short horizontal lines represent each a part of the compound subject. They are connected by dotted lines, which stand for the connecting word. The × shows that a conjunction is understood. The line standing for the word modifier is joined to that part of the subject line which represents the entire subject. Turn this diagram about, and the connected horizontal lines will stand for the parts of a compound predicate.

Oral Analysis. *Wives, sisters* and *mothers* form the compound subject; *anxious* is a modifier of the compound subject; *and* connects *sisters* and *mothers.*

Parsing. *And* is a conjunction connecting *sisters* and *mothers; ah* is an interjection, expressing a sudden burst of feeling.

Figure 1.6   The Sentence Diagram. (From Alonzo Reed and Brainerd Kellogg, *Higher Lessons in English,* 1909; first edition, 1877.) "As a means of discipline nothing can compare with a training in the logical analysis of the sentence."

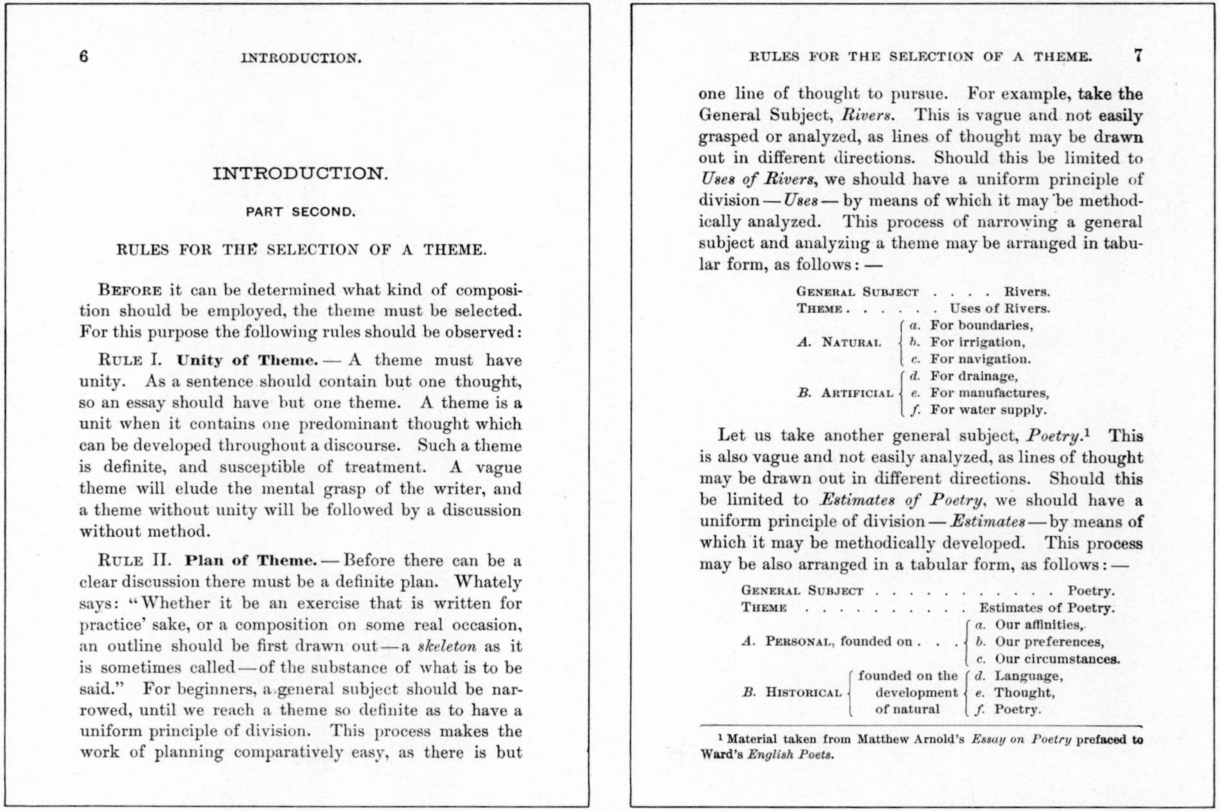

INTRODUCTION.

PART SECOND.

RULES FOR THE SELECTION OF A THEME.

BEFORE it can be determined what kind of composition should be employed, the theme must be selected. For this purpose the following rules should be observed:—

RULE I. **Unity of Theme.** — A theme must have unity. As a sentence should contain but one thought, so an essay should have but one theme. A theme is a unit when it contains one predominant thought which can be developed throughout a discourse. Such a theme is definite, and susceptible of treatment. A vague theme will elude the mental grasp of the writer, and a theme without unity will be followed by a discussion without method.

RULE II. **Plan of Theme.** — Before there can be a clear discussion there must be a definite plan. Whately says: "Whether it be an exercise that is written for practice' sake, or a composition on some real occasion, an outline should be first drawn out — a *skeleton* as it is sometimes called — of the substance of what is to be said." For beginners, a general subject should be narrowed, until we reach a theme so definite as to have a uniform principle of division. This process makes the work of planning comparatively easy, as there is but

one line of thought to pursue. For example, **take the** General Subject, *Rivers*. This is vague and not easily grasped or analyzed, as lines of thought may be drawn out in different directions. Should this be limited to *Uses of Rivers*, we should have a uniform principle of division — *Uses* — by means of which it may be methodically analyzed. This process of narrowing a general subject and analyzing a theme may be arranged in tabular form, as follows:—

GENERAL SUBJECT . . . Rivers.
THEME . . . . Uses of Rivers.
A. NATURAL { a. For boundaries,
             b. For irrigation,
             c. For navigation,
             d. For drainage,
B. ARTIFICIAL { e. For manufactures,
               f. For water supply.

Let us take another general subject, *Poetry*.[1] This is also vague and not easily analyzed, as lines of thought may be drawn out in different directions. Should this be limited to *Estimates of Poetry*, we should have a uniform principle of division — *Estimates* — by means of which it may be methodically developed. This process may be also arranged in a tabular form, as follows:—

GENERAL SUBJECT . . . . Poetry.
THEME . . . . Estimates of Poetry.
A. PERSONAL, founded on . . { a. Our affinities,
                              b. Our preferences,
                              c. Our circumstances.
B. HISTORICAL, founded on the { d. Language,
  development of natural   e. Thought,
                               f. Poetry.

[1] Material taken from Matthew Arnold's *Essay on Poetry* prefaced to Ward's *English Poets*.

Figure 1.7 Nineteenth-Century Composition Textbook. (From T. Whiting Bancroft, A *Method of English Composition*, 1884.)

Nineteenth century teachers were also deeply concerned with training for correctness and developed the red-penciling of themes to a fine art (Figure 1.8). At Harvard College, students in English "A," the forerunner of modern freshman English classes, wrote daily, weekly, and fortnightly themes, all of which the teacher corrected as vigorously as the one shown and sent back to the student for revision. The Harvard composition faculty made it no secret that it wished secondary school teachers would pursue an equally rigorous course of instruction.

The teaching of literature was a relative latecomer to the English cur-

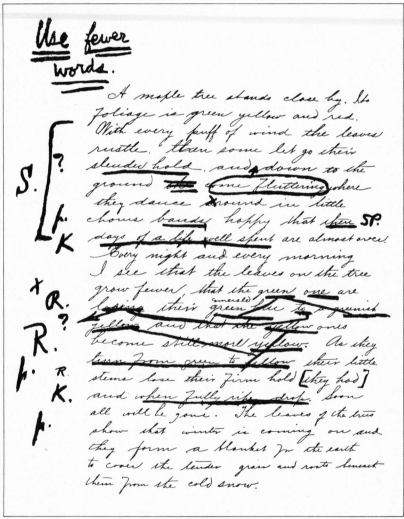

Figure 1.8   How to Correct a Theme. (From C. T. Copeland and H. M. Ridout, *Freshman English and Theme Correction at Harvard College,* 1901.)

riculum, being added to the secondary curriculum only during the final quarter of the nineteenth century. Although *reading* had been a part of American schooling since Colonial times, the study of literature had been largely limited to the Greek and Roman classics, studied in the original language. But growing literary nationalism coupled with the increasingly "practical" emphasis of public school education led in the 1870s and 1880s to the introduction of selected works by American and British writers. By 1880, *Silas Marner* had found a place for itself in the curriculum, and a collection of Shakespearean plays—*Julius Caesar, As You Like It, Macbeth, Hamlet, The Merchant of Venice*—had become established as a standard repertory for study by high school students.

The schools, however, were much more concerned with literary history, biography, and criticism than with the actual content of literature; and the last quarter of the century saw the development of the literature "compendium," a handbook of information on authors and their works. Although the youngsters who studied Jennie Ellis Keysor's *Sketches of American Authors* might never have *read* anything by James Fenimore Cooper, they would know that Cooper's literary style was "pure, simple, strong, breathing of untrammelled outdoor existence; weakest in portrayal of character and strongest in description of scenes and narration of events," and they would learn that Cooper himself was "truthful, fearless, uncompromising, sensitive, impulsive, pure-minded, partisan, aristocratic, [and] ingenuous" (Figure 1.9).

By the end of the nineteenth century, the so-called "tradition" in English was established. English consisted of three major components—language, composition, and literature. *Language* meant grammar, including parts of speech, the nature of the sentence, parsing, diagramming, and/or sentence correction exercises. *Composition* consisted of the study of prose structures, followed by practice themes and error correction. *Literature* centered on the examination of selected great works from a historical-critical point of view. This tradition has been challenged over the years, and it is certainly under considerable fire today. But English teachers should recognize that the roots of this tradition are quite deep.

From time to time during the twentieth century, minor and major revolutions have attempted to alter this tradition. In 1917, a committee of the newly organized National Council of Teachers of English (NCTE) and of the National Education Association (NEA) chaired by James F. Hosic reflected the growing progressive education movement and expressed concern at the academism and sternness of English and an emphasis on preparation for college. This "Committee of Seventeen" declared that English was preparation for life, not college, adding that the best preparation for all students would probably be the best preparation for college. Unfortunately, these recommendations suffered in translation to classroom practice. Undercutting its own position, the committee offered a circular argu-

QUESTIONS ON COOPER.

How much younger was Cooper than Irving?
What new era in our national development began with his birth?
Where was he born? What fact in his father's life accounts for this?
Where is Lake Otsego? Describe the scenery about this lake.
Where is Cooperstown and why so named?
Give several reasons why this region was well adapted to be the residence of such a novelist as Cooper.
Speak of Cooper's opportunities at the Academy.
What sort of schools were the old Academies?
How was Cooper further fitted for College?
What college did he enter? What of his career there?
What business was selected as Cooper's life work? How was it learned in those days? How is it learned to-day?
Of what value was it to Cooper in his story writing? Illustrate your answer.
What can you say of the relations of Captain Lawrence and Cooper?
Why did Cooper give up his business?
Speak fully of his wife and her family.
What can you say of Cooper's home life?
Describe the incident which started Cooper in his career of writing?
What was his first book? What can you say of its success?
What largely caused this result?
What difficulty did Cooper have to contend with that never troubled Scott?
What were some of the things which made "The Spy" a success?
Why did Cooper move to New York?
What was "The Bread and Cheese Club?"
Who were some of its prominent members?
Who was "Leather-Stocking"? What books are called by the name of this character and why?
What development did Cooper work out in this character in the course of the series?

What can you say of the pay Cooper received for his books?
When did Cooper go to Europe and how long did he stay?
How did he defend us while abroad?
What features of the old country pleased him and how did he profit by them?
What country was his favorite? What city?
How did America impress him on his return? What reasons were there for this condition of things?
How did he show his disapproval of American manners?
What led to the famous quarrel with his neighbors?
How did the quarrel result? Was Cooper justified in the quarrel?
Why did interest in Cooper's novels decline during his last years?
Explain the difference between the *novel of adventure* and the *domestic novel*.
It what other kinds of writing did Cooper excel besides the novel?
What are some of the strongest points in Cooper's literary style?
What is his greatest work?
What character did he *create*?
Make a list of the good points in Cooper's character.
Name some of the bad points and show how the former outweighed the latter.
Where would you look for Cooper's grave?

SUBJECTS FOR LANGUAGE WORK.

1. The Scenery of Otsego Lake.
2. A Day with Leather-Stocking.
3. Cooper, Our Defender Abroad.
4. Cooper, Our Censor at Home.
5. Cooper and His Critics.
6. Cooper and His Neighbors.
7. Cooper and Irving Contrasted.

OUTLINE OF COOPER'S LIFE.

I. Birth in 1789, the beginning of the Constitutional period in United States History.
   1. At Burlington, New Jersey.
   2. Of Quaker parentage.

Figure 1.9   Nineteenth-Century Study of Cooper. (From Jennie Ellis Keysor, *Sketches of American Authors*, part of *The Young Folks Library of Choice Literature*, 1895.)

ment: Since classic literature was "great," it ought to be good preparation for life and appeal to all students; if it didn't, something was wrong with the teachers and their methodology. Thus teachers continued with a rigorous literature program—basically a college preparatory curriculum—but were made to feel inadequate if they could not persuade students in the

---

LITERATURE, GRADES 7—12

5. PRIMARY OBJECTIVE: To observe man's industrial expansion.
   ENABLING OBJECTIVES: To compare industry as it was before our time with our own industrial age; to participate vicariously with men and women who worked and are working under conditions both good and bad; to analyze our present economic system, and to compare it with systems of other days.
   Typical Materials: Silas Marner (Eliot); David Copperfield (Dickens); The Last of the Mohicans (Cooper); The Slave Ship (Johnston); The Luck of Roaring Camp (Harte); Roughing It (Twain); Two Years Before the Mast (Dana); A Son of the Middle Border (Garland); The Oregon Trail (Parkman); The Crossing (Churchill); Seven Iron Men (de Kruif).

6. PRIMARY OBJECTIVE: To observe the effects of widening trade horizons on our daily lives.
   ENABLING OBJECTIVES: To see how new frontiers and new customs were the direct result of the desire of man to increase his trading area; to catch some idea of the need for invention, investigation, and discovery; to note the organization of big business and the resulting efficiency and economy which it implies.
   Typical Materials: I Hear America Singing (Whitman); Modern Pioneers (Cohen and Scarlett); Pete of the Steel Mills (Hall); Making of an American (Riis); Our Foreign Born Citizens (Beard); "The Thinker" (Braley); Andrew Carnegie's Own Story (Brochhausen); At School in the Promised Land (Antin); Greatness Passing By (Neibuhr); The Pit and The Octopus (Norris); The Harbor (Poole); I Went to Pit College (Gilfillan).

Figure 1.10   Teaching Literature by Patterns, Themes, and Ideas. (From *An Experience Curriculum in English,* 1935.) Note that in addition to expanding literary study into social domains, the Committee on the Experience Curriculum also drew on a wider *range* of literature, including contemporary works. At the same time, the tradition—here represented by *Silas Marner* and *David Copperfield*—continued as a strong component in the program.

commercial tracks that this literature would help them through life.

A second revolt from tradition appeared in the pages of *An Experience Curriculum in English* (NCTE, 1935). The report presented the work of a committee chaired by W. Wilbur Hatfield. It was somewhat more successful in breaking with tradition than were the efforts of the Hosic committee. The *Experience Curriculum* strongly emphasized both the social values of English and the role of the student's experience in learning English. Perhaps its two most significant developments were its emphasis on

---

WRITING EXPERIENCES, GRADES 7—12

A. SOCIAL LETTERS

1. SOCIAL OBJECTIVE: To write appreciative and tactful notes of thanks.

    ENABLING OBJECTIVES: To evidence cordial and sincere gratitude for the gift or favor or hospitality and appreciation for the consideration of the tastes and interests of the recipient. To write prompt acknowledgment as an evidence of appreciation. To use adjective prepositional phrases to add color unobtrusively (I.G.U. 11). To use appropriate paper with matching envelope, and ink, never pencil. To say "Dear John," or "My dear Mary," but never "Dear Friend." To end the letter "Sincerely yours," or "Cordially yours," avoiding "Respectfully yours."

2. SOCIAL OBJECTIVE: To write informal and courteous notes of invitation and acceptance or regret.

    ENABLING OBJECTIVES: To write interesting, persuasive invitations. To make definite and concise statements concerning place, time of arrival, and extent of visit. To specify the type of entertainment and the size of party, which will suggest appropriate dress. To give directions and suggest convenient transportation. To arrange items in orderly sequence and to express them with direct simplicity. To omit confusing items and superfluous words. To accept or to decline graciously and sincerely so that appreciation for the invitation is evidenced. To capitalize important words in titles. To use infinitives as subjects for variety and vigor (I.G.U. 13). To capitalize proper adjectives.

Figure 1.11 Teaching Socially Useful Skills. (From *An Experience Curriculum in English.*)

teaching literature by patterns, themes, and ideas (Figure 1.10) and its emphasis on teaching socially useful skills like letter writing and conversation (Figure 1.11). Although overly concerned with correctness (and with promoting the life style and values of middle-class whites), the *Experience Curriculum* presented a unique opportunity for English education to broaden its base and move into new domains.

The promise of the *Experience Curriculum*, however, was never realized. Some educational historians feel that the outbreak of World War II and an ensuing interest in teaching English as part of the war effort blunted the effects of the new program. Others believe that the *Experience Curriculum* was too "permissive," too exclusively focused on social skills rather than on academic knowledge, so that its "softness" led to its dissolution. In any event, the 1950s dawned with the traditional curriculum firmly in place. A few components of the *Experience Curriculum* remained in the schools, most notably, the concern for teaching social graces like answering the telephone (Figure 1.12). The familiar chronological-historical approach to literature was back, and the thematic focus of the thirties survived only in modified form in a few junior high school texts (Figure 1.13). The new look of the fifties was often graphic, not pedagogical (Figure 1.14). Texts came printed in several colors, with "amusing" drawings illustrating rules and principles that were the same as ever. Textbooks tried to stress the *fun* in English, as illustrated by such series titles as *Enjoying English* and *Enjoying Life Through Literature*.

Interestingly enough, however, the most influential textbook of the fifties emphasized neither fun nor graphics; it was a stern little volume called *Handbook of English*, written by John Warriner (Figure 1.15). It is said that in the early nineteenth century, Lindley Murray's books were so widely used that his name became synonymous with "grammar," and students talked of studying their "Murray." The same can be said of "Warriner's" in our own century. Equally interesting are the great similarities in content between Murray's and Warriner's books. Both men taught the "basic" structure of English, and each succeeded with his book because he told about this structure more clearly than anyone else in his time.

A third major challenge to the tradition was quite literally "launched" in 1957, when the Russians opened the space era ahead of the United States by sending the first earth satellite, "Sputnik," into orbit. The American government and the public were greatly alarmed: No one had imagined the Russians possessed such technological skill, which incidentally could be used to launch nuclear warheads at an enemy. Suddenly, American education found itself blamed for the "missile gap." If the schools had not been so "soft," so "progressive," it was argued, students would have learned more and American technological supremacy would have been preserved.

Initially, this concern and anger was directed toward teachers of the

WHAT'S YOUR TELEPHONE SCORE?

Do you?	YES	SOME-TIMES	NO
1. Answer promptly			
2. Greet the caller pleasantly			
3. Identify yourself properly			
4. Explain waits			
5. Leave word where you're going			
6. Ask questions tactfully			
7. Take the message			
8. Signal the operator slowly			
9. Know the number			
10. Allow time to answer			
11. Ask if convenient to talk			
12. Speak in a natural tone			
13. Visualize the person			
14. Say "Thank you" and "You're welcome"			
15. Listen attentively			
16. Use the customer's name			
17. Speak directly into transmitter			
18. Apologize for mistakes			
19. End the call properly			
20. Replace receiver gently			
Total			

Figure 1.12   Answering the Telephone. (Reprinted by permission of Harper & Row, Publishers, Inc. From *Building Better English 9,* by Mellie John, Paulene M. Yates, and Edward N. De Laney. Copyright © 1961 by Harper & Row, Publishers, Inc.)

The Concord Hymn

By the rude bridge that arched the flood,
   Their flag to April's breeze unfurled,
Here once the embattled farmers stood,
   And fired the shot heard round the world.

The foe long since in silence slept;
   Alike the conqueror silent sleeps;
And Time the ruined bridge has swept
   Down the dark stream which seaward creeps.

On this green bank, by this soft stream,
   We set today a votive stone;
That memory may their deed redeem,
   When, like our sires, our sons are gone,

Spirit, that made those heroes dare
   To die and leave their children free,
Bid Time and Nature gently spare
   The shaft we raise to them and thee.

Discussion

1. What makes this poem especially appropriate for the occasion for which it was written?
2. What is a "votive stone"?
3. To whom do the pronouns "them" and "thee" in the last line refer?
4. What does Emerson mean by "the shot heard round the world"?

Research

1. The Battle of Concord was an event of historical importance. Look up the facts and prepare a brief report.
2. Concord is important in literary and political history. Prepare a written report on both aspects of its history.

Figure 1.13   Chronological-Historical Approach to Literature. (From Gunnar Horn, *A Cavalcade of American Writing,* 1961 edition. Copyright © 1961 by Allyn and Bacon, Inc. Reprinted by permission of the publisher.) In contrast to the methodology recommended by the *Experience Curriculum,* the approach shown here makes no reference at all to the experiences of the student. The poem is treated as a historical artifact for analysis and research.

PRINCIPAL PARTS   PARTICIPLES AND INFINITIVES

Present Tense: *see* ⟶ Present Participle: *seeing*
⟶ Present Infinitive: to *see*
Past Participle: *seen* ⟶ Perfect Participle: having *seen*
⟶ Perfect Infinitive: to have *seen*

Practice 3 **Using the Principal Parts**

For each of the verbs below make two charts like those above. Use *I* as the subject of the verb when you write the tenses. Several pupils may each write the charts for one verb on the board.

1. go
2. lie
3. sell
4. walk
5. come
6. hear
7. swim
8. take
9. bring
10. sever
11. write
12. choose
13. shrink
14. acquire
15. discuss
16. flutter

Practice 4 **A Verb's Progress in Outline**

Write the forms of any six of the irregular verbs listed on page 173. Follow the model below.

Example: PRINCIPAL PARTS

Present tense: Today I *take*
Past tense: Yesterday I *took*
Past Participle: For a long time I have *taken*

Present tense: I *take*   Present perfect tense: I *have taken*
Past tense: I *took*   Past perfect tense: I *had taken*
Future tense: I *shall take*   Future perfect tense: I *shall have taken*

Figure 1.14 Graphics and Grammar. (From Don M. Wolfe and Josie Lewis, *Enjoying English 10,* 1964 Copyright © 1964 by L. W. Singer Company. Reprinted by permission of Random House, Inc.)

Handbook
of English

JOHN E. WARRINER
Head of the English Department,
Garden City High School, Garden
City, Long Island, New York

The English Workshop Series

HARCOURT, BRACE AND COMPANY

NEW YORK   CHICAGO

Figure 1.15   Title page from the first edition of Warriner's *Handbook of English*, 1951. (Reprinted by permission of Harcourt Brace Jovanovich, Inc.)

sciences and mathematics. In 1958, Congress funded the National Defense Education Act, which provided federal funds for curriculum development and teacher in-service training in mathematics and science. The act completely ignored English. However, not content to see the profession ignored, the NCTE argued for the centrality of literacy studies in the schools. *The National Defense and the Teaching of English,* published in 1961, forcefully presented the case, and the effort was rewarded when, a year later, Congress provided for a series of curriculum study centers in English.

"Project English," as this network of research and demonstration centers was called, led to the exploration of all aspects of the English curriculum. Virtually all the centers agreed that "the tradition" had failed: Teaching grammar had not taught students to read or write better; redpenciling student themes had not brought about improvement in composition; treating literature as fodder for historical study had not made good readers or lovers of literature.

A variety of "new English" programs emerged. At one extreme, educators looked to the transformational grammar of Noam Chomsky to provide a focus for English. This, in turn, led to the publication of a number of "linguistic" programs for high schools, most short lived because of their complexity and their remoteness from actual language use (Figure 1.16). Other educators looked to what was called "student-centered" education, which developed a curriculum on young people's growth and development, rather than on the structure of the disciplines. Textbooks growing from this conviction featured high interest, easy reading materials along with writing that emphasized expression of self rather than mastery of set forms. Textbooks took on a bright, graphic look (Figure 1.17).

The revolution was catalyzed by several related developments in education:

> In the mid-1960s, a group of "romantic" critics of education—John Holt, Jonathan Kozol, Herbert Kohl, and George Leonard, to name several—wrote indictments of the schools for being oppressive places for children to be. Learning, the critics argued, is natural, positive, and pleasurable.
>
> Paperback books became acceptable in the schools in lieu of hardbound textbooks and anthologies. The "paperback revolution" in publishing made a wide range of new titles, including classic literature, available to teachers at low cost. Thus teachers were able to break away from the content of anthologies and began to exercise much more imagination and originality in the development of courses than they had previously.
>
> An Anglo-American Seminar on the Teaching of English held at Dartmouth College (1966) emphasized the role of language learning in personal growth, stressing, for example, the importance of self-expression in writing and personal response in literature. The "Dartmouth Seminar" demonstrated the importance of experiences such as drama and role playing in the education of children.
>
> English teachers discovered elective courses. In the spirit of the 1960s

Syntax — **Number**

We will note one other optional element that may occur in the determiner of the noun phrase. This is **number**:

Det → (pre-article) + Art + (demonstration) + (number)

As the rule shows, **number** occurs after D_1 or D_2, if they occur, and in any case after **article**.

Number is of two sorts:

number → cardinal
               ordinal

cardinal → one, two, three, four, five . . .
ordinal → first, second, third, fourth, fifth . . .

With the inclusion of number, we can account in the grammar for noun phrases of the sort shown in the following:

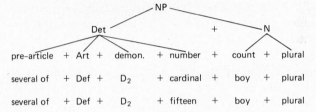

What will Def + D_2 become when the following noun is plural? What is the actual noun phrase represented by the K-terminal string?

Draw a tree for the noun phrase **many of these twenty girls**.

Since **number** may be **ordinal** instead of **cardinal**, we may also have a structure such as the following:

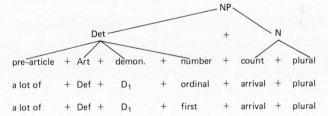

What noun phrase is represented by the K-terminal string? Draw a similar diagram for **most of those second floors**.

Figure 1.16   (From Paul Roberts, *The Roberts English Series* [Complete Course], probably the most widely used of the 1960s "linguistic" approaches to a "new" English. Copyright © 1967 by Harcourt Brace Jovanovich, Inc.)

You can also tell about yourself by describing some of your favorite things. In *The Book of Myself* make a list of your "favorites", including your favorite

song
singer
singing group
sport
school subject
item of clothing
athlete
musical instrument

food
color
car
animal

Are there any other "favorites" in your life? What does each of these tell about you? If you wish, share your list with someone else and talk over your favorites.

One way you can describe your personality is by making comparisons between yourself and other things. For example, if someone asked, "What kind of animal are you like?" you might answer in several ways:

"A *dog,* because I am friendly and agreeable."

"A *cat,* because I am very independent."

"A *fish,* because more than anything, I enjoy swimming."

What kind of animal *is* like you? Write down the answer and then explain why. Then answer some of these comparison questions and put your answers in *The Book of Myself:*

What kind of *automobile* is most like you? (an old-fashioned model-T Ford? a bright red Triumph Spitfire? a blue Chevrolet sedan?)

What kind of *flower* or *plant* or *tree* is most like you? (Are you like an oak tree? a rose? a cactus? a poison ivy bush? In what ways?)

What piece of *furniture* is closest to your personality? Why do you think so?

If you were a pair of *shoes* what would you be like? (an old pair of sneakers? a dusty set of loafers? a freshly shined pair of dress shoes?)

Describe a *day* that is like your personality. (Are you a rainy day in March? a pleasant day in October? a blazing August day? a blizzardy day in December? Why?) What other comparisons can you make between yourself and other living things or objects? Write these in the *Book of Myself* too.

The Creative Word III   **19**

Figure 1.17   (From *The Creative Word 3,* by Stephen Judy. Copyright © 1973 by Random House, Inc.)

and early 1970s, elective English came into vogue, replacing the traditional high school courses—English I, II, III, IV—with a wide range of courses from "Shakespeare" to "Supernatural Literature." Even schools with small English departments managed to produce an array of elective choices. In schools offering electives, students often took even more than the required basic English courses.

As the 1970s dawned, then, a revolution from the tradition seemed, if not complete, at least solidly under way. The traditional tripod of literature, language, and composition, with common course content for all students, seemed to have been replaced by student-centered courses based on a wider range of reading materials than had ever been seen in the schools.

But the revolution was by no means complete; nor, as it turned out, had schools entirely discarded tradition.

For one thing, much revolutionary activity took place only on the pages of professional journals and in the meeting rooms of conferences and conventions. Teachers "in the know" were often department heads who kept up with the latest in professional ideas. The classroom teachers, too busy to read the journals and not having their way paid to conventions, inherited only the trappings of student-centered learning. They placed the desks in circles, and they spoke of the need for creativity along with correctness. But in large numbers, they kept on teaching their Warriner's.

Further, beneath the glitter, the "new English" had some obvious weaknesses. Students often found that the choices offered in elective programs were limited to course selection only; once enrolled in the course, students found the content fixed. Frequently, the material in those courses was no different from that presented in traditional English I, II, III, IV courses. The only thing new was a course title. Electives also tended to mask what teachers were doing; if only one section of a course was offered in a school, nobody ever really knew what the single teacher presenting the course was teaching. Under the elective system, teachers who wanted to avoid composition, for example, could do so without fear of exposure.

Even as these new programs were being introduced, some unfamiliar terms began to crop up in the professional literature: "behavioral objectives," "accountability," "assessment," "mandated goals." While some English educators had been moving toward a "new English" based on student needs and the principles of language growth, others had been looking toward assessment and quantification as a means of creating a more effective, more efficient school curriculum. Robert Mager's influential *Preparing Instructional Objectives* (Figure 1.18), originally written as an instructional guide for preparing programmed learning materials, articulated a call for increased specificity of school objectives. The "behavioral" objective became linked with state- and nationwide assessments of educational progress and the preparation of lists of minimum objectives for young people. Many English teachers agreed that programs should have clear statements of purpose. But the language form of the "behavioral" objective meant that most of the aims of the "new" English wouldn't fit in. On the other hand, the goals of traditional English, particularly grammar instruction, could easily be translated into the often complex language and terminology of the accountability movement (Figure 1.19). Behavioral objectives, in short, tended to make the curriculum conservative. The development of accountability models spread rapidly, so that in the early 1970s, state after state and district after district introduced new objectives and testing programs. While the proponents of behavioral objectives—in-

$1.75

PREPARING

INSTRUCTIONAL

OBJECTIVES

ROBERT F. MAGER

A book for teachers and student teachers ... for anyone interested in transmitting skills and knowledge to others.

Figure 1.18 (From *Preparing Instructional Objectives,* first edition, by Robert F. Mager. Copyright © 1962 by Fearon-Pitman Publishers, Inc., Belmont, California. Reprinted by permission.) This book represents the origin of the "behavioral" objective.

cluding Mager himself—argued that such programs need not be limited to rote skills or simple learnings, the fact is that in most cases, the new curricula concentrated solely on the "minimum essentials."

This conservative movement gained enormous strength when, in 1973, the College Entrance Examination Board announced that scores on the Scholastic Aptitude Test verbal test had been dropping for over a decade, having fallen off some 40 points (on a scale of 800) during that time. As had happened 16 years earlier, the public and the media were aghast. In contrast to Sputnik, however, this time the reaction was against "new" methods and an allegedly dropping level of student achievement.

Newsweek devoted much of an issue to the so-called "crisis" in literacy and claimed:

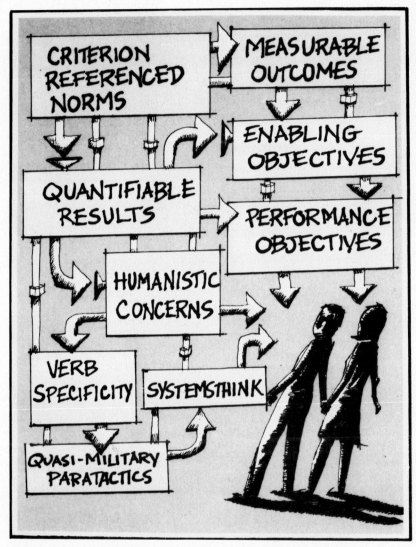

Figure 1.19   A satirical representation of the conflict between the accountability/assessment movement and the student-centered approach to English. (David Kirkpatrick's cover for *The English Journal,* April 1975. Copyright © 1975 by the National Council of Teachers of English. Reprinted with permission.)

If your children are attending college, the chances are that when they graduate they will be unable to write ordinary, expository English with any real degree of lucidity. If they are in high school and planning to attend college, the chances are less than even that they will be able to write English at the minimal college level when they get there. If they are not planning to attend college, their skills in writing English may not even qualify them for secretarial or clerical work. And if they are attending elementary school, they are almost certainly not being given the kind of required reading material, much less writing instruction, that might make it possible for them eventually to write comprehensible English. Willy-nilly, the educational system is spawning a generation of semiliterates. (December 8, 1975, p. 58. Copyright 1975, by Newsweek, Inc. All Rights Reserved. Reprinted by Permission.)

While the analysis offered by *Newsweek* lacked fundamental accuracy about the nature of language and language learning, the impact on the teaching profession was marked: In large numbers, sometimes forced by the administration, often of their own volition, teachers went back to the basics. (Some teachers, obviously, had never left.) Schools replaced elective courses with global English courses stressing grammar and punctuation; the bright new anthologies disappeared, and publishers brought out new editions of programs that had been largely discredited by the research of the "new English" years. (In conjunction with the Bicentennial in 1976, Harcourt Brace put new covers on John Warriner's *Handbook* and called it the "Heritage Edition"; the book enjoyed its best sales ever.)

Not all teachers responded by retreating into traditional approaches. Many argued the the "new English" was not responsible for the test score decline. Teachers pointed to the success of paperback reading programs and the great interest in student writing as evidence that new methods had not failed. As the decade of the 1970s came to a close, the profession of English found itself deeply in conflict, within itself and with the public.

In many respects, English teachers today find themselves split into "two personalities," as described by Charles Bonnici in *The English Journal* (September 1978): one personality that of a mechanic concerned with teaching the rote mastery of "basics," the other part "artist," dealing with human concerns on a more subjective basis through the teaching of literature and writing.

That the two personalities need not make teachers schizophrenic is a central premise of this book. In the chapters that follow, I will show that teaching the basics of language is not in conflict with self-expression by young people, that the reading of literature can be as disciplined as any other activity. Whether in the 1980s English teachers will be able to bring about a fusion of their subject, treating it as an integrated whole, or failing that, will allow the English teaching profession to be split hopelessly into two personalities must be of continuing concern us to all.

EXPLORATIONS

• Throughout the history of English teaching, a number of central issues and questions have been debated. Why are we teaching English? How can we teach students to write? What good is literature? Where does language study fit in? Answers have been offered, tested, modified, accepted, and rejected—sometimes following repetitious cycles.

Here are a number of statements about the teaching of English made over the past two centuries, and they constitute a brief overview of the kinds of questions this book will explore. Write down your own reactions to each of these statements. Do you agree or disagree? In what ways? Save your notes and use them as a bookmark. When you have finished working through *Explorations in the Teaching of English*, come back, reread the statements, see whether your own thoughts on the teaching of English have changed. (Note: Don't let the vintage of these statements shape your opinions. Not all good ideas are new, and not all of our contemporaries have profited from the mistakes of history.)

Purity of language expresses and aids clearness of thought: vulgarity, profanity, coarseness, carelessness in language, deepen the characteristics they express.

J.M. Blodgett, *Journal of the Proceedings of the National Education Association,* 1870

"When I use a word," Humpty Dumpty said in a rather scornful tone, "it means just what I choose it to mean, neither more nor less."
"The question is," said Alice, "whether you *can* make words mean so many different things."
"The question is," said Humpty Dumpty, "which is to be Master— that's all."

Lewis Carroll, *Through the Looking Glass,* 1872

The province of the preparatory schools is to train the scholar, boy or girl, and train him or her thoroughly in what can only be described as the elements and rudiments of written expression—they should teach facile, clear penmanship, correct spelling, simple grammatical construction, and neat, workmanlike mechanical execution. And this is no slight or simple task. . . . It demands steady, daily drill, and drudgery of a kind most wearisome. Its purpose and aim are not ambitious—its work is not inspiring.

The Committee on Composition and Rhetoric of the Harvard College Board of Overseers, 1898

Language is acquired only by absorption from contact with an environment in which language is in perpetual use. Utterly futile is the attempt to give a child or youth language by making him learn something about language. No language is learned except as it performs the function of all speech—to convey thought—and this thought must be welcome, interesting and clear. There is no time in the high school course when language will be learned in any other way.

Samuel Thurber, Girls' Latin School, Boston, 1898

[In literature] the pupil should be given experiences that have intrinsic worth for *him,* now. No matter how much the story may thrill us sophisticated adults who make and teach the courses, no matter how much the play may inspire us or the poem charm us, if it is beyond the intellectual and emotional range of our pupils, we are worse than wasting time to attempt to impose it on them.

An Experience Curriculum in English, 1935

Ideally the teacher should not only read every paper and mark its formal errors, but should write detailed comment. The comment should not necessarily be complete for each paper read, but it should always be constructive and specific, showing the student exactly what he might have done to improve the theme and what has been done successfully in the theme presented. In the course of a year, the comment should make as coherent a progress as the classroom teaching, directing each writer to examine and correct his worst faults, one by one, so that at the end of the year he can look back on measurable improvement.

The Commission on English of the College Entrance Examination Board, 1965

For the sake of both proficiency and pleasure the student should be able to understand implied as well as surface meanings, to make critical judgments as a basis for choice in his own reading, to recognize the values presented in literature, and to relate them to his own attitudes and values. He should be familiar with the "reservoir" literature that forms a common background for our culture (classical mythology, European folk and fairy tales, Arthurian legends, the Bible, etc.), with a range of selections from English and American literature and with some from other literatures in good translation. So far as possible, he should have some "time sense"—not a detailed, lifeless knowledge of names and dates, but an imaginative sense of the past.

Study Group on "Response to Literature," the Anglo-American Seminar on the Teaching of English, 1966

Standard English is not just a bourgeois dialect, after all, but the most common and widespread form of English, and no education for life in a democracy can be complete without some knowledge of it. Call the preference for it ignorant or snobbish, the fact remains that it is the language of educated people everywhere, and no person can hope to talk or write effectively for all his purpose unless he can use it with a fair degree of naturalness and correctness. Democratic idealism itself calls for the teaching of it to all children as an essential means to sharing the heritage of their society and the opportunities for realizing their potentialities, bettering themselves, both intellectually and socially. Refusing to teach it to poor children would automatically condemn most of them to remaining poor and underprivileged, seal the division into sheep and goats.

Herbert Muller, *The Uses of English,* 1968

We affirm the students' right to their own patterns and varieties of language—the dialects of their nurture or whatever dialects in which they find their identity and style. Language scholars long ago denied that the myth of a standard American dialect has any validity. The claim that any one dialect is unacceptable amounts to an attempt of one social group to exert its dominance over another. Such a claim leads to false advice for speakers and writers, and immoral advice for humans. A nation proud of its diverse heritage and its cultural and racial variety will preserve its heritage of dialects. We affirm strongly that teachers must have the experiences and training that will enable them to respect diversity and uphold the right of students to their own language.

Conference on College Composition and Communication, 1974

Diagramming sentences is out, no one teaches Shakespeare any more, and there are all those kids talking and rapping with each other, not knowing how to examine what they think in one discursive sentence.

James Knapton, *Newsweek,* 1975

. . . teaching literacy must employ joy, inquiry, openness, appreciation of difference and divergence, of ambiguity and paradox, or the literacy we achieve will be rote, mechanical or subservient to rules and order. . . . these latter achievements would be the "literacy" of machines, a literacy hardly worth the price of an education . . .

Seymour Yesner, *The English Journal,* 1978

And a final thought, this one on the English teacher:

The teacher who has not a passion and an aptitude for imparting instruction in English, who does not feel it is a great thing to live for, and a thing, if necessary, to die for, who does not realize at every moment that he is performing the special function for which he was foreordained from the foundation of the world—such a teacher cannot profit greatly by any course of training, . . . he lacks the one thing needful.

G. R. Carpenter, F. T. Baker, and F. N. Scott, *The Teaching of English,* 1909

2
Language, Experience, and the Teaching of English

> . . . I am waiting
> to get some intimations
> of immortality
> by recollecting my early childhood
> and I am waiting
> for the green mornings to come again
> youth's dumb green fields
>   come back again
> and I am waiting
> for some strains of unpremeditated art
> to shake my typewriter
> and I am waiting to write
> the great indelible poem
> and I am waiting
> for the last long careless rapture
> and I am perpetually waiting
> for the fleeing lovers
>   on the Grecian Urn
> to catch each other up at last
> and embrace
> and I am awaiting
> perpetually and forever
> a renaissance of wonder.
>
> *From* "I Am Waiting" (last stanza). Lawrence Ferlinghetti, *A Coney Island of the Mind.*
> Copyright © 1958 by Lawrence Ferlinghetti. Reprinted by permission of New Directions.

One summer evening some years ago my three-year-old son was standing on the balcony of the apartment, resting his chin on the railing and staring off into the sunset—one of those rare quiet times for a preschooler. His mother, concerned about paint-and-lead poisoning, called out to him, "Stephen, are you chewing on that railing?" He thought about that for a moment, then turned and said, "No, I'm *wondering* on it."

I found that to be an exciting use of language. It was creative, and it was highly effective. It was natural metaphor. I wished I'd said it.

During that same year I helped out from time to time in a cooperative preschool and I was constantly amazed by the ways in which the children used language and were delighted by it. Adults too often seem to dislike writing, to feel embarrassed or inarticulate when speaking in public, and to prefer *not* to read. Preschoolers, by contrast, love to make things in language—playing with words, making rhymes, listening to and telling stories, role playing, and pretending to write and to "read" books. Young children not only are deeply involved in the process of learning language, but they are also having a good time doing it.

These observations also made me wonder—in particular, about what happens to the ability young children have to "wonder" with language, to use it playfully and experimentally, operating on the fringes of grammaticality to make new meanings for themselves and others. That ability seems to diminish as young people grow. By the time their schooling is complete, all too many of them have been reduced to speaking and writing what Ken Macrorie has labeled "Engfish," a kind of faceless, dull, standardized, jargon-laced prose.

A NAME FOR IT
A student stopped me in the hall and said, "Do you think I should submit this to *The Review?* I have this terrible instructor who says I can't write. Therefore I shouldn't teach English. He really grinds me."
I looked at the first two lines:

> *He finks it humorous to act the Grape God Almighty, only the students in his glass lisdyke him immensely.*

and thought they seemed like overdone James Joyce. I said I had better take the paper home and give it several readings before reacting. But she pushed, and I read the next lines,

> *Day each that we tumble into the glass he sez to mee, "Eets too badly that you someday fright preach Engfish."*

I wanted to hug that girl. She had been studying Joyce in another class and had used his tongue to indict all of us Engfish teachers. I didn't believe I had lisdyked my students all those years, but I had indeed tumbled them into a glass every day and fright preached Engfish at them. This girl had given me a name for the bloated, pretentious language I saw everywhere around me, in the student's themes, in the textbooks on writing, in the professors' and administrators' communications to each other. A feel-nothing, say-nothing language, dead like Latin, devoid of

the rhythms of contemporary speech. A dialect in which words are almost never "attached to things," as Emerson said they should be.

There is no need to romanticize childhood or to suggest that we all
should talk and act like preschoolers. One reason children can make creative leaps is that their language categories are not so refined and explicit
as those of adults. As children grow, as children learn more and think
more, their language use becomes sharpened and refined; they use language more precisely and at the same time lose some of their ability to
make broad, poetic jumps. This increase in the precision of children's language use is an important part of growing, and thus it is natural for some
children's "wondering" capacity to disappear.

When Stephen was eight, his language growth had taken on a different direction. While pedaling our bikes down a back street, we paused to
watch a mangy, battle-scarred tomcat sniff through the contents of a garbage can. Stephen observed, thought, then asked, "Is this an alley?"

In this case, he was using language not to create a metaphor, but to
pin down a definition and to understand a metaphor by attaching the
"right" kind of label to that cat. As both semanticists and logicians have
noted, the more mature and sophisticated our labeling systems, the less
able we become to jump outside the restriction imposed by our own language.

But one must also examine the effects that *schooling*—specifically the
teaching of English and the language arts—has on children, because despite good intentions and carefully planned curricula, book reports and poetry discussions, weekly themes and careful evaluation, the schools have
rather consistently blunted peoples' use of language and created an un-
healthy fear of language in adults.

THE CONCERN FOR ADULT STANDARDS

One clue to the problem is the general attitude that many people have
toward the young and the process of growing. Back in the 1950s, Art Linkletter's afternoon television program provided some interesting insights
into adult attitudes through the daily interview feature involving young
children, "Kids Say the Darndest Things." What struck Linkletter and his
adult audience as being funny or cute were children who said adultlike
things without fully knowing what they meant: "Out of the mouths of
babes. . . ." The same principle proves to be a major source of the humor in
Charles Schulz's "Peanuts" strip. Charlie and Lucy and Linus and

Schroeder have "adult" problems and often use the language of adults. If Schulz aged the characters 30/40 years, "Peanuts" would be no more humorous than "Mary Worth" or "The Heart of Juliet Jones."

Adults like children who are "little men" and "little women," who "act their age," who show signs of a "normal" progression toward adulthood; and the schools seem to have taken to the task of pushing children into adulthood as quickly and efficiently as possible.

In the teaching of English, this position has led to an overwhelming concern for adult language standards—what adults say, do, read, and write—with the schools requiring young people to meet these standards as early as possible.

The adult standards model is shown in Figure 2.1. The adult stands at the top of the stairway of learning, the child at the bottom. Since adults perceive adulthood as a generally desirable end product, the adult knowledge is parceled out along the K–12 stairs. Children pause at each level to learn the required materials—this year, nouns and topic sentences; next year, gerunds and the three-paragraph theme. Sometimes children get stuck and must spend an extra year on a step; occasionally, a bright child comes along who can take the steps two at a time. In terms of the school system, the diploma symbolizes the attainment of adulthood.

In English classes, this adult standards approach creates an obsession with "good English" and leads to grammar and usage lessons, vocabulary and spelling drills, and endless correction of "errors" and "blights" in student writing. In teaching reading, it creates the "reading group" and leads to a peculiar absorption with reading grade levels. (Recall the prestige given to the fifth grader who scores at the tenth grade reading level.) At the upper levels it creates the belief that allowing children to choose their own reading matter will destroy their "progress" and fail to develop their "taste."

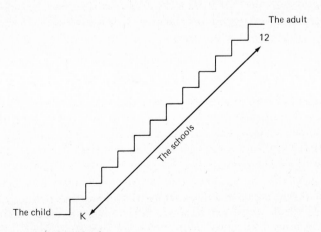

Figure 2.1   Adult Standards.

Teaching adult standards has been approached with all the directness and efficiency that teachers once employed in teaching multiplication. Under the "old math," there was no nonsense about learning to multiply. We were first taught times tables, a clearly established set of relationships among numbers, and shown the principles of multiplication: how to arrange figures in columns, where to place the multiplier and the multiplicand, how to move one column to the left for each row of figures. Next we were given exercises, page after page of figures to multiply. These were inspected by the teacher, and if we were erring—perhaps because we didn't know the times tables or because we couldn't remember which was the multiplicand and which was the multiplier—we received remedial instruction. It was the familiar pattern of teach-test-reteach.

In composition, instruction often begins with the adult standard: fundamentals of sentence structure, paragraphs, and organization—the "times tables" of our profession. Next the teacher provides writing practice, an assignment that enables the student to demonstrate mastery of the skill. Finally, the teacher evaluates and comments on the writing, suggesting appropriate remedial work or revision. Teach-test-reteach, study-write-revise. In reading, the "times tables" consist of phonics and word attack skills, taught from grade one and tested through the medium of the reading group. In literature, instruction includes the fundamentals of criticism and literary structure, with testing done through discussions and essays that reveal whether students can produce acceptable, adult-like interpretations of important works.

WEAKNESSES IN THE ADULT STANDARDS APPROACH

The adult standards approach seems direct, uncomplicated, and efficient. It "ought" to work. Yet the public and teachers continue to lament that Johnny and Jane can't read and write, and by almost any measure one can name our children come out less literate than we want them to be. Why hasn't this direct approach worked?

To the extent that one can sort out reasons, the problem can be traced to several false assumptions and oversimplifications that teachers have made about language, thought, and experience. For instance, the concern for adult standards clearly implies that adult language behavior is both fixed and exemplary; because adults think and talk one way, future generations must continue to do the same. This assumption fails to take into account the flexible, changing nature of language and dialect by decreeing that the speaking and thinking style of one generation must become that of the next. But language changes from year to year, from decade to.decade, and contrary to popular mythology, change seldom represents decay. By stressing the language of adulthood as a fixed model, the adult standards approach attempts to cut down on language excursions and explorations, the very sort of "wondering" with language that is so vital to children.

A second weakness deals with the relationship between thinking and language. The adult standards approach has consistently drawn on the metaphor that "language is a mirror of thought." The relationship between language and thought has been seen as being so close that many teachers believe that "unclear" or "ungrammatical" speech represents unclear thinking or reasoning. This belief, in turn, has created an almost moralistic tone in language instruction; teachers of English are not simply teaching language forms, they are teaching *right thinking* through the medium of language. If the mirror of thought—language—is not shiny and spotless, the mind of the child is dull and blighted. English texts have thus made heavy use of the metaphors of disease, warfare, and gardening, as teachers "diagnose and cure" language ills, "attack and defeat" illogical language and "weed out" undesirable words. The mirror metaphor at best oversimplifies the thinking/speaking relationship, ignoring, for instance, such phenomena as intuition, uncomprehended experience, and subconscious thought.

Perhaps the most damning indictment, however, is that the adult standards approach denies the language competence of young people. In Figure 2.1, the child is shown at the *bottom* of the stairway, far removed from the ideal of adulthood. Yet we know that virtually all children perform competently with language in many situations just as soon as they can talk. Granted, they occasionally misuse syntax or grope for words or fail to make their meaning clear. Sometimes they say "he don't" or "him and me." But young people of school age—five to seventeen—exhibit a remarkable amount of language competence. They send most of their messages successfully, to adults as well as to one another. They talk, chat, and gossip; they question, challenge, and inquire. When you think about it, in a short span of time, young people have mastered an incredible number of language processes and skills.

But the adult standards approach sees *any* error, *any* deviation from the ideal, as something wrong, rather than as a groping toward something in an experimental way. Thus, the adult standards approach amounts to a doctrine of *anticipatory remediation,* calling for every student to be treated as a *remedial adult,* even though he or she is still in the process of reaching adulthood. If adults applied the same hypercritical standards to their *own* language, they might find themselves placed back on the bottom step of the stairway of learning.

THE RELATIONSHIP BETWEEN LANGUAGE AND EXPERIENCE

In order to see the problems with the adult standards approach even more clearly, teachers should look at a more complex model of language learning, one derived from contemporary research in education, linguistics, and psychology. It is represented in Figure 2.2.[1] The model consists of four central parts: 1) *experience* (here represented by the "real" world, a globe), 2) *perceiving*, 3) *thinking*, and 4) *languaging*. A fifth component, shown at the center of the model, is the *child*. In contrast to the previous stick figures, the child shown here is fully dimensional. This representation stresses that although one can talk about the cycle in general terms, it is unique for every individual. The cycle gains its power—is "energized" so to speak— by the fact that, as James Moffett states, "The human child was made to symbolize." Children and adults constantly use symbols in all phases of experiencing, perceiving, thinking, and using language.

The human child was made to symbolize. Language is one especially useful way to do so because it parcels out, labels, and links material reality according to social practicality.

From James Moffett, "The Word and the World," *Language Arts,* February 1979, p. 115.

Experiencing and Perceiving

We frequently speak of the world out there as "the real world," yet all of us know that we perceive the world differently. The seventeenth-century empirical psychologists got themselves into a true dilemma, in fact, by claiming that the only reality is a person's perceptions, so that there is no way one can prove that the world exists independently of his or her own perceptions. Bishop Berkely was famous for refuting those empiricists by kicking a stone—to show its reality—though in fact he may merely have proven that he was himself capable of perceiving pain.

For practical purposes, however, we are able to reach agreements about external reality. We can agree that the sky is "blue"; that it gets "dark" at night; that the "Chevy" pulled into the intersection first. Obviously, the use of language is inextricably bound up with the process of establishing mutual realities. Walt Whitman writes of the child that "went forth every day" to look upon objects and to become those objects. But as Ernest Cassirer points out, becoming a part of the "objective world" in-

---

[1] This model is based in part on studies of language and thinking by Jean Piaget, L. S. Vigotsky, and Kornei Chukovsky; the general semantics of Alfred Korzybski; the cultural linguistics of Benjamin Whorf and Edward Sapir; the language acquisition studies of Colin Brown, Martin Braine, Ursula Bellugi, and others; and the pedagogy of John Dewey, James Britton, John Dixon, James Moffett, and many others. A selected bibliography is given at the close of the chapter.

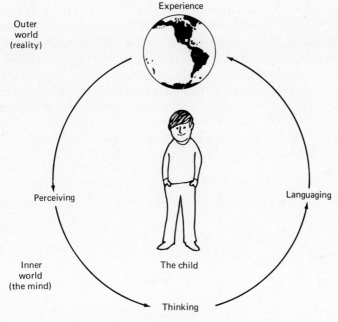

Figure 2.2   The Language/Experience Cycle.

volves both naming and conceptualizing. Language becomes a link between what we perceive in the world and the concepts and thoughts we store in our heads. Language, then, is not simply useful for sending messages. It involves tabulating, classifying, naming, conceptualizing, as well as establishing and presenting the "self."

> There was a child went forth every day,
> And the first object he look'd upon, that object
>   he became,
> And that object became part of him for the day
>   or a certain part of the day,
> Or for many years or stretching cycles of years.
>
> *From* Walt Whitman, "There was a child went forth."
>
> By learning to name things a child does not simply add a list of artificial signs to his previous knowledge of ready-made empirical objects. He learns rather to form the concepts of those objects, to come to terms with the objective world.
>
> *From* Ernest Cassirer, "An Essay on Man."

This role of language has long been fascinating to linguists and psychologists. In the early part of this century, they believed that language systems placed limits on perception, so that, for example, people who spoke "primitive" languages were capable only of "primitive" thought. However, as linguists have become more sophisticated, they have discovered a reciprocal arrangement: Human beings create symbols to represent their experience to themselves, and because of the human need to symbolize, people find ways of representing *anything* that finds its way into their experience. In other words, language systems expand to accommodate people's experience.

At the same time, there is a danger that once linguistic symbols have been established, they can become a substitute for reality itself. For example, earlier in this chapter I wrote, "The sky is blue," something that generally passes as a truism. Yet as I write, the Michigan sky outside my window is a bleak, midwinter gray, and even if the weather were bright and sunny, any painter will tell you that using a blue pigment in pure form is at best a crude approximation of what the sky "really" looks like.

To say that the sky is blue is a useful verbal shorthand that will do nicely for most purposes. Yet language users must regularly test their verbal abstractions against the reality of what they are seeing, hearing, and feeling. A good user of language—the child at the center of Figure 2.2— will thus come to learn that although language can simplify the process of recording experience, it must be used with great caution as well.

Thinking

> I think, therefore I am.
>
> **Descartes**

Descartes might just as easily have said, "I use language, therefore I am," as a proof of his identity, for just as perceiving is a linguistic process, what we label as "thinking" involves language as well. To begin with, the words we use generate some of the raw material for our thinking. We "talk to ourselves"; we think in language (or possibly in several languages); we rehearse what we are going to say before we say it; we review what we have said after we have said it.

And just as it was with perception, language both simplifies and endangers clear thinking. For example, the more abstract a word becomes, the less direct are its connections with reality. Compare the specificity of "animal" (abstract) to "dog" (more specific), of "dog" to "poodle" (more specific still). Then consider the amount of abstraction involved in a term like "freedom" or "equality" or "professionalism" or "justice." Abstract language of this kind is useful in dealing with broad issues and problems; yet at the same time, it is terribly easy for one's thinking to go astray because of inaccuracies induced by the abstracting process. It is thus a legitimate concern of the English class to take up and monitor *thinking* (that term itself an abstraction that describes thousands and thousands of interconnected mental processes).

Languaging

The final phase of the language/experience cycle is the area where the schools and English teachers have traditionally spent the most time: the actual creation of language. It is important to recall, however, that beneath utterances lies much previous linguistic activity. Through perceptions and thinking, we structure a view of reality and a view of ourselves. When it comes to creating language for others, we present a view of ourselves for public scrutiny. Languaging, then, serves a function for the speaker or writer as well as for the listener or reader.

To see these functions more clearly, it is useful to draw on the work of James Nimmo Britton, a language researcher from the University of London, who divides the functions of language into three categories:

1. *Expressive language* is very close to the inner worlds of perceiving and thinking, and it is presented not so much for the benefit of a listener or reader as to help the language user clarify the sense of self and of reality. For example, writing in journals and diaries is largely a matter of expressive language, allowing one to pin down thoughts and ideas for analysis. For many people, gossip and chat are principally expressive, done not so much to gain or to give new information, though that is obviously a central part of the process, but to express inner thoughts and to get them out in public where they can be studied.

2. *Transactional language* is concerned with carrying a message to another person, with transacting business through language. This form has probably received most attention in the schools, particularly through instruction in essay writing. But it is important to note that messages can be sent and business transacted in many forms of discourse—including film, television, video, song, poem, and story—so that the schools must be cautious about overstressing the essay.

3. *Poetic language* is not, as the term might imply, simply poetry or so-called "creative" writing. Indeed, one wishes that Britton had chosen a different label, for this one causes some confusion. Poetic language, he suggests, is language in which structure, style, and tone matter as much as content, and perhaps more important, it is language in which the reader or listener is invited to contemplate another's ideas. Much literature falls into

this category, but a great deal of student writing and speaking fits here as well, even though the young person may not be creating a poem or a novel.

With the creation of language, the experience cycle is completed; the speaker/writer reestablishes contact with the "real world." The use of language, then, is bound up with one's sense of reality. When we create language we ask a fundamental question: "Is my sense of the world an accurate one?" While that question sometimes leaves us at the mercy of our audience, it is much more sensible than kicking rocks to prove that we are alive.

The language/experience cycle, at first glance a simple one, is, in fact, quite complex. This complexity is shown in Figure 2.3, where the various processes I have described have been overlaid on the original diagram.

On that figure, too, I have sketched in the traditional components of the language arts program—reading, writing, listening, and speaking. These provide a shortcut or short circuit past "the real world." For though it is important for us to remain in touch with reality, we constantly use language to substitute for reality. If we want to fix a car, we don't just open the hood and start pulling wires and removing bolts. Rather we read a

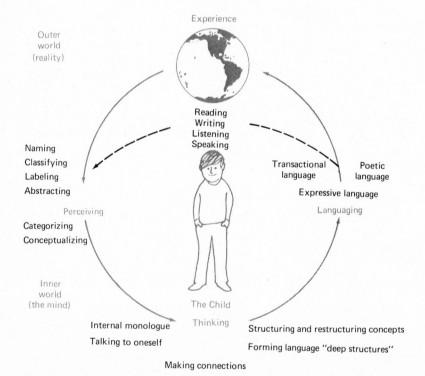

Figure 2.3   The Functions of Language.

book or ask a friend to tell us what to do. It is not necessary for us to experience every human emotion in order to be sensitive people. We can read novels where such ideas have been stored in poetic language.

The diagram helps to show, then, why the adult standards model is simplistic. "English" is far more than mastering parts of speech and the conventions of adult language. It involves complex processes and skills, all of them basic not only to communication, but to living as a fully functioning, creative human being.

Everyone is an artist. Whoever creates is an artist; and who does not create? This conversation is an art product. Back of our talk is our secret mind fabricating animated thought that does not even appear in speech. . . . Living things are creative artists every second of the time.

From Hughes Mearns, *Creative Power* (Garden City: Doubleday, 1935), p. 157. Cited by Roderic Botts, "The Student Comes of Age in the English Classroom," *The English Journal,* September 1973, p. 888.

PRINCIPLES OF LANGUAGE LEARNING

The relationships among thinking, feeling, and languaging are considerably more complex than the adult standards approach admits. Instead of regarding language instruction as a bits-and-pieces, lockstep, assembly line affair, teachers need to recognize that they are dealing with a complicated process, one that no simple mechanism will describe. As an alternative to the adult standards pedagogy, then, I want to present three basic premises about the language-learning process. Like the language/experience cycle, these premises are derived in part from the work of the various authors listed at the close of the chapter.

1. *As people grow, their language grows with them.* This growth is most obvious in the way young children master the basic grammar of English. No one needs to "motivate" the two-year-old to learn the basics of language; in fact, there is no way one can prevent a normal child from learning them. From the start, the young child searches for ways to communicate, to make contact with people, to express needs; and this drive for communication continues throughout life.

As people gain in experiences, they naturally assimilate what has happened to them and share it with others. In doing so, they search for the language that will help them say what they want. Language is not a *limit* to what people can think and do, but an outgrowth of their thought and experience. Nor is language a mere reflection of thought patterns; both mind and syntax are far more complex than that.

2. *The learning of language is a naturalistic process.* Given time, almost all people will discover a way of saying what is important, just as a baby, trying to find a way to describe his or her needs, discovers all kinds of strategies for communicating with others—especially at 2 A.M. No one gives the baby "babbling lessons." In fact, by the time children begin to string two words into "sentences," they are creating new, original speech. Through a complex process of probing, testing, receiving feedback, listening, and absorbing language patterns, children learn the complex rules of English.

It appears that the same process takes place in other kinds of language learning, even in complex matters of structure and style. Language learning is a process of wondering and exploring, of discovering the conventions of language in society so that people can use language successfully for their own purposes. One of the greatest problems with the adult standards approach has been to underestimate this enormous capacity people have for learning language or anything else that interests them.

I do not believe that language, in any of its manifestations, is regarded as something "different" by children. Children do not learn language differently from the way they learn anything else. Nor are they motivated to learn about language for different reasons. Indeed, children do not want to learn "speaking," "listening," "reading," and "writing" as isolated skills or abstract systems; they want to understand the world in a far more general sense and to achieve their own ends in a far more general sense, and the learning of language in any of its external aspects is entirely coincidental. Language only becomes complicated and difficult to learn when it is separated from other, more general, nonlanguage events and activities in the world.

From Frank Smith, "The Language Arts and the Learner's Mind," *Language Arts,* February 1979, p. 119. Copyright © 1979 by the National Council of Teachers of English. Reprinted by permission of the publisher and the author.

---

3. *People learn language only when the language is being used for real purposes.* "Real" purposes in this case means using language for self-selected reasons. No one learns very much about language either by studying language or by completing practice exercises that are isolated from real life. Spelling drills, vocabulary, composition lessons, reading lessons will accomplish little if the student does not see them as "real"; and no end of motivating, threatening, challenging, encouraging, or browbeating will make the unreal real. In other words, one cannot teach language unless the setting for its use is important to the learner.

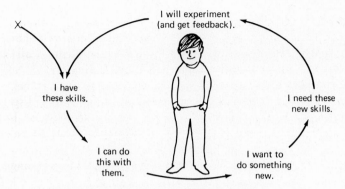

Figure 2.4   The Process of Acquiring Language Skills.

SKILL LEARNING: A MODEL

The idea of language learning as "naturalistic" is unsettling to many teachers. It seems to imply that language learning happens "by magic," without any intervention from the outside. Since many of us were reared in school systems that used the traditional approach, we wonder where the teacher fits in. To gain a sense of the relationship between learner and teacher in an experience-based program, it is useful to look at another model, this one of the process of skill acquisition.

Alec Hinchliffe has suggested that "skill getting" and "skill using" are reciprocal and interdependent processes.[2] Only as we use present skills, Hinchliffe suggests, do we create a need to develop *new* skills. Further, as we search for new skills, we strengthen and refine our existing ones.

Borrowing from Hinchliffe's model, we can visualize a cycle of skill acquisition, as shown in Figure 2.4. The cycle helps to show how language skills—from basics to rather complex thinking skills—grow and develop. Speakers or writers, whatever their age, have an intuitive knowledge of their bank of skills—that is, what they can *do* with language. "I have these skills," they say to themselves, "therefore I can do these kinds of things." But no member of the community of language is static; each person is growing, so speakers or writers come to feel, "I want to do new things to express and share my growing experiences." Thus they conclude, "I will need new skills to accomplish this task." As they attack a new task, they reinforce their present bank of skills while adding to it.

How are the skills actually *learned?* Obviously many complex processes operate, but three main sources, in order of importance, can be identified.

[2] Alec Hinchliffe, "In Search of Splendour," ed., in Leslie Stratta, *Writing* (London: National Association of Teachers of English, 1968). Hinchliffe acknowledges D. H. Parker as a source of his ideas.

Imitation and Synthesis

Imitation is perhaps the strongest language-learning mechanism that human beings have: We absorb language from our surroundings and learn how to create new structures based on the same model.[3] Sometimes the imitation is direct, but most of the time, it is rather like osmosis—after being around and in language for a period of time, we automatically begin to pick up its characteristics. Many people have experienced this when they have visited an area with a dialect different from their own; after a day or two, most people start to talk like the natives. Similarly, foreign languages are learned most easily in a country where the language is spoken, because in being immersed in the language environment, the imitation/synthesis cycle operates at full strength.

Closer to home, we can see the process at work in the language acquisition of babies. At first babies coo and gurgle aimlessly. But they also hear adult sounds and receive rewards for imitating them. (Anything my babies said that sounded even faintly like "dada" was greeted with high praise.) Largely through imitation, children learn to make single words and then to string two and three words together to create sentences. But almost as soon as children are capable of generating these minisentences, they begin to make new combinations that they have never heard before. Thus babies do more than just imitate like a parrot; they figure out the scheme of language to use it creatively.

In this way, language grows. By the time children are four or five, they have mastered literally thousands of linguistic transformations and tens of thousands of words that give them access to the full range of English. All this is done without a single lesson in grammar, without a textbook or schoolteachers, without exercise sheets and drill.

But schooling has a role in the process, too, and as I will suggest, the teacher is vital in fostering and promoting the imitation/synthesis of new language structures.

Trial and Error

Closely bound up with the imitation process is experimentation, testing out new language structures to see whether they work. The baby experiments with one- and two-word utterances, babbling and cooing and shifting sounds until its language gets some results. Young people and adults experiment as well: In oral language, we watch for cues in body language and quiz our listeners—"Y'know what I mean?"—to make certain our message is coming across. In writing, we draft and revise, trying to find the

---

[3] This paragraph should not be taken as offering support for the so-called "models approach" to writing in which students copy the styles of famous writers. Slavish imitation stultifies rather than helps a person become a more creative language user.

words we want, and after the writing is done, we seek feedback: "Did you like it?" "Could you understand it?"

The schools have been much too eager to assist children with the "error" part of "trial and error." Teachers would be a good deal more effective if they concentrated on helping students arrange some good, realistic experiments, some possibilities for using language where both the errors and successes would be evident.

Information Sources

Obviously, many language activities involve skills that cannot be picked up entirely by imitation and trial and error. In reading, for example, it seems evident that students need to be told something about the print code in order to be able to crack it, and similarly, the conventions of spelling are such that direct instruction is sometimes more efficient than relying on a naturalistic learning mechanism. Still, one should not underestimate the extent to which even these conventions can be learned through imitation, synthesis, and exploration. A great many readers are self-taught, and a high percentage of our vocabulary grows directly through reading rather than from studying word lists.

In the traditional classroom, teachers devote a great deal of time to telling students how language works, providing information about it. In a classroom using the naturalistic approach, the teacher concentrates on creating an environment where students can find the help and instruction they need at the time when they need it.

Many teachers doubt that students will spontaneously ask questions about such matters as spelling, mechanics, and usage. But students are intensely aware of the effect that errors have on an audience. In fact, while doing a study of student writing, Robert Graham discovered that most young people are so tense about being correct that they are almost totally unable to do expressive or creative writing in any situation that remotely resembles a test (unpublished doctoral dissertation, Michigan State University, 1971). Not only are students aware of errors, they are often as obsessed with them as are their teachers and parents; and like the teachers and parents, young people need to put error consciousness in proper perspective.

If asking for help is encouraged rather than penalized, if it is welcomed and is met with practical advice, then seeking help becomes quite natural. But when students ask for help or identify a problem, they need prompt, useful help, not a lecture on adverbs. The materials that students find helpful vary widely, and the teacher therefore needs to have a wide variety on hand. Reference copies of basic texts—dictionaries, handbooks, grammars—may be useful for some students. Others may find a brief conference—30 seconds to see how the comma or paragraph works, for instance—much more helpful. Many students learn most satisfactorily from one another, and the teacher might want to learn about and publicize the names of members of the class who are good spellers, good punctuators, and good theme organizers, and set them up as resident experts. Teachers and students can also develop and collect games and puzzles that will appeal to people with different learning styles. With a bit of imagination, the teacher can invent materials that will be much more interesting than the usual textbook fare.

Another concern many teachers have is whether or not students will ask the right questions: "How can students know what to ask if they don't know what it is that they are asking about?" It may be that initially the students won't ask all the "right" questions. What they will ask is questions about what they perceive to be problems standing in the way of their success.

However good the children are, they will not produce adult work. Their work will be essentially child-like, and to assess this work anyone is up against a very real difficulty. For though he was a child once, though he may have made a serious study of child psychology and development, though he may have spent years at work among children, the fact is inescapable that he is an adult now. His memories of childhood are remembered with an adult memory, his knowledge of children is an adult's knowledge, and his conception of what is child-like is adult, too. The absolutely impossible thing for most people is to see anything as a child sees it, unclouded by maturity, and not through the mirror of assimilated experience. So in being critical he must beware of judging by what *he thinks* a child should do, or what a child should like; the criterion is what the child does do, and what he likes. The ability to turn again to childhood and see the world truly through childish eyes is given to very few men. . . .

From Sybil Marshall, *An Experiment in Education.* Copyright © 1963 by Cambridge University Press.

As Sybil Marshall has suggested, it is difficult for an adult to predict what a young person will or will not see as vital at any given moment. What seems most important is that teachers concern themselves less with whether or not the student will ask the right questions (i.e., the adult questions) than with providing useful answers to the questions that are asked. If students begin to develop confidence in their ability to ask questions and to find workable answers, if the teacher gives them confidence in their skills and a feeling of security about exploring new territory, they will, as time goes by, ask more and more sophisticated questions—naturally moving to the point where their questions are the "right" ones.

SOME IMPLICATIONS FOR EDUCATION

Perhaps the most important implication in what I have been writing is that education in general and language education in particular must focus on the personal growth of young people, not simply on the transmission of facts and skills. It is a cliché that education should concern itself with "the whole child," but cliché or not, few educators have practiced it. As writers like Erik Erikson, Edgar Friedenberg, and Paul Goodman have suggested,[4] adults have consistently short-circuited or warped the process of coming of age through the impositions they make on young people.

No real-world ostrich buries its head in the sand when frightened, but real-world educators do. And, when one's head is firmly buried, the problems of growing up are invisible. This out-of-sight, out-of-mind stance of educators is an ancient one. In 1900, when the high school dropout rate was nearly 93 percent, the "problem children" indeed disappeared: they drifted unprepared into the larger society that absorbed them. As our society matured—became urbanized, technological, and affluent—we began to get serious about compulsory education for all the people; head burying no longer worked to shut out the real world.

As our society tries to organize in the turmoil of fear, drugs, protest, and violence, and as our cities burn, each of us must face the truth that there is no place to hide. We must finally look hard at the way it really is and hope it is not too late to abandon the old and learn to live with the new. The wrenching process of change is upon us; if we do not adapt, the bones of education will bleach alongside those of the dinosaurs of previous millennia. We must look closely at current, largely unacknowledged problems of early adolescents and deal with them within our education system.

From Elton McNeil, "Early Adolescence—Fact and Fantasy," in Stephen Dunning, ed., *English for the Junior High Years.* Copyright © 1969 by the National Council of Teachers of English. Reprinted by permission of the publisher and the author.

When the growing up process is distorted, the end product—the adult—is also likely to be distorted. A distressing number of adults are not self-fulfilling. Rather, society is filled with people who have torn egos, who are dependent on the opinions of others and on the accumulation of material possessions to establish their own self-esteem. Often people are incapable of loving in any real sense; they are incapable of establishing goals for themselves and cannot expand their lives beyond the routine of job and

[4] Erik Erikson, *Childhood and Society* (New York: Norton, 1963); Edgar Z. Friedenberg, *Coming of Age in America* (New York: Random House, 1963); Paul Goodman, *Growing Up Absurd* (New York: Random House, 1960).

home. Too many Americans lack what John Gardner calls the capacity of "self-renewal," and once they reach adulthood, they become unchangeable and static, with no potential for further growth.

"Keep on growing," the commencement speakers say. "Don't go to seed. Let this be a beginning, not an ending."

It is a good theme. Yet a high proportion of the young people who hear the speeches pay no heed, and by the time they are middle-aged they are absolutely mummified. Even some of the people who make the speeches are mummified.

As we mature we progressively narrow the scope and variety of our lives. Of all the interests we might pursue, we settle on a few. Of all the people with whom we might associate, we select a small number. We become caught in a web of fixed relationships. We develop set ways of doing things.

As the years go by we view our familiar surroundings with less and less freshness of perception. We no longer look with a wakeful, perceiving eye at the faces of people we see every day, nor at any other features of our everyday world.

When we have learned to achieve . . . self-renewal . . . we shall have discovered one of the most important secrets a society can learn, a secret that will unlock new resources of vitality throughout the society. And we shall have done something to avert the hardening of the arteries that attacks so many societies. Men who have lost their adaptiveness naturally resist change. The most stubborn protector of his own vested interests is the man who has lost the capacity for self-renewal.

From John W. Gardner, Self-Renewal. Copyright © 1964 by John W. Gardner. Reprinted by permission of Harper & Row, Publishers, Inc.

Because living and using language are so intimately related, the language capacities of these adults also tend to be blunted and distorted. The end products of the linguistic coming-of-age process are often inarticulate people, incapable of anything more than basic writing, unable to sustain a detailed conversation, uninterested in reading.

This line of thinking suggests that educators and parents should stop trying to propel children through the schools toward adulthood at increasingly accelerated rates. Rather, teachers should concentrate on helping students gain in experience in order to become as full and rich as they can be at their present level. Instead of worrying about getting students ready for third grade (when in second) or college (when in sophomore year in high

school), teachers should work toward providing a full set of living and languaging experiences. The child begins the educational process as a self-renewing, self-motivating person using language creatively. If the teacher
sustains that capacity for self-renewal by providing new directions, opportunities, and experiences, students will not only sustain their powers of self-
renewal, they will extend them. Students who have participated fully and
diversely in a variety of language experiences will easily outstrip those
whose instruction in English has been limited to indoctrination into the linguistic standards of adulthood.

THE COMMUNITY OF LANGUAGE

We can visualize the young person as a growing, inquiring member of a
community—humankind—linked together by its use of language. Each of
us participates in the language community for our own ends and purposes.
Each of us gives *to* the community by sharing ideas, thoughts, and experiences with other people when it is clear that they want to listen to us and
when it serves our own needs. Each of us also takes *from* the community
through language that provides information, ideas, aesthetic or affective
experiences, and confirmation of our own beliefs.

Young people are quite like adults in their participation in the community of language. But the extent and range of that participation differs.
The baby in the cradle participates only to a minor extent, making contact
with one or two persons in limited ways, sharing with them and learning
from them. As young people mature, as they meet new people and probe
into new ideas, their participation in the community of language naturally
broadens until it becomes full and "adult." In coming of age, young people
learn the language that supports their communication needs.

The schoolroom provides a model but by no means an unreal version
of the language community. It is a place where students can explore their
experiences and ideas through language. The English teacher is anything
but passive in this classroom, as subsequent chapters will show. The use of
language is natural and pleasurable, and any reasonably normal person en-
joys life in the community of language. A central aim for the English
teacher must be to help students participate in the community of language
to the fullest possible extent by providing situations and experiences that
allow them to use language naturally and pleasurably. This is no small task.

EXPLORATIONS AND RESOURCES

- In *Teaching as a Subversive Activity*, Neil Postman and Charles Weingartner list
  the following traits of a "good" learner:

  Good learners have *confidence* in their ability to learn.
  [They] tend to *enjoy solving problems*.

[They] seem to know what is relevant to their survival and what is not.

[They] prefer to rely on their own judgment.

[They] are not fearful of being wrong.

[They] are emphatically not fast answerers.

[They] are flexible.

[They] have a high degree of respect for facts (which they understand are tentative).

[They] know how to ask meaningful questions.

[They] are persistent in examining their own assumptions.

[They] use definitions and metaphors as instruments for their thinking and are rarely trapped by their own language.

[They] do not *need* to have absolute, final, irrevocable resolution to every problem.

The sentence, "I don't know," does not depress them.[5]

Some of these traits—such as the ability to ask good questions—directly involve language. Others draw on language, as part of perceiving, thinking, or languaging. Review the list by considering the role of language. How much or how little does skill in using language affect one's ability to be a "good" learner?

• Make a list of your principal encounters with language during a busy hour of your life, say, the first hour of the day or en route to school. What division do you note among various language forms—the amount of language you receive orally, in print, or through the media? Ask some young people to do the same and lead a discussion on the ways in which we receive language and how it shapes experience.

• Do the same activity with your own production of language. What proportion of your language is oral? Written? Break down your language use into the three categories described by James Britton: *expressive* (for yourself), *transactional* (for sending messages), and *poetic* (for contemplating experience). Which forms do you use most regularly? Have some students keep the same sort of record and compare ideas. [Note: This is an interesting experiment to try at various times during the day.] How does your ratio of, say, *expressive* to *transactional* change from when you arise to when you are directly engaged in your work for the day?

• Choose a nonverbal medium—photography, painting, clay or junk sculpture, drawing, montage—that you have never used before and compose an "essay." Keep note of the skills that you master in the process of composing. Where do the ideas come from? Could a teacher have helped you before you started? In what ways? What questions would you ask someone skilled in that medium if that person were here?

• Observe a class (someone else's or your own) and do an analysis of the skills exhibited and learned (or not learned) during, say, a 20-minute period. If it seems to be a good class, take note of the components that make this language community work. If it is unsuccessful, plot out some of the changes needed to make it a skill-learning environment.

• Education textbooks and school curriculum guides are often prefaced with statements about what children "ought" to know and do and about the school's

[5]*From* Neil Postman and Charles Weingartner, *Teaching as a Subversive Activity* (New York: Dell [Delacorte Press], 1969), p. 45.

"duty" to the child. Often these statements are based on adult standards and are remote from the immediate needs and interests of children. Without falling into the writing of clichés and bromides, write a description of what you think the English class ought to do for young people in terms of language growth. You might start with a list of the traits of a good *language* learner.

- Here is a letter of complaint to a daily newspaper. Like many such letters, this one makes its point, but does so through extreme statements and by ranting. Analyze this letter and its language. If schooling should have some carry-over into adult life, what did the schools owe this writer?

To the Editor:

In response to Mrs._____'s letter about the Foundry: I realize that the factory is noisy but there are a lot of men and their families who depend on that noise for a living. My husband is one. One thing you don't know is the terrible heat and heavy lifting all the guys do there.

Also, we live about a mile from the airport and talk about noise and not being able to hear tornadoes. Those big jets sound just like a tornado. We are right in the take off and landing pathways and if one ever comes down God help us. So you may have noise but the Foundry isn't going to drop on your home.

I am not saying stop the planes and put a lot of men out of work. So you see, Mrs._____, we all have things we don't like but we have to think of others too.

Mrs._____

Related Readings

The two most comprehensive and valuable discussions of what English is, can be, and should be are John Dixon's *Growth Through English* (Urbana: National Council of Teachers of English, 1975) and James Moffett's *Teaching the Universe of Discourse* (Boston: Houghton Mifflin, 1968). Both explore some of the models and approaches that have been used over the years and make recommendations for the establishment of "personal growth" and "student-centered" curricula. My own *ABCs of Literacy* (New York: Oxford University Press, 1980) provides a discussion of the aims and dimensions of literacy education in America, both from a historical perspective and in terms of recent concern over a possible decline in literacy. Every teacher should, at one time or another, look at some of the classic background work that supports a naturalistic language-learning approach: John Dewey's *School and Society* (Chicago: University of Chicago Press, 1956), Jean Piaget's *Language and Thought of the Child* (New York: Humanities Press, 1962), L. S. Vigotsky's *Thought and Language* (Cambridge: MIT Press, 1962), and Kornei Chukovsky's *From Two to Five* (Berkeley: University of California, 1962).

In this chapter, I have placed strongest emphasis on the productive language skills—writing and speaking. However, the language/experience model is also applicable in the complex field of reading. Frank Smith's *Un-*

derstanding Reading (New York: Holt, Rinehart and Winston, 1971) is an outstanding study of the process of mastering reading skills and extends much of what was said here into the area of reading. Even if they are not concerned with teaching initial reading, teachers can gain a great deal by examining *Learning to Read Through Experience* by R. V. Allen and Dorris Lee (Englewood Cliffs, N.J.: Prentice-Hall, 1966), a book that shows the natural integration of reading and writing skills. Finally, John Holt's *How Children Learn* (New York: Pitman, 1967) though a bit dated in some of its rhetoric, offers some fascinating informal studies of the learning process in young people and implies that the skill acquisition model discussed here is valid not only for talking and reading, but for games, sports, art, and mathematics.

3
The Dimensions of the English Curriculum

Abolish English? Those are strong words. The man can't be serious. English has been around forever and will be around forever. It's as American as . . .

When August Franza wrote his essay "Abolish English," he generated a storm of protest. An English teacher himself, his purpose was to satirize some of the failings of the English curriculum. But a great many people thought his proposal was genuine and wrote strong letters of protest.

His tongue-in-cheek argument presents a number of points that could be taken seriously by teachers, administrators, and parents. For example, many people have argued that English is irrelevant in the age of media. Kids watch television nowadays and don't read books. They pick up a telephone and call long distance rather than write letters. And if adults write, it is often oral, through a dictation unit, and their reading is limited to cereal boxes. While people obviously need to learn to read and write, the critics argue, the age of English, with its emphasis on books, pens, and paper, is over. If we teach anything, critics suggest, we ought to teach "media literacy," the how to's of "reading" and "writing" in film, video, tape, photography, and even computer languages.

Other people cast a different argument for the abolition of English. English, they say, is too filled with frills and nonessentials like the historical study of literature or vague goals like the "appreciation" of literature as art. Let's stick to the basics; abolish English and teach something called "communications skills": how to send and receive messages clearly and precisely. List the basics you want to teach; teach them; then measure your students to see whether you've succeeded.

I have no particular quarrel with the integration of media in the English classroom; nor am I opposed to ensuring that students who graduate from our schools have competence in basic communications skills. It seems to me however that critics err badly when they claim that print is dead and when they imagine that future cultures will rely on electronic communications media to the exclusion of reading and writing. Further, those people who would reduce English to a laundry list of basic skills are ignoring broad areas of competence in their zeal to make English functional.

Even though it seems fair to suggest that English teaching has had many failures, one must still ask, "To what end have all these methods and techniques and strategies been tried? What were people trying to accomplish with paperbacks or anthologies or formal writing or no writing or anything they could get away with?" The answer that comes back is clear. Whether using the new technology or the old, paperbacks or hardback anthologies, teachers have consistently and steadfastly had the adult standards discussed in Chapter 2 in mind.

For instance, when the use of film-as-art recently became popular in English classes, one of the first texts to appear on the market was a glossary called "A Grammar of Film." The assumption—very old and really quite traditional—was that until students knew about film terminology—"pan," "fade," "wipe," "dolly in," "zoom," "cut," "take"—they couldn't properly understand or appreciate a film. Similarly, although the paperback revolution brought interesting, relevant literature to the English class, one still has the feeling that many teachers introduce paperbacks only as a new route to an age-old goal: "If we let them read what they want, perhaps we can eventually get them back to the 'good' books." Musical lyrics too often enter the classroom only as an oblique way of presenting poetry: "These popular song lyrics, class, are actually *poetry*. You see, poetry *is* something you've been enjoying all along without even knowing it. Now, let's look at the metaphors in the first line of this song . . ."

Marshall McLuhan has noted that we approach the future by looking in a rearview mirror. New media, he says, are often filled with the content of the old rather than used for fresh purposes. And so it is with innovation in education. Teachers discover film, then use it to teach traditional literary terms; curriculum reformers decide that it is innovative to make teachers list objectives, then settle for objectives whose origins are two hundred years old and whose underlying principles have long since been discredited. Under such circumstances, it is hardly surprising that "new," "revolutionary," "innovative" ideas don't seem to work better than did their predecessors.

If the teaching of English is to grow, and if the critics are to be answered, English teachers must deal with some first principles, asking themselves precisely what they are about. "What is English?" is a question that provokes debate whenever it is raised, but it is a question that must be considered by English teachers every time they enter their classrooms. What the teacher does—whether teaching film grammar or trying to get students to write about their personal experiences—defines the subject not only for the teacher, but for the student as well.

The most articulate answer to the question of "What is English?" that I have ever encountered was written by Benjamin DeMott, a professor of English at Amherst College. While it is somewhat lengthy, it bears reprinting *in toto*.

"English" is not centrally about the difference between good books and bad. It is not centrally about poetics, metrics, mysteries of versification, or the study of balance and antithesis in the Ciceronian sentence. It is not centrally about the history of literature, not centrally about changes in moral and philosophical systems as these can be deduced from abstracts of selected Great Works. Still more negatives: the English classroom is not primarily the place where students learn of the majesty of Shakespeare and alas for Beaumont and Fletcher. It is not primarily the place where students learn to talk about the structure of a poem or about the logic of the octave and sestet, or about the relation between the narrator and author and speaker and mock-speaker and reader and mock-reader of the poem. It is not primarily the place where students learn to mind their proper manners at the spelling table or to expand their vocabulary or to write Correct like nice folks. It is not a finishing school, not a laff riot with a "swinging prof," not an archeological site.

It is the place—there is no other in most schools—the place wherein the chief matters of concern are particulars of humanness—individual human feeling, human response, and human time, as these can be known through the written expression (at many literary levels) of men living and dead, and as they can be discovered by student writers seeking through words to name and compose their own experience. English in sum is about my distinctness and the distinctness of other human beings. Its function, like that of some books called great, is to provide an arena in which the separate man, the single ego, can strive at once to know the world through art, to know what if anything he uniquely is, and what some brothers uniquely are. The instruments employed are the imagination, the intellect, and texts or events that rouse the former to life.

From Benjamin DeMott, "Reading, Writing, Reality, Unreality . . . ," in James Squire, ed., *Response to Literature* (Urbana: National Council of Teachers of English, 1968), p. 36. Copyright © 1968 by The National Council of Teachers of English. Reprinted by permission of the publisher and the author.

DeMott's statement is a remarkably coherent and complex observation. It is important to note that he does not discard the traditions of the English profession. He values studies as diverse as the reading of Great Works and the learning of vocabulary. Yet he is unwilling to let the traditional studies completely dominate the discipline. English, he says, is centrally about humanness as it can be known and explored through language.

As I demonstrated in the previous chapter, language interpenetrates every part of our lives. DeMott is right in saying that there is no other place in most schools where the concern for the individual human being and his or her language is central. Most important perhaps is that he puts the various components of English into perspective by relating them to the personal growth of the individual. Does "correctness" matter? Of course it does, but it cannot be allowed to engulf students in mechanical matters so that the human voice is lost. Should students study the media? Of course, since the media play an important role in structuring and shaping our lives; but students should study other human uses of language as well, including reading and writing.

If we accept the concept that English is a study of humanness—of humanity—we can see some important implications for the English program:

1. *"English" is more than just reading and writing.* While the first two Rs are a major concern of English teaching, the subject must broaden its scope to include *all* uses of language, from informal chatter to formal discussion, from short memos to long examination papers, from the "language" of television to the language of computers. English can not afford

to limit itself to the writing of school essays and the reading of school textbooks.

2. *"English" is not limited to the English classroom.* In his influential *Hooked on Books* (New York: Berkley, 1976), Daniel Fader calls for "diffusion" of English throughout the school, so that every teacher is concerned with English. Actually, that goal is not new but has been an ideal since the nineteenth century. Still, at the present time, schools at all levels seem to be moving in the direction of interdisciplinary studies, and even in schools where interdepartmental cooperation is not easy, English teachers can take it upon themselves to include other subject fields in their work, inviting students to read about science, to write about social studies, to roleplay and dramatize from history, to talk about consumer concerns, politics, and world affairs.

3. *"English" is a way of perceiving, knowing, learning, and becoming.* English is not simply a matter of mastering the language, for language is a part of all aspects of human experience. Martin Nystrand has described the English class as a place where one uses "language to know," not just studies the uses of language. Actually, the two are bound up with each other.

Order can be created *through* language use, not just studied *in* language, imposed catechismically through a canon of rules. We can use *language to know*, not just *study to know language*.

From Martin Nystrand, ed., *Language as a Way of Knowing* (Toronto: Ontario Institute for Studies in Education, 1977), p. 12.

Borrowing from Benjamin DeMott, we can say that English as a school subject is "not centrally" about the learning of language, either language structures or applications, that it is "centrally" about the processes of perceiving, knowing, learning, and becoming as these involve language. The point of connection, of course, is that in learning to use language to explore, to know, to become, one also masters the forms and structures of the language as well.

THE ENGLISH CURRICULUM: THE STATE OF THE ART

The heretic spoke: "The only thing holding most educational institutions together is the brickwork and the heating and plumbing. Schools find it convenient to centralize the purchase of books, fuel oil, and hamburger meat, and economical to gather children in blocks of five hundred or two thousand for the purpose of educating them. But aside from these considerations (and perhaps a winning football team), most schools are simply physical conveniences—like bathrooms—with no spiritual or intellectual relationship to draw people or to hold them there."

"Hold on there!" Up the aisle came the assistant superintendent for instruction, struggling under the weight of a heavy volume. "This book provides our unity here. It is the curriculum guide that we have developed."

The book that the superintendent displayed was three hundred mimeographed pages long, bound in pale green paper, and held together with oversized brads. The preface included a letter from the school board, thanking the members of the curriculum committee for their dedication and long hours of work in preparing the guide, along with a note from the principal adding some comments about the tradition of quality that the school had long enjoyed. Inside the guide could be found a pie diagram showing the components of English, a list of the textbooks shelved in the book room, charts of grammar objectives by grade levels, a list of senior high English electives, a bibliography of books approved for free reading, sample lesson plans for teaching *To Kill a Mockingbird*, a list of spelling demons, and a map showing fire escape routes.

The guide had been written in 1974.

Had anyone asked, it would have been noted that the assistant superintendent's was the only extant copy, the others having been lost or misplaced as early as the fall of 1975.

Examining a typical curriculum guide often reveals an incredible amount of inconsistency and disarray, carefully masked by a good typing or printing job. In preparing this chapter, I reviewed approximately three dozen curriculum guides from elementary, junior, and senior high schools around the country, guides I collected at national meetings or through one of the national information retrieval systems. While there is obviously no national curriculum or "typical" school, I think it might be useful to present some generalizations about the common characteristics of these guides in order to create a view of the current state of the English curriculum.[1]

The Elementary Years

"English" does not exist for the elementary teacher. It is either called "language arts" or is broken down into its various components: reading, writing, spelling, vocabulary, etc. And here is perhaps the greatest weakness of the elementary curriculum, for despite the opportunity for integrated studies presented by the self-contained classroom, elementary teachers

[1] I want to emphasize that I am generalizing here. There are many good schools in North America that do not resemble the school I will describe. Still, I will stand by this description as being fairly representative of school curricula today.

tend to fragment language, presenting it to children in small bits and pieces. "Spelling" becomes a component all to itself (9:20 on Tuesdays and Thursdays). "Writing" becomes penmanship, which is different than composition. Elementary school children even pick up these distinctions. When my son Stephen was in third grade, he was careful to distinguish "reading," which meant going to the library, from "reading workbook," which involved learning how to alphabetize. While a great many elementary school teachers do a superb job of teaching language, I believe it is fair to say that in all too many cases, the English curriculum of the elementary grades is dominated by workbooks, work sheets, and fill-in-the-blank activities rather than by actual language production.

The Junior High/Middle School Years

At the risk of alienating a number of good, well-organized school staffs, it appears to me that the junior high English curriculum can best be characterized as "Basic Hodgepodge." While some middle schools and junior highs have established topical or thematic courses, most simply have an "English" or a "Language Arts," a general course, with teachers moving from one instructional unit to another without purpose or focus. This leads to a blend, or hodgepodge, characterized by the following list of units from a junior high school curriculum:

> Building Blocks of Communication
> Curtain Up!
> Focus on Life
> Man in Conflict
> Power of the Paragraph
> Western Sampler
> Reinforcing Language Skills
> Aquanauts and Astronauts
> Communications Through Mass Media
> Encounter and Insights
> Laughter and Legends
> Power of the Paragraph
> Creative Composition

I do not wish to detract from the content of these units, for many seem sound, clever, and imaginative. The flaw it seems to me is the inconsistency in the definition of "English" that emerges from the list. Why must "Creative Composition" be isolated from the literature units? Why must instruction in language basics always be isolated in "Building Blocks" units? If mass media are important, why are they set apart in a unit of their own rather than integrated with either literature or composition work? Children characteristically take many, many such units of work during their junior high years, but I fear that often in the schools, there is no real cumulative effect, no real sense of purpose and direction in the English that students "do."

The Senior High Years

Now I will risk alienating the English staffs of some top-notch schools by generalizing that in contrast to the junior highs, the senior high English curriculum comes off as being "Advanced Hodgepodge."[2] Most commonly, high schools offer a "general" or basic first-year English course, sometimes offered in different sections with students grouped by ability levels. Such courses have a twin aim of remediating what the high schools commonly conceive of as the misspent years of elementary and junior high schools, plus providing material to prepare students for the coming years. The content of the course may range from mythology—so they will understand classical allusions in literature—to grammar—so they will presumably learn to write and speak "correct" English. Like the junior high curriculum, the general courses tend to alternate a series of units in literature, language, and composition, often without apparent connections.

For upper-level students, and in many cases for the entire school, the high school English curriculum is usually based on limited numbers of elective courses. Electives are something relatively new, having first appeared in a significant number of high school curricula about 1970. Prior to that time, the upper-level courses tended to be yearlong surveys of British, American, and world literature. Elective courses broadened the offerings but in many cases presented too many choices so that topics and decisions overwhelmed the students. Too, in the heyday of electives, many courses of dubious intellectual merit with only marginal content in English crept into the curriculum. In recent years, the trend has been toward consolidation, eliminating some of the spurious choices, and, in some instances, replacing electives altogether and returning to the traditional survey.

One attempt to control the profusion of elective offerings was through the concept of *phasing*, in which the difficulty levels of courses were identified, the course difficulty often following a five-level designation developed at the Trenton, Michigan, high school. Phase I courses were for remedial students and tended to be fundamental courses such as "Practical English," "Jobs and Business Problems," and "Study Habits and Note Taking." At the upper level, Phase V courses were strongly academic, designed

---

[2] As a university person, I may be accused here of patronizing the schools. I do not intend to patronize and for the record, I will characterize the typical university curriculum as "Arrogant Hodgepodge," put together by people who should know better. The university catalog is perhaps the worst of the curriculum guide genre, a potpourri of conflicting demands and ideologies, duplicated efforts, idiosyncratic courses, and paper monuments to special interest groups. The university "curriculum" is, in fact, merely a compilation of the messy results of years of independent planning, growth, accretion, and accident.

REPRESENTATIVE HIGH SCHOOL ELECTIVE COURSES

Effective Listening and Speaking
Fiction: Struggles and Conflicts
Studying the News
Seeing with the Camera
Man and the Car
Girl Talk
Practical English
Jobs and Business Problems
The Novel
Writing Stories
Heroes
The Art of the Motion Picture
Individualized Reading
Modern Books
Successful Writing
Plays
Mass Media
Search for Meaning
Rebellion and Conformity in
   America

The American Dream
Study Habits and Note Taking
Creative Writing
World Literature
Early English Writers
Modern British Realism
Mythology
Advanced Composition
Science Fiction
Research Seminar
Great Ideas
Linguistics
What Makes a Classic?
Poetry
The Oriental Mind
Literature Concerning Africa
The American at War
Pulitzer Prize Winners
Shakespeare
Business English

for accelerated and highly motivated students, covering topics like "Early English Writers," "Modern British Realism," and "What Makes a Classic?" While this phasing scheme made some sense out of the elective hodge-podge, it also had the effect of tracking students, so that vocationally oriented students and many minority and second language students found themselves in lower-phase courses, while the college-bound, often the children of white professionals, pursued the upper-level, advanced courses.

Despite the problems inherent in elective curricula, a return to the conventional survey course hardly seems like a solution. What is required in the teaching of English at all levels, it seems to me, is not another round of restructuring and reordering of the traditional components of language study, but a reexamination of both the discipline (What is English?) and the concept of curriculum (What do we mean by "curriculum"?)

In any case, real change can only occur when teachers change what they *do* in a classroom with *any* given curriculum. That is, a "classical" curriculum does not preclude an "experience-centered" approach. Electives do not guarantee student choice. Required courses do not eliminate the possibility that students may make many selections as part of their education. While some curriculum patterns make good teaching easier, no curriculum or guidebook can effectively prohibit teachers from asking basic questions about their subject and teaching on the basis of the answers they discover for themselves.

CURRICULUM: NOUN OR VERB?

In a great many elementary, junior high, and senior high schools (as well as the colleges), the curriculum is static. When asked about the school's curriculum, many teachers will produce a *document*, a listing of courses, aims, and requirements, rather than describe what people *do* in the school. Thus "curriculum" has become a noun—an object—that is changed only when the documents are rewritten. Often a rewriting really means a reshuffling, so that all the old familiar parts settle, largely undisturbed, into new, but more comfortable settings.

By contrast, curriculum can be conceived as a verb—something dynamic and changing—consisting of a set of flexible relationships and activities that evolve from a group of adults—the teachers; a larger number of young people—the students; and a set of resources—bricks and mortar, books, desks, pencils and paper. When these parts function well together, they produce a community of language, a place where students read, write, and talk about concerns of their own, steadily increasing the range and complexity of their language skills. The English curriculum, in short, is a *process*—something *happening*—rather than a product or object, and its dimensions grow and shift just as surely as the needs and interests of the students change.

In order to become a verb instead of a noun, a curriculum must be both *collaborative* and *experimental*. Too few teachers in the schools and colleges seem to be exploring their teaching systematically. As often as not, "innovation" consists of adopting a new textbook, that covers the old material in new, or superficially different, ways. Few teachers are willing to experiment and share the results of their experiments with other teachers. Teachers tend to work alone, in silence, often masking their failures and sharing only their successes.

A faculty must find a common meeting ground where people can talk to one another, share their successes and failures openly, and search productively for new ways to solve common problems. This common ground does not mean that the faculty must be monolithic. To the contrary, the most productive schools are those that are not only diverse, but that capitalize on the diversity of their members.

An experimental curriculum involving collaboration among teachers will obviously lead to constant development, evolution, and sharing. Although curriculum artifacts—written statements of ideas, units, aims, goals, and approaches—will be available, there may not be any single, dated "guide." Ideally, no formal revision will take place either, because revision will be constant, and the members of the department will look forward to new experiments rather than back to the documentation of a tradition.

It is also obvious that no standard curriculum will do for all or even for most schools. Any evolutionary curriculum will be shaped around the qualities of the participants. One can, however, talk about the curriculum-building process and about some of the stages through which faculties need to proceed as they evolve the curriculum and courses.

FORMING A THEORY OF INSTRUCTION

In *Toward a Theory of Instruction* (Belknap, 1967), Jerome Bruner makes a valuable distinction between a "theory of instruction" and a "curriculum." A *theory of instruction*, he suggests, is a consistent, coherent, if tentative, statement about what young people need to learn and about how they learn it, "a theory of how growth and development are assisted by diverse means." A *curriculum*, on the other hand, is a specific set of goals, methods, and materials.

Unfortunately, many educators are reluctant to deal with the necessarily difficult and abstract issues that come up in the process of developing a theory of instruction. Rather, they prefer to get to the "nuts and bolts," the practical business of mapping out a course of study. It is understandably tempting to avoid the "idealistic" stage in order to get on with the course outlining and the text adoption. But dealing with basic issues is critical, and unless a faculty is willing to grapple with them, the time spent planning is often wasted. Without a theory of instruction—even one that sometimes says, "We don't know" or "We can't agree"—the curriculum becomes fragmented.

The actual form that a theory of instruction takes is variable. It may consist of an essay about English teaching written by one member of the faculty; it may be a collection of individual statements submitted by individual teachers; or it may be an inventory of teacher talents in which the members of the faculty describe what they feel they can bring *to* the language community. Perhaps most useful, it may be an unwritten spirit of understanding that grows among staff members as a result of discussions and debates. What it cannot or should not be is the typical broad statement of "philosophy" for a school system—something so vague that any member of the department can seek refuge under it—a statement laced with meaningless platitudes about citizenship, morality, and the basic skills of language.

Gray Cavanagh has evaluated some of the questions that departments typically consider when planning curriculum. The questions for concern that he *rejects*—"How can the teacher best teach?" "What are the best ways of teaching the student our literary heritage?"—are the nuts and bolts questions. The questions he proposes instead—"How can the student best learn?" "What curriculum approach best assures the emotional and imaginative development of the student?"—are the broader questions that are the concern of a theory of instruction. Only *after* those have been answered adequately should the department begin moving on to more practical matters.

The Questions for Concern Should Not Be	The Questions for Concern Should Be
How can the teacher best teach? What is the best course of studies?	How can the student best learn? What are the most effective ways of involving the student in the learning experience?
What are the best texts for teaching English?	How can the student be motivated to develop a taste for reading a wide range of books and magazines?
What are the best ways of teaching the student our literary heritage?	How do we teach the student to select and to teach himself those elements important to his personal understanding of the past and present?
What is the best way and sequence in which to teach the basic skills of English?	How do we lead the student to master the processes necessary to his full development and to accept his responsibility to himself to select and perfect these skills in a developmental pattern?
How do we make the student learn efficiently those subjects and skills in which he is weakest?	By what approaches can we best enable the student to develop his talents and abilities in his areas of greatest interest and aptitude?
What curriculum approach best assures the cognitive development of the student?	What curriculum approach best assures the emotional and imaginative development of the student?
By what methods can the student best be taught standard English usage?	By what methods can the student best learn to express himself orally and in written form with power and individuality?
How can teachers best work together to produce a valid course of studies?	What are the most effective ways in which the student can be enabled to direct his own learning?

LEARNERS AND THEIR LANGUAGE

Perhaps the most neglected aspect of curriculum building has been the learner. Though most guides and catalogs are filled with statements about what the school plans to do with, to, about, and for the students, one seldom sees any overt indication of the teachers' understanding of the students and what they bring to school. Lack of concern with the learner is characteristic of the adult standards approach, since the overwhelming interest of that approach is not in what the student *is*, but in what he or she supposedly should be.

In *Sense and Sensitivity* (London: University of London Press, 1965), J. W. Patrick Creber has argued that failing to look at the student has led to a split between "the interests of the pupil and the interests of the discipline." Curricula are constructed with the *discipline*—grammar, rhetoric, criticism—at the center, and students and their interests simply must be fit in around this center.

The whole approach to [English] has encouraged [the child] to pass over vast areas of familiar but interesting experience—to bury it forever, without realizing its significance, without ever having an inkling of its connection with the subject he has been trying, so painfully, to learn.

We cannot, however, accept any such sacrifice—any dichotomy between the interests of the pupil and the interests of the subject. Such a distinction seems based on the false premise that the two are mutually exclusive or radically opposed. On the contrary, that method which is of greatest benefit to the child seems to be precisely the method which makes for the greatest vitality and sensitivity of language.

From J. W. Patrick Creber, Sense and Sensitivity. Copyright © 1965 by J. W. Patrick Creber. Reprinted by permission of the publisher, The University of London Press.

Creber contends that the needs of students and the knowledge of the discipline *must* coincide. If they do not, he suggests, then the *discipline* or *course content* must be reshaped to fit the needs of the individual student.

This view leads Creber to a simple but ingenious approach to developing a course of instruction. First, the teacher must study the students in terms of their psychological, emotional, cognitive, and linguistic development. Then he or she can sensibly select experiences that will both meet the students' needs and help them develop within the disciplines of English.

Following this approach, once a department has developed a theory of instruction, it should take a very close look at the students it serves. One way of doing this, of course, is through interest inventories and surveys. A survey might include the following kinds of questions:

What are the principal common interests of the students at this age: animals and pets? sports? boys? girls? the world outside? college?

What are the principal concerns that the students feel? What do they worry about most: themselves? their relationships with peers? their relationships with adults?

Where are they in the process of becoming adults? In what ways are they adultlike? In what ways are they operating under different patterns?

In addition, teachers should draw on their own experiences with students at the appropriate grade level, using all of their past experiences to focus on what can be happening in the English class.

Which books, poems, stories have proven "sure fire" with this group? Why?

Which books appeal to special interests?

What kinds of writing topics and speaking topics have worked well? What kinds haven't? Why?

Given completely free choice of language activities, which ones will students choose? What does this tell us about these students?

Teachers might also want to look directly at the language skills that the students already have mastered to discuss the direction those skills seem to be taking. One way to approach this would be for the teacher to think in terms of ten or so students whom he or she would regard as competent users of language for their own purposes at their present age, students who seem to be getting along well in the community of language—talking comfortably with peers and adults, writing successfully in the tasks they select, reading and generally enjoying it. Then the teacher might ask himself or herself:

What are the skills in language that these students have mastered to date?

What can they do with language? What are they learning to do?[3]

From this discussion will emerge a developmental portrait of young people, a rather complex and detailed one if the curriculum group is serious about trying to determine student needs. Like the theory of instruction, it will be tentative; and it will recognize, furthermore, that not all students will or should fit precisely into the pattern that has been identified.

[3] Obviously this list of skills will differ markedly from the skill distribution in textbooks, being based on the students' use of language, rather than on adult expectations. I find it both amusing and disturbing that in the recent move toward assessment and accountability, no group (to my knowledge) has taken this approach to setting standards. No one actually looks at children's writing, so the skill expectations set by assessment groups are often little more than wishful thinking, bearing no relationship to the real languaging worlds of young people.

ESTABLISHING THE CURRICULUM PATTERN

This kind of planning sets the stage for actual curriculum development based directly on students' needs. With such data one could, for example, apportion elective courses not by their difficulty, but by the kinds of student interests that they meet. Quite a few school systems have done something like this, creating sequences of "selectives," so that students' work is both directed toward particular needs and sequential through related term courses. Or if teachers were designing general English courses, they might choose units to mesh with a particular stage of student development rather than assigning topics in a hodgepodge fashion. (Three model curricula designed this way are given a following section.)

In a follow-up to the article cited previously, Gray Cavanagh and Ken Styles have suggested in "Design for English in the 1980s" (*The English Journal*, September 1978, pp. 40–44) that curriculum design in the future will consist of three basic elements:

1. *Core program elements as determined by governmental education authority.* In this country, for example, both state and local boards of education have engaged in preparing lists of minimum basic skills for each grade level. Often such lists cover *just* a bare minimum. A curriculum planning group will need to include those skills but make certain they do not dominate the curriculum.

2. *Local program elements determined by team planning and individually by the classroom teacher.* There are two components that need to be considered:

   a. *Team planning.* The local group—school staff, English faculty, districtwide planning group—meets to make some basic curriculum decisions. Such planning should go beyond adopting a series of textbooks or approving a free reading list. A good planning team will take into consideration the surveys described in the previous section and will be concerned with meeting student needs and monitoring growth, not just with sequencing course structures.

   b. *Teacher planning.* At the very best (or worst, depending on one's point of view), the government-mandated and locally planned curricula will account for perhaps 25 percent of a teacher's time. The individual teacher always has done and probably always will do the bulk of planning.

3. *Personalized program projects designed and contracted by students working individually or in small groups.* Styles and Cavanagh involve students in the curriculum design, allowing for individualized and student-intitiated work done individually or in small groups.

(A diagram of the Styles-Cavanagh program, including a balance of reading/writing/listening/speaking projects, is shown in Figure 3.1.)

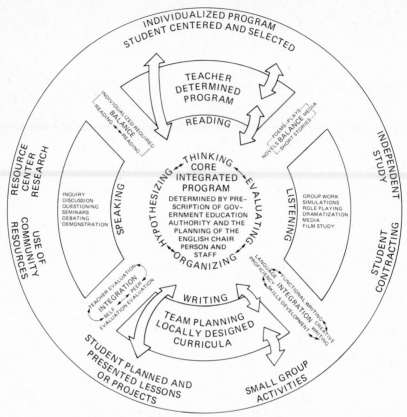

Figure 3.1 English Curriculum Components. (From Ken Styles and Gray Cavanagh, "Design for English in the 1980s," chart appearing in *The English Journal,* September 1978, p. 40. Copyright © 1978 by the National Council of Teachers of English. Reprinted by permission of the publisher and the authors.)

The Curriculum Design

The next step is to select a curriculum design or "package," a way of dividing students and teachers into units or courses of a workable size and content. In the secondary schools, the most common design is either *elective courses, general courses,* or a combination of the two. Within the elective pattern, courses may be completely free choice or a mix of required and elective.

But many more curriculum options exist at all levels, and curriculum groups should probably consider some of the following possibilities.

Curriculum Options

• *The Self-Contained Classroom.* A mainstay of elementary school, the self-contained classroom is really a variation of the one-room schoolhouse, where students meet with a single teacher for all their subjects. At one time self-contained classrooms were popular at the junior high school level as well, but more recently they have been replaced by subject-divided classes and teachers. Many people have argued that the loss of intimacy of the one-room school house has reduced the quality of education. Self-contained classrooms also make interdisciplinary teaching relatively easy, while at the upper levels, where this curriculum plan is not widely used, the various disciplines become fragmented and isolated.

• *Team Teaching.* Fashionable in the sixties, interest in teaming seems to have declined in the schools, partly because it often degenerated into lecture swapping, with team members taking turns lecturing to hordes of students on specialized topics of the team member's choice. The advantage to teaming is flexibility of grouping and the capacity for individualizing instruction. Through "buying time" by means of making presentations to large groups, the team members create more time for seminars and individual conferences. Thus, without disturbing schedule makers, schools create a kind of flexible scheduling. Many variations on teaming are possible. An appealing idea is that of clustering teachers of differing skills and experiences in single classes—a team consisting of master teacher, new teacher, a teacher aide, and perhaps a student teacher or group of tutors.

One area where teaming is on the upswing is in the middle school, usually grades 6, 7, and 8, where cross-age, interdisciplinary teams are growing in popularity. Junior high and senior high teachers might well study these experiments to see if they are applicable at the higher levels as well.

• *Small Group/Large Group.* This scheduling system allows the teacher to meet with a class as a whole once or twice a week and then in tutorial sessions several more times, usually for shorter periods of time. Such a plan allows for a high degree of individualization and helps to get the teacher out of the lecture mode.

• *Modular Scheduling.* Instead of relying on traditional 50-minute periods, modular scheduling breaks the day into a number of 15- or 20-minute modules. These "mods" can be combined in various ways to create long or short "periods" for small or large numbers of students.

• *School-Within-a-School.* Not all schools can or will achieve the kind of departmental unity that is necessary to achieve an integrated curriculum. The school-within-a-school provides room for consistent experimentation by interested members of a faculty, so that the department members who *can* agree on a course of study are able to work together within the school, establishing what amounts to an alternative curriculum. The obvious disadvantage, like that of the electives, is the potential for fragmentation and the creation of special interest groups. One can shudder at the thought of a grammar-oriented school functioning happily alongside of an experience school, each pleasing its own little clientele of students and parents. However the S-W-S program provides potential for rapid change and broad experimentation without disrupting the routine of the school.

• *The Infant School or Open Classroom Model.* The British infant schools are open activity centers, places where children go to talk, read, write, experi-

---

THE MOFFETT K–13 CURRICULUM
(Summary of Principal Writing Forms)

GRADES   **LANGUAGE ACTIVITIES**

K–3	Pantomime	Dictating and telling stories
	Acting out stories	Song writing
	Free improvisation	Writing captions
	Informal discussions	Writing observations
	Show-and-tell	Calendars and letters
4–6	Guessing games	Writing about pictures
	Charades	Diaries and letters
	Enacting stories and music	Written show-and-tell
	Taking dictation	Writing directions
	Writing from memory	Fables
7–9	Drama workshop	Writing short scripts
	Enacting scripts	Writing dialogue
	Improvisation	Dramatic monologue
	Panel discussions	Autobiography and memoir
	Journals and diaries	Poetry of observation
10–13	Autobiography and memoir (more complex)	Reflection
		Generalization and theory
	Interviews	Literature as script
	Reportage and research	Formal drama
	Profiles	Chamber theater

Abridged from James Moffett, *A Student-Centered Language Arts Curriculum, K to 13* (Boston: Houghton Mifflin, 1968).[4]

---

[4]A more recent edition of Moffett's book, co-authored with Betty Jane Wagner (Boston: Houghton Mifflin, 1976), features a new arrangement that deemphasizes the grade-level assignment of various language activities. This change made the book more accessible to teachers at all levels but eliminated what had been an excellent curriculum design model.

ment, and listen—to explore in an environment where free and open learning is invited. Extending and modifying the model, the open classroom curriculum consists of classes—or more accurately centers—where students go for language experiences. These centers can be divided by grade levels or by grade-level groupings (e.g. 7–8, 9–10, 11–12). The class structure emerges from the materials stocked in the center and from the interests of the students. The open classroom has recently come under attack for allegedly being "unstructured." However, teachers who have explored the concept or employed it in their work have discovered that this plan simply increases the amount of responsibility children take for planning their own education, while reducing reliance on the governmental or locally planned elements.

Three Model Curricula

English curricula can be designed and focused in a number of ways to bring about a degree of continuity in instruction. The three models that follow are based on the common principle of finding the structuring elements for the curriculum within the students' developmental patterns.

The Moffett K–13 Curriculum

By far the most ambitious, detailed English curriculum design available is found in James Moffett's A Student-Centered Language Arts Curriculum, K-13 (Boston: Houghton Mifflin, 1968), and its accompanying theory of instruction, Teaching the Universe of Discourse (Boston: Houghton Mifflin, 1968). Moffett's plan is based on seeing the communications situation as a relationship between "I"—a speaker or writer—"you"—a listener or reader—and "it"—the material under discussion. His developmental scheme, drawn in part from the work of Jean Piaget and L. S. Vigotsky, argues that as students mature, they increase their ability to do abstract thinking (dealing with more and more abstract "its"), while simultaneously learning to discourse over wide and more complex "I-you" distances. Thus, for the youngest children, K–3, he emphasizes such close kinds of communication as storytelling, sharing, and reportorial writing. At succeeding age levels, the writing and speaking activities gradually become more abstract and formal: transcription, memory writing, fiction writing for grades 4–6; monologues, dialogue, narratives, poetry of observation, journals for grades 7–9; autobiography, reportage, research, generalization for the upper-level students. Moffett would select appropriate literature from those genres as the students experience different kinds of writing.

Schools drawing on the Moffett model usually begin by presenting reading and writing activities centered on the discourse forms that have been described as appropriate for each level. Thus as children mature, their literacy skills become more and more complex. However, one weakness in the Moffett model is its very emphasis on literary and composition genres, e.g. dialogues, autobiography. This emphasis leads to develop one-dimensional teaching units or courses that draw on a single form rather than a rich variety of reading/writing types.

Creber's Program for Imaginative Work

J. W. Patrick Creber's curriculum procedure in *Sense and Sensitivity* (see earlier discussion) leads him to a program of "imaginative work" for students. After analyzing the interests and needs of his students, he perceives three developmental levels: the "rediscovery of the familiar" for 11-year-olds, "the expanding consciousness" for 12- and 13-year-olds who are entering puberty and becoming more aware of themselves in relation to others, and "imagination and morality" for the older students who are expanding their interests and concerns to encompass more and more of the world. Having selected these broad themes, Creber then chooses literature and writing activities that will help students explore the theme. Although Creber works from the point of view of *themes* and includes both literature and writing, his program has some interesting parallels to Moffett's. Both Moffett and Creber emphasize observation poetry and the rediscovery of the familiar for junior high youngsters and both move toward more abstract, essay-like writings—generalization, theory, and morality—at the upper levels.

CREBER'S PROGRAM FOR IMAGINATIVE WORK

FIRST YEAR [AGE 11]: THE REDISCOVERY OF THE FAMILIAR

"For several reasons the training of the imagination to recapture visual impressions is a good starting point with children entering the secondary school. In the first place, such children tend to interpret the injunction 'use your imagination' in a purely visual sense. . . . Secondly, the visual element is very obviously dominant in our society, particularly in entertainment. . . . One often has the feeling, when dealing with fourteen- and fifteen-year-olds, that much adolescent inarticulateness has its roots in a visual incapacity, or at any rate in a blunted sensibility; children appear to grow up without really seeing anything. . . ." (p. 23)

Topics for imaginative work:

    Concentration exercises
    Memories from nature (rainy days, Christmas morning)
    Responding to pictures and photographs from nature
    Responding to nature poetry

SECOND AND THIRD YEARS [AGES 12-13]: THE GROWTH OF CONSCIOUSNESS

"The stages outlined here are somewhat arbitrary and the division I am now making between the work for first- and second-year children is a case in point. Nevertheless, this division may serve to emphasize two general truths about children's development:

1. in this second year we may expect to see the nascence of adolescent self-consciousness
2. by this time the children are readier to be "art conscious"—to look at their work more critically and to learn some simple concepts of form and style.

... Though the main characteristic of this year's work will be its increased complexity, it will also differ from what has gone before in its greater stress on *people* as opposed to *things.*" (p. 48)

Topics for imaginative work:

Scenes describing people, especially familiar people
Descriptions of their own feelings in real situations
Descriptions of feelings in imagined situations
Critical or workshop examination of writing

THE FINAL STAGE [AGE 14]: IMAGINATION AND MORALITY

"Children of this age are becoming, as they move into the difficult period of adolescence, much more vividly aware not only of internal stresses but also of their relations with other people, whose behavior interests them deeply. The greater complexity and disintegration of their lives and the sharper intensity of their personal problems lead normally to a much greater degree of inhibition and self-consciousness. . . . A further characteristic of this age is of fundamental importance. Morality, for most children . . . as for most adults . . . is largely a matter of precepts and rules of thumb, which, though they may be modified or even rejected, are very rarely questioned fundamentally. . . . I believe that the only satisfactory method of making a real impact on the moral standards of the children is through the imagination by utilizing their already lively interest in people's behavior. They should now be ready to attempt subjects the aim of which is to make 'reciprocity of viewpoint' part of their own attitude to people." (pp. 73-75)

Topics for imaginative work:

Responding to literature of human experience
Objectifying some of the difficulties of adolescence through literature
Thinking and writing about people in other situations
Dramatization of diametrically opposed roles
Writing from the point of view of others

From J. W. Patrick Creber, *Sense and Sensitivity.* Copyright © 1965 by J. W. Patrick Creber. Reprinted by permission of the publisher, the University of London Press.

The Creative Word

The Creative Word is a six-volume English program with an emphasis on literature that I designed as part of the Random House English Program. In the manner of Creber, I based it on broad thematic-rhetorical emphases at each grade level, but with a number of appropriately chosen "units" within each grade. The units themselves contain literary selections, art and photographs, and detailed options for composing activities. Grade 7 emphasizes both close observation (the rediscovery of the familiar) and imagination, fantasy, and language play. Grade 8 stresses young peoples' expanding interests and provides a kind of transition between writing that is principally personal and writing that is more public—moving from monologue to dialogue, diary to narrative. The focus in grade 9 is on reportage, memory writing, and storytelling, while grades 10 and 11 deal with the students' expanding interests in their world. Grade 12 rounds out the cycle, dealing with broad issues in society and encouraging the students to look at and think about the world they are on the brink of entering.

Although this series is based on teaching units rather than complete courses, I believe *The Creative Word* offers a useful model for systematic development of English elective programs. Instead of merely offering courses in wild profusion, the English department can consider clusters or groups of related electives from which students can choose at any given level. Thus the topics of Book 5—"Values," "Making Judgments," "Taking a Stand," "Reason and Emotion," "Commentary," and "Exploring the Media of Persuasion"—are turned into a series of related courses open to, say, juniors and seniors. The material in Book 3—"Writing About Yourself," "Seeing People," "The World We Live In," "Actions and Reactions," "Friends and Relationships," and "Spinning Narratives"—can be used to create a series of course choices appropriate for younger students, say, in grades 9 and 10. Thus the principle of basing the curriculum on the cognitive, emotional, and linguistic development of children can be maintained, along with the obvious value of giving students choices through elective programming.

THE CREATIVE WORD

Book 1 (*Grade Seven*). Written by Geoffrey Summerfield. Emphasis on close observation, fantasy and imagination, and language play.

  Making lists of sensory observations
  Observation activities, seeing the unseen and unnoticed
  Playing with language in poetry and prose
  Seeing relationships
  Personal writing

Making up codes
Writing short playlets and stories
Doing interviews

Book 2 (*Grade Eight*). Written by Richard Peck. Emphasis on the expanding consciousness of the adolescent: internal thoughts, external and expanding relationships.

Making contact with other people
The animal kingdom
Survival and staying alive
Telling stories
Growing up
Telling opinions

Book 3 (*Grade Nine*). Written by Stephen Judy. Emphasis on seeing, describing, and telling about a personal world.

Writing about yourself
Seeing people
The world we live in
Actions and reactions
Friends and relationships
Spinning narratives

Book 4 (*Grade Ten*). Written by Patrick Courts. Emphasis on probing beneath the surface to see how things work, on examining how the world is put together.

Motives
Human relationships
Seeing points of view
What makes things tick?
Problems and solutions
Prophecy

Book 5 (*Grade Eleven*). Written by Stephen Judy. Emphasis on evaluating what the student sees happening in the world; expanded focus on problems outside the immediate life of the student.

Values and the individual
Making judgments
Taking a stand
Reason and emotion
Commentary
Exploring the media of persuasion

Book 6 (*Grade Twelve*). Written by Stephen Judy and Patrick Courts. Emphasis on the world a student is about to enter; a look at universal issues and problems from the point of view of the individual.

Who am I? or How do we become what we are?
Values in society today

Problems in society: Psychological knots, media, isolation, dehuman-
ized technology
Popular culture: art or trash?
You, your world, and tomorrow

From The Creative Word (New York: Random House School Division, 1973, 1974).

EVALUATING A CURRICULUM

This chapter concludes with a list of 20 questions I have found useful in examining elementary and secondary school English and language arts curricula. The questions are designed so that the more positive replies given,
the "better" the curriculum. However, not all curriculum specialists and
teachers would agree that all the components and elements described are
desirable. For example, though I believe basic skills instruction should be
integrated throughout the program, many people are persuaded that skills
must be taught in isolation to guarantee that they are properly covered.
Thus people evaluating an English curriculum should revise, adapt, and
rewrite the list to fit their own theory of instruction and particular interests.

QUESTIONS FOR CURRICULUM EVALUATION

1. Does the curriculum have a clearly stated, specific philosophy or
   theory of instruction?
2. Does the theory of instruction grow from observation and research
   into the growth and development of young people?
3. Does the philosophy reflect current, "state of the art" theory and
   research on language learning?
4. Do course and curriculum objectives grow from the philosophy so
   that they are consistent with it?
5. If a common core of objectives is supplied by either the school district or the state, do the objectives go beyond mere basics to encompass the full range of language activities?
6. Do common objectives leave room for individual teachers to develop
   courses around the individual needs of their students?
7. Does the curriculum reflect the expressed concerns and interests of
   parents and other community members?
8. Does the curriculum reflect the stated interests and concerns of the
   students?

9. Does the curriculum provide opportunities for students to assume some responsibility for their own education?
10. Do the courses or instructional units integrate the language arts rather than isolating them as separate components, that is, reading, literature, writing, skills?
11. Are students encouraged to read and write in a wide variety of discourse forms?
12. Are oral language activities—speaking, listening, dramatics, role playing—an integral part of language arts courses and units?
13. Are contemporary media—film, television, radio—a natural part of English work?
14. Does the curriculum include provisions for interdisciplinary work, either within English courses or through interdepartmental units and courses?
15. Does the curriculum make connections with the "real" world through community-based activities?
16. Does the curriculum directly or indirectly state or imply a concern for lifelong literacy?
17. Is the curriculum fully multicultural?
18. Does the curriculum pattern (e.g., grade-level English, electives, self-contained classroom) provide for sequence, growth, articulation, and natural relationships from one course or unit to another?
19. Does the curriculum provide for evaluation and assessment, both of students and the curriculum itself?
20. Does the curriculum provide for and encourage its own evolution?

EXPLORATIONS AND RESOURCES

- Articulate a response to August Franza's modest proposal to abolish English.
- What is your answer to the question, "What is English?" Consider it from one or several points of view:

  What *was* "English" for one of your favorite English teachers in high school or college? How did his or her teaching define it?
  What *is* "English" for you now, either as you are experiencing it in courses you are taking or as you define it through your teaching?
  What *could* "English" be if it fulfilled its potential? What do you *want* it to be for future generations of students?

- What is your own theory of learning, your "theory of how growth and development are assisted by diverse means"? You might find Gray Cavanagh's list of "questions for concern" given in the chapter helpful in pinning down your answers.
- The administrative structures of a school both simplify instruction and make it more complex. In your opinion, which of the following structures are worthy of

being preserved or saved? Which should be discarded? Which would, with some modification, be useful? To whom?

	Preserve	Discard	Modify
Schools	( )	( )	( )
Classes	( )	( )	( )
Courses	( )	( )	( )
Grades	( )	( )	( )
Teachers	( )	( )	( )
Academic departments	( )	( )	( )
Diplomas	( )	( )	( )
Semesters or terms	( )	( )	( )
Administrators	( )	( )	( )
Class periods	( )	( )	( )
Counselors	( )	( )	( )
Recess	( )	( )	( )

- The Canterbury Schools Simulation. This game simulates the development of an English/language arts curriculum for the public schools of Canterbury, U.S.A. The superintendent of schools, Alton Grandstaff, has invited educational consultant firms to submit designs for the curriculum in any of the district's three schools: Chaucer High, Pardoner JHS, and Pilgrim Elementary School (Figure 3.2).

A minimum of ten people can play this game as part of a college "methods" class or as a school or departmental in-service activity. Divide into teams of three, four, or five members. One group will role play the Panel of Judges, whose duties are described below.

Each of the other groups becomes an educational consultant firm, and chooses a name for itself like *Creative English Associates, Supergrammar Think Tank, Tomorrow's Words Today*, etc. In a predetermined period of time (ninety minutes to two hours seems to be a minimum), the educational consultant firms develop a proposal for the Canterbury school closest to the members' area of interest, either elementary, junior high, or senior high. Each firm makes a 20-minute presentation to the Panel of Judges. The panel may select "best" proposals from among those submitted or merely quiz and question the presentors, asking them to explain and justify their decisions and proposals. The Panel of Judges must represent all segments of the Canterbury population as well as the superintendent's office. A typical cast for a panel of five might include:

1. A representative of the superintendent's office: a bright young person with a fresh Ph.D. in Administration and Curriculum. Reform is this person's stock in trade; nothing is good unless *innovative*.
2. A representative of the minority groups, preferably someone fairly militant and activist.
3. A member of the white blue-collar work force, someone who sees the schools as functional and doesn't want to see hard-earned tax dollars wasted.
4. A liberal parent from a professional background who wants to see the schools in Canterbury become just as imaginative as those in Kensington Hills, a neighboring wealthy suburb.

```
                    THE CANTERBURY PUBLIC SCHOOLS
                        Canterbury, U.S.A.


Alton P. Grandstaff, Superintendent

        NEW INSTRUCTIONAL PROGRAM IN ENGLISH


Deeply concerned about the quality of literacy education, the Board of Education
of Canterbury, U.S.A. is authorizing the development of new English/language
arts curricula for Geoffrey Chaucer Senior High School, Pardoner Junior High
School, and Pilgrim Elementary School.  The Board seeks proposals from reliable
educational consultant firms for the new program.

The town of Canterbury has been described as "Everytown" and was once named an
All-American City by the national Chamber of Commerce.  It is supported through
a variety of forms of industry.  It is known internationally as the Safety Pin
Capital of the world, and the city also manufactures clocks and watches, lip-
stick cases, link chains, and comic books.  This industry has also created an
active business district and a need for a number of professionals in law, medi-
cine, and related fields.  In short, the town and its schools represent all walks
of life.

Twenty-four percent of the students in the schools are members of racial or
ethnic minorities, and the school district is committed to equality of educational
opportunity for all.  Approximately fifty percent of the graduating class of
Chaucer High will go on to college, many to Canterbury Junior College, but a high
percentage to the State university or other four-year colleges.  Most of the
remaining fifty percent will receive some form of vocational or career training
after they graduate.  The district is concerned about meeting the future needs
of all students.

The Board of Education has no particular model or pattern of instruction in mind
and invites consultant firms to develop highly imaginative, but sound innovative
programs.

Proposals will be discussed at a public hearing.

                                        Alton P. Grandstaff
                                        Superintendent
```

Figure 3.2   The Canterbury Public Schools.

5. A representative of the English teachers, someone well-informed about new trends in the field.

While the consultant firms are at work on their proposals, the Panel of Judges meets to develop a list of criteria for evaluating the proposals, possibly drawing on the evaluative questions listed previously. It must decide what kinds of educational features it sees as important, and it needs to settle on some ideas concerning whether or not the program is meeting the needs of the Canterbury students.

Related Readings

The reader interested in the three curriculum models presented in the chapter might want to examine the original sources in detail: James Moffett, A *Student-Centered Language Arts Curriculum, K-13* (Boston: Houghton Mifflin, 1968, 1976); J. W. Patrick Creber, *Sense and Sensitivity* (London: University of London Press, 1965); Stephen Judy and others, *The Creative Word* (New York: Random House, 1973, 1974). The concept of English across the curriculum is explored in depth in Nancy Martin and others, *Writing and Learning Across the Curriculum* (London: Ward Lock Educational, 1976, distributed in the United States by the National Council of Teachers of English), which is especially good at showing the relationships between students' personal lives and feelings and their learning of various school subjects. No large-scale study of the state of the English curriculum exists to replace the well-known James Squire-Roger Applebee study of *High School English Instruction Today* (Englewood Cliffs: Prentice-Hall, 1968). However, A *Survey of Teaching Conditions, 1977* by Arthur Applebee (Urbana: National Council of Teachers of English, 1978) reviews some of the same schools as the 1968 study and provides an interesting picture of the present shape and form of the English curriculum. Perhaps the most current information is available through the National Council of Teachers of English, whose Committee to Review Curriculum Bulletins annually solicits exemplary curriculum guides and publishes an informal review. Schools interested in having their curriculum guide reviewed can do so at no cost through that Committee: c/o National Council of Teachers of English, 1111 Kenyon Road, Urbana, Illinois 61801.

4
Creating Instructional Units

The term *units* is one that teachers use rather loosely. "I've just finished a unit on vocabulary," says Teacher A, who has spent five days reviewing a basic word list. "I'm about to start my popular culture unit," says Teacher B, who will spend the next eight weeks having her students study mass media. "I'm falling behind in my New England Poets unit," explains Teacher C, who is just halfway through a chapter in a literature anthology. An instructional unit can be almost anything from a few days of concentrated study to an entire course. Some teachers may have several units going at once: a Fridays-only writing unit, mixed with a Monday–Wednesday literature unit, combined with a Thursdays-only free reading unit.

In this chapter, I use the term to mean all of the above, consistent with popular usage, but I will place particular emphasis on long units for a simple reason: The longer a unit is, the more likely it is to be poorly planned. It is fairly easy to put together short units where the end is in sight right from the beginning. But working over a period of many weeks or several months, teachers often have difficulty planning and structuring. For one thing, there is simply the pressure of time placed on the typical teacher. Faced with several preparations and up to six classes, the teacher simply hasn't the time to figure out the fine details of a unit. It's easier just to select a textbook or two, launch into teaching, and then plan day-to-day as the term proceeds. The unit then becomes a long string of loosely related activities, and, to borrow from Shakespeare, "Tomorrow and tomorrow and tomorrow creeps at this petty pace from day to day."

Of course, there are some very good reasons for not knowing exactly where a unit will finish. If teaching is truly individualized, then some of the outcomes of an instructional unit will emerge as the needs, interests, and abilities of the students dictate. Still, it is one thing to individualize within a well-designed unit framework and quite another to teach day-to-day, hand-to-mouth, with no real sense of direction. This chapter presents a pattern for planning units—whether a ten-day "mini-unit" or a full-term course—which allows for careful, comprehensive design, yet still allows room for meeting individual needs.

Much of unit building depends upon the teacher and his or her individual style and values. Teachers must discover patterns of organization and activity that are comfortable for them while still being productive for students.

It is also important to note two parallels between unit building and the curriculum planning process described in the previous chapter:

> Like curriculum planning, unit building must be based on a solid, consistent (if tentative) theory of instruction—in this case, a theory of instruction that includes the teacher's own assessment of what a class can and cannot do.
>
> A unit should be based on intimate knowledge of students' needs and interests, on knowing the learner not simply by grade level ("Ninth graders are interested in _____") but by name ("Although Charlie is interested in _____, Scott certainly isn't").

TOPICS FOR UNITS

An instructional unit can be created on just about any topic in the known, or for that matter unknown, universe. Traditionally in English programs, units have been centered on the following:

> *Literary history* covering periods in British, American, and world literature.
>
> *Literary genre* focusing on a particular kind of literature: poetry, fiction, the novel, or a subgenre like science fiction.
>
> *Elements of language and composition* ranging from "the sentence" to "the paragraph" to "building blocks for communication."

While very good units can be built using any of these structuring principles, in fact, each kind places some serious limitations on the concepts and materials that a teacher can comfortably introduce. Thus, in a literary history unit, matters that go outside historical interest are often ignored, and literature is presented from a single point of view: its location in a chronological parade of literary works. Genre units tend to become "self-centered," dealing only with a single genre and ignoring connections with other literary forms. Language and composition units are notorious not only for isolating composition from literature but for breaking language and composition into fragments rather than treating them as an organic whole.

A much more useful way to structure and organize materials is through the *thematic* or *topical* unit. In the 1950s, when the term *thematic unit* first emerged, "theme" referred exclusively to *literary* themes: "courage," "identity," "the westward movement." Such units, like genre studies, tended to become self-centered, with the theme providing the cen-

TYPICAL TOPICS FOR THEMATIC UNITS

I Am Woman, You Are Man: Sexual Identity
"Alive but Alone . . .": Loneliness and Alienation
I Hear America Singing: American Folklore
Supernatural Literature: Launching Pad to Inner Space
Is Today Tomorrow?: Science Fiction
"We Are But a Moment's Sunlight . . .": Death and Dying
Whodunit?
Coping with Life: Survival
Teaching About Energy: Choices and Their Consequences
". . . Gonna Study War No More": Peace Studies
Life Experience: Biography
It's No Laughing Matter: A Study of Humor
Violence: As American as Apple Pie?
Let the Voice of the People Be Heard (American labor)
The Art of Criticism
The New Journalism and the Student Voice
Is Anyone Out There? (life on other planets)
Living with Difference (the handicapped)
The Exodus Theme in Black American Literature
Divorce
Dreams and Nightmares (American technology)
Twain and Vonnegut
Gods and Goddesses: Exploring Greek Mythology
American Ethnic Studies
Thinking About Things (a study of objects)
The Eskimo and His Literature
Literature from Prison
People in Crisis
Working
Kawps (police stories)

This list is drawn from three publications: *Miniguides,* by the editors of Scholastic (New York: Citation Press, 1975); Sylvia Spann and Mary Beth Culp, eds., *Thematic Units in Teaching English and the Humanities* (Urbana: National Council of Teachers of English, 1977); and Susan Judy, ed., "The *EJ* Curriculum Catalog," *The English Journal,* September 1977, p. 53.

tral quest and with teachers and students looking for little beyond it.

More recently, the concept of theme has broadened so that thematic units take on a wide range of issues and topics. As the preceding list shows, units can center on topics as diverse as the American labor movement and Eskimo literature. Well-constructed thematic units seem to me to have three principal advantages over conventional units.

1. *They accommodate a wide range of literary and other materials.*

Not limited to any genre, a thematic unit can contain poetry, prose, non-fiction, drama, and essays as well as media materials: films, videotapes, television programs. In the unit, "Violence: As American as Apple Pie?", for example, students would certainly explore the theme of violence in literature, but they could just as easily make a study of contemporary television programming.

2. *They are naturally interdisciplinary.* A unit on "Dreams and Nightmares" (a study of technology and its side effects) could easily include a historical component, tracing industrial growth back into early American history; a science component, examining scientific and technological progress and problems; a manual arts emphasis, studying the effect of labor-saving devices on the quality of products produced; a social studies element, reviewing the impact of automation on the American labor movement; a sociology focus, discussing the effects of industrialization on family life; and even a future studies emphasis: "Where is our technology taking us?"

3. *They allow a natural integration of reading, writing, listening, and speaking.* The traditional unit often isolates the parts of English: literature is studied alone; language is treated by itself; writing is separated from both. Thematic units, by contrast, invite students to apply all the language arts to the topic at hand. One day they write or talk about it; the next day they read or listen.

It should be noted, too, that thematic units can be easily worked into conventional curriculum patterns. For example, if teachers are in a school system that requires a full-year course in American literature, they can create topical units, say, "American Identity," "City Life and Country Life," "The Quest for Technology," and "War in American Life," all of which draw on the strengths of thematic teaching. A genre course on the short story or the novel can similarly split its content into themes, which, in turn, allows the teacher to bring in materials for enrichment from outside the central genre. Even composition courses can be structured thematically, replacing "the paragraph" and "the whole composition" with "Writing About Personal Interests," "Writing About Human Relationships," or "Writing About Issues and Attitudes." (See the description of *The Creative Word* English program in Chapter 3 for one example of a writing curriculum constructed along thematic lines.)

SETTING OBJECTIVES

Objectives are a highly controversial topic these days. Ever since the publication of Robert Mager's *Writing Behavioral Objectives* (Belmont, California: Fearon-Pitman, 1962), the schools have been in controversy over how objectives should be stated and how the success or failure to reach them should be measured, rewarded, and penalized. Consistently absent from discussions of objectives has been a concern for the underlying theory of instruction and the nature of the learners whose lives are to be shaped by those objectives. Whether good or bad, objectives come from two major sources that require separate discussion: *mandated* or *imposed* objectives, and *teacher-created* objectives.

Mandated Objectives

These are the objectives that, for teachers, are "givens," a fixed part of the curriculum. Traditionally, these common objectives grow from curriculum development committees at the building or, possibly, the district level. Increasingly however, state departments of education have created lists of skills to be covered at specific grade levels. Mandated objectives tend to be weak, possibly because they are created by committee and thus lack consistency, but more likely because they are far removed from particular young people in particular classrooms. Such objectives tend to concentrate on isolable skills—spelling, punctuation, handwriting—and to fragment the curriculum into innumerable pieces.

Nevertheless, given a mandated list, teachers must ask, "What do we do now?" One response is to design a teaching unit for each of the skills on the list, but "that way madness lies." Teachers would quickly find themselves teaching a fragmented curriculum—"thank you" letters one week, "listening skills" the next—without any sense of purpose or connection. But in many systems, particularly those in which students are tested for mastery of the mandated minimums at regular intervals, that is precisely what teachers have been doing. Predictably, the skills list becomes the entire curriculum, a curriculum built on bits, pieces, and fragments.

It is much more satisfactory for teachers to incorporate the mandated objectives within their own list of goals, as described in the next section. Most basic English skills—from spelling and punctuation to reading for comprehension—are covered not once, but dozens of times during an English course. A good strategy is for the teacher to post or list the common objectives, then check off each one as it is met through class activities. In this way, the mandated objectives are not allowed to dominate instruction, and the teacher remains in full control of the course.

Teacher-Created Objectives

Valid criticism has been directed toward English teachers because of their failure to make their objectives explicit. "I want my students to *appreciate* literature," a teacher says.

"Define 'appreciate'," requests the critic. "How will I know that your students can 'appreciate'?"

"It can't really be defined," the teacher responds, "but I know when my students are doing it!"

The critic, perhaps rightly, concludes that the teacher doesn't really know what the objective is or how it can be achieved.

Actually, the problem may not be that the teacher doesn't know what he or she is doing, but that the goal isn't described clearly enough. "Appreciation" is something that James Hoetker calls a "may-do" behavior, involving synthesis of a variety of skills in a new situation. When students face a new literary work, the teacher hopes that they "may" be able to respond to it creatively and imaginatively, to "appreciate" it.

There are three sorts of behaviors that educators are concerned with. I am going to call these "can-do" behaviors, "may-do" behaviors, and "will-do" behaviors. "Can-do" behaviors are those specific things that a student can do at the end of a particular unit that he could not do at the beginning of it; in terms of Bloom's *Taxonomy,* the "can-do" behaviors include knowledge, comprehension, and the application of knowledge in familiar situations. "May-do" behaviors are things a student may be able to do in a novel or unfamiliar situation because he has mastered certain "can-do" behaviors. These would include, among cognitive behaviors, the application of abstractions in novel situations, analysis, synthesis, and evaluation; plus, among affective behaviors, attending, responding, valuing, and in some cases, organizing. "Will-do" behaviors are the choices and preferences that describe the quality of an adult's life, and which are present only fractionally during the school years. . . . Traditional education is concerned with "can-do" behaviors—skills and knowledge. Progressive or radical educators are more concerned with "may-do" behaviors. But all educators profess to believe that the can-do and may-do behaviors they shape from day to day lead to the development of desirable patterns of will-do behaviors. . . .

From James Hoetker, "Limitations and Advantages of Behavioral Objectives in the Arts and Humanities," in John Maxwell and Anthony Tovatt, eds., *On Writing Behavioral Objectives for English* (Urbana: National Council of Teachers of English, 1970), pp. 49–50.

In seeking clarification, the critic may well ask the teacher to describe some "can-do" behaviors, the individual, *demonstrable* skills or processes or activities that make up the more complex, "may-do" skill.

This problem of specifying goals led to the popularity of the so-called "behavioral" objective, which has a teacher describe objectives in terms of an expected outcome, usually a can-do skill; the conditions under which the behavior will be observed, as in a test or in a class discussion; and an acceptable level of performance, as achieving 90 percent correct or satisfying a judge or teacher. Behavioral objectives work adequately for skills such as punctuation and spelling, where the conditions and the performance level can be easily stated: "I want the students to be able to put commas in the right place nine out of ten times on a test." But a global skill such as "appreciation" doesn't lend itself easily to quantification. (Some have suggested that appreciation can be measured by whether students check books out of the library or by whether students can explain why they like or dislike a particular piece of literature, but such quantification only measures the desired behavior indirectly.)

As teachers try to translate their goals into behavioral terminology, they become frustrated, for no matter how they try to translate a "may-do" skill into "can-do" behaviors, they come up with only approximations of what they want. In such processes as "appreciating," the whole is very clearly greater than the sum of the individual component skills.

A way out of the dilemma is to worry less about the form of objectives than about their content and rationale. The lack of focus in instruction that worries many proponents of behavioral objectives results not from a lack of proper statement, but from a failure to develop a rationale for teaching. The question should not so much be "What is appreciation?" as "Why are you trying to teach appreciation in the first place?" Any objective needs to be clearly justifiable in terms of some of the following questions:

Is this objective consistent with the theory of instruction—what we have identified as the nature of the learning process and the function of schooling?

Is there any evidence (from research or intuition) that having students do this will actually help them use language more successfully?

Is this goal consistent with the developmental pattern of the learner we have developed?

Is this goal based on real expectations (i.e., what we know of what students *do*) rather than on teacher expectations (what we think students "ought" to do)?

If these criteria are met, the objective can be stated in any of a number of ways:

As a list of skills or processes that students will master during the course.

As a list of course activities: what students will read, talk about, write about, or experience.

As a description of "end products": the actual course projects the students will complete.

As a list of "exit skills": activities that the students will be able to perform after the course is over.

Objectives can be phrased as infinitives ("to learn," "to read," "to write") or imperatives ("you will_____"). Sometimes objectives can be written as aims for teachers, sketching out what they intend to accomplish in a course. Some teachers I know write a "scenario" instead of a list of objectives, describing what they want to have happen in the class. Others put their aims in the form of a letter to students and parents, describing exactly what the expectations of the course will be and how the student can meet his or her responsibilities successfully.

In themselves, objectives are a dime a dozen: "Gimme a topic and I'll give you 20 objectives—make that two hundred objectives." Clearly stated objectives that mesh with a thoughtful theory of instruction are not so easily produced because one is constantly thrust back to the real question: "Is this objective a *good* one?"

CHOOSING MATERIALS

Like objectives, materials for an instructional unit come from two sources that need to be discussed separately: *adoption* of materials by a school or district and *teacher-selected* materials.

Adopted Materials

The adoption of texts and other materials serves several functions. Adoption allows schools to guarantee a degree of consistency in courses that are taught by a number of different teachers; it ensures some continuity between grade levels when materials are bought in a series; it simplifies the selection of materials for teachers; and it cuts down on paperwork in ordering. Unfortunately, adopting textbooks creates at least as many pedagogical problems as it solves. For one thing, educational publishers see that big money is to be made in getting books adopted. Thus many textbook companies concentrate on producing major series rather than on individualized and enrichment materials that may yield smaller sales. Too, the massively adopted series are designed to satisfy large numbers of teachers and to be as inoffensive to as many people as possible. Thus they often tend to be on the traditional, conservative, "safe" side. Adopting can be time consuming for a school staff, and once completed, it locks the district or building into a fixed curriculum for the length of time it takes the books to wear out.

Still, if done thoughtfully, adoption can provide a solid core of good materials. (The outline in the box provides a procedure for adoption that was developed by the National Council of Teachers of English.) In any event, whether the materials are good or bad, a majority of teachers will find themselves using some form of adopted books as a starting point for their classes and units. The question then becomes: How do I make use of the material selected?

The boxed material, "Evaluating Textbooks," presents a sequence of questions I have given teachers to use in assessing textbooks. It begins by having teachers assess the aims of the textbook. Do the aims mesh with one's own? Too many teachers let their course or unit objectives evolve

SELECTING INSTRUCTIONAL MATERIALS

1. IDENTIFYING THE PARTICIPANTS

Identify the persons who have an interest in and a right to participate in the business of selecting instructional materials:

Parents	Taxpayers
Students	Teachers
Principals	Superintendents
Supervisors	Board Members

2. DEFINING THE NEEDS

Define the need for instructional materials from responses to certain questions:

What curricular goals are some students not now achieving?

What students are not being served by the present instructional materials?

What materials, demonstrably helpful in meeting certain goals, need replacing?

What course changes, to better meet certain goals, could be made with new instructional materials?

What learning processes could be improved with new or different instructional materials?

3. ESTABLISHING THE INTERPLAY AMONG THE COMPONENTS OF SETTING

Relate selection of materials to district statement of philosophy and goals.

Identify religious, cultural, ethnic considerations.

Specify applicable state laws and regulations.

Identify local criteria and process lists.

Record steps of compliance with district policies.

Review conflict of interest codes.

4. MAKING THE SELECTION

Provide for each selection:

A statement of title, author, publishing company, price, publication data, number ordered.

Names, titles of recommending individuals, groups, committees, reviewers, tryer-outers, approval granters.

Means by which this selection is recommended: need statement, rationale, student responses, parent recommendations, results of tryout ratings.

Identification of students, grade levels, for whom the selection is intended, restrictions on use.

Program goals, learning processes, modes, and objectives this selection will serve.

All applicable laws and regulations, as well as long-range plans considered in making this selection.

Sources of professional legitimacy for your selection.

5. FOLLOW THROUGH

Develop and carry through processes and procedures for:

Orderly distribution and inventory.
Initial and replacement cost records.
Storage and access.
In-service education.
Information and sample copies available to parents.
Evaluation and appraisal based upon student performance.
Citizen and professional staff requests for reconsideration.
Regular review for obsolescence.

From "Selecting Instructional Materials," written by James W. Sabol on behalf of the Secondary Section Committee of the National Council of Teachers of English, *The English Journal,* January 1977, pp. 9-14. Copyright © 1977 by the National Council of Teachers of English. Reprinted by permission of the publisher and the author. Abridged and adapted. For the statements in item 4, Sabol credits the *1973-74 Resource Guide to Reading and Language Arts Programs* (New York: MacMillan, 1973) and *NCTE Guide to Teaching Materials for English 7-12* (Urbana: National Council of Teachers of English, 1976).

from whatever the textbook seems to dictate. It is also important for teachers to look for hidden objectives and inconsistencies among goals that are revealed upon close examination of the text. Next, teachers can examine the content of the book. The crucial question to discover here is whether the content fits in with the teachers' theory of instruction and with the aims of the course. The textual "apparatus"—introductions, study questions, discussion questions, drills and activities—should also be reviewed. All too often, books drift into a kind of textbook talk that is insulting to students and quite unlike language any living adult would employ in chatting with young people. Finally, teachers should look at the adopted book from the point of flexibility. Is it constructed so that it must be followed page by page, or can it be reworked to fit one's ideas of what the course can and should be?

Whether teachers must "follow the textbook" varies widely from one school district to another. In some places—a very limited number in my experience—teachers must base their courses directly on the adopted book, and their job will be in jeopardy if they don't. Most districts however have a more liberal policy that encourages teachers to use some of the basic material, but not all, and to rearrange units and selections to fit their needs.

Most important however is that whether or not teachers choose to use the book as is, to modify it to suit the course, or to let it sit on the back shelves as a reference tool, they should know precisely how it relates to the course that is being planned. No textbook should ever be allowed to determine what a teacher shall teach.

EVALUATING TEXTBOOKS

1. AIMS AND OBJECTIVES

What are the stated aims? (Find these in the teachers' manual or the preface.)

What are the implied values of those aims?

What are the true aims as deduced from analysis of the textbook itself?

Are the aims consistent from one section or chapter to another?

Are the aims supportable in terms of good teaching?

Do the aims mesh with your own? Are any differences minor or irreconcilable?

2. CONTENT

Is the content current, up-to-date, pedagogically sound?

(For literature texts) Are selections representative of the topic? Are the best pieces of an author represented? Are minority literatures present in more than token amounts? Are the selections readable for most of your students? Are the selections enjoyable reading for your age group?

(For language/composition texts) Does the book present the facts about language accurately? What stand does it take on grammar and usage? Is this consistent with linguistic scholarship? Are materials for writing lively and interesting? Does the rhetoric of the book accurately describe good contemporary writing? Does the book teach writing through actual composition or through rule study and exercises?

Does the content relate to what you want to do in your course or instructional unit?

3. APPARATUS

Is the language to the student clear? Does it patronize or sound "schoolish"?

Is the apparatus needed? Could a teacher provide the same information or questions?

Does the apparatus include any busywork unrelated to the content of the text (e.g., drills, homework)?

Does the apparatus integrate literature, language, and composition, or does it treat them in isolation?

4. FLEXIBILITY AND ADAPTABILITY

What kind of course or unit structure is implied by the book?
Must the book be taught in sequence?
Can it be rearranged to fit many different course plans?
Can it fit into *your* course?
How much would you have to compromise your own teaching style if
you used it "as is"?
If it were not on an adopted list, would you use it anyway?

Teacher-Selected Materials

The development of elective English courses in the 1960s and 1970s did a great deal to promote the selection of materials by teachers and to deemphasize the role of the central, adopted textbook. It is a trend one hopes will continue for several reasons: First, because it allows teachers to maintain greater control over the courses they teach; second, because it permits greater individualization; and, third, because, by and large, teacher selection of paperback materials tends to be more economical than the purchase of large, hardbound anthologies.

Chapter 8 will discuss teaching a multiple text approach in detail. For the moment, it is sufficient to suggest that in selecting materials for an instructional unit, the teacher will probably want to consider using all the following:

Class sets of single titles for common reading.
Clusters of four or five titles for small groups.
Individual titles for free or guided reading.
Books already available in the school library as well as new materials.
Nonbook, print materials, such as newspapers and magazines.
Nonbook, *non*print materials: films, filmstrips, slide-tapes, television programs.
Human and community resources: speakers, consultants, guests.

Before putting something on a booklist or a resource list, a teacher should be prepared to:

Demonstrate how the material supports the course or unit objectives.
Provide a rationale for its selection.
Indicate whether the material is meant for whole class or individualized use.
Show that it is not objectionable to special interest groups, if it will be required of all students.
Document that it has been approved or recommended by a professional organization or that it is listed on a well-known bibliography.

STRUCTURING A UNIT

Few words in the language have undergone as many meaning changes and assumed such diverse connotations as has "structure" in education. In the late fifties, following the Russian launching of Sputnik, many people found a spokesman in Vice Admiral Hyman G. Rickover, "father of the nuclear submarine," who felt that "progressive" schools that emphasized "life adjustment" were creating a "cultural lag" and were utterly failing to prepare students for life in a modern, technological society. Education, he claimed, is "our first line of defense," but he felt that unless the schools returned to a structured plan, the United States would fall hopelessly behind the Russians.

A year or two later, at the beginning of the sixties, there was a new interest in a different kind of "structure," and this interest was focused through Jerome Bruner's influential book *The Process of Education*. For Bruner, "structure" was less a matter of intellectual rigor or school discipline than a way of seeing subject matter: "Grasping the structure of a subject is understanding it in a way that permits many other things to be related to it meaningfully. To learn structure, in short, is to learn how things are related."[1] Writing of the importance of structure, Bruner explained that the schools needed to reject traditional patterns of instruction and to search for new ways of structuring and teaching subjects so that children could more successfully come to discover the relationships within various disciplines.

Following Bruner, curriculum builders began to create "structured" curricula that would allow students to relate the components of the discipline in systematic ways. The search for structured, sequential curricula led to numerous metaphors for the relationships that exist among the components of English. At one curriculum conference, for example, the following English designs were described, each accompanied by appropriate maps, charts, and diagrams:

> Tri-component or tripod design
> Hierarchical articulation design
> Functional Reaction design
> Spiral Cone
> Bi-Polar
> Bi-Polar Multi-Component[2]

Obviously the metaphors are those of science and technology, reflecting the desire of English educators to systematize their discipline.

At the same time, however, a kind of anti-structure movement was

---

[1] *From* Jerome S. Bruner, *The Process of Education* (New York: Random House, 1960), p. 17.
[2] *From* Howard Zimmer, ed., *Ideal Designs for English Programs* (Toledo: University of Toledo, 1968).

springing up. Influenced by writers like Herbert Kohl, James Herndon, Jonathan Kozol, and John Holt, many people began to argue that the schools were *over*structured, authoritarian, and often destructive institutions. This concern for freedom led to the "free" and alternative schools movements and to the rejection of structure that marked "open" classroom teaching. Unfortunately, many of the open classroom advocates overstated their case, quite possibly for rhetorical effect. Within the movement a number of excesses took place, epitomized by the statement I once heard: "I am totally unstructured in my teaching, for after all, I find I have nothing to give to children."

These excesses, coupled with occasional willful misunderstanding and a conservative trend in the nation, led toward a reaction against openness and "permissiveness" and a concern for reintroducing "structure." The debate between pro-structure and anti-structure forces continues. The problems and ambiguity that surround the word "structure" can perhaps best be illustrated by two English classes that I visited.

The first was an elementary school class where the teacher obviously got along well with the children, and they enjoyed being in the class. The classroom was relaxed and informal. Students were working on a variety of individualized and group projects, and they wandered freely about the classroom, talking with one another and the teacher, who also drifted from table to table, giving suggestions and advice and answering questions. But I also discovered some interesting inconsistencies in the class. Although the students were working on "independent" projects, I learned that in almost every case the project ideas had originated with the *teacher*. The students, moreover, seemed almost desperate for the teacher's approval, and many of the questions that they asked were not inquiry-oriented; they were simply designed to elicit approval—step by step—for the "correctness" of their work.

The second class was conducted in a high school by a teacher who claimed to be "one of the old guard who still believes in standards." This teacher ran a tight ship. The desks were in straight rows and the students were at work in stony silence. As I walked around the class and talked with the students, I learned that they were all pursuing independent study projects. But in contrast to the elementary class, these senior high students *had* created the project ideas themselves (and submitted those ideas, in writing, by a rigid deadline). The students were doing some careful, thorough, highly creative work.

I present these two examples not to defend the old guard or to attack freely structured classrooms. On the contrary, I found the second teacher's class a very uncomfortable one despite the obviously good work that was being done. But they do show the extent to which appearances can be deceiving. Often structures aren't quite what they seem, and one must look below the surface to discover structures and their effect.

Multiple Structures

Most people tend to think of structure in simplistic terms—a teacher is either structured or not—when there obviously are *many* kinds and degrees of structure possible in a classroom, each of which needs to be considered independently. In fact, it is debatable whether we ever should use such terms as "unstructured" or "nonstructured," since they reinforce this two-value way of thinking.

Any unit a teacher creates will contain a number of structures, and when the unit is put into practice, additional stuctures will be added. Some of these will relate to the actual content of the unit: "I want you to discuss this poem." Others will relate to discipline and classroom management: "No talking, please, while somebody else is talking." "If you want credit, you must get your paper in on time." It is especially important that the content structures not be confused with management structures. The former are generally planned well in advance and modified as a class develops. The latter tend to be imposed during specific teaching situations as problems arise.

Types of Structures

In creating plans for a unit, the teacher will probably want to choose from among the following kinds of content structures:

• *Whole Class.* Meeting the class as a whole is the time-honored mode of teaching. It allows the teacher to convey common content efficiently, and if handled well, it creates a sense of community. The obvious disadvantages of whole class teaching are that it tends to force the teacher into a dominant role, that it allows for very little student interaction, that it permits little individualization. In my own teaching, I seldom use whole class sessions for presentation of material; rather, I use class meetings either as show-and-tell session for presentation of students' work or to organize along the several patterns that follow.

• *Small Groups.* A student in one of my high school classes once remarked, "This is the 'groupinest' class I've ever been in." I like to use groups, and I find them an effective compromise between whole class instruction and a totally individualized program. Groups usually involve a high degree of interaction among students, yet control is still maintained. The major disadvantages of small groups are that the teacher cannot always tell what is happening within them and that students don't always know how to work well in groups (a problem that will be taken up in Chapters 8 and 12).

• *Individual or Independent Study.* Individualizing instruction has long been a goal in education, one complicated by the economic necessity of clustering students in groups of 30 or 35 for efficiency. It's tough to individualize an English class with close to three dozen students in it, especially if one has four or five other classes the same size. At the same time, the use of multiple text approaches has gone a long way toward simplifying the task, for if a classroom is filled with resources, the teacher can more easily match the individual student with an individual book or magazine and, in turn, can create individualized assignments for topics and projects. Individualization can, of course, be taken too far. Some schools in the 1970s developed programs based too heavily on individualized study and found that not only was it unmanageable but both students and teachers became downright *lonely*. Although individual study may be important, education seems to require the sharing of ideas and information as well.

• *Peer Learning and Tutoring.* Jean Jacques Rousseau's educational ideal was an adult working one-to-one with a child. Contemporary educators have discovered that face-to-face learning need not always involve an adult, that young people of almost any age have much to learn from one another. Babies who have older brothers and sisters learn to talk more rapidly than those who don't. Why? Because the older siblings interact with the baby and help the infant to learn to talk. In elementary school classes, peer learning can be used on everything from spelling to reading. In the secondary schools, peers can assist one another with reading and writing assignments and can learn from one another as they explore thematic topics. We are just beginning to understand how peer learning works; it is an area that deserves exploration and experimentation in English classes.

• *Contracts.* Extremely popular as a form of organizing individualized classes, contracts require that the teacher and student agree on an amount of work to be done by the student to receive a certain grade. Quality controls are built into the contract so that students must do more than simply "knock off" assignments or breeze through the reading and writing work. In some schools, projects have point values assigned—e.g., 10 points for a book report, 15 points for an essay—with grades depending on point accumulation. Contracting sometimes has the effect of generating work simply for its own sake—the more students do, the higher their grade—but handled cautiously, it allows teachers to control individualized work and manage it effectively in rather large classrooms. Further, it offers clearly defined structures and expectations for students who may get lost in completely individualized classrooms.

• *Activity Centers.* An activity center allows a teacher to create an informal learning environment using resources rather than assignments as a way of organizing. A room will have locations where the students go to write, read, listen to records, dramatize, talk, work on projects, or edit their writing. In a less ambitious project, a teacher offering a course or unit on, say, science fiction might create an activity center that would include supplementary readings, recordings of science fiction literature, and possibly a number of suggestions for writing.

"Orchestrating" an Instructional Unit

How these various structures are woven together to combine with materials—both adopted and teacher-selected—and objectives—both mandated and those written by the teacher—is more a matter of art and intuition than of science and cold rationality. I call it "orchestrating" a unit, and it involves creating a sequence of materials and activities that allows the course objectives to be met while providing an interesting mix of activities for the students. In my own teaching, patterns of orchestration run along several sequences.

1. *From large group to small group.* Initial class sessions describe the course or unit, stake out the ground rules, clarify objectives, and provide some common experiences such as reading several stories or poems or writing on a common topic.

2. *From assigned work to individualized projects.* I want my students to explore topics on their own terms, so the thrust of the course is away from teacher interests or assignments toward areas where students can exercise choice.

3. *From small group or solo work back to large.* Following group or individualized work, students have ideas, projects, writing to share. This sharing helps the class to operate as a cohesive group, rather than as a collection of individuals or subgroups.

Teaching is an art, not a science, and individual teachers must develop their own patterns, their own techniques and strategies for developing and presenting instructional units. But art is seldom improvised. All of the advice, suggestions, and techniques of this chapter can be condensed into a single imperative: Plan.

I would like to end this chapter by presenting one, or possibly several, detailed, well-designed unit plans selected from the many I have collected from teachers over the years. But space limitations preclude reprinting such documents, which sometimes run twenty or thirty pages. Instead I will reproduce an encapsulated course description that was published in *The English Journal.* Deborah Rosen's "American Nonfiction" course seems to me well planned, with thoughtful objectives, a good solid reading and media list, and a sensible course sequence.

AMERICAN NONFICTION DREAMS AND NIGHTMARES

DEBORAH ROSEN

Coconut Creek High School, Coconut Creek, Florida

Man has always been in search of utopia ever since he was expelled from the first one in the Garden of Eden. *Dreams and Nightmares* is a one-semester course that explores the utopian dream in world literature. This prominent theme has its earliest roots in Plato's *Republic* and continues into the 18th and 19th centuries where a mood of optimism produced an explosion of utopian literature. The 20th century reversed this trend and ushered in an increase in the dystopian nightmare as the dominant type of literary speculation about the future. The suggested reading list and activities provide an historical framework as well as a social and literary perspective with which to trace the beginnings of utopian thought up to its status today.

OBJECTIVES

To explore the history of utopian thought; to explore the differences between the utopian and dystopian vision; to determine the reasons for the decline of the utopian hope and an increase in cynicism and pessimism about man's future; to find practical solutions to obvious social problems; to determine the problems of planning a utopia.

MATERIALS

Designs of Famous Utopias: Materials for Research Papers, Donald Gray and Allan Orrick. This source includes condensed versions of the most important classical utopias, discussion questions, and composition assignments. Excerpts are from Plato, More, Bacon, Bellamu, Hertzka, Morris, Wells, and Skinner.

Fahrenheit 451, Ray Bradbury, 1950. A dystopian future where book-burning and censorship are a way of life.

Childhood's End, A. C. Clark, 1964. Aliens from another solar system impose a utopia on earthlings.

"The Machine Stops," E. M. Forster. Short story. (Check *Short Story Index* for exact location.) Mankind is forced to live underground where a machine completely operates this luxurious society.

Lost Horizon, James Hilton, 1933. A group of explorers in the Himalayas get lost and find the mystical, utopian Shangri-La.

Brave New World, Aldous Huxley, 1932. A classic dystopia. This novel derives its inspiration from American pop culture where the average man wants nothing more than to be happy.

This Perfect Day, Ira Levin, 1970. A horrifying vision of the future where a computer named Uni controls everyone. (Beware of censorship problems with this novel.)

1984, George Orwell, 1949. 1984 has become a catchword for totalitarian nightmare. The story of one man against a superstate. A classic.

Anthem, Ayn Rand, 1946. Equality 7-2521 lives in the dark future where asking too many questions leads to severe punishment.

Walden II, B. F. Skinner, 1948. An experimental farmland somewhere in the U.S. is conceived and put into operation by a psychologist who believes that man has a means of conditioning himself to accept the good life which is available to him.

We, Eugeunii Zamiatin, 1924. Short story. The world of D-503, a mathematician of the One State, is a sterile, highly organized society which is isolated from all nature.

"The Unknown Citizen: To JS/07/M/378: This Marble Monument Is Erected By the State," W. H. Auden. Poem found in many anthologies.

Films for rent: *Future Shock; 1984; 2001: A Space Odyssey; THX-1138; Metropolis; Fahrenheit 451.*

Science Fiction Survival Simulation Game, designed by Martha Pine and Ginger Larson. Available from Martha Q. Pine, St. Louis Park Senior High, 6425 W. 33rd Street, St. Louis Park, Minnesota 55426.

COURSE SEQUENCE

Begin by exploring the reasons for studying the utopian dream and its relevancy. Discuss current social problems (education, loss of a family structure, pollution) and possible solutions (communal living, social conditioning). After reading excerpts of classical utopias, discuss the philosophical schemes and recurring elements in the utopian vision. Using *Walden II* as a link between the romantic idealism of the utopians and the pessimism of Huxley and Orwell, discuss the reasons for the increase in the nightmare vision of the future. Conclude by reading and discussing *Childhood's End,* a science fiction novel that can be interpreted as utopian or dystopian depending on the student's philosophy of the universe, human nature, and man's ability to change himself. Assignments: Composition topics are unlimited; have students read supplementary material on experimental utopias, classical utopias, current dystopias, current social criticism such as *Future Shock.* Have students set up an experimental utopia on paper; have students participate in the science fiction game to attempt to solve major international crises in moments.

EXPLORATIONS AND RESOURCES

- Learn about mandated objectives in your school, district, or state. Do common basic skills lists exist? Is there a core of goals that every teacher is expected to cover? Is mastery of these goals measured or monitored in any way? Evaluate the list in terms of your own knowledge and beliefs about the teaching and learning of language. Are these good goals?

- Find a copy of a textbook that has been adopted in a school district near you or where you teach. Evaluate it along the lines recommended in the box "Evaluating Textbooks."
- Create a list of thematic or topical units that you think you would like to teach. How might such units be worked into a traditional course structure, say, a one-year study of American or British literature?
- Learn about the textbook adoption procedures for a school district. How often are books adopted? For what kinds of courses? Who decides which books are chosen? Does the district have a written adoption procedure? Also investigate the restrictions that are placed on supplemental or teacher-selected materials.
- Choose a topic that you would like to teach and explore various ways of writing objectives for it. How can you most comfortably and most explicitly state what you want the outcomes of a unit to be?
- Develop a unit along the lines suggested in this chapter.

Related Readings

The professional literature is surprisingly sparse when it comes to course and unit planning. It is almost as if it is assumed that through experience, teachers will somehow know how to put together a well-organized, coherent instructional unit. *The English Journal* publishes outlines of courses and units from time to time. In addition, the National Council of Teachers of English publishes *Thematic Units in English and Humanities,* which is updated from one year to another through supplements. Many commercial publishers have created teaching guides to go along with paperback titles; these are available free and often provide excellent supplementary reading lists. (One cautionary note: The publishers tend to build their reading lists solely out of their own titles.) Albert Oliver's *Maximizing Minicourses* (New York: Teachers College Press, 1978) is an excellent little book on creating short-term units, and many of its ideas can be extended to full-term courses. George Posner and Alan Rudnitsky's *Course Design* (New York: Longman, 1978) is less helpful because of a tendency to drift into educationese and to misapply systems terminology to school instruction. Finally, in *The English Teacher's Handbook* (Cambridge: Winthrop, 1979), Susan Judy and I have devoted a full chapter to unit planning and development from the point of view of creating full-term courses.

5

An Environment for English (Or, What Can You Do Before the Students Come?)

Success in teaching English depends on what the teacher makes of the students who walk in the door on that first day of school, students who present a diversity for which the teacher cannot completely prepare. Something a teacher *can* do well in advance is to take steps to ensure that when the students arrive, they will step into an environment that invites them to participate in the community of language. To a surprising extent, the physical setting can shape this participation.

The environment in which learning takes place has been a neglected aspect of education. Whether one considers the institutional lime green of hallways or the uniformity of cinder block classrooms, the school environment is too seldom interesting or attractive. Industrial psychologists have long recognized that the pleasantness (or unpleasantness) of an environment strongly influences peoples' motivation and productivity. Teachers too seldom consider the broad effects the school environment may be having on their students.

There seems to be no reason why any language arts classroom *must* be bleak. John Artman, an English teacher from Keokuk, Iowa, has tried to fight the problem by making himself an "interior decorator"; he has used student work and posters to transform the environment of his classroom. In addition to covering the walls, his practice provides a substantial audience for student work and displays models on which students can draw for future projects and ideas.

> . . . if you come to my classroom you will see that I have become an accomplished interior decorator. . . .
>
> Hanging on the wall, hanging from the ceiling, and scattered all over the floor of the room are projects which the senior Individualized Reading classes have made. At the end of this one semester course, the students are asked to interpret in some art form (model, mobile, drawing,

painting, or sculpture) the book they enjoyed the most. Leaning against the blackboard in the back of the room is a large oil painting of *In Cold Blood*. It shows a black shotgun leaning against an orange wall that has blood splattered on it. To the right of the shotgun, on the scales of justice stand Perry and Richard. Another picture on the blackboard is of *Alas, Babylon*. It is painted in bright yellows, oranges, red, and blues and shows a mushroom explosion and distorted people gathered in a circle in front of it.

Hanging from the ceiling is a mobile representing *Exodus*. It is a round ball of barbed wire with a yellow wooden star of David hanging in the center of it. On one of the shelves of a huge bookcase is a wooden model of *The Bad Seed*. A wooden body with black wire legs and arms has a black seed in its stomach. From one of the arms hangs a pair of shoes. Another arm has a burnt match and an ax. Long strands of gray hair are twisted around the arm. Also in the bookcase is a huge stone literally covered with faces cut out of magazines and glued on. It represents *A Single Pebble*.

Besides these Individualized Reading projects, there are posters hanging on two bulletin boards that students asked to make. These posters are for Individualized Reading, and they show one or more scenes from a book. Again these are not required. The students become fired up over a book and want to paint or draw a poster. At present there are two student posters on the board. One is a huge one of *All Quiet on the Western Front* and the other is *On the Beach*. The first one shows death dressed as a German soldier standing in a trench. The second one shows an Australian officer standing outside a building. He is waiting for the end of his world.

As you stand in my room, you exclaim, "How do you ever get around in this room?" I say, "I don't. I stumble through, but it's nice stumbling."

But decoration alone is not sufficient to redo the total environment—physical or intellectual—of a class. The English teacher cannot change the environment simply through cosmetology.[1] An environment influences behavior in many different ways, and teachers need to look at the total environment of their classes in terms of their program and what they want to accomplish.

[1] *Mad* magazine once ran a satiric spread on "The Senior Prom," in which a class spends a small fortune renting the ballroom of a local hotel, then spends days painstakingly decorating it to look just like a high school gymnasium. People often become locked into environments, with a subsequent decrease in their powers of imagination and originality.

I'D RATHER DO IT MYSELF: THE ENGLISH TEACHER AS SCAVENGER AND BUILDER

Although a good environment for English can be constructed using regulation schoolroom furniture and supplies, a more satisfactory classroom can be created by an English teacher who likes to sew, paint, or build things, or, better, by the students in the class who like to do these things. One of the best ways of getting a class started, in fact, is to ignore "English" for a few days and to allow the students to get acquainted by working on projects to transform the environment.

The materials involved can be inexpensive—many of them collected over the summer from scrap piles or remnant sales. Both teachers and students need to become scavengers. Some places to visit in search of materials might include hardware and paint stores, furniture stores, fabric shops, bookstores, magazine stands, construction sites, lumberyards, travel agencies, office supply stores, and resale shops. Look for equipment, materials, and odds and ends that are left over, used, broken, damaged, free, or cheap. Tell potential contributors you are constructing an "Experimental Learning Environment" and ask for their help. You can also involve the services of art, business, and shop teachers and quite possibly the skills of interested parents.

Scavenging is inexpensive, but often you can persuade an administrator to share a slice of the supplies budget for purchase of a few items. The best single course of funds is the regular school furniture budget. If you can dissuade the administrator from buying standardized, formica-topped school furniture, you will save enough money to improve the classroom environment and have enough cash left over to buy some paperbacks or magazines.

THE GATHERING PLACE

Here it is, Room 331, 25'x35'. Over the summer, the janitor has waxed the floor and scrubbed all the graffiti off the desks or slapped a coat of yellow varnish on the wooden desks if you're in an older school. The desks have been lined up to face front, flag, and lectern. It is an environment potentially hostile to the English class as a community of language because its structure tends to inhibit a free flow of discourse. Even if equipped with movable desks—"stations" as they are ironically called—Room 331, the typical English classroom, is a place where it is difficult to move about, difficult to achieve a bit of conversational privacy, difficult to put people into groups for discussions.

What to do? For step one, you *might* call the janitor and have him remove the desks. The typical school desk occupies about 6 square feet. Thir-

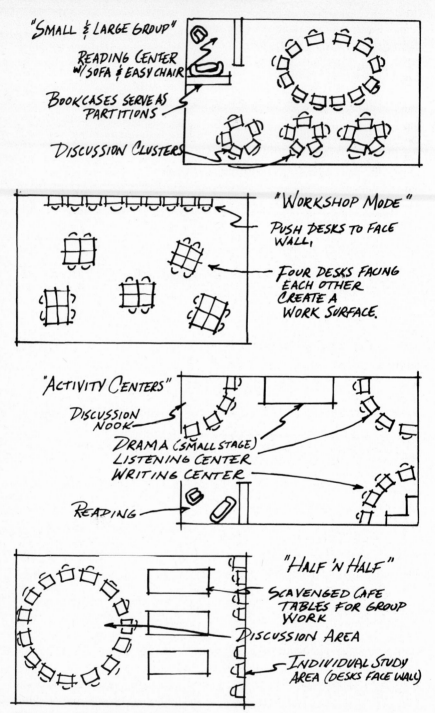

"SMALL & LARGE GROUP"

READING CENTER w/ SOFA & EASY CHAIR

BOOKCASES SERVE AS PARTITIONS

DISCUSSION CLUSTERS

"WORKSHOP MODE"

PUSH DESKS TO FACE WALL,

FOUR DESKS FACING EACH OTHER CREATE A WORK SURFACE.

"ACTIVITY CENTERS"

DISCUSSION NOOK

DRAMA (SMALL STAGE)
LISTENING CENTER
WRITING CENTER

READING

"HALF 'N HALF"

SCAVENGED CAFE TABLES FOR GROUP WORK

DISCUSSION AREA

INDIVIDUAL STUDY AREA (DESKS FACE WALL)

Figure 5.1 Classroom Floor Plans.

ty of them take up 200 square feet, or 40 percent of the total space in the classroom. They are simply not that useful. But it if you can't get rid of the desks, at least push them against the wall for a while to get a look at the available space.

The actual floor plan of Room 331 can vary infinitely as projects, students, and furniture come and go to meet various needs. What all interesting floor plans have in common is avoiding the traditional classroom grid. Desks can be pushed into patterns of circles, semicircles, grape clusters, horseshoes, and bananas to create functional designs for small- and large-group discussion, workshops, and activity centers. Even if you can't throw out the old furniture, you can supplement it by bringing in an old sofa or easy chair, or finding scraps of carpet or large cushions for additional leisure seating. Some classroom floor plans are shown in Figure 5.1.

If you can, bring in some tables. These seat five or six and are far more efficient than individual desks. Round tables are better than square ones because of the atmosphere of a "roundtable" setting. Don't overestimate the amount of actual surface space you need in the form of tables or desks. Many tables are larger than they need to be and simply invite clutter. If you can break out of the mode of lectures, common writing assignments, and examinations, you will find there will be very few times when an entire class needs to use a desk surface at once. (You can also have a supply of lapboards for such occasions.)

The simplest and cheapest round table is a discarded cable spool that you can get free or at nominal cost from electric and telephone companies. Use individual chairs with these—folding chairs or stackable furniture is ideal. Other tables (and various kinds of chairs and benches) can be built from scratch by interested parents and students or by the shop. Some possibilities are sketched in Figure 5.2.

In addition to the tables, investigate the possibilities of other kinds of comfortable furniture for the class—inflatable chairs and couches, coffee tables, beanbag chairs, and cushions. The shopping malls often provide helpful examples of inexpensive furniture in their casual waiting areas. So do playgrounds, bank lobbies, and airport terminals. Places which depend on peoples' goodwill for survival tend to develop comfortable environments. One seldom finds interesting lounges in schools or city halls.

USING THE WALLS

Walls are the most neglected space in a classroom; after all, they probably have thrice the square footage of the floor. Of course you should hang things on walls—pictures, posters, and student work. But as the designers of ships and pullman cars have long known, you can do a great deal more with walls. You can fold things into them and out of them. You can lean

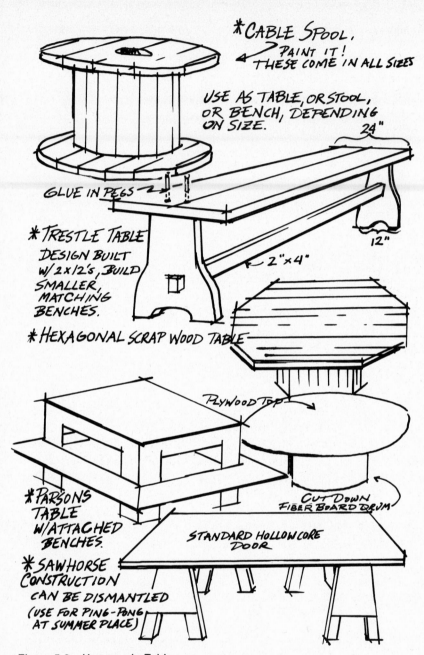

*CABLE SPOOL,
PAINT IT!
THESE COME IN ALL SIZES

USE AS TABLE, OR STOOL,
OR BENCH, DEPENDING
ON SIZE.   24"

GLUE IN PEGS

*TRESTLE TABLE
DESIGN BUILT
W/ 2 x 12's, BUILD
SMALLER,
MATCHING
BENCHES.   12"

2"x 4"

*HEXAGONAL SCRAP WOOD TABLE

PLYWOOD TOP

*PARSONS
TABLE
W/ATTACHED
BENCHES.

CUT DOWN
FIBER BOARD DRUM

STANDARD HOLLOW CORE
DOOR

*SAWHORSE
CONSTRUCTION
CAN BE DISMANTLED
(USE FOR PING-PONG
AT SUMMER PLACE)

Figure 5.2   Homemade Tables.

things against them and suspend things from them. It is only tradition that prevents us from using walls better.

For instance, a student working alone does not have to face the open space of a central classroom. If private work spaces are created facing the wall, the center area of the classroom is left free for community activities. In most rooms, corners are simply the dead space where two walls meet. Building a wall installation that bends around a corner can create a "room within a room," using the former dead space as a *focal* point for an activity center. Figure 5.3 shows designs for centers built for wall installations that serve a number of purposes. All of these can be put together with scrap and recycled materials.

Although cosmetology alone cannot create the environment, it can help, and a few decorator touches may help to transform 331. Visit the Old Mill Inn, the Schnitzel Haus, Kirby's Pub-Erin, and the Lighthouse Inn to study the techniques decorators have used to create atmosphere. Some teachers have even selected a motif for a classroom: The students of Sister Mary Clare Yates, Our Lady of Mercy High School, Farmington, Michigan, designed a classroom along the classical partition of the elements into fire, earth, air, and water; some of their visualizations are shown in Figure 5.4. These "constructions" naturally tie in to various literary works: *air* to *Walden, fire* to Frost's "Fire and Ice," *water* to *Two Years Before the Mast, earth* to *The Good Earth*. At the elementary level, tie-ins could include *Peter Pan* (air), *Snow White* (earth), "Hansel and Gretel" (fire), and "The Legend of Atlantis" (water).

Of course, even if teachers do not have the time or the resources to make elaborate constructions or built-ins, the walls can be used for decoration and display. Elementary school teachers are past masters of the bulletin board, and secondary teachers would be wise to study some of their techniques. As a sample, a professor at California State College in Pennsylvania, Eleanor Hibbs, reports seeing a bulletin board of a giant shark with huge teeth fastened in with *Velcro* tape, allowing the teeth to be removed. On the back of the teeth were writing assignments based on the thematic unit, "Creatures of the Deep." (More suggestions for bulletin board displays are given in Chapter 10.)

RESOURCE AND ACTIVITY CENTERS

In addition to arranging furniture to enhance communication, the teacher can make the English classroom a place where students have ready access to the tools and materials of literacy. Materials can be collected and stockpiled over the summer, then made available to the students in the fall. One way of organizing materials is through the development of resource or activity centers—actually just corners of the room that are set aside for certain purposes.

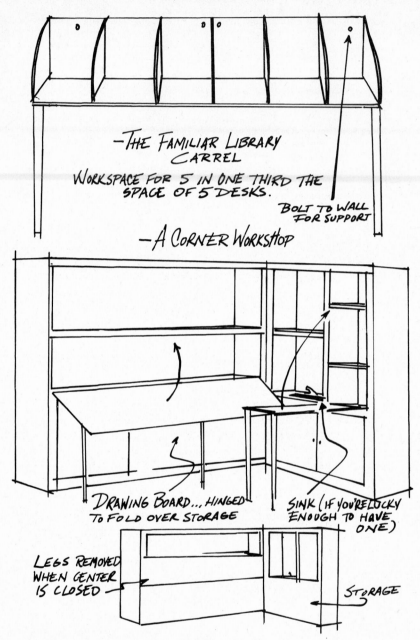

—THE FAMILIAR LIBRARY CARREL

WORKSPACE FOR 5 IN ONE THIRD THE SPACE OF 5 DESKS.

BOLT TO WALL FOR SUPPORT

—A CORNER WORKSHOP

DRAWING BOARD... HINGED TO FOLD OVER STORAGE

SINK (IF YOU'RE LUCKY ENOUGH TO HAVE ONE)

LEGS REMOVED WHEN CENTER IS CLOSED

STORAGE

Figure 5.3   Using Walls and Corners.

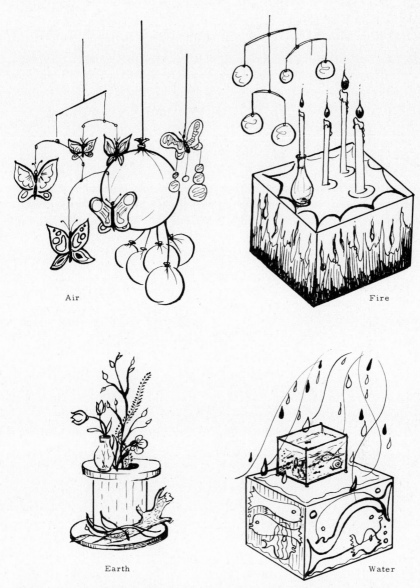

Air

Fire

Earth

Water

Figure 5.4   Fire-Earth-Air-Water Visualizations. (From Sister Mary Clare Yates, "Choose Your Environment," in Stephen Judy, ed., *Lecture Alternatives in Teaching English.* Copyright © 1971 by the Michigan Council of Teachers of English.)

A Reading Center

Central to a good, individualized English program is engaging students in a "free" or guided reading program in which they select and pursue books on topics of their own interest. The resource center to support this program should be a place where students can relax comfortably to read, and possibly to listen and talk. Ideally, the center might be equipped with some comfortable furniture—an easy chair or an old sofa—or rugs and cushions for seating. In addition, it should have reading and related resources available.

• *Paperback Display Areas.* Paperback distributors have recognized that displaying books with covers face up attracts a readership. To the greatest extent possible, the classroom library holdings should be presented in open-faced shelves or bookracks.

• *Bins and Files.* This center should be an open filing system where students can find materials quickly. The organization of a bins-and-files system will depend on the materials you have, but a set of boxes or baskets, appropriately marked, can be kept in the resource center. Perhaps the easiest filing system is by material type like pamphlets or photographs, but a more useful arrangement may be by themes or topics—animals, ecology, current events. Once students learn the system, they can clip and file materials they find in their reading.

• *Current Magazines.* Survey your local paperback store and review magazines, particularly those that appeal to special interest or hobby groups: coin collectors, model railroaders, Civil War buffs. If your school cannot supply subscriptions to a few of these, speak to the paperback distributor in your area and see whether you can get back issues and unsold copies given to the school free.

• *Newspapers.* Have the local paper plus at least one large city paper made available to your students. Like magazines, unsold papers, just a day old, are often available free.

• *Reference Books.* Stock your reading center with a good dictionary, a one-volume encyclopedia, the almanac, a copy of the *Guinness Book of World Records,* catalogs from mail-order houses, *1001 Things You Can Get Free,* and so on.

• *Book Carts.* The school librarian or media center director may be willing to prepare a cart with 40 or 50 titles on a theme for your class. Book carts increase the supply of materials available and can be changed from time to time to keep interest in your reading center fresh.

• *Recorded Literature.* The enormous volume of recorded literature is often neglected. Records placed in a free reading center along with a record player and earphones will attract "readers." If the school record collection is sparse, try the public library. This center can also contain literature written and recorded by students. Many schools have successfully built up large collections simply by making a systematic effort to record the best dramatic performances and readers' theater events around the school.

A Writing Center

The writing center serves several different purposes, which need to be discussed separately:

• *Ideas for Writing.* "What can I write about?" is a common question asked of the English teacher. The writing center can be a place where students go to find idea starters.

> Activity or index cards with writing ideas and suggestions on them. The Illinois Council of Teachers of English once published a list of 1000 topics for composition. Such a list—which could easily be gleaned from professional publications—would make the start for an excellent set of writing cards.
> Samples of writing, either by other students or by professional authors, with suggestions for related projects.
> Photographs or posters to serve as inspiration.
> "The Topic of the Day/Week/Month," set by the teacher as a subject of common interest for a period of time.

• *Help with Editing.* When students have completed the draft of a paper, they might go to the writing center to

> Talk with others about their writing.
> Work on a revision, alone or with other students.
> Examine reference books for help with mechanics, usage, style, and form.

• *Graphics Materials for Final Copy.* Much school writing is done on cheap paper, with the student using either a smudgy #2 pencil or a ball-point pen that leaves ink spots. We have all seen and spilled coffee on the stacks of papers that result. They are at best unattractive, and if a student's hand-

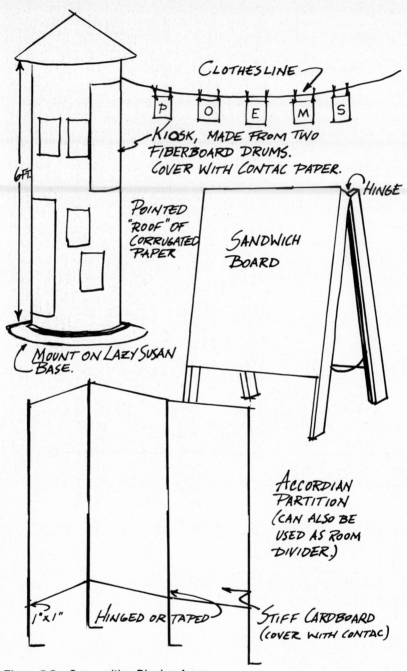

CLOTHESLINE

P O E M S

KIOSK, MADE FROM TWO
FIBERBOARD DRUMS.
COVER WITH CONTAC PAPER.

6 FT.

POINTED
"ROOF" OF
CORRUGATED
PAPER

SANDWICH
BOARD

HINGE

MOUNT ON LAZY SUSAN
BASE.

ACCORDIAN
PARTITION
(CAN ALSO BE
USED AS ROOM
DIVIDER.)

1"×1"   HINGED OR TAPED   STIFF CARDBOARD
(COVER WITH CONTAC)

Figure 5.5   Composition Display Areas.

writing is poor to begin with, they are downright ugly. After all the pain and care of creating something, the student produces an object nobody wants to look at. No wonder young people hate writing.

The writing center can encourage students to make their final copy look as attractive as possible, reflecting the hard work that went into its preparation. Supplies for the center can include construction paper in a variety of colors, scraps of poster board, felt tip pens in a rainbow of colors, string and yarn for binding books, magazines for cutting up, and paste, glue, and scotch tape. To show the various results of these graphic efforts, a display area can be constructed (Figure 5.5) or the teacher can create a bulletin board display. Sheila Murphy, a member of the New York Teachers and Writers Collaborative, has described the materials she used in creating a writing center. Her list is shown in Figure 5.6.

A list of suggestions:

1. Have writing equipment: pencils, paper, manual typewriter. All kinds and shapes of paper—including large rolls of wrapping paper and newsprint. Paper could be on large rolls and spools, much as other supplies in the room are displayed.
2. Paper cutter.
3. Tape recorder (cassette would be best).
4. A tape library with tapes of:
children talking
   reading their writing
   improvising
teachers talking
   reading their writing
   reading kids' writing
   giving dramatic readings
music, without lyrics, for background
   blank tapes.
5. Bins with old magazines for cutting up.
6. Bins with pencil pieces and erasers.
7. Picture books without words. . . .
8. Word books without pictures.
9. Large dowel frame for collaborative stories, poems, thoughts. Make frame about 4 feet high. . . . I can't describe it, here:

A Drama Center

All kinds of dramatic activity—creative dramatics, improvisation, reader's theater, dramatic interpretations, and oral presentation of students' work—should be woven into any English program. The tools of this trade need not

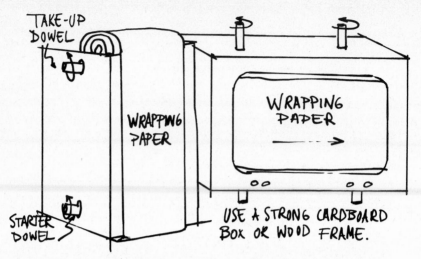

Figure 5.6 Materials for a Writing Center. (From Sheila Murphy, "Garbage Picking," *The Teachers and Writers Collaborative Newsletter,* May–October, 1971. Copyright © 1971 by the Teachers and Writers Collaborative. Reprinted by permission of the publisher.)

be terribly complex, and many drama activities will require no equipment at all. The ease of play making and the effects of drama, however, can be heightened with a few supplies and pieces of equipment.

In many classes, the stage may simply be an area of the floor cleared away for the purpose. But a simple stage is not difficult to construct. A raised platform can provide a basic stage, and underneath can be stored risers, flats, and furniture that can be used to create levels, rooms, partitions, and the like (Figure 5.7). When not in use as a stage, the platform can be rearranged to serve as an informal reading or discussion center.

Reader's theater and oral readings are aided by tall stools, so readers can sit and still be seen, and music stands, so students can rest their manuscripts and, quite possibly, hide their shaking hands. Unpainted stools are inexpensive; music stands can often be appropriated from the band room.

Lighting can also add to a stage production by making it something different from the ordinary class scene. Make a basic stage light out of a #10 tin can, a 60 watt bulb, and a light fixture. These lights can be placed at the base of the stage or suspended from the ceiling or a simple canopy. An inexpensive dimmer switch to raise and lower the lights can be installed by the custodian.

For elementary students, a costume box is an excellent resource and will prove to be a good drama starting point in itself, with dramatic play spontaneously emerging when students try on new costumes and identities. As students grow older, they are less likely to be interested in the costuming aspect of drama, and by the time they are seniors they will do most

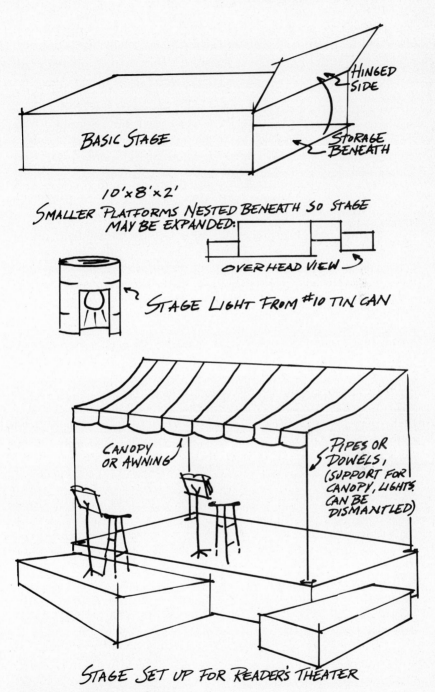

HINGED SIDE

BASIC STAGE

STORAGE BENEATH

10' x 8' x 2'
SMALLER PLATFORMS NESTED BENEATH SO STAGE MAY BE EXPANDED:

OVERHEAD VIEW

STAGE LIGHT FROM #10 TIN CAN

CANOPY OR AWNING

PIPES OR DOWELS, (SUPPORT FOR CANOPY, LIGHTS CAN BE DISMANTLED)

STAGE SET UP FOR READER'S THEATER

Figure 5.7   The Drama Center.

dramatic activity in street clothes, because as people mature, they need fewer and fewer aids and props to participate in a dramatic experience.

ALTERNATIVES FOR THE PERIPATETIC TEACHER

In many schools, some teachers, especially new ones, are "peripatetic"; they are not assigned to any single classroom and thus must move from room to room. Obviously such an assignment seriously limits the teacher's ability to create the kind of English classroom I have described here. Too, in some schools either the administrators or the custodians will not permit drastic rearrangment of furniture or the use of furniture that is not school issue. One needs, then, to keep in mind some alternatives for "the real world."

Even wandering teachers can create a more interesting environment than that which exists in most classrooms. The transient teacher can expect to use a share of bulletin board space for student writing, and it might be that the teacher can get display space in the halls for combined showings of students' work.

In addition, one can make materials and centers that can be quickly and easily stored away. If a full-sized reading center is not possible, the teacher can still stash several boxes of books and clippings away in a closet. A writing center can be created using several bright plastic washtubs picked up at a variety or discount store: one to file writing ideas, one to hold graphic supplies, one to store reference books. While having an actual stage might be pleasant, students can rearrange a few desks in 30 seconds to create anything from the graveyard of *Spoon River Anthology* to the ballroom of "Cinderella." A simple costume box can hold materials for dozens of roles and can be toted from class to class when needed.

The various centers that I have sketched in this chapter are meant to serve as models—or perhaps ideals—toward which a teacher might aim. Even in the best of circumstances, the English classroom will not be ideal however, and teachers can use their ingenuity to create a unique environment for English.

EXPLORATIONS AND RESOURCES

Explore the many inexpensive kinds of building materials and objects that are available to construct an English environment. Consider the possible uses of some of the following materials. Better yet, obtain and make something from them.

rope	tin cans	an old parachute
scrap wood	Christmas lights	wall paper
styrofoam	coat hangers	pasteboard drums
beans	cloth remnants	chicken wire
cardboard	orange crates	theater flats

- Design some furniture for an English classroom—yours or one you'd like to furnish someday. Perhaps the single best source for building ideas is *Sunset Magazine* (Lane Publications, Menlo Park, California), which describes well-designed furniture, built-ins, wall coverings, patio furniture, children's rooms, and the like. *Sunset's* designs are both inexpensive and practical; further, the editors test them out and they *do* work. Many of the *Sunset* ideas are gathered into book length collections. Three that are directly applicable are *Children's Play Rooms and Play Yards, Furniture You Can Make,* and *Storage.*
- Another superb source of ideas, unfortunately now out of print, is *Farallones Scrapbook* (Farallones Designs, 1971; distributed by Random House). This is a report, complete with diagrams, of a group of teachers and students who experimented broadly with classroom environments. It contains expecially useful ideas on reworking classroom space, building carrels and cubicles from cardboard and plywood, making playground equipment, and scavenging.
- Scavenging is an art, and is not learned overnight. Make a list of some of your needs and start exploring sources. What can you scavenge from hardware stores, plumbers, army-navy stores, flea markets, auctions, demolitions, neighbors, and your attic?
- Design a floor plan for a classroom that would let you do what you want to do. Figure out how to make that plan work even if you won't have all the equipment you need.
- Activity centers, or resource boxes, can be developed on almost any topic, and need not be limited to reading, writing, and drama. Below are listed some possible topics for centers. Choose one and develop a list of materials and resources. Or pick a topic of your own and do the same.

Language Play	Biography
Language History	Media Study
Discussion	Media Production
Creative Writing	Short Stories
One-Act Plays	Script Writing
The Nature of Language	Current Events
Careers	Business Writing

6
Getting Started
(Or, How Do You Begin Once
the Students Come?)

Synergy is a state in which a number of separate parts act in concert to create a strong structure. Buckminster Fuller's geodesic domes are synergistic structures, with individual parts—tubes, pipes, panels—linked in a geometric design to produce a strong, lightweight structure. The human body is also a synergistic unit, with separate organs working on different tasks for a common purpose.

Teaching language arts class can be perceived as the task of creating a synergistic structure using *people*. On the opening day of class, the teacher is faced with students of widely diverging interests and expectations. Each of these students has special strengths and weaknesses, and the teacher's task is to figure out how to fit the students together into a class, creating a strong unit without having any parts left over. If the class comes together and works well, it will become self-supporting—like a geodesic dome. Unfortunately, unlike dome builders, teachers don't know quite what the final structure will look like. As much as they would like to produce a smooth, symmetrical unit, the class will probably be more like the human body: subject to malfunctions and disease—with parts that need glasses, or braces, or occasional shots to keep operating. But like the body, a class is capable of doing some marvelous, unanticipated things.

OPENINGS

Where to begin? Given all the pieces and parts, how does the teacher start the class-building process? Teachers often underrate the competencies of young people, failing to see the abilities and skills they have. Perhaps one of the first things a teacher should do is discover the human resources of the class.

It is well known that the youth of the television generation are well-informed, but the amount of information that any group of 30 students brings to a class is staggering. As a test, put together a trivia quiz:

Who knows what the dust on a butterfly's wing is?
Who can splice a rope?
Who can recite the second verse of "The Star-Spangled Banner"?
Who were the pitchers in the second game of the 1978 World Series?
Why is a sewing machine bobbin called a bobbin?

In almost any class you will find that most of these (or any equally trivial) questions can be answered from the community storehouse of knowledge.[1]

More important, the students have language skills they can use in the class. Some are good talkers; others are good writers. Somewhere in the class is a potential spelling champion and a student who is a walking dictionary. The class probably has one or two crossword puzzle addicts, along with a few students who read and write poetry on the sly. One student likes to type; another does hand lettering. Someone has read the Bible cover to cover, and somebody else has read every single Tarzan book.

The experience and language of the students should interact constantly. In the synergistic classroom, everything a student knows or does through language becomes a critical contribution to the class. Sharing knowledge and experience is an important event for the language community.

The task of those first few weeks of school is, first, finding the skills and interests each student brings and then shaping a climate where the students will share freely with each other. This is no easy task, and the first few weeks of any class are likely to be rocky and rather unpredictable—a period of trial, error, and groping—with the teacher looking for something, but never knowing quite what.

GETTING TO KNOW YOU

Although some students may know one another already, in large schools many of the students will be strangers. The teacher may also be a stranger to the students. Before the class will function as a unit, the students and teacher will need to get to know one another—not only by name, but as personalities.

There are many different ways this can be done, the most common one being "going around the circle," with members of the class—including

[1] Many community learning centers are run on the principle of shared competencies. On a bulletin board people advertise what they can teach and when they will teach it: "Sally Kenyon will teach italic script writing on Thursday morning." "Bill Jefferson will show what he knows about guitar on Tuesdays." The interested members of the community sign up for "classes." As it turns out, in any group of people almost anyone who wants to learn something can find someone else who will teach it. Ivan Ilich has even proposed that we should "deschool" society and rely on shared knowledge for education. While his proposal does not seem particularly practical, there is no reason why the basic principle of peer and group teaching should not be incorporated within the schools.

Figure 6.1 Making Silhouettes.

the teacher—talking a bit about themselves and their interests. Though this device is useful, it is usually not enough. To become thoroughly acquainted, people have to work and talk together, exchanging ideas and information. On the next few pages are four starter activities that supply opportunities for the students to work together on cooperative ventures while eliciting expressions of interest, abilities, and problems.

1. SILHOUETTES

Materials:

Construction paper
Scissors
Glue
Light source: a slide or overhead projector

Procedures:

Have students pair off with other students in the class whom they haven't met. Using contrasting colors of construction paper, each partner makes a cutout profile silhouette of the other, using the source of light to cast a shadow on the paper. (See Figure 6.1.)

After the silhouettes have been completed, have each person interview the partner about interests, beliefs, ideas, background, etc., and then write a thumbnail sketch of the person directly on the silhouette.

Hang the completed silhouettes with written commentary on the board for a week or two. This display provides an interesting and colorful "rogues gallery," but in addition proves to be a help in learning names.

2. GONFALONERY

Materials:

Dowel rods
Felt scraps
Burlap or cloth remnants, or construction paper
Glue
String or cord

Procedures:

The gonfalon originated in medieval times as a banner or standard; it is simply a decorative wall hanging.

Making gonfalons can be done by small groups of students (or if you prefer, on an individual basis). Members of the group work out a design for a gonfalon in which members of the group have special symbols that they use to represent themselves. The steps are shown in Figure 6.2.

The entire class will enjoy seeing the various gonfalons and trying to determine who is represented by each symbol. The banners make good wall hangings, helping to individualize the classroom environment.

3. SKILLS EXCHANGE DAY

All students have some things they do very well—hobbies, sports, outside interests. Skills exchange day consists of arranging for students to share those skills with one another. There are many ways of organizing this activity; perhaps the simplest is to split the class into several groups and to run the activity for several consecutive days.

On the first day, each member of group 1 sets up a "booth" where he or she will demonstrate the skill to anyone who comes by. Groups 2 and 3 rotate about sampling the presentations.

On the remaining days, the other groups put on their presentations.

To add to the interest, try carnival decorations or advertisements. Also, skills exchange can be taken "on the road" to other classes, thus helping to build solidarity within your class.

4. "WRITING" AN ENVIRONMENT

Lavonne Mueller of DeKalb, Illinois, has tried this idea with writing classes, and I think it might make an interesting starter activity:

> I met my classes in a large room covered with butcher paper and the students were told to write anywhere they wished: on the wall, on the floor, half on the wall and extended to the floor, alternatively the wall and then the floor—a sort of expanded exercise in graffiti-writing with a serious purpose.
>
> The students wrote quite eagerly, seemingly uninhibited by their surroundings. I wanted to see how they worked beyond the literal dimensions of a sheet of loose-leaf paper. The edge of the wall or floor, or room, I thought, would provide a far more precise caesura; here the world of the student would end and the world of the reader, or experiencer, would begin. By making mural-scale stories, or poems, the writers ceased to be writers only, and merged into their environment. Entangled in the web of words to some extent, and by moving in and out of the skein of lines, students experienced a kind of spatial extension. What resulted was writing which tended to lose itself out of bounds, and filled a student's world with itself.
>
> In some other classes I asked the participants to bring in something other than pen and pencil. They wrote with crayons, magic markers, chalk, and lipstick. A few brought different writing surfaces: a paper bag, a light fixture, a jar, a piece of cloth. They noted that the friction of a new surface offered the path of their hand an interesting kind of energy; and ultimately, a new tone emerged from their lines.

From *Convention Concerns* 1971, The National Council of Teachers of English.

TELL ME ABOUT YOURSELF

These starter activities help the students get to know one another and in the process elicit expressions of self-perception, interests, and beliefs. But there remains much that a teacher can learn by encouraging the students to talk directly about themselves, their problems, and their ideas. On the next few pages are some additional activities and games designed for individual rather than group use. Since these are a bit more personal than activities like "Silhouettes" and "Gonfalonery," the teacher needs to use discretion in deciding whether they should lead to public sharing of ideas. In

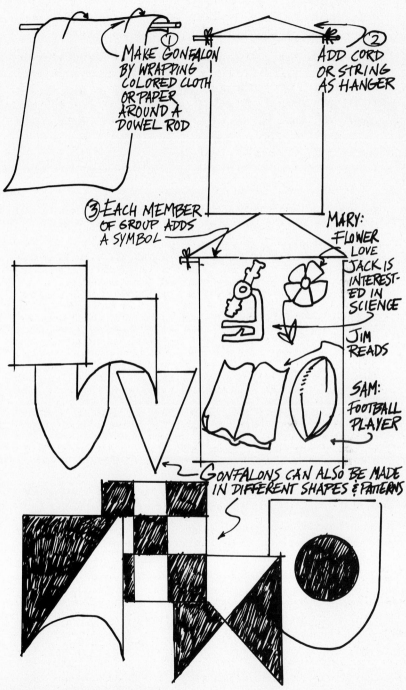

Figure 6.2 Making a Gonfalon.

any event, the teacher should use these activities chiefly as sources of information about interests and not use the data to psychoanalyze students.

1. *Signatures* is a short activity that all students—even those with bad handwriting—seem to enjoy.

Have students try writing or signing their name different ways:

Which signature seems to reflect the student's personality best? Why?

2. *If I Were*, shown in Figure 6.3, involves students in an assessment of their own personality through making odd comparisons between themselves and such things as animals, objects, plants.

3. *The Admiration Ladder* (Figure 6.4) encourages students to describe their own tastes and values by having them talk about other people. If you limit the names on the ladder to nationally known people (e.g., movie stars, sports figures, public leaders, and the like), you will have lively material for whole class discussion. On the other hand, if you permit the use of local names, the results of the ladder are probably best kept personal.

One way of clarifying what you want to do and be is through an indirect method, a game called "If I were . . .".

For example, suppose you were not a person but an animal. Would you be a lion or a mouse, a skunk, a deer, a hippopotamus, or some other kind of animal? Why? Because you're powerful or meek, unpopular or graceful?

Pair off with another person and try this—writing down the name of the one animal you think represents you most closely and the one that most closely represents your partner. Your partner should do the same. Compare notes and decide how close you came to each other's judgments.

Now try the game in other forms as a way of telling others who you are; and explaining why.

If I could be an automobile, I would be a (Volkswagen, Ford, Cadillac, Pontiac, Mustang, Porsche, etc.) because I am . . .

If I could be a flower, I would be a (violet, lily, aster, sunflower, petunia, etc.) because I am . . .

If I could be a bird, I would be a (cardinal, eagle, robin, bluebird, hawk, vulture, seagull, etc.) because I am . . .

If I could be a tree, I would be a (maple, oak, apple, sumac, dogwood, walnut, hickory, ash, etc.) because I am . . .

If I could be a street, I would be (Main Street, High Street, River Road, Broad Street, Happy Lane, etc.) because I am . . .

If I could be a building I would be a (beach cottage, a department store, a skyscraper, an office building, a ranch house, a library, etc.) because I am . . .

If I could be a game I would be (baseball, Monopoly, cribbage, basketball, hockey, football, tennis, darts, etc.) because I am . . .

You are welcome to add new categories to the game if you think they can tell still more about you. Talk over your choices and reasons.

Figure 6.3   (From Alfred Alschuler and Diane Tabor, *Who Am I?* Adapted from Achievement Motivation Development Project, Harvard University. Copyright © 1970 by Education Ventures, Inc. Reprinted by permission of the publisher.)

The person I admire most:

What I admire most about this person:

Admiration Ladder. This exercise should be done in the form shown below. Use any names you want except those of people from the class or group in which you are working. You might write in the names of nationally known people or the names of people from your own community or school. The names should cover a range from "admire most" to "dislike most". In other words, names in the middle should be those of people toward whom you don't have much feeling of admiration or dislike, while those at top and bottom should be names of people toward whom you have strong feelings.

After you have written in ten names on the form, write *your own name* in on the step where you think it belongs. You can do this by deciding which person named on the ladder is closest to you in being worthy of respect and admiration.

Now that you see where you stand on the ladder, do you want to change your position? What would you have to do to be as worthy of admiration as the next person up the ladder? How would you go about changing yourself so that you could climb upward? If you want, compare your ladder to those made by others in your group.

The person I admire least:

What I dislike most about this person:

Figure 6.4

AUTOBIOGRAPHY

At one time or another during the first few weeks of class, the teacher may want to give the students a formal questionnaire about their experiences and concerns. In *Values in Teaching* (Columbus: Merrill, 1966), Louis Raths, Merrill Harmin, and Sidney Simon developed a list of 40 possible questions of this kind. No teacher would include *all* these items and most teachers will reject some and add others. Many of these questions provide good discussion topics, and the autobiographical questionnaire might be used to initiate classroom talk in large or small groups.

AUTOBIOGRAPHICAL QUESTIONNAIRE

1. Name
2. Birth date   Age in years
3. Address   Phone number
4. What other schools did you go to? Tell me something about them.
5. Who are the people in your family? If you had to use two sentences to describe each person, what would you say about each member of your family?
6. Have you ideas about what you would like to do when you grow up?
7. What possibilities have you talked over with your parents?
8. What does your father do for a living?
9. What are some of his interests, hobbies, etc. What does he do when he isn't working?
10. Does your mother work?
11. What are her interests, hobbies, etc.?
12. How do you spend your time after school?
13. Of all the things you do in your free time, which do you like most?
14. Which do you like least?
15. What does your family usually do for Thanksgiving? Christmas?
16. What have you done the last two summers?
17. What have you done the last two Christmas vacations?
18. What magazines do you read regularly?
19. Do you subscribe to any yourself?
20. What are your favorite TV shows?
21. Have you seen any movies in the last few months which you particularly liked?
22. Tell me a sentence or two about each movie and why you liked it.
23. What are your favorite sports, if any?
24. If I were to ask you what books you've read which you've liked the best, what would you answer?
25. Do you work after school or on Saturdays? Where? What are you using the money for?
26. What do you like best about school?

27. What do you like least about school?
28. If you could change some part of your educational program, what would it be?
29. If you were a teacher, how would you teach your classes?
30. Have you a hobby which takes up a lot of your time? What is it?
31. How did you get interested in it?
32. Which of your friends are interested in it with you?
33. Who are some of your friends who aren't interested in this activity?
34. Is there an adult outside of school whom you dislike intensely? Why?
35. Are there some adults outside of school whom you admire intensely? Why?
36. Do you have some good ideas about things which you might like to mention?
37. Have you ever invented anything? What?
38. What is there about you which makes your friends like you?
39. Is there something you want badly but can't quite afford right now? What?
40. Of all the people you know who have helped you, who has helped the most? How did they go about it?

From Louis Raths, Merrill Harmin, and Sidney Simon, *Values in Teaching.* Copyright © 1966 by Charles Merrill Books. Reprinted by permission of the publisher. For information about current values clarification materials or a series of nationwide training workshops, contact Values Associates, Box 43, Amherst, Mass. 01002.

A LITERACY ATTITUDE SCALE

The teacher will probably want to find out how the students feel about the main content of the course—reading, writing, and speaking. Elton McNeil developed an attitude scale for the *Hooked on Books* reading program that can be used for this purpose (Figure 6.5). In addition to helping the English teacher learn how students see the importance of reading and writing, as compared with cars, television, sports, and food, this scale can be used as an informative pretest for an English class. Administered again at the end of the course, the literacy attitude scale will presumably show that the students think better of reading, writing, and speaking than they did when they entered the class. Since research has shown correlations between skill performance and the attitude of the student, showing such improvement in students is a helpful bit of evidence of a teacher's competence.

Teachers will probably want to adapt this device to their own classes, adding some items and eliminating others. One notable omission from McNeil's list is reference to the listening/speaking/dramatizing domain of English. One might add items like:

Example			Money is			
very good	good	sort of good	not good or bad	sort of bad	bad	very bad
very weak	weak	sort of weak	not weak or strong	sort of strong	strong	very strong
very interesting	interesting	sort of interesting	not interesting or dull	sort of dull	dull	very dull
very small	small	sort of small	not small or big	sort of big	big	very big
very important	unimportant	sort of important	not important or unimportant	sort of unimportant	unimportant	very unimportant

Test Items (using above dimensions)

1. Cars are	2. Television is	3. Classes are	4. Newspapers are
5. I am	6. Sports are	7. Writing is	8. Food is
9. This place is	10. Reading is	11. Tests are	12. Teachers are
13. Home is	14. Magazines are	15. Work is	16. Books are

Figure 6.5   (From Daniel Fader and Elton McNeil, *Hooked on Books*. Copyright © 1966, 1968 by Daniel Fader and Elton McNeil. Reprinted by permission of the publisher, Berkley Publishing Corporation.)

Talking with friends is _____ .
Class discussions are _____ .
Seeing plays is _____ .
Debating questions is _____ .

One could also add specialized questions about particular kinds of reading and writing:

Poems are _____ .
Writing stories is _____ .
Writing letters is _____ .
Reading about people's lives is _____ .

ASSESSING ABILITY LEVELS

Much has been written about the use of diagnostic tests and assessments to determine individual pupil needs. While I strongly support the idea of learning about students' needs on an individual basis, a great many commercial tests are not especially helpful and are even detrimental to establishing rapport with a class.

Reading tests, for example, generally offer students a series of passages for silent reading followed by a number of comprehension questions. Depending on whether they remember the facts of the passage, students are given a reading grade-level score or shown to be weak or suspect in various reading skills. In a similar manner, writing per se is seldom tested, but one can find on the market many tests of so-called "writing skills," meaning the elements of sentence mechanics and "proper" usage.

The use of such tests is suspect on two counts.

First, the results—too often given as some sort of raw score or percentile—tend to bias teachers about the skills and abilities of their students. Johnny becomes labeled a "second grade reader" in the teacher's mind and remains that way throughout the year. Jane is perceived as "having language skills two years above norm" and has her linguistic growth ignored as a result. The scores are too easy to substitute for actual observation of young people and their language.

Second, the tests themselves are inaccurate. No collection of passages followed by a series of questions even begins to measure adequately what children can read. Can they read street signs? the daily paper? TV ads? the textbook? These are the crucial questions that are not answered by a diagnostic test score. Similarly, the so-called "basics" of writing as measured by tests are not necessarily basic at all. While it may be convenient to know whether Jane can distinguish between *sit* and *set* on sample questions in a test, the real question is how well she uses language. Does she write successfully in school? Does she write outside of school? Does she enjoy writing? Can she compose poems? plays? stories?

The answers to such questions will emerge naturally over a semester or term, but the teacher needs to do some preliminary assessment as well. To that end, I suggest that that teachers conduct a kind of test sequence, presenting a broad range of activities and ideas to students. In doing so, teachers can both "define themselves" for the students and show the dimensions of the class.

Test Sequence

• *Poetry Reading and Discussion.* The teacher spends a day on a good contemporary poem, something with unstructured verse form dealing with an issue or theme of current interest to students: e.g., poems by Ferlinghetti, Jarrell, Lear, Cummings. Through discussion and response, the teacher learns about the students' attitudes toward poetry. How deep-set are their biases?

• *Short Story Reading.* The same kind of survey as for poetry, using a good lively short story—preferably one involving a young person about the same age as the students.

• *Play Reading.* The teacher brings in a recording of a play, or invites volunteers to read. How do the students respond?

• *Free Reading.* One day the teacher brings in a bundle of reading materials: magazines, paperbacks, pamphlets and brochures, advertisements. The students are given a browsing period and the teacher observes the materials they select. Alternatively, each student brings in something for a free reading period. The teacher makes a list of the titles and holds a class discussion. How many students share common reading interests? One can assume, too, that whatever the students bring in, they can read. Thus the teacher observes the level and complexity of the books and magazines, and if it is necessary to estimate skill levels, these observations, rather than a diagnostic test, can be used.

• *Free Writing.* John Holt has suggested the "Writing Derby," or nonstop word-production contest, which leads to open, unstructured writing. An alternative approach is that of playing a record (Bartok and Stravinsky work well) and letting the students free-associate for 20 minutes. Use this raw writing for finding out about students' interests and abilities.

• *Letter Writing.* Susan Judy has had success meeting new groups of students by providing a letter-writing activity. Students are given a range of audiences to whom they can write, ranging from personal and private (write a letter to yourself) to public (write a letter to the mayor or governor) to the imaginary (write to a Martian who is thinking about visiting our planet).[2] Students can write anything from personal narratives to discussions of world issues. By studying topic choices, audience, and the quality of writing, the teacher can make significant statements about the abilities and interests of the students.

• *Expository Writing.* The teacher can bring in a controversial newspaper article and ask the students to write a reaction, a letter to the editor, or a countereditorial. How do they handle "straight" writing? What are their values?

• *Language Awareness.* The teacher asks the students to analyze the appeal of an advertisement or commercial. To what extent are they aware of the way in which language works them over? Are they sensitive to language? Are they interested in words? Do they enjoy talking about language?

• *Activity Centers.* The teacher establishes four activity centers: a reading center, well-supplied with books and magazines; a listening area, with records of music and the spoken arts; a discussion area, with several "primer" topics written on cards; and a writing center, with a list of suggestions. While the students browse, the teacher studies their selections.

[2] *The Writing Interests of Children and Adolescents,* doctoral dissertation, Michigan State University, 1975.

• *Individual Conferences.* Finally, the teacher can have private conferences, perhaps while students are having a reading hour. Here student's individual goals are discussed:

> What do you think are your strongest and weakest skills in English?
> What would you like to accomplish in this class?
> What can I do in class that will be most interesting or helpful to you?

Evaluating the Test Sequence

The test sequence should be followed by evaluation through questionnaires or class discussion.

> Which of the activities proved most interesting? Why?
> Which *didn't* you care for? Why?
> From which activities do you think you learned the most? (Be cautious about answers to this question, since most students have come to think of all "real" learning as painful.) Which were least helpful?

From the answers, the teacher can proceed by means of related questions:

> Which kind of activities would you like to continue?
> What other kinds of things should we be doing in an English class?
> Are there special issues or topics you would like to take up?

The kind of sequence I have proposed is obviously time consuming: helping the students get to know one another, assessing their interests, running the test sequence, and discussing the results. This use of time may be frustrating to many teachers, and, for that matter, to some students.

Yet, this seems to me time well spent. My own experience has suggested that classes where getting started is done carefully and thoroughly tend to be more productive than those where the preliminaries are gotten over with quickly. People are not interchangeable like the parts of a car; the "breaking in" period of a class is necessarily less mechanical and more time consuming. Too, it seems to me quite debatable that the policy of getting quickly down to business has accomplished much in the past. Getting started is not an *alternative* to the "real" content of a course; it *is* a basic part of the program, though a first stage. It is the foundation of a strong synergistic structure, not a diversion from the main business of the class.

A NOTE ON TEACHER EXPECTATIONS

WHO OWNS THIS SCHOOL?

Surprisingly, you do! This building and its equipment, including the busses, was paid for by tax dollars contributed by your parents. Thus you and your family own a share in the school, and it is your responsibility to protect that investment for your family. This means that you must take care of all school property—books, desks, and classrooms—as if it were your own, and if you see other persons damaging or defacing the school, you must turn them in to the proper authority. Remember, MOST TROUBLE STARTS AS FUN.

From a freshman orientation booklet of a large urban school.

Surprisingly, the students to whom this message was delivered resisted the temptation to dismantle the school—brick by brick—and to split it into equal shares. This message, prepared no doubt in an honest attempt to cut down vandalism, is typical of the negative attitudes that many adults have toward young people. It is coy and patronizing. Instead of coming directly to the point, it plays a game, trying to trick the students into feeling that they have a stake in the school. The final sentence is the giveaway, presenting an image of the stereotypical young person, whose "fooling around" invariably leads to catastrophe. The expectations of the adult who wrote this are low, and they are plainly communicated to the students who read it.

Young people understand such messages, both the real and hidden meanings. In significant research into teacher attitudes, Robert Rosenthal and Lenore Jacobson have demonstrated that students are sensitive to what the teacher perceives as their capabilities.

One of the central problems of American society lies in the fact that certain children suffer a handicap in their education which then persists throughout life. The "disadvantaged" child is a Negro American, a Mexican American, a Puerto Rican or any other child who lives in conditions of poverty. He is a lower-class child who performs poorly in an educational system that is staffed almost entirely by middle-class teachers.

The reason usually given for the poor performance of the disadvantaged child is simply that the child is a member of a disadvantaged group. There may well be another reason. It is that the child does poorly in school because that is what is expected of him. In other words, his shortcomings may originate not in his different ethnic, cultural, and economic background but in his teachers' response to that background.

If there is any substance to this hypothesis, educators are confronted with some major questions. Have these children, who account for most of the academic failures in the U.S., shaped the expectations that their teachers have for them? Have the schools failed the children by anticipating their poor performance and thus in effect teaching them to fail?

Are the massive public programs of educational assistance to such children reinforcing the assumption that they are likely to fail? Would the children do appreciably better if their teachers could be induced to expect more of them?

We have explored the effect of teacher expectations with experiments in which teachers were led to believe at the beginning of a school year that certain of their pupils could be expected to show considerable academic improvement during the year. The teachers thought the predictions were based on tests that had been administered to the student body toward the end of the preceding school year. In actuality the children designated as potential "spurters" had been chosen at random and not on the basis of testing. Nonetheless, intelligence tests given after the experiment had been in progress for several months indicated that on the whole the randomly chosen children had improved more than the rest.

From Robert Rosenthal and Lenore Jacobson, "Teacher Expectations for the Disadvantaged," Scientific American, April 1968. Copyright © 1968 by Scientific American, Inc. Reprinted by permission of the publisher.

Although the work of Rosenthal and Jacobson emphasizes the so-called "disadvantaged," the concept that people come up to expectations is widely applicable. It is clear that in day-to-day teaching, we communicate to students—directly and indirectly, verbally and nonverbally, through tone, appearance, language, and action—exactly what we think they are. These messages may be translated into self-fulfilling prophecies, and children become what they are expected to be.

This is not to suggest that all teaching failures are a result of negative expectations, or that, conversely, by stating high expectations at the beginning one can achieve results.[3] But if the teacher operates with a concern for adult standards—seeing children as essentially *in*complete, *in*capable, and *in*articulate—he or she will often be strongly influenced by that expectation. Nowhere is this more evident than in classes of general, average, or remedial students, who have such totally negative self-concepts that they are initially unteachable. More than once I have heard of general students telling a teacher, "You're wasting your time trying to do something interesting with us; we can't learn anyhow."[4]

[3]One can visualize many teachers abusing the Rosenthal-Jacobson research simply to raise their standards higher than ever: "I *know* you can read Shakespeare, Charles, I *expect* it of you."

[4]Though less obvious in its effects, teacher expectation also operates negatively on the successful students—the "As" and "Bs" and honors students. Although they are meeting expectations—doing what the teacher wants—in the process these students come to look toward the teacher's expectations as the guiding force in their lives. Though they are performers, their capacity for independent learning and self-direction may be destroyed.

There is no way in which anyone can persuade a teacher that young people are fundamentally positive, capable creatures, and no amount of study of psychology or children's writing can substantially change a negative attitude toward the young. It is critical that the teacher see students as positive, without at the same time falling into the trap of praising all virtues—real or imagined—and ignoring all faults.

Young people are highly competent in many areas, and it is one of the tragedies of education that teachers seldom encourage them to use that competence inside the classroom. For example, most young people are well informed about music—knowing songs, groups, and musicians with a thoroughness that teachers would envy if it were in the field of literature. Students also know much about cars, sports, films, fashion, and world affairs. They are skilled in social relationships, managing to master complex codes, rituals, and rules in dealing with one another.

However, in each of these areas they are able to set their own expectations or to meet expectations established by the peer group or people whom they respect or admire. When placed in the classroom situation, with the teacher stating low expectations or establishing goals that the students do not see as important, their work may become marginal. Indeed, it is an ironic proof of young people's basic competence that they are skilled in discovering the real expectations of any situation and meeting them at a minimal level.

THE ROLE OF TEACHER EXPECTATIONS

[Pippi is a nickame for the heroine of this passage, Pippilotta Delicatessa Windowshade Mackrelmint Efraim's Daughter Longstocking.]

"Now," said the teacher, "suppose we test you a little and see what you know. You are a big girl and no doubt know a great deal already. Let us begin with arithmetic. Pippi, can you tell me what seven and five are?"

Pippi, astonished and dismayed, looked at her and said, "Well, if you don't know that yourself, you needn't think I'm going to tell you."

All the children stared in horror at Pippi, and the teacher explained that one couldn't answer that way in school.

"I beg your pardon," said Pippi contritely, "I didn't know that. I won't do it again."

"No, let us hope not," said the teacher. "And now I will tell you that seven and five are twelve."

"See that!" said Pippi. "You knew it yourself. Why are you asking then?"

The teacher decided to act as if nothing unusual were happening and went on with her examination.

"Well now, Pippi, how much do you think eight and four are?"

"Oh, about sixty-seven," hazarded Pippi.

"Of course not," said the teacher. "Eight and four are twelve."

"Well now, really, my dear little woman," said Pippi, "that is carrying things too far. You just said that seven and five are twelve. There should be some rhyme and reason to things even in school. Furthermore, if you are so childishly interested in that foolishness, why don't you sit down in a corner by yourself and do arithmetic and leave us along so we can play tag?"

From Pippi Longstocking by Astrid Lindgren. Copyright 1950, copyright © renewed 1978 by the Viking Press, Inc. Reprinted by permission of Viking Penguin, Inc.

Astrid Lindgren's fictional character, Pippi Longstocking, is adept at seeing through the web of teacher expectations. But she is naive and responds literally to the teacher's comments and questions. Unlike Pippi, most children find it more comfortable to slip into what some have called "the school game," answering whatever questions the teacher supplies. In the process, the students meet whatever expectations the teacher has established.

There are no set rules for a teacher to avoid setting poor or false expectations at the beginning of a class, but it is important to stress that young people are far more skilled and competent than adults have given them credit for. Given this conceptualization of young people, a number of useful metaphors for the teacher come to mind. The teacher, for instance, may be a coach or catalyst, a resource person, adviser, guide, or listening ear. Perhaps the most useful metaphor that I have heard is that of teacher as midwife—a midwife being one who assists in the process of bringing something forth, but who does not directly participate in the process herself. As a midwife, the English teacher is constantly at work helping students "bring forth" their work with language. The birth metaphor is neither erroneous nor accidental. And like most times of birth, the beginning of a class should be one of great, not small expectations.

EXPLORATIONS AND RESOURCES

• It is a Tuesday night, the day before school opens, and an English teacher sits at her desk, writing with a quill pen on foolscap. She is working on her opening comments to her first period class.

"Hello, boys and girls," she writes, "My name is Ms. Hendall and I'm your English teacher. We'll be seeing a lot of each other this year."

That won't do, of course, and she scratches it out and begins again:

"Hiya, kids. I'm Ms. Hendall. Call me Becky!"

That doesn't do it either. In desperation:

"Good morning, class. Who can tell me why it's important to study English?" Enough. What *does* a teacher say on the very first day of class? Work out some tentative opening lines. Ignore everything you've ever heard about these: "Let 'em know who's boss," "Never turn your back to the class on the first day," or "Don't smile until the second week of class."

- The various inventories, questionnaires, and activities in this chapter seek answers to questions that I feel are important for the teacher to ask about students. No doubt your list of questions differs. Develop some questions that you think need to be answered during the getting started stage, then invent some activities that will reveal the answers.

- A test sequence can also serve as an overview of what your English or language arts program will offer, thus giving students a preview. Design a specific test sequence for your teaching, whether science fiction, basic composition, American literature, or third grade language arts.

- In a tutorial or small group situation, talk with one or several students about their feelings concerning reading and writing. Survey their interests and their sense of their own skills. Then look up the record of their performance in English as measured by grades and standardized test scores. To what extent do your own observations conflict with or confirm the formal record? How might your expectations have been different if you had looked at the records first?

- Also in tutorial or small group meetings, interview students about their out-of-school pastimes, from TV watching to art or music. What language-related skills do they demonstrate in each? For example, TV watching requires that one respond to a plot, no matter how banal; playing a musical instrument requires that one have an intuitive sense of the "togetherness" of a piece, much like that required to a read a poem. How might these skills be applied in English? Is there evidence that skills are transferred, or do out-of-school and in-school skills remain isolated?

- *Four Case Studies.* Here are four hypothetical situations where teachers must make decisions about beginning a class. What kinds of getting started activities would you recommend for each?

  1. *Julian Harris* takes over a reportedly "wild" tenth grade class after that group has driven the previous teacher to the edge of madness. Julian discovers that the previous teacher had been drilling the students in workbooks and spending much of the time simply trying to maintain order. How should he begin?

  2. *Mary Anthony* is teaching the honors seminar in World Literature. These students are go-getters; they come to class with sharpened pencils, and if Mary comments about the weather, the students will write it down in their notebooks. What kinds of getting started activities should she try? To what end?

  3. *Benjamin Lewis* gets the "C"-stream eighth grade class, a group of disadvantaged students, most of whom have reading difficulties. Their favorite answer to questions is, "I dunno." Their second most favorite is, "I forgot my book." They don't or won't do homework; they don't talk in class unless forced; they don't seem interested in reading or writing or anything. In short, they are brilliantly living up to the expectations previous teachers have placed on them. Propose some ideas for Benjamin to try with the students.

4. *Lorrie Knight* teaches a fourth grade class in an affluent suburb. Almost every student has had advantages like ballet lessons, symphony concerts, and world travel. Two or three students, however, represent those who live "across the tracks." How does she plan for this class?

Related Readings

Values in Teaching, by Louis Raths, Merrill Harmin, and Sidney Simon (Columbus: Merrill, 1966), is concerned with teaching strategies that help students clarify their own values. It contains numerous activities and ideas that can help a teacher become conscious of students' beliefs and interests. *Hooked on Books*, by Daniel Fader and Elton McNeil (New York: Berkeley, 1976), contains quite a few interesting questionnaires and evaluation instruments in a section called "Hooked on Research." The series *Teaching Achievement Motivation*, by Alfred Alschuler and Diane Tabor (Wesleyan: Education Ventures, 1970), includes both activities and teachers' guides for helping students and teachers identify hopes, aspirations, and talents. Samples from all three books have been included in this chapter.

Walter Lamberg, a reading and English specialist, has prepared a sequence of inventories described in "Helping Reluctant Readers Help Themselves: Interest Inventories" *(The English Journal,* November 1977, pp. 40-44). Teachers concerned about the validity of testing as a way of assessing students and establishing expectations should review the October 1978 issue of *The English Journal,* "Standardized Tests and Their Alternatives."

7

Personal Engagement with Reading and Literature

SOME QUESTIONS FOR THE TEACHER OF READING AND LITERATURE[1]

Did people read to you when you were a child? What stories did they read? Can you remember the place where this happened?

Who taught you to read? What can you recall from those days? What were the first books you read by yourself?

[1] In this chapter, I will use the terms "reading" and "literature" both together and interchangeably. In doing so, I want to break down the traditional distinction between those two components of English. "Reading skills" are not separate from "literary skills"; rather, the two are inextricably bound together. I am also reluctant to accept any distinction between "literary" materials and "reading" materials that implies that the reading process for "great" books differs substantially from reading a contemporary magazine or a detective thriller.

How many nursery rhymes can you recall from childhood? How many Shakespearean sonnets can you recite?

How many of the Nancy Drew, Cherry Ames, Tom Swift, or Hardy Boy books did you read? How many did you read twice?

Did you ever go on reading jags—voraciously consuming book after book—when you were young? What guided your choices?

Do you ever go on reading jags now? What do you read?

Who was your best elementary junior, or senior high school literature teacher? What made that teacher good?

Can you remember the titles of any books on which you gave oral or written book reports?

What is the all-time best book you ever read? Why did you like it? Who introduced you to it?

That you either teach or are interested in teaching English suggests that your engagement with reading and literature has generally been positive. The vast majority of English teachers come into the profession because of their love of literature. Teachers' interest in sharing literary experiences with young people has consistently led to literature as the core of the language arts curriculum, with language, oral English, and especially written composition trailing along.

Unfortunately, though the literary experiences of teachers may be rich, those of many public school graduates are not. The schools have aimed at producing people who love great literature, who can read skillfully, who know the great ideas and values of civilization. Instead, the schools have created many book haters and functional illiterates. As most practical humanists will admit, the reading of literature seems to have had almost no impact on our nation's values and mores.

Some teachers respond by blaming the problem on the influence of mass media—particularly films and television—on the way young people spend their time. Although few people take Marshall McLuhan's assertion that "print is dead" literally, in many areas of society the media have taken over many tasks formerly given to the printed word.

At the same time it is important to observe that reading is still valued by many. As G. Robert Carlsen has commented in an articulate defense of reading, "We are literature-creating and literature-consuming animals." The act of reading is natural and pleasurable, and as the growth of paperback book sales demonstrates, it remains an intrinsically motivating activity even in an age of mass media. Print is neither dead nor dying.

But the schools have not helped much. From the time children begin their education, reading is often a threatening matter. Children must read aloud, and the teacher will correct them if they haven't mastered their fundamentals. They will be grouped and categorized according to their reading ability, and their survival will be largely dependent upon their

Every once in a while groups of self-appointed intellectuals get themselves up tight about the status of literature and the status of reading in
a culture. They feel that something must be done to defend a fragile
flower against the trampling of barbaric boots. Really this seems nonsense to me. Literature is not so delicate that it needs any special protection . . . nor is reading. If it were, then no outside defense would do
much to nourish it back to health.

Man is basically a *maker* (the literal meaning of the word poet).
After satisfying the basic physical needs of living and sometimes even in
the process of satisfying them, he creates. From the depths of his nature comes the need to decorate, to rearrange materials into patterns,
and to imitate and represent the world as he perceives it. He creates
with the pigments of the earth, with his own motions and sounds, and
sooner or later, with his language.

Man, we are told, is a tool-making animal. I suggest that equally we
are story-making animals . . . And something deep within us impels us to
cherish the product of the writer. I have watched it happen over and
over. Given a modicum of reading skill, some free time, and accessibility
to literary materials, people read . . . not every person, but most. People
read in cramped bunks under the arctic ice. They read 40,000 feet above
the earth. They read as they have their hair cut or dried, and while they
wait for the dentist. People read in bed, in the bath tub and occasionally,
sitting upright in a chair.

We are literature-creating and literature-consuming animals.

From G. Robert Carlsen, "Literature IS!" *The English Journal,* February 1974, p. 24.
Copyright © 1974 by the National Council of Teachers of English. Reprinted by permission of the publisher and the author.

ability to process print in school. Even though we live in a multimedia
world, the smaller world of the school makes use of a single language: the
language of print. Help for the nonreader is often punitive, with the student being sent to a remedial center that sometimes serves as a detention
hall for discipline problems.

. . . in most schools throughout the country, there exists an equation between intellectual ability and reading skill. Even if we were not living in an
electronic age, I think this equation would be incorrect . . . thinking ability and reading are not necessarily related.

From Neil Postman, "The Ecology of Learning," *The English Journal,* April 1974, p. 59.

In literature classes, which ostensibly aim to present new experiences, students often find that there is little relation between the world outside and the world presented to them through literature.

Ivanhoe, Silas Marner, Christmas Carol, The Merchant of Venice, Julius Caesar, Lady of the Lake: The names of these books are familiar to us. Why? Have these books ever been on the best seller list? Have we ever seen them being bought up feverishly at the newstands? Are these books the ones that our friends recommend? No! We know these books only because they are the sole stock of the English Book Room. . . . Someone long ago told that long dead original department head that those were the only truly good authors. This false idea has been perpetrated from year to year and remains with us today.

—High School Student

From Diane Divoky, ed., *How Old Will You Be in 1984?* (New York: Discus-Avon, 1969).

Literature programs have consistently ignored the individual experiences and interests that young people bring to their reading. Instead, teachers have concentrated most of their attention on what amounts to a specialist's interest in literature as an academic discipline. Until recently, most courses have been structured around historical periods, Colonial literature, eighteenth century, the survey; genres or literary types, the novel, poetry, drama, or romantic literature; and geography, British, American, world literature—a pattern of organization that is a monument to the interests of college English professors. Even under the newer high school elective programs one still finds that the majority of courses are being given titles and contents out of this traditional framework, and the course catalogs of many schools have come to resemble miniature versions of college English department listings.

Too often these secondary literature classes focus solely on analysis and explication, on wringing all possible meanings and interpretations from a text. Teachers have been more concerned about teaching critical analysis—the making of "acceptable" judgments about literary works—than about whether students are actually enjoying reading. Too many teachers think students are getting away with something if they are allowed simply to say, "This book is terrible" and to put it down without further commentary. "Why did you dislike it? You must give me your reasons!" In such a case there are probably a number of good reasons for students to reject a book: perhaps the book strikes too close to some of their personal fears; perhaps it is simply a book that has nothing to say to them;

or perhaps it is one of those books arbitrarily deemed "great" by the long-dead department chairman. But such explanations are seldom acceptable to the teacher, who keeps at the students until they mumble something about "weak plot" or "unreal characterization."

Under the traditional approach, we can visualize the literature curriculum as a giant vat or cauldron containing all the great works, all the accumulated literary scholarship and criticism, and all knowledge of form, style, genre, figures of speech, meter, versification, plot, prosody, and characterization. The cauldron gurgles ominously from time to time as new critical discoveries break loose and bubble their way to the top. Like children in a Dickens orphanage, the students line up and pass by, each to receive a draught in a battered tin cup. The younger children pass by first, and the teacher draws off the lighter liquids for them; only the older, more mature students are allowed to drink of the dark, viscous fluids from the bottom.

This may seem an unnecessarily bleak and negative description of what happens in literature classes, but the effects of that tradition are clear. Those of us who are lovers of literature may have a good deal of difficulty understanding the feelings of those who don't share our interest. I have often wondered, for example, whether the parental desire to censor books may be a result of the possibility that very few people who pass through the schools ever have an animating, exciting personal experience with literature. Not understanding what a significant literary experience can or cannot do to a person, the graduates of our English programs blindly try to control the effects of reading on their children.

LITERATURE AND THE READER

What are the alternatives to a vat-and-tin-cup approach? One is to look toward both *reader* and *response* rather than concentrating on explication and authors' lives. If we look at the experience of literature from the point of view of a reader, we realize that reading is an active, dynamic activity—no less creative, than say, the writing of a poem or story.

Marshall McLuhan has articulated this idea by adapting his famous claim that "the medium is the message;" that is, a communications medium—print, television, film—shapes the content of its message. He has also argued that the *receiver is the message* (*Atlantic*, October 1971). McLuhan is suggesting that meaning is not something fixed and stable that resides permanently "out there." A message depends on the experiences, biases, and perceptions that the receiver brings to it. A poem has vastly different meanings for an 8-year-old, a 13-year-old, a 21-year-old, and 50-year-old. When a reader and a book meet, they bump against each other. The book passes meanings, ideas, and emotions to the reader, and the reader brings meanings, ideas, and emotions to the book. The result is something new and original—not simply a transmission of a standard message to a standard receiver.

Louise Rosenblatt has suggested that in this respect, literature is a "performing art." Not only do books "perform" for a reader, the reader also "performs" upon a text to create meaning. As readers become more experienced in responding to texts, their performances become more and more complex.

No one else can read a literary work for us. The benefits of literature can emerge only from creative activity on the part of the reader himself. He responds to the little black marks on the page, or to the sounds of words in his ear, and he makes something of them. . . . Out of his past experience, he must select appropriate responses to the individual words, he must sense their interplay among one another, he must respond to clues of tone and attitude and movement. He must focus his attention on what he is structuring through these means. . . . The amazing thing is that critics and theorists have paid so little attention to this synthesizing process itself, contenting themselves with the simpler task of classifying the verbal symbols and their various patterns in the text.

From Louise Rosenblatt, *Literature as Exploration* (New York: Noble and Noble, 1968).

The role of literary education, then, becomes far more than filling students' heads with nuggets of literary wisdom and cultural history. It is a matter of helping individual readers improve their ability to engage with books successfully. While it is important to perceive the reading process as a whole, for purposes of discussion I want to consider four areas of reading and literature as shown in Figure 7.1:

1. Reading skills.
2. The process of response.
3. Analysis and criticism.
4. Knowledge of literary and cultural history.

The figure places a young person—the individual reader—at dead center. The message I shall repeat throughout the chapter is that whatever teaching we offer must keep the reader in mind. We must guard against the tendency for instruction to take precedence over actual reading or for the teacher's well-meant assistance to become an end in itself, destroying the intrinsic pleasure in reading.

READING SKILLS

It is unfortunate that reading and literature have become separated in the professional mind. Reading even has its own organization, The Interna-

Figure 7.1   The Elements of Reading and Literary Study.

tional Reading Association, while literature is generally given over to teachers who belong to the National Council of Teachers of English. This division has isolated something called "skills" from something called "content," with reading teachers responsible for the former and language arts teachers taking care of the latter.[2] English teachers generally don't know much about the "skills approach" and thus remain mildly in awe of or mystified by it. In practice, they often ignore reading problems or penalize the students who have them.

At the risk of seeming simplistic, I want to argue that English teachers need to be deeply conscious of students' reading "problems," but, at the same time, the importance of a "skills approach" to remediate such problems has been greatly overemphasized. The language arts teacher can do much to assist readers within the class, without an in-depth background in

[2] In the elementary grades, reading and literature are taught by the same teacher, but frequently the same sort of isolation takes place. Reading skills are taught apart from the books children read for pleasure. Sometimes pleasure reading is limited to the library and free time, while the other reading—skill instruction—is stressed in more formal classes.

teaching reading. Peter Sanders has observed that reading problems are often more a matter of poor student self image than actual skill deficiencies. The task of the teacher is not to reteach reading skills, but to persuade students they can read and to help make reading worth their while.

The number of students who *can not read* is small. The number of students who *will not read*, who have been taught again and again to think of themselves as inadequate, slow, and disabled—and who therefore behave as if they are—is considerable. We are not always successful in distinguishing between the two.

This "disabled" reader . . . is quite likely to be an authority on the subjects of failure and frustration. Where print is involved, he has long since learned that his chances for success are minimal. He has been conditioned to expect, though not necessarily to accept, embarrassment and even ridicule. His self-image, his ego, have been severely bruised. Small wonder, then, that he may also have learned that it is oftentimes easier to permit and, indeed, even to encourage his teachers to say, "Well, he can't read . . . ," than it is to risk once again his sense of who and what he is.

Within the English class, one can "teach" reading in three major ways.

Match the Student and the Book

The next chapter will discuss individualized reading programs. At this point, it is sufficient to suggest that a major cause of reading "malfunctions" is reading material that is inappropriate for the student: too tough, too distant, or too removed from experience. Teachers must use books and other materials that, as John Steinbeck has remarked, "have some points of contact with the reader."

Sometimes, the point of contact will be the student's own interests and problems reflected in the book, but it may also be the free play the book gives to the imaginative or fantasy world of the student. Teachers cannot require books simply because they represent "good" or "classic" literature. As a teacher gains experience with students and books, a sense of appropriateness grows. But new and experienced teachers can find help with book selection is available, particularly from librarians and young adult reading bibliographies. The next chapter provides a list of the latter.

> A man who tells secrets or stories must think of who is hearing or reading, for a story has as many version as it has readers. Everyone takes what he wants or can from it and thus changes it to his measure. Some pick out parts and reject the rest, some strain the story through their mesh of prejudice, some paint it with their own delight. A story must have some points of contact with the reader to make him feel at home in it.
>
> From John Steinbeck, *The Winter of Our Discontent* (New York: The Viking Press, 1961).

Fitting books to students' interest and needs does not, however, mean simply letting the students read any old thing, not offering them anything new or challenging. Teachers should make certain students establish contact with their reading, but they also should systematically introduce students to new ideas and materials to stretch both their minds and their reading skills.

Provide a Purpose for Reading

People read for many different reasons: to learn, to be entertained, to escape the world, to seek solutions to problems. They seldom read simply for the sake of learning to read better. Yet a great many reading programs are based on the assumption that reading is done for practice. Students read passages and answer questions as a way of proving that they have understood; they read literary classics and write essay exams to show that they have mastered the central ideas. However, if we recall that the reader must be kept at the center of the process (Figure 7.1), we can see that unless reading serves a purpose, it is not likely to improve either reading skills or attitudes towards books.

If the match between student and book is a good one, the student will naturally sense a purpose for finishing the book, if only to find out what happened. But the teacher can also assist by making the end of the reading process something other than recitation or book reporting. Students can share responses, write journals and diaries, compose literature of their own, seek applications of literature in their own lives, or look for other books on the same topic. By providing a variety of outlets for the student's response, the teacher brings reality to the reading process, making it part of the student's conscious concerns, not just a schoolroom exercise.

Provide Support for Reading Process

A vast number of so-called "reading skills" are not unique to reading at all. Most young people are able to find the main idea in a television program or summarize the plot of a film they have seen, so it is redundant to teach such skills as if they were a unique part of reading. Further, from grade one on, most students are capable of basic decoding—translating printed words into sounds, either orally or silently—and need little help with phonics. They need practice *reading*, and they need to have that practice in an environment that supports the naturalistic development of reading abilities. A teacher can take various steps to promote and sustain reading:

> Present a rich variety of reading materials: classic and contemporary novels, poetry and play collections, short story anthologies, books written for young adults, newspapers, magazines, monographs, brochures, phamplets.
>
> Provide time for students to read. Young people don't have a lot of time to give to reading; by providing in-class time, the teacher not only supports reading but also creates an opportunity to offer specific help to students who need it.
>
> Include recorded literature in a classroom library for those who find reading difficult or for those who simply enjoy listening to a good story.
>
> Use oral presentations and classroom drama to bring literature to life. Students should not be forced to read or dramatize if they find it extremely difficult, but in most classes, many students enjoy dramatic work. (See also Chapters 10 and 13.)
>
> Provide prereading warm ups. Before students plunge into a new book or story, provide them with appropriate background and discuss the key issues and problems. Give students a preliminary sense of what is likely to happen so they don't become lost.
>
> Use television and film tie-ins. Draw on novels-for-television and films made from books. Look for film versions of classic and contemporary books to show to the class.
>
> Let students quit reading books that they are not able to comprehend or enjoy. With hundreds of thousands of books in print, the teacher can usually find acceptable alternatives.
>
> Read aloud to students regularly, letting them follow along in the text or just plain listen.
>
> Provide help with difficult textbook assignments. There are times when students will need to read material they do not find especially appealing as part of their course work. But rather than have them struggle in silence, the teacher can offer help for both English and other assignments. Create tutorials, partnerships, or discussion groups. Many English departments now supplement their instruction by establishing learning centers (not simply remedial centers) where all students can go for help with reading problems.
>
> Praise students when they succeed at new and difficult reading tasks.

RESPONDING TO LITERATURE AND READING

An alternative to the vat-and-tin-cup metaphor for literary study suggested itself some years ago as I watched my son playing with two lumps of modeling clay: one yellow, the other red. As he worked with the two lumps, a third color emerged—orange. In literature, the same kind of transformation occurs: a new color results from the mixing of red—the book—and yellow—the students' previous experiences. Orange then represents involvement in literature. If the mixing is successful, a very bright shade of orange results; the students literally change, coming to know themselves better and growing through their experience with literature.

Encouraging students to relate to literature in these deeper ways is not easy. Many students are accustomed to classes in which the principal goal seems to be discovering acceptable answers—the teacher's answers—and it will require considerable work before these students can develop their ability to relate to books in personal terms. If the teacher begins with an open, affective question, "What did you feel about this poem?" the student will, as often as not, reply, "I dunno," "I forgot to read the assignment," or something else—anything else—to avoid having to answer such a question.

English teachers are not the only ones facing this difficulty. Hilda Taba, who was at one time a student of John Dewey, felt that this reluctance was a problem in history and social studies classes, where students become oriented toward factual, cognitive responses and lose the ability to react in personal terms to historical experiences. Consequently, she devised a series of teaching stategies, sequences of questions teachers can raise to lead students away from strict cognitive responses.

Many of Taba's ideas are applicable in the English class too. I have adapted some of her strategies to four levels of questions that the teacher can use in leading discussions of literature. Although the questions are listed by numbered levels, this is not a sequence that should be followed strictly or rigidly.[3] Nor is one level necessarily higher or better than another. How these questions are actually used will depend on the individual teacher, the class, the literary work, and the intangible variables that surround any teaching situation.

———————————————————————————————

Level I: Understanding. The teacher asks questions to make certain the students have understood the basic meaning of the poem, play, or story.

SAMPLE QUESTIONS: What happened? What happened after that? What do

---

[3] The Taba strategies are sometimes presented as a formula for lesson planning. Though there might be some value to practicing writing questions at the various levels, it would be naive to assume that any catechism of questioning will work at all levels in many teaching situations. Many graduates of Taba workshops come out adept at question writing, but their teaching becomes quite wooden.

you think the poet is saying in the first two lines? Were there any parts you didn't understand?

THE ANSWERS: Questions like these tend to have single, right-wrong answers. The teacher asks only enough questions to make certain that understanding has taken place. Although most teachers want to avoid questions that have only single answers, some group dynamics experts have noted that asking a few short questions of this type at the beginning of a discussion often helps to break the ice, providing opportunities for several students to speak and initiating a flow of dialogue.

_____

The first level deals with understanding, with the teacher conducting a brief survey to ensure that students understand the essence of the plot of a story or play, or the basic content of a poem. The teacher wants to make certain all members of the class can follow the subsequent discussion. No member of the class should be left behind because of vocabulary problems or obscure meanings. The purpose is not to find out who did or didn't read the assignment. The aim is checking understanding, not conducting a police action.[4] With some literature, a question or two will assure the teacher that students have gotten the meaning. With other pieces—say, an e. e. cummings puzzler or a complicated short story—a class may need to spend a fair amount of time figuring out meanings. However, if discussion at Level I takes up an unusual amount of time, the teacher might want to question the choice of literature. After all, it's probably true that one can drag junior high students to the point where they understand the language and meaning of a sophisticated adult play or novel, but is it a good idea to try? To force reading of difficult works violates the principle of matching the student to the book discussed previously.

_____

Level II: Interpreting. The teacher asks these questions to help the students explore the relationships within the literature.

SAMPLE QUESTIONS: How do you think X felt? What did Y mean when she said Q? Why do you think he reacted that way? What evidence did you have to suggest that Z was going to happen? Why do you think the poet said R? What do you think might happen next if we continued the story?

THE ANSWERS: A variety of opinions will come out in this discussion. In most cases a class will be able to come to a consensus view, since the text itself provides evidence to support various interpretations. Nevertheless, the

[4]Neither should these questions be equated with the typical comprehension questions that teachers often ask as a test of reading skill. Forcing students to remember things simply to prove that they can decode a printed page does considerable damage to the reading process.

questions are generally open ended, creating opportunities for sustained discussion.

_____

The second level deals with seeing relationships between the parts of a poem or story. It calls for understanding characters beyond the surface, seeing levels of meaning, and probing into the parts of a work of literature to see how it is put together. Most students will enjoy this kind of discussion *if* the teacher doesn't overdo it by running an exhaustive analysis. Further, it has been the case traditionally that analysis is the *end* of the process—the draught of liquid from the vat of literature. However, if students see a connection between their own experiences and those described in a play, for example, they will be a good deal more interested in analyzing the play in depth.

_____

Level III: Relating. The teacher encourages the students to bring their own values and experiences to the literature.

SAMPLE QUESTIONS: How did you like X? Do you think you would want this character for a friend? What would you have done? Has anything like this ever happened to you? What did you do? Why did you want it that way? Would you do it that way again? Why do people act that way?

THE ANSWERS: Obviously these questions are wide open. There are no right answers to them (although each student will have some answers that are personally right). Some of the questions direct the students toward the text; others send them into their own experience. Occasionally the teacher can touch base with the story, bringing the student's experiences and those of the literature together: "That's an interesting reply, John, but don't you remember what happened to X when he tried something like that?"

_____

At this third level—relating—the students bring meaning *to* literature. The teacher encourages students to put themselves and their values into the story or poem, drawing on their own experiences, concerns, interests, and ideas. Typically in college, Level III questions are discussed only in dormitory rooms or over coffee at the grill, because much literary criticism is not prepared to deal with open-ended questions to which only the reader has the answers.

_____

Level IV: Exploring Beyond the Text. Using the literature as a jumping-off point, the teacher searches for related ideas and ways of extending the discussion into new areas.

SAMPLE QUESTIONS: What other questions does this bring to mind? What additional issues do you want to take up? What should we do about it? Who is interested in writing a play (or poem or story or essay) that expresses our view? Would a small group like to investigate more? Here are two poems that also take up the idea—what is your reaction?

THE ANSWERS: Unpredictable and unlimited in direction.

At Level IV, the literary experience extends *beyond* the text as the students explore additional ideas that grow from their response. Formalist critics might throw up their hands at this kind of questioning, arguing that such discussions have nothing to do with literature. However, if the teacher has been able to get students stretching and exploring, moving into new areas of experience, the literature will have served its purpose well—the students will have grown as a result.

The explorations that grow from literature need not be limited to talk, and teachers probably greatly overuse discussion as a means of analyzing and assessing students' reactions to literature. The teacher should encourage students to experiment with many different ways of describing their reactions to reading. Sometimes the best approach will simply be to suggest more reading—another book by the same author, a magazine on the same topic, a biography or an autobiography, or some writing by other students. At other times it may be appropriate for students to see or make films, prepare posters, satirize what they have seen, or participate in dramatic experiences. If the teacher supports a range of different reactions, the students will become interested in one another's work. At this point, the traditional distinction between literature and composition vanishes. A class will flow freely from reading to creating to reading its own creations. The students' own work becomes part of the literature under examination.

Approaching a Poem

To illustrate how engagement with literature can happen in a class, I will present a hypothetical lesson based on a poem I have used with success with students—Stephen Spender's "My Parents Kept Me from Children Who Were Rough":

> My parents kept me from children who were rough
> Who threw words like stones and who wore torn clothes.
> Their thighs showed through rags. They ran in the street.
> And climbed cliffs and stripped by the country streams.
>
> I feared more than tigers their muscles like iron
> Their jerking hands and their knees tight on my arms.

> I feared the salt-coarse pointing of those boys
> Who copied my lisp behind me on the road.
>
> They were lithe, they sprang out behind hedges
> Like dogs to bark at my world. They threw mud
> While I looked the other way, pretending to smile.
> I longed to forgive them, but they never smiled.[5]

Most students react strongly and directly to this poem, because they can make contact by bringing a number of personal experiences to it.

Because of its brevity and content, the poem is a good one to read aloud to a class. It is straightforward, and thus there is probably little need for detailed discussion at the understanding level. As a prereading activity, the teacher might want to check on one or two unusual words—"lithe" and "salt-coarse," for instance—to help guarantee understanding. One or two questions would probably be enough to convince the teacher that the students understand the poem:

> What image do you have of the boys Spender is talking about?
> What did they do to him?
> What did he say and think about them?

Interpretive questions (Level II) may be a bit more challenging to the students, because some of Spender's attitudes and feelings are not explicit in the poem. In the discussion, the teacher might use some of the following questions:

> How do you think Spender felt toward these boys?
> Why did he say he "longed to forgive them"?
> How do you think he felt toward his parents?
> Does he seem to be saying that his parents did something wrong in keeping him from children who were rough?

That last question would lead quite naturally to some Level III discussions.

> Do you think Spender's parents should have kept him from rough children? Why?
> How would you have handled it if you have been one of his parents?
> How would you have reacted if you had been Spender?
> Would you have "longed" to "forgive" the boys?

If the students respond well to these questions, the teacher might ask some additional, more personal questions at Level III:

> Can you recall having been pushed around by rough children when you were younger? How did you feel? How did you react?

[5] From *Collected Poems 1928–1953*. Copyright 1934, renewed 1952 by Stephen Spender. Reprinted by permission of Random House, Inc.

Have you ever done this kind of thing to someone else?
How did you feel then?
Have you ever had to call on your parents to interfere on your behalf?
Have you ever had the feeling that your parents protect you too
much?

The order of questions is not rigid. In an actual class, the discussion
would range freely from one level to another. The teacher might begin the
discussion by asking, "How do you think Spender felt toward these boys?"
(Level II) or "Do you think Spender's parents should have kept him from
these kids?" (Level III). In fact, the teacher might even want to conduct a
brief discussion before asking the students to look at the poem: "Have you
ever seen big kids pushing around little ones? Why do people do that?
Here is a poem that talks about it."

Benjamin DeMott refers to this latter approach as introducing the
poem as a "third voice" in the classroom conversation. I like both the notion of a literary work as a "voice" and the idea of a literary experience being a "conversation" among teacher, students, writer—with the implication that the three are equal, each with a set of experiences, under-
standings, feelings, and reactions. (See Benjamin DeMott, "Reading,
Writing, Reality, Unreality . . . ," in *Response to Literature*, James Squire,
ed. [Urbana: National Council of Teachers of English, 1968].)

There are also many possibilities for extending this discussion into additional areas (Level IV). The teacher might want to bring in other poems
and stories related to the theme. For instance, Richard Wright's *Black Boy*
contains a number of scenes in which Richard fights back against both
young people and adults, black and white, to gain acceptance or to avoid
being crushed. In fact, literature is filled with stories or confrontation of
this kind at many levels. Some other possibilities include John Steinbeck's
The Winter of Our Discontent, Jack London's "Lost Face," and Yevgeny
Yevtushenko's *Precocious Autobiography.*

Another natural outcome from this lesson might be role playing, with
improvisations on a range of related issues and problems:

A student who is getting pushed around by some older students talks it
over with his or her friends.
A student feels he is receiving unfair treatment from a teacher and
goes to discuss it. What stand should he take?
A new student comes to school, and the other students decide to test
her to see how she is going to fit in.

Other topics and explorations might include:

Interviewing other students and parents to develop ideas on whether
youngsters nowadays are overprotected.
Writing a short story or play that illustrates the problem.

Writing real or imaginary letters to younger people giving them advice.

Conducting a panel discussion or debate on the process of raising children.

The possibilities for such activities are unlimited, provided the teacher can find ways of leading students to the point where they feel comfortable and involved in the issue.

ANALYSIS AND CRITICISM

Criticism—talk about likes and dislikes—is a natural part of making contact with literature, something that will emerge at *all* levels of discussion for students of all ages. Given a chance, students will talk openly about good stories and bad ones, poems they like and poems they don't like, and if the teacher does not push or use such comments as an excuse to teach taste, those evaluations will become more sophisticated as students read and talk more. The kind of evaluation that evolves naturally might be called "informal criticism," to set it apart from new criticism, mythic criticism, historical-biographical criticism, and psychological criticism. Informal criticism deals with human reactions to literature. Some questions that the informal critic will raise: "So all in all, how did you like it?" "Suppose you had been writing the play, how would you have ended it?" "Let's see if we can't improvise a more satisfactory scene." "What feelings do you have toward the author? Would you like the author as a friend? Would you like to read something else by this writer? Would you like to read some similar poems?"

In his book on the response-centered literature curriculum, *How Porcupines Make Love*, Alan Purves notes that the objectives of a good program involve helping students come to understand why they respond the way they do and why other people's responses differ from their own.

FOUR OBJECTIVES OF A RESPONSE-CENTERED PROGRAM

a. An individual will feel secure in his response to a poem [or other literary work] and not be dependent on someone else's response. An individual will trust himself.

b. An individual will know why he responds the way he does to a poem—what in him causes that response and what in the poem causes that response. He will get to know himself.

c. An individual will respect the responses of others as being valid for

> them as his is for him. He will recognize his differences from other people.
> d. An individual will recognize that there are common elements in people's responses. He will recognize his similarity with other people.
>
> From Alan Purves, *How Porcupines Make Love* (Lexington: Ginn/Xerox, 1972).

These objectives provide a bridge between purely personal, idiosyncratic reactions and the responses of large numbers of people that in effect come to stand as the critical judgment of a literary work. While acknowledging the validity of the individual's reaction—a reaction that will differ with that person's tastes and past experiences, both literary and personal— Purves also insists that the readers must take time to see how and why their responses differ from those of other people.

When the teacher moves in the direction of evaluating literature, it may be useful to introduce some literary terminology. Examining students' reactions may be simplified if the group can use terms like "plot" or "character." But it is important to emphasize that knowledge of literary terminology is no substitute for the experience of literature. What matters is that the students understand and enjoy the plot and the characters, not that they learn definitions. Further, just because some students have mastered the terms and can employ them with a degree of expertise is no measure of their ability to respond to literature. The upper levels of colleges are filled with students—many of them destined to become English teachers—who can speak and write the language of criticism but who have lost the ability to respond directly to literature in personal, human ways.

Analysis and criticism are not in opposition to a reader-centered program. Rather, they occur naturally as students develop—as they read, react, and articulate their responses. But skill at analysis is not the principal aim of a school literature/reading program, and it must be placed in the context of—really in subservience to—the young person's engagement with the material.

CULTURAL AND LITERARY BACKGROUND

In Chapter 1, I sought the reader's opinion of a statement written by the Study Group on "Response to Literature" at the Anglo-American Seminar on the Teaching of English, held at Dartmouth:

For the sake of both proficiency and pleasure, the student should . . . be familiar with the "reservoir" literature that forms a common background for our culture (classical mythology, European folk and fairy tales, Arthurian legends, the Bible, etc.), with a range of selections from

English and American literature and with some from other literatures in good translation. So far as possible, he should have some "time sense"— not a detailed, lifeless knowledge of names and dates, but an imaginative sense of the past.

For a long time that statement puzzled me, and it still strikes me as possibly inconsistent with the findings of the Dartmouth seminar and its emphasis on personal response to literature. The "reservoir" alluded to sounds surprisingly like the "cauldron" that I satirized earlier, and rather than offering a new approach to literature, the statement seems to be calling for a return to a more classical, less student-centered form of education.

But a key word in the statement allows for alternative interpretations. In the first sentence "should" can be taken to mean either "compelled to" or "given the opportunity to." If the intent of the study group was to compel all students to swim in that deep reservoir, I would have to mark the statement, "strongly disagree." One simply cannot force literary history and culture on students and expect them to respond positively. Such has been the nature of the teaching of literature for over a hundred years, and it obviously hasn't worked.

I suspect, though, that the study group had "opportunity" in mind, suggesting that in any good literature program, students will encounter works not written in their own time, works that naturally take them into other eras and countries. If "opportunity" was the intent, then I change my answer to "strongly agree."

Students fail to appreciate literary history and culture principally when materials are presented for information and enculturation rather than for assistance in reading a book. Young people seem generally fascinated with life in Shakespeare's time and enjoy the historiography of the plays, but not if the unit becomes an exercise in memorization of dates and places. Students enjoy reading myths of many cultures and can appreciate myth as a way of coming to grips with mysteries in the universe, but a number of mythology units have been wrecked by teachers who taught myth principally as a means to recognizing allusions in British literature.

There is a fine line between cultural history that enlightens a reading and that which becomes extraneous to the students' response. One key is the length of time required. If teachers must spend almost as much time providing background as they actually spend on the work, then the background seems to have gotten out of hand. In addition, teachers should recall that in-depth historical and cultural analysis is basically an adult or college-level activity. Relatively few students will reach a stage where background study becomes an interesting end in itself.

Still, while down playing the role of such studies in school English and language arts classes, I want to reemphasize that in the course of a response-centered curriculum in literature, students "should" gain a great deal of cultural background. Some students will read and delight in Dickens and gain historical insights into the periods in which he wrote and into his literary styles. Some students will read science fiction and discuss current cultural problems as they emerge in intergalactic sagas. Some will read travel and geography books; others will read history and social science. Probably just about every student will read or watch a Shakespearean play and learn something of that culture. Probably everyone will read some myths, some portions of the Bible, and perhaps an Arthurian legend. Kept in context, as a means, not an end, the careful use of historical and cultural materials should enhance engagement with literature and reading, not diminish it.

EXPLORATIONS AND RESOURCES

- Think about the ways in which you respond to literature. How do you react when you are reading a good book? How does a book work you over? What happens after you have finished reading (i.e., how do you act as a result of your literary experience)?

     Additional thought: To what extent does your formal literary training help you respond when you are engaged in private, personal reading?
- Find some people who are interested in the teaching of English and start an argument by declaring: "Print is dead; we ought to abolish literature classes and teach media literacy." What kinds of justifications, if any, do they offer for the teaching of literature and reading? Are these arguments sufficient?
- Give a poem to a small group of students and let them discuss it with no teacher present. Tape-record the discussion. Study its ebb and flow. To what extent do students stay with the poem? How do they work in their own experiences and concerns? How can this kind of discussion be developed and refined in the classroom?
- Choose a poem or short story that you think students will like and teach it to several groups, varying your approach each time. One time plunge right in by asking students to respond in personal terms (Level III in the schema presented in this chapter). Another time, take the questions in order. Experiment with the amount of historical information you present with an older poem.
- Study students' explanations of why they like or dislike particular literary works. What patterns do you detect in their responses? Can you discover any critical principles—for example, the nature of the plot or characters—that underlie their reactions? Working with several other people, choose a poem or story or play and brainstorm for teaching techniques. Prepare an exhaustive catalog of what you could do with the work in a literature class. Then split up the ideas, try them out, and compare notes.
- Start a file of students' reactions to books for use in the future.

Related Readings

Louise Rosenblatt's *Literature as Exploration* (New York: Noble and Noble, 1968) is a powerful book on teaching literature and deserves a full reading. *Response to Literature*, edited by James R. Squire (Urbana: National Council of Teachers of English, 1968), grew out of a Dartmouth seminar study group and contains a number of useful essays. One of Hilda Taba's books, *With Perspective on Human Relations* (American Council on Education, 1955), will prove valuable to those interested in discovering other areas of affective education to explore. A very practical book on response-centered teaching is Alan Purves's *How Porcupines Make Love* (Lexington: Ginn/Xerox, 1972), which includes chapters showing connections between literature and composition, drama, and media.

Teachers interested in learning more about reading might begin with Frank Smith's *Understanding Reading: A Psycholinguistic Analysis of Reading and Learning to Read* (New York: Holt, Rinehart and Winston, 1971). The November 1974 issue of *The English Journal* focused on reading for the classroom teacher, including an outstanding article, "The Rip-Off in Reading," by William S. Palmer, which exposes such reading frauds as "The Skills Sleuth," "The Medicine Man," and "The Panacea Pusher." The March 1979 *EJ* also focused on reading and includes a piece by Pat Rigg and Liz Taylor, "A Twenty-One-Year-Old Begins to Read," which reviews a number of support techniques that can be used with older students.

If the reader is interested in the relationship between subjective response and more formal kinds of criticism, see Walter Slatoff's seminal *With Respect to Readers* (Ithaca: Cornell University Press, 1970) or David Bleich's *Subjective Criticism* (Baltimore: Johns Hopkins, 1978). Those who know Rosenblatt's *Literature as Exploration* may also want to examine her *The Reader, the Text, the Poem* (Carbondale: Southern Illinois University Press, 1978), a book that offers a theoretical and critical explanation of the more practically oriented earlier book.

8
Organizing a Literature Program

HELPING TO READ: A PROPOSAL

I propose that we abandon the concept of reading as a subject and, as a consequence, the complex that has grown up around it. I propose, in short, that we stop "teaching reading." I propose that we adopt instead the concept of reading as an act, an act that children perform of their own volition, and that we develop a new set of practices to implement the concept, that is, to help children perform the act . . . .

First, a look at the kindergarten. Many children enter kindergarten already familiar with books. Their parents have read to them and the children have looked at books by themselves. In the kindergarten their teacher reads to them and they are free to look at books in the room collection. They experience many highly satisfying activities in their daily living and they find the activities reflected in the books. Before long the teacher arranges for them to take books home. Looking at books eventually becomes so engaging that the teacher and the class occasionally set aside a time to do just that.

Concurrently a number of other reading-related developments are taking place. One is that the children are acquiring myriads of concepts from their experiences. Another is that they are hearing language associated with the concepts and are using oral language extensively themselves. Still another is that they are experiencing reading in its origin: writing. They see the teacher writing on many occasions of practical importance and they become aware that reading what the teacher writes is the same as reading what is printed in books.

Of course in none of this kindergarten program is the teacher requiring the children to look at books. In none of it is he requiring them to speak or write. In none of it is he assigning, pressuring, checking, correcting, marking, testing. In none of it is he judging, labeling, grouping, or—certainly not—rejecting. In none of it is he using basal readers, workbooks, phonics charts, linguistic materials, individualized reading, language-experience reading, or any other method, means, approach, or system of "teaching reading." He is, in short, not "teaching reading" at all.

Yet several significant facts with respect to reading are soon making themselves apparent.

1. Without exception the children are continuing to use books. . . . The facts are that they do like the stories and information that come from books, that they will use books, and that they will continue to use them without harassment from us.

2. Using books means that the children are reading. . . . Ability ranges all the way from none at all to complete mastery. There is no practical value in trying to determine either extreme. The important fact is that after some zero point children are reading in some degree. They may be reading no words but they are getting meaning from the book and this is reading. And they do soon come to recognize titles and single words without instruction of any kind.

3. It is clear that when children choose books they choose them for certain purposes—their own purposes. We can interfere and force them to read for our purposes—to read what we think they should read, but the children's needs will be best served when the children are permitted from the beginning to read for their own purposes and therefore to select their own reading.

4. Children grow in their ability to read. They learn to read by reading. Each child learns as fast as he is comfortably capable of learning, given opportunity and help. He constantly pushes himself to keep abreast of his expanding interests and experiences.

From Beecher Harris, "Helping to Read: A Proposal," *Phi Delta Kappan,* May 1969. Copyright © 1969 by Phi Delta Kappa. Reprinted by permission of the publisher.

Beecher Harris offers an intriguing idea. Stop "teaching" reading. Arguing that reading is a naturalistic process, Harris looks at the free-and-easy way kindergartners use books for their own purposes. He suggests that teachers should adopt the same approach. If we abandon reading programs, he claims, a number of exciting things will happen:

More children will read better.
More children will read more.
More children will read more intelligently and with better taste.
Reading clinics and remedial reading will disappear.
Behavior problems now caused or aggravated by the pressurized reading program will no longer occur.
The money now spent on materials, gadgets, devices, and extra personnel will be entirely saved or partially channeled into libraries.

If only half of Harris' claims prove valid, his idea seems well worth adopting. But if Harris is right, one can properly ask: "Why raise the topic of reading programs at all? If reading growth takes place without teaching, what is the point of even talking about the 'teacher' of reading and literature?"

I will suggest two answers, one that is pragmatic, the second that delves somewhat deeper into the nature of literature than Harris does in his broadside.

First, for practical purposes, simply leaving students alone to read doesn't work. Even though learning to read is a more naturalistic process than most teachers have imagined, without some structure in the schools, reading is not likely to be done in significant amounts. While Harris's point that reading programs have become overstructured is well taken, his program (or nonprogram) may well go to the opposite extreme.

Second, and quite possibly more important, Harris fails to acknowledge that reading and responding to what one reads are often community activities. The sharing of responses to reading is at least as important as the actual comprehension of print. A completely unguided program, then, fails to create opportunities for individuals to *do something* with what they read.

LITERATURE IN THE CLASSROOM

In *Response to Literature* (edited by James Squire, NCTE, 1968), D. W. Harding described three "modes of approach" to literature, suggesting that in any class, literature will be presented and "used" in different ways:

1. *Presentation of literary material accompanied by discussion.* This mode is the formal examination of literature with which most of us are familiar from high school and college literature courses. It is guided by the teacher, but it need not be academic, dull, or divorced from the students' experiences, as I suggested in the previous chapter.

2. *Literature as group experience.* In this mode, the class members share a common literary experience—"storytelling, folksongs and ballads, film viewing, listening to what others have written, creative dramatics, choral reading, oral interpretation, dramatic interpretation, role playing [or] listening to recorded literature" (p. 17). This is a shared experience, Harding suggests, with a concern less for intellectual analysis than for a kind of "communal response."

3. *The individual child with the individual book.* This, for Harding, is free reading—self-selected—with the teacher serving as a resource person. In this mode, the teacher tends to remain apart from the process, leaving students to read and respond as they see fit. This is also the mode that Harris recommends in "Helping to Read."

It is fair to say that in the past, the presentation of literary material accompanied by discussion has been allowed to dominate the literature curriculum, almost to the exclusion of group and individual reading experiences. By contrast, a good literature program will not overstress or ignore *any* valid mode of reading and responding and will thus achieve a balance among *whole class, group,* and *individual* approaches.

THE WHOLE CLASS APPROACH

Generally this approach involves assigning a single literary work—poem, short story, novel—to the class so that every student reads the same material. If the teacher assumes the role of lecturer or critic, the whole class approach can be deadly dull. However, the common class experience with a work of literature can also provide students with models of response that can be carried over to their small group work. In this respect, the instructor becomes not so much a teacher as a participant in the process.

Elaine Konigsburg has discussed some of the pleasures and complexities of sharing in the reading process with young people. People generally enjoy talking about books with friends, and there is no reason why the adult book nut—the teacher—shouldn't join in. As Konigsburg suggests, one doesn't discuss books with youngsters for selfish reasons—improving their taste or helping them find the "right" meaning—but at the same time, nothing will help to reinforce students' reading habits as quickly as being able to talk with the teacher, freely and openly, about some of the interesting things that happen in books.

Benjamin DeMott has described literature as a "third voice" in the classroom conversation. (See Chapter 7.) The teacher is the second voice. As an adult—one who has experienced more and done more than the students—the teacher can help the students sharpen and refine their own involvement with literature. The teacher serves as a guide, sometimes pointing out things that have not been noted and sometimes describing personal reactions and experiences. The second voice helps students improve in their ability to make contact with literature without necessarily teaching it to them or butting in on their private and personal responses.

A BOOK IS A PRIVATE THING

As I was growing up I used to read in the bathroom a lot. It was the only room in our house that had a lock on the door, and I could run water in the tub to muffle the sounds of my sobbing over Rhett Butler's leaving Scarlett. Reading was tolerated in my house, but it wasn't sanctioned like dusting furniture or baking cookies. My parents never minded what I read, but they did mind *when* (like before the dishes were done) and *where* (there was only one in the house). I used to read a lot of trash. My own children aren't so lucky.

I share my children's reading. . . . I bring books home from the library and strew them all over the house because there are some books that I can hardly wait for them to read. I like to talk about books. It is almost as much fun as gossip, gossip being spicier only because it has two built-in dangers: being caught and being quoted. If one of my children takes the bait, it's apt to provoke a lively book discussion like this:

ME *(eagerly)*: Did you like it?
SHE: Yeah.
ME: Did you like the part where she hid in the closet?
SHE: Yeah.
ME *(brows knitted slightly, voice lowered)*: Did you cry at the end?
SHE: Mo— —ther!

I shouldn't have asked; crying at the end is a private affair even when you have a room of your own and don't have to run water in the tub.

When my children discover a book that they have enjoyed, one that they found for themselves, especially one that I haven't read, they tell it to me, but they don't discuss it. They tell the whole thing starting at the climax and then ping-ponging from Chapter One to Chapter Last. Wanting to discuss books is an okay selfish motive for butting into my children's reading; unfortunately, it doesn't work.

From Elaine L. Konigsburg, "A Book is a Private Thing," *Saturday Review,* November 9, 1968. Copyright © 1968 by Saturday Review, Inc. Reprinted by permission of the publisher.

The use of literature as a common class experience also creates problems in book selection. One wants to choose books that are close to, but possibly just outside the range of materials students would pick for their own reading, yet the literature must be accessible to a mixed group of 25 to 35 young people.

Interested in knowing about the kinds of selections teachers make, Susan Judy and I conducted a poll of "English Teachers' Literary Favorites" through *The English Journal.* The results are summarized in the box. In addition to the simple tabulation of favorites, our study of the questionnaires submitted led us to some observations about the kind of literature selected and teachers' reasons for choosing it.[1]

1. *English teachers don't especially like to teach British literature.* It was clear from the frequency of responses as well as marginal comments that teachers generally find American literature to be more accessible to their students. At the same time, William Shakespeare dominated the favorite playwright category more than any other writer in any category, so that our ties with England have not been lost.

---

[1] These observations are an expanded version of some remarks first drafted for *The English Journal,* February 1979, p. 6. Unfortunately, our survey population was limited to secondary school teachers. It would be very useful to have parallel information from elementary teachers as well.

2. *English teachers avoid using best sellers.* Why, we were not certain. It may be that contemporary best sellers contain too many four-letter words for teachers to use them comfortably. It seems that English teachers see best sellers as appropriate for individualized but not common core materials.

3. *Minority literature remains just that.* We were disappointed to see few minority writers appear on this list. The only winner was Alex Haley, author of *Roots*, whose book also had the advantage of being promoted through a media blitz in connection with the televised saga. English teachers ought to be much more conscious of minority writers and should include them in the common class reading experience much more frequently than they do.

4. *Similarly, teachers seldom select books by and about women.* Here, too, we feel that English teachers ought to do a better job of expanding students' literary horizons.

5. *English teachers like to teach their personal favorites.* Our survey asked teachers to distinguish between "personal" and "teaching" favorites. We were both surprised and pleased to see that teachers either choose books they like to teach or like the books they are assigned to teach. Thus teachers enjoy reading *Huckleberry Finn, The Grapes of Wrath, Catcher in the Rye,* "The Road Not Taken," "Our Town," and "A Rose for Emily." That teachers like what they teach seems very healthy.

6. *At the same time, many teachers teach books that are far more difficult than the ones they like to read.* This situation seemed to us potentially dangerous. A surprising number of teachers listed as personal favorites works of writers who are contemporary (e.g., poet William Stafford and playwright Neil Simon) but said that they preferred to teach older and more difficult writers (e.g., Melville and Ibsen). It may be that teachers see whole class reading as an opportunity for enculturation and enrichment rather than the sharing of responses.

This latter phenomenon is perhaps the greatest weakness in the whole class approach. For generations, teachers have variously sought or compelled students to read books and poems and plays that are remote from their interests. When that happens, whole class reading may become painful.

How does one avoid the many problems inherent in teaching common literary works to an entire class? I asked a group of experienced teachers in a workshop at Michigan State University to write down their suggestions. Here is a selection of their responses.

Teach short works rather than long ones, preferably choosing poems, plays, and stories that can be taught in one or two periods.
Don't teach classics just for their own sake. Teach books that will carry their own weight with young people.

Supplement readings with films, filmstrips, and recordings whenever possible.

Link classical and contemporary literary works together (e.g., *Romeo and Juliet* and *West Side Story*) so that students can see connections between great books and their own lives.

Accept the students' responses, even when they differ from your own. At the same time, students should have to explain why they respond as they do.

Pick and choose from the required anthology. Teach the works *you* want to teach. Never teach an anthology cover to cover.

The common experience provides great opportunities for the teacher to enrich the literary experiences of young people, to provide them with a model of sharing and response, and to help them encounter literature they might miss in their own individualized reading. But it also is fraught with difficulties, and if not done well, it can damage the literature program more than it helps.

ENGLISH TEACHERS' LITERARY FAVORITES

ENGLISH NOVEL

A Tale of Two Cities (Dickens)
Lord of the Flies (Golding)
Jane Eyre (Bronte)
Brave New World (Huxley)
Lord of the Rings (Tolkein)
Return of the Native (Hardy)
Rebecca (DuMaurier)
Animal Farm (Orwell)
Tess of the D'Urbervilles (Hardy)
Great Expectations (Dickens)
Wuthering Heights (Bronte)
Pride and Prejudice (Austen)

AMERICAN NOVEL

Huckleberry Finn (Twain)
Of Mice and Men (Steinbeck)
To Kill a Mockingbird (Lee)
The Great Gatsby (Fitzgerald)
The Old Man and the Sea (Hemingway)
A Separate Peace (Knowles)
Look Homeward, Angel (Wolfe)
The Grapes of Wrath (Steinbeck)

A Farewell to Arms (Hemingway)
Catcher in the Rye (Salinger)
The Sound and the Fury (Faulkner)

CHILDREN'S BOOK

The Velveteen Rabbit (Bianco)
Charlotte's Web (E. B. White)
A Wrinkle in Time (L'Engle)
Alice in Wonderland (Carroll)
Winnie the Pooh (Milne)
The Wind in the Willows (Graham)
Where the Wild Things Are (Sendak)
The Bat Poet (Jarrell)
Grimm's Fairy Tales
The Seuss books
The *Little House* series (Wilder)
The Wizard of Oz (Baum)

YOUNG ADULT BOOK

The Outsiders (Hinton)
The Pigman (Zindel)
Catcher in the Rye (Salinger)
To Kill a Mockingbird (Lee)
A Separate Peace (Knowles)
Lord of the Flies (Golding)
The Chocolate War (Cormier)
A Day No Pigs Would Die (Peck)

POEM

"The Road Not Taken" (Frost)
"Richard Cory" (Robinson)
"The Love Song of J. Alfred Prufrock" (Eliot)
"Birches" (Frost)
"The Raven" (Poe)
"The Highwayman" (Noyes)
"Fern Hill" (Thomas)
"Dover Beach" (Arnold)
"Death of a Hired Hand" (Frost)
"Traveling Through the Dark" (Stafford)
"Do Not Go Gentle Into That Good Night" (Thomas)

SHORT STORY

"The Necklace" (de Maupassant)
"The Lottery" (Jackson)

"A Cask of Amontillado" (Poe)
"The Secret Life of Walter Mitty" (Thurber)
"Flowers for Algernon" (Keyes)
"The Telltale Heart" (Poe)
"Tomorrow and Tomorrow" (Vonnegut)
"A Rocking Horse Winner" (Faulkner)
"A & P" (Updike)
"Silent Snow, Secret Snow" (Aiken)

PLAY

"Death of a Salesman" (Miller)
"The Glass Menagerie" (Williams)
"The Crucible" (Miller)
"Our Town" (Wilder)
"Pygmalion" (Shaw)
"Macbeth" (Shakespeare)
"Romeo and Juliet" (Shakespeare)
"Hamlet" (Shakespeare)
"A Raisin in the Sun" (Hansberry)
"A Man for All Seasons" (Bolt)
"Who's Afraid of Virginia Woolf" (Albee)
"Inherit the Wind" (Lawrence and Lee)
"She Stoops to Conquer" (Goldsmith)

INDIVIDUAL AND IDIOSYNCRATIC FAVORITES

Category	Nominee(s)
Ancient Philosopher	Marcus Aurelius
Original Poet	Gerard Manly Hopkins
Great American Novelist	Mark Twain
Humorist	James Thurber, Robert Benchley, P. G. Wodehouse, Erma Bombeck
Dictionary	*The Oxford English Dictionary*
Magazine	*Mad, National Geographic, The New Yorker, People, Ms.*
Cartoon	"The Wizard of Id," "Doonesbury," "Peanuts"
Overrated Author	Robert Heinlein, Richard Brautigan, Ernest Hemingway, William Saroyan
Teacher	Socrates
Mystery Writer	Arthur Conan Doyle, Agatha Christie, Ngaio Marsh, Edgar Allan Poe
Feminist Book	*Our Bodies, Our Selves*
Literary Character	Hamlet, Portia, Scarlett O'Hara, Heathcliffe, King Arthur
Textbook	*Writing to Be Read, The Elements of Style*

Underrated Writer	Walker Percy, Walt Whitman
Writer Born on Another Planet	Woody Allen
Trash Author	Jacqueline Susann, Grace Metalius, Xaviera Hollander, Erich Segal
Reread Novel	*Pride and Prejudice, Lord of the Flies, The Chocolate War, A Bell for Adano*
Epic Poem	"The Aeneid"
Speech	Clarence Darrow, "The Scopes Trial"; Jonathan Edwards, "Sinners in the Hands of an Angry God"
Male Chauvinist Writer	Ernest Hemingway
One Book to Teach All Year	"The Odyssey"

Adapted from Stephen Judy and Susan Judy, "English Teachers' Literary Favorites," *The English Journal,* February 1979, pp. 7–9. Copyright © 1979 by the National Council of Teachers of English. Reprinted by permission.

SMALL GROUP READING AND DISCUSSION

Examining full-length books with an entire class can become difficult. I have personally reached the point where I seldom, if ever, compel a whole class to read a long work in common, preferring to limit the common class experience to short works. However, the teacher can often find several students in any class who would like to examine a single book and work together on it. Small group work also has the advantage of being self-supporting, with the group members, rather than the teacher, supplying the principal motivation and direction.

In-common reading experiences, if wisely planned and carefully directed, are valuable for teaching literature/reading skills, of course. They become tools for teachers who wish to assist groups of young people to become independent readers. However, students whose reading experiences are selected almost exclusively by the teacher—often from a book which at least half the class cannot read independently and which may offer content of marginal interest to a minority of class members—may begin to associate even the reading of imaginative literature with failure, pain, duty—anything but pleasure. It is ironic and sad that so many teachers who feel it their duty to tour the anthology and its outlying paperbacks with their students (and who may do so with considerable flair) often work very hard to prepare students for other trips, trips those students will choose not to take.

From Terry C. Ley, "Getting Kids into Books: The Importance of Individualized Reading," *Media and Methods,* March 1979, p. 24. Copyright © 1979 by North American Publishing Company.

In moving toward small group reading, the teacher uses a multitext approach, having students read a number of works simultaneously rather than studying a single text. Multitext teaching can be as complex as a totally individualized reading program with every student reading a different book, or relatively simple, with students reading two or three different books in small groups. A comparison of multitext and single text approaches is shown. As Roberta Riley and Eugene Schaeffer note, there are many advantages to using more than one book, most notably that the teacher can be reasonably certain that students are reading books they will find profitable. It also raises problems, particularly in terms of record keeping.

A COMPARISON OF APPROACHES

MULTITEXT APPROACH	SINGLE TEXT APPROACH
1. The problem of different levels of ability within a classroom can be addressed through content as well as activities.	1. Since this content is the same, if the teacher chooses to relate to varied abillity levels, activities are the principal means.
2. Materials are diverse.	2. Material is easy to keep track of.
3. Participation in selection can be broad based and individuals or groups responded to simultaneously.	3. Participation in selection may be narrow, idiosyncratic, and often determined by people outside the group concerned.
4. Group members become familiar with a wide range of varied books.	4. Intensity and in-depth study may be enhanced.
5. Teacher preparation and involvement can be personal and individual.	5. Teacher preparation can be focused on content rather than people.
6. Reading for pleasure and out of interest can be encouraged.	6. Reading for structure and analysis is likely to be the focus.
7. Reading interests of the group may be expanded through variety of materials available and through use of peer recommendations.	7. Reading interests are directed toward a few prominent and well known works.
8. Documentation of student learning can be highly specialized and individual. Rec-	8. The task of evaluation is simplified because it is focused on a single work; often paper

ord keeping may be a teacher's initial, dominant concern. On the other hand, some teachers are just glad students are reading anything and precisely what they are learning or the depth of learning is not their main concern.

and pencil tests are used.

9. Occasionally, censorship may become an issue.

9. Books are usually approved.

10. Enrichment is possible with this approach as well as time for the teacher (and possibly other students) to work on with students who cannot read.

10. Learning is rarely differentiated.

From Roberta Riley and Eugene Schaeffer, "No Secrets: The Process of Sharing," *The English Journal*, February 1979, p. 29. Copyright © 1979 by the National Council of Teachers of English. Reprinted by permission of the publisher and the authors.

A convenient way to begin multitext teaching is to introduce several common readings to the whole class—four poems on a theme, three stories by a particular author—then to extend the range by having the students break into small groups to read several different full-length novels on the theme or to examine longer works by the same author. Students remain in their groups for a period of time for reading and discussion, then meet with the class as a whole to share their responses.

The teacher does not simply turn the students loose to proceed any which way but prepares a reading or study guide—perhaps following the levels of response suggested in the previous chapter—so that they have a sense of direction in their reading. As students become more experienced at this sort of small group work, the teacher can reduce the amount of direction.

I also like to structure these groups by having the students read for the purpose of solving problems or finding answers to questions which they themselves have raised. Many of us have had enough bad experiences with research papers that we tend to ignore the fact that people read to learn things. In fact, most of us do the bulk of our day-to-day reading for functional reasons. If students' reading is task oriented—aimed at learning things—and if the tasks and titles are selected by the students, an enormous amount of reading—fiction, nonfiction, poetry, drama—will take place. Small group reading for problem solving makes this use of reading comfortable and natural for many students.

Individualized Reading

Individualized or free reading programs are relatively new in education, having become popular about the time the paperback revolution of the late 1950s and early 1960s made quality literature available inexpensively. Up to that time, the common class reading of literary materials was the dominant mode of instruction.

Like multitext teaching, individualized reading calls for new roles for English teachers. Instead of being a lecturer, the teacher is often a book or reading resource, working closely with students to learn about and to suggest titles they will enjoy reading. Individualized reading programs also involve a fair amount of bookkeeping, and the teacher must develop some sort of manageable procedures to record student progress. Solutions to that problem range from cumulative reading folders that the students maintain themselves to large posters or charts on which the teacher or students can note the titles that have been read.

Contrary to some published statements, most notably, Daniel Fader's *Hooked on Books*, launching an individualized reading program is not simply a matter of supplying books in profusion, then letting the students have at it. Most teachers find they need to supply additional structure to make the program work.

Sometimes individualized programs can be linked to thematic or other kinds of instructional units. After the class has examined some common literary works each student launches off on a personal reading program. In this way, the books read by individual students are related to the common interests of the class, creating a natural audience for sharing.

Many teachers have adapted the basic instructional idea behind *Reading Ladders for Human Relations*, a book first developed by the American Council on Education many years ago, currently in its sixth edition (Eileen Tway, editor. National Council of Teachers of English, 1980). The "ladders" consist of book titles, arranged by difficulty level, on a single topic or theme. Students can thus follow a series of titles that continually expands their interests. Most school and public librarians know of the concept of reading ladders and are willing to help the English and language arts teacher develop similar sequences.

In some schools, individualized reading programs become formal courses, frequently with a title like "Reading for Pleasure." Such courses have been controversial and have come under attack from both parents and other teachers. "Why should kids get credit just for reading for fun?" is the question most often raised. As far as I am concerned, the more fun connected with reading courses the better. Given the wealth of reading materials available at all levels, K–12, there is no reason why the reading act need be unpleasant at any time.

My principal concern about free reading *courses* centers on the effects on the rest of the curriculum. Too often, individualized reading is slotted into the reading course only, while other courses continue with a one book, whole class approach. In some schools, the "Reading for Pleasure Class" has become associated with students of low motivation or low reading ability. When this association happens, the free reading course is seen as a last resort, as a course to be recommended when the student cannot be compelled or cajoled into reading teacher-selected material. An individualized reading program should be well integrated into the entire English or language arts curriculum.

A free reading program also opens unique opportunities for the teacher to individualize in other areas. For example, students may spend two or more days a week in silent or individualized reading. During this time the teacher is free to consult with students about other areas of their work, including writing, and to find conference time that is otherwise scarce. In a related phenomenon, as student reading is individualized, it becomes easier for the teacher to differentiate writing assignments, even to the point where every student in the class is writing on a unique topic. This differentiation in turn creates potential audiences for student writing, a topic that will be taken up again in Chapter 10.

THE TEACHER AS A READING RESOURCE

Obviously, as one moves toward multitext, individualized programs, the role of the teacher changes. Instead of simply selecting and then defending classics, the teacher needs to be a person who knows a great deal about reading resources for young people and who can help each student find appropriate reading material. In theory, one could simply turn students loose in the library and allow them to locate what they need, but such a process would be time consuming and frustrating for many students. The reading process is supported more strongly if a teacher is present at the right times to suggest titles, without pressuring the students to accept recommendations.

In sheer quantity, the resources that should be made available to students is staggering. Paperback catalogs and book lists provide literally thousands of book titles that are appropriate at various levels of the schooling process. At last count some 25 thousand magazines were being published regularly in this country, many of which are useful to a teacher of English. Brochures, pamphlets, flyers, and booklets are readily available and should be brought into a class at the appropriate times. A teacher also needs to know nonprint media, in order to serve as a resource person on films, television, recordings, and radio.

This variety means that the English teacher must be bibliographically agile. If a student develops a sudden interest in cacti or Strindberg or stage direction or poetry, the teacher needs to be able to help locate material that will satisfy those interests—even to the point of suggesting alternative sources to reach the student's reading level. Teachers of literature must know far more than the books covered in four years of college English. They must know and have access to many reading resources that may interest a growing member of the community of language.

For basic help in selecting materials, I recommend a collection of four books. Three are annotated book lists for elementary, junior high, and senior high, published by the National Council of Teachers of English: *Adventuring with Books* (edited by Mary Lou White, 1980), *Your Reading* (edited by Jerry L. Walker, 1975), and *Books for You* (edited by Kenneth Donelson, 1976). These books are prepared by committees of teachers and librarians, and in my experience, the annotations are informative and accurate. Teachers can select books they haven't read and assign them with confidence on the basis of these lists. The fourth reference is a bibliography of bibliographies, *Book and Non-Book Media: A Selection Guide for Educational Materials,* edited by Flossie L. Perkins (Urbana: National Council of Teachers of English, 1972). This publication tells the teacher where to find materials and book lists on such topics as science, art, books for children, award-winning books, history, and government publications. To supplement these book lists, most school libraries have other selection resources available as well.

But for many teachers, the problem is not so much locating titles as getting the actual books into the classroom. Book budgets are slim and are often consumed by the purchase of adopted anthologies. Brainstorming on this problem, a group of my students in an adolescent literature class came up with a list of suggestions.

Contact your local paperback distributor for free or sample copies and for unsold back issues of newspapers, magazines, and even books.

Visit garage sales. Often you can find quality paperbacks at rock-bottom prices.

Sponsor book swaps, where students can exchange titles.

Rip apart anthologies and group by genre, theme, author.

Seek donations from the community and from the students. Many paperbacks rest on home bookshelves unread, and they can easily be brought into the school.

Raise money to buy books: bake sale, car wash, talent show.

Set up an in-school paperback bookstore with the assistance of your local paperback distributor.

Encourage students to join some of the paperback book clubs that are advertised through such magazines as *Scholastic*. These clubs supply books at bargain prices.

Write to the government with questions. These inquiries will often bring back a rich supply of pamphlets.

Rotate classroom libraries with other teachers.

There are many clever ways to get a supply of books inexpensively. For example, at MacDonald Middle School in East Lansing, Michigan, the principal hit on the idea of a nickel book drive/book sale. The students were paid five cents for each paperback book they brought in; at the sale, they could buy as many books as they wanted for a nickel apiece. The students brought in thousands of good, readable books. Parents were informed of the drive and told they must approve of the books their child brought in, thus solving the censorship problem. Students who couldn't afford to buy books were given a handful of nickels privately by a teacher, so that every child in the school was able to buy new reading material. The unsold books were then divided among the English teachers for use in classroom libraries.

Overall, the advice to the teacher who is just moving into the area of individualized reading is to start small and expand. Initially, a classroom library may contain only 25 to 50 titles. That number can be gradually increased as the teacher locates new book sources and becomes more skilled at keeping track of individual student readers.

THE TEACHER AS READING PROPAGANDIST

Implicit, too, in multitext and individualized programs is the role of English teacher as book promoter, one who unabashedly "hypes" literature and reading to young people, telling them about books, placing books in their hands, reviewing books, sharing responses. One clue to the importance of this role is suggested by the success of TV novels. Such books, ranging from the *Star Trek* books to *Roots* to *The Little House on the Prairie*, sell well as a result of the publicity they receive. Apparently, most readers want to know something about the book before they plunge into it.

Again I will draw on some of my former students and present some of their suggestions for propagandizing about literature:

Put up attractive book posters advertising interesting reading.

Include many short books in your class library.

Always include free or individualized reading as part of elective English courses.

Offer speed reading or developmental reading courses on the side for extra credit.

Have "hot" books to the extent that school and community standards will allow it. Even books for young adults are fairly explicit about language and sex. Without opening a porno shop, you should realize that students want to read material that treats life realistically and speaks to their own concerns. "Hot" books do just that.

Include series books: *Hardy Boys, Nancy Drew, James Bond,* Seuss books, the *Wizard of Oz* books.

Put up book advertisements in odd places.

Provide frequent reading periods.

Provide book talks periodically, telling students what's available in an area or field.

Sponsor field trips to bookstores and libraries.

Make audio-visual helps readily available: filmstrips, records, even filmed versions of books.

Another excellent list of suggestions is provided by Donna Brutten and her students.

HOW TO DEVELOP AND MAINTAIN STUDENT INTEREST IN READING

How can we, as English teachers, motivate our students to read? In order to find possible solutions to this dilemma, we asked one thousand pupils at Nathaniel Hawthorne Middle School, Bayside, New York, the following two questions: *What has a teacher of yours done to interest you in reading? What could a teacher of yours do to interest you in reading?* The most frequent cited responses are listed below:

1. Let us choose our own book.
2. Tell us interesting stories.
3. Show filmstrips or films about stories.
4. Let us act out exciting scenes from stories and plays.
5. Suggest names of interesting stories.
6. Let us read along with taped stories.
7. Play records that tell stories.
8. Have free reading periods.
9. Assign creative projects, such as posters, collages, dioramas, and montages instead of book reports.
10. Have contests to see who reads the most books.
11. Assign different types of books.
12. Tell only the beginning of interesting stories.
13. Let us read comic books, magazines, and newspapers.
14. Have group discussions and panel discussions.
15. Let us tell the class about exciting books that we have read.
16. Decorate the room with interesting posters, book displays, and students' projects relating to books.
17. Take us to the school library.
18. Play reading games.
19. Award prizes.
20. Have a classroom library.
21. Bring book clubs, such as TAB or AEP, to the attention of students.
22. Prepare teacher and/or student annotated book lists.
23. Don't assign everyone the same book.
24. Let us read at our own pace.
25. Assign relevant literature.

ORGANIZING THE LITERATURE PROGRAM

Over the years, four principal ways of focusing literary study have predominated in the colleges and the schools:

1. *The Historical/Chronological Approach,* featuring survey and period courses and a concern for literary history. (Often these surveys are done by individual nations, e.g., British literature.)
2. *The Author Approach,* with a concern for the collected works of a single writer and the relationships between his biography and his evolution as a writer.
3. *The Genre Approach,* which directs literary study through the examination of the principal forms of writing: poetry, essay, drama, fiction.
4. *The Masterpieces* or *Great Books Approach,* which unifies its study through the choice of widely accepted classics.

In any college or secondary school curriculum, one often finds any number of courses based on one of these four organizing features.

Without rejecting the value of dealing with literature in terms of history, biography, genre, or classic titles, I want to suggest that none of these provides an especially good or convenient starting point for involving students in literature, because each takes the content of literary scholarship rather than human experience as its starting point. If one is teaching a genre unit such as poetry or drama the common denominator of instruction is still the elements of a literary form, leading the teacher inevitably to such questions as, "What is the 'definition' of 'poem'?" "Why is *Dr. Zhivago* a 'better' film than *Gone With the Wind?*" "What is drama?" In a survey or period course, discussion emphasizes historical matters, concentrating on knowledge of times and writings. Each of the other approaches similarly initiates discussion in terms of critical content, and the student's personal involvement naturally gets second billing.

To some extent, a fifth approach, *Humanities,* has broken the tradition of criticism-centered courses by focusing on issues and ideas. Yet in practice, humanities courses are often simply grand survey courses in the historical/chronological mode, or they reduce truly interdisciplinary questions to a mere comparison of artistic genres.

Thematic courses provide a sixth alternative, which focuses, first, on issues and problems, and, second, on literature. If a literature program begins with people and ideas rather than with literary patterns, types, or histories, the teacher can effectively involve students' experiences in the reading process. By centering on an idea or topic rather than a form of literature, the teacher is free to bring in multiple resources in many forms and media and to provide direction for reading by allowing students to read for their own purposes. (A short list of topics for thematic units and courses is given in the next box.)

Feelings and Emotions	War and Peace
The Sea	Illusion and Reality
Animals	Ecology
Friendship	Futurism
The Supernatural	Coming of Age
The Seasons	Prison Reform
Holidays	Cities
First Relationships	Isolation
Anomalies	Dissent
Persuasion	Racism
Fantasies	Prophecy

A good many teachers, however, find themselves thrust into curricula that are patterned along traditional lines, with course titles like "American Literature," "The Short Story," or "Romantic Poetry." Obviously, curricula like these place limits on thematic teaching. But before the teachers surrender, they ought to explore how the traditional curriculum can be shaped along thematic lines. Though not an ideal arrangement, courses can be oriented more directly to students' needs.

For example, a teacher I know was once assigned a "Poetry" elective course. "I'll be damned if I'll concentrate only on meter and rhyme scheme and versification," she told me. "The kids have had enough of that sort of thing and they hate it." Her solution was to purchase one copy each of the fattest paperback poetry collections at the bookstore—an out-of-pocket cost of under $20 for a dozen books. She then ripped off the book bindings and found herself in possession of a loose leaf collection of about two thousand poems. She parceled out this collection along the lines of some thematic topics that she felt would be of interest to her students—Reminiscences, Coming of Age, and The Generation Gap, to name a few. Her poetry course was then structured in topical ways, and it proved to be a major success.

The same strategy can be applied to other courses. Thematic courses can be constructed from materials that are exclusively American, or exclusively British, exclusively drama or exclusively in the classics. One could build a topical course or unit around the works of a single author—say, Shakespeare or Mark Twain—by dividing the works into thematic units.

CREATING A LITERATURE RESOURCE UNIT

Whether one is teaching a topical, genre, chronological, thematic or an interdisciplinary course, it is useful to prepare resource materials in advance to help structure the course, materials that promote a balance among the basic ways of presenting literature: whole class, small group, and individualized.

Unit Components

A unit can consist of three main components:

• *The Common Class Readings.* You can use a good commercial anthology for this or create your own. Use short selections—poems, stories, essays, one-act plays—for the common readings. The function of these readings is to give the students a common background for the issue under discussion. These materials should have broad appeal and high readability. They are discussed by members of the class at intervals, once or twice each week, while the unit is in progress. The approach to discussion sketched out in Chapter 7 is most appropriate here.

• *The Resource Center.* This center is the heart of a program and the most interesting part to construct. It is based on the assumption that if teachers concentrate enough resource materials and enough project ideas in one place, they will be able to strike a spark with each student. The resource center should contain:

1. *Reading Materials.* Select short to mid-length selections for the most part, and include all forms and genres: poems, articles, brochures, pamphlets, magazines, etc. Tear up some paperback anthologies and pull out the appropriate material. Clip appropriate articles from newspapers and magazines. Save your most interesting junk mail. When possible, dry-mount or glue the materials on construction paper, adding appropriate photographs. Make construction paper covers, envelopes, folders, and the like.

2. *Other Materials.* Include photographs, prints, posters, comics, games, puzzles, records, filmstrips, film loops, tapes.

3. *Suggestions for Speaking, Writing, and Projects.* Often these ideas can be typed or printed right on your selection. Ideally, every selection in the resource center might have three or four suggestions for student activities. There can be ideas for creative and expository writing, interviews, related reading. Some activities might involve small groups. Materials can be cross-referenced: "If you liked _____, then have a look at _____." The key is to provide enough ideas and alternatives to pique the interest of each student.

• *The Book List or Class Library.* Prepare an annotated list of books related to the topic and/or bring in a class library of titles for free and individualized reading. In addition to books, the list can include magazines, records, and films.

The resource unit can be used in many ways in a class or course. One pattern might be to begin with several days of common class reading and discussion, after which the students would have several sessions to examine the individualized materials. Eventually, the students settle on some specific projects or topics that they want to examine, either on an individual basis or with several other students, and the teacher and students work out agreements about when the work will be completed. At this point, the class enters a workshop mode, and the teacher sets aside project days for the workshop, perhaps alternating with some common reading days. As the students begin to complete projects, of course their work will become the focus of the common class days, and more and more the class will be taken over by the students and their work.

As described here, building an experience-centered resource center may seem enormously time-consuming—impossible for the teacher who has a full course load. Without attempting to minimize the amount of work involved, I want to stress that it is not as complex as it looks, especially if one starts *early* and organizes the project. It also helps to form a unit builder's collaborative within the school. If each teacher agrees to build and share one resource kit, a large supply of materials can be rotated among members of the staff. In a workshop of a week or two, a small group of teachers can easily construct several kits—enough for a semester or more of work.

Finally, it should be noted that as a unit like this is used, it will grow. Much of what the students write or tape or film should go back into the resource kit so that student work becomes mixed with the materials that the teacher originally found. Many teachers discover that students enjoy adding their own suggestions for activities. If the unit is at all successful, the teacher will be faced with a problem of cutting and editing, not rebuilding.

Individualized Reading Packs

As a supplement to the literature program, the teacher can develop individualized, multidisciplinary reading packs, a smaller version of the unit described in the previous section. The individualized packs center on both practical topics and subjects in other fields and disciplines. In a period when the schools are becoming more and more concerned with both career education and interdisciplinary learning, developing a set of individualized reading packs can help English teachers meet the demands being placed upon them.

Sample topics for individualized packets (these topics were developed by my students simply by asking them to list their interests outside the field of English):

Music	Politics
Crafts	Cacti
Philosophy	Calligraphy

Religions	Two-Cycle Engines
Theater	Pollution Control Devices
Parachute Jumping	Sewing
Knitting	Disc Jockeying
Printing	Terrariums
Jobs	Yoga
Making Snow	Plants
Communications	Journalism
Government	Cooking
Botany	Swimming
Sociology	Advertising
Girls' Sports	Almanacs

Individualized packets can range in size from an envelope containing a half-dozen essays to a box with several hundred related pieces of reading material. As with the more formal resource unit, the teacher should include topics and projects in the packet that involve both reading and writing, in order to help students find direction in their work.

These reading packs are not enough to sustain a class for an entire term. Ideally, they should be developed as a satellite to other units and materials under examination by a class, and from time to time, the teacher might pause in the regular work of the class to allow the students to work on individualized materials for a spell.

Developing reading packs is even easier than constructing a formal unit, since reading matter of the slightest conceivable interest to the students can find its way into one pack or another. An afternoon spent cutting up the bulky Sunday *New York Times* will provide you with enough material to begin two dozen packs, as will an evening spent browsing through back issues of magazines you probably already have lying around home.

A Student-Built Unit

Another intriguing possibility for the literature program is a unit in which students take principal responsibility for locating reading materials and for defining and executing their own assignments. Teachers are thus freed to move to a consultative or resource role more quickly than if they were carrying primary responsibility creating the unit.

One such unit is called a "Probe." To initiate the unit, the teacher simply asks "What concerns you as a class and what do you propose to do about it?" From a guided discussion emerges a concerted effort on the part of the class to learn about an issue or problem and to take action on it. Some successful "Probe" topics include:

Noise	Civil Rights
Waste	Liberation
The Government	Censorship

Victorian Morals	Clocks
Our Town—100 Years Ago	Russia (or any country)
Old Age	Religions
Human Relationships	Earthquakes
2050	Electronics

Some of the basic steps in organizing "Probe" include the following:

1. *Choosing a general chair.* This student will serve as a coordinator for the program. Often the chair will need one or more assistants or helpers.
2. *Brainstorming.* Working in groups of four or five, the students talk over three main questions:
   What do we know about this topic already?
   What do we want to know?
   Where can we find out what we want to know?
3. *Setting priority questions.* The fruits of the brainstorming session are evaluated by the whole class and reduced to, say, six or eight main questions or issues. The students break up into teams according to interests, each team with the central task of finding an answer to its question.
4. *Probing.* The teams probe the question—reading, interviewing, watching, observing—following plans worked out by the team and approved by the chair. The teacher serves as a consultant to each team, at the team's request.
5. *Production.* Each team produces things—perhaps essays, films, tapes, or advertisements—that help translate its findings for the class. Depending on the nature of the "Probe," the teams may present material to the class or go outside the class to take action.

The kinds and amounts of reading and writing which the students do will, of course, vary with the topic. Some "Probe" topics will lead principally to reading in expository prose; others will focus more on drama and poetry and fiction. The teacher will need to help the students see alternatives and possibilities, and guide them toward new and unperceived directions.

THE INTEGRATION OF THE LANGUAGE ARTS THROUGH LITERATURE

It is probably clear by now that the literature programs described here are, in essence, *English* programs—they involve at least as much composing, speaking, and listening as they do reading and literary study. This integration seems to me highly desirable; teachers should encourage a natural flow from one form of language use to another. By offering writing options as part of a literature unit, the teacher makes the *producing* of language a comfortable outcome of *consuming* it. Similarly, when reading is focused toward an actual task—learning something or persuading someone—it too becomes natural and purposeful and leads easily to related language arts activities.

Indeed, it is perhaps inaccurate to call these *English* units at all, since they involve experiences outside the dimensions of the traditional English course. In the history of education, English has often been the umbrella subject, with the unfortunate English teacher trying to hold the umbrella straight while teaching basic reading, the history of Western civilization, spelling, the business letter, the necessary skills for success in college, and the difference between the Elizabethan and Petrarchan sonnet. I suggest that teachers use this umbrella to advantage as a way of enlivening English and providing students with useful training for other fields. There seems to be no reason why the English teacher should not lay claim to the materials of science, history, math, business and industry, politics, psychology, sociology, vocational education, art, music, journalism, and theatre—since they can be used to provide a genuinely humane, broadly practical literature and reading program.

EXPLORATIONS AND RESOURCES

- To run a good literature course, one must be bibliographically agile, knowing sources. Teachers need not always know the fine details of what is in the literature, but the knowledge must be sufficient to allow them to make recommendations with confidence. Here are three projects that a teacher can undertake to develop bibliographic agility:

  1. *Spend time browsing in a paperback bookstore looking at books that might be useful with students.* Don't limit your thinking to traditional literature. Check out the sociology section, the history paperbacks, the jokebooks, and the science section. Examine the handicrafts department and the sports books. Check cookbooks. Practice scanning for content so you can form quick, reliable judgments about a book's applicability.
  2. *Do the same with the magazine section of a bookstore.* There are a phenomenal number of magazines upon which you can draw regularly. Check such titles as *Gem Collector* and *Czechoslovakia Today* for possible use.
  3. *Learn about pamphlet and brochure sources.* Enormous amounts of such material are printed each year in this country. For starters, familiarize yourself with the publications available from the Superintendent of Documents in Washington, D.C., and from your state's printing office. Then check travel agencies, public service institutions, universities, county agriculture agents, and the pamphlet files at your local library.

- Pick a topic that you think would interest students of the age you like to teach and create a reading ladder—in effect, a book list—of related books of increasing sophistication and difficulty.

- Learn how to give a book talk, a 15- to 30- minute review of books on a topic for young people.
- Try letting a class (or a few students) embark on a totally free reading program, with you serving only as a guide or coach. Stay with it long enough to see patterns of growth and development emerging. Do students grow as readers when left on their own? Do they enjoy the program?
- Design a record-keeping system for an individualized reading program.
- Choose a book that you think a small group of students could read on their own and develop a study guide to assist them in their reading.
- Get together with two or three others teachers and build a resource unit, just to find out how it's done and how much or how little work it involves. Flip a coin to see who gets to test it first.
- Study a conventional literature anthology in terms of its adaptability to thematic teaching. For example, if you find a British literature anthology is organized chronologically, consider ways in which its literary selections could be restructured along thematic lines.
- Start your collection of individualized reading packs.

Related Readings

D. W. Harding's essay "Response to Literature" (in *Response to Literature,* edited by James Squire, National Council of Teachers of English, 1968) is a concise and practical discussion of literature and reading programs. Note especially Harding's comments on the ways in which reading patterns change as students grow, thus creating the need for the teacher to alter the modes of approach to literature. Daniel Fader and Elton McNeil's *Hooked on Books* comes up again as a useful reference because of its comments on ways of saturating a school with reading matter—especially newspapers and magazines. Geoffrey Summerfield's *Topics in English* (London: Batsford, 1965) is the single best practical guide available for the development of experience-centered programs; in addition to an excellent section on conducting project work, it contains sample units (for such widely diverse topics as "Snakes and Reptiles" and "Loneliness").

In addition to the book selection sources mentioned in the chapter, teachers may want to consult "A Book Selection Primer," by Barbara Blow and Linda Waddle *(The English Journal,* January 1974, pp. 76–79), which lists over 40 review sources. That same issue of *EJ* also includes an exhaustive bibliography of multiethnic literature prepared by Alleen Pace Nilsen (pp. 41–72). Magazines like *The English Journal, Language Arts* and the *Newsletter* of the Adolescent Literature Assembly contain brief reviews of newly published books that keep the teacher up to date.

9
The Process of Composing

Scott BAtes

I would like to start out by saying, "I hate
wrighting." But there one thing I like is
Math. I like to play baseball. I was
an a teem last year. I was on the
KAWANis club. But I dont do that
good in it that much. I batted 200.
Every body call me Babu so thats
my nich name. Chess is a good
game to play, I am good in that.
                              mAStike
I know how to (cheek) mant in 3
moves. I tell you, I hate wright.
I have never wrote an a letter
to knowbody. But once I was going
to wright to my brouther in Kansas
City to play chess by mail. It would
tath a (tach) about 3 per mouths to play
one game.

Thats all I got to say.

185

The process of composing[1] is a difficult and complicated one. Even the most dedicated writers have times when they agree with Scott Bates in saying "I hate wrighting." But professional writers usually get over their hate with time, while the attitude expressed by Scott Bates seems to stay with students. When we interview young people about their attitudes toward composition, we find a substantial number who see it as exceedingly unpleasant; only math gets worse reports. Were it not for the expectations of the worlds of business and college, most students would be delighted to see composition dropped from the curriculum altogether.

Part of the dislike of composing grows from the fact that it *is* hard work.

Like any creative effort, composing in language requires energy and time. Few writers are able to dash off something in final form and most of us find writing rather a struggle. Further, in composing, people put a bit of their soul down for close scrutiny by others, something that can be quite uncomfortable.

At the same time, there are many processes in a young person's life that require complex skills, an investment of time, or public exposure: mounting a butterfly, mastering a bicycle, playing football, painting a picture, being in a play. Although composing differs in many ways from these activities, there seems to be no reason why students who are willing to invest time on diverse activities seem to find the single task of composing so difficult.

An obvious explanation is that composing has the distinction of being the only one of those activities that usually takes place in a schoolroom, and there can be little question that much of the distrust and fear young people have about composition has grown from previous classroom experiences. Often when students have opened up their souls in writing, the teacher has merely commented on spelling. While busy preparing students for college, teachers have overemphasized the value of impromptu writing, implying that to be good, a writer must be able to bat out polished prose within the span of 40 minutes or an hour. Writing activities have often been aimless: "For tomorrow, I want you to write four paragraphs comparing and contrasting the poetic styles of John Keats and Percy Bysshe Shelley." Why? I leave it to the reader to fill in the explanation: "_____."

One consistent exception to the "I hate writing" syndrome is the writing journal, a form that has received great attention in the past few years. Teaching techniques vary; but in general, the journal is based on writing that is *free* (the students can write about anything they choose), *private* or

[1] In this chapter, I will be dealing chiefly with *written* composition, which, despite a growing concern in many schools for work in the media and nonverbal composing, will continue to be the major form of composition in schools. However, as I will stress throughout the chapter, writing should not be isolated from such other composing forms as talk, drama, film making, and nonverbal expression. These specialized areas will be taken up in Chapters 12–14.

semiprivate (the teacher is usually the only other person who can read the journal, and even then the student can turn down private pages), and *nongraded* (usually the only grade is a blanket grade for successful completion of the task).

In my experience, student response to the journal has been almost universally positive, making it the closest thing yet to a surefire teaching device. The so-called nonwriters like to write in journals, while writers go berserk writing in them. Teachers generally enjoy reading journals. All of the problems traditionally associated with writing seem to be almost magically solved when teachers use the journal.

One exception: A teacher told me she had tried the journal and abandoned it. "Didn't work," she said, somewhat sourly. I pressed her for further information, and she explained, "Well, they wrote very well in the journals—better than they ever had written before—but I found there was no transfer of writing skills to their Chaucer papers." The "failure" was not surprising. This teacher had seen the journal as something apart from the mainstream of the English—as a gimmick or time killer, not as a regular form of instruction. My proposal—one that she rejected as "antiacademic"—was that if something had to be dropped in the class, the ominous Chaucer paper ought to be the first to go.

Since the journal seems to work, teachers need to find ways of applying its techniques to the regular work of composition. This does not mean giving students a 12-year diet of journal writing; the teaching of composition defies such simplistic solutions. In many schools, in fact, the journal has been so overworked that it no longer provides a satisfying experience for students. As often happens with educational innovations, teachers have emphasized the trimmings (the loose-leaf binding and diary format) and ignored the essence of the journal (its freedom and naturalness). Surely there is nothing so unique about free writing in a notebook that the principles of success cannot be discovered and applied elsewhere.

WRITING: PERSONAL AND CREATIVE

It is a cliché that "the best writing comes from personal experience," and for decades teachers have offered students the advice, "Write about something you know." Unfortunately, this has often led to "My Summer Vacation," in which the personal experience tends to be routine or standardized.

One reason the journal works is that it allows the students to draw not only on personal experience but on *substantial* experience—things that hurt and worry, that delight and please.

As Donald Murray has observed, we teach writing because it is a useful skill, both inside school and outside. But most important is that writing involves self-discovery and satisfies a person's need to communicate.

WHY TEACH WRITING?

1. *Writing is a skill which is important in school and after school. . . .*
2. *Writing for many students is a skill which can unlock the language arts.* Students who have never read before often begin to read in the writing program. They have to read their own words to find out what they've said and decide how to say it more effectively.
3. *Writing is thinking. . . .*
4. *Writing is an ethical act, because the single most important quality in writing is honesty. . . .*
5. *Writing is a process of self-discovery. . . .*
6. *Writing satisfies man's primitive hunger to communicate. . . .*
7. *Writing is an art, and art is profound play. . . .*

Abridged from Donald Murray, "Why Teach Writing—And How?" *The English Journal,* December 1973, pp. 1234-1237. Copyright © 1973 by The National Council of Teachers of English. Reprinted by permission of the publisher and the author.

Composing provides an important way for students to sort through their experiences, to make sense of their world, and to share their observations with others. When students are deeply engaged in this process, it is often revealed in the intensity and vibrancy of their language. It is little wonder that writing skills don't seem to transfer from the journal to pseudo-academic papers. Unless composing is real and personal, it is aimless, and people learn nothing from it.

Another way to phrase this idea is to borrow another cliché, one that has been ignored in actual practice: "All writing is creative." The distinction between "creative" composition and its opposite (uncreative? non-creative? countercreative?) is an unfortunate one. There are obvious differences in form and process between composing a poem and an essay, but the similarities are also great. Creative writing involves a writer successfully assimilating a personal experience and sharing it with another person. A good memo, for instance, is a creative piece of writing. The results of a teacher-imposed sonnet-writing lesson often aren't.

Evoking personal, creative writing in the classroom is not easy. Students are accustomed to looking for "what the teacher wants," for in the past, this has been the route to successful grades. One way of describing these creative topics is to suggest that they grow from basic open-ended questions about human experience:

How do you feel?
What are you thinking about?
What puzzles or bothers you?
What interesting things do you know?

If teachers ask these questions they will be getting at the personal experience that leads to strong writing. The journal accomplishes this by not stating any topics, thus forcing the students back into the reservoir of personal experience. But the teacher can encourage the students to speak out on subjects of personal concern. Many of the "getting started" activities in Chapter 6 were designed to do precisely that—to create situations in which the teacher can demonstrate interest in making the classroom an arena for the discussion of personal experiences.

TRYING TO READ AN ENGLISH ED TEXTBOOK (THE CHAPTER ON COMPOSITION) WHILE SITTING ON A SEAWALL AT LOW TIDE: AUTUMN

It's amazing how much windier it gets as you cross town.
(Come to think of it, there was *no* wind across town.)

The shoreline is never perfectly straight, is it?
And the whitecaps never converge, or run in unison, or fizzle
    out at the same time. They don't obey the human
    impositions on life.
(Still, they all disappear on the same shore, and I guess
    that's close enough for some people.)

A Seagull hovers, so close I can almost count its feathers!
(So, why am I worried about it being too directly overhead?)

I close the book of ideas-for-getting-students-to-write-from-
    their-own-experiences
And take a walk: along the seawall, over the bridge to the
    causeway,
And stop halfway to look back.
The royal palms laugh warmly over where I was sitting.
Then they turn and laugh at me.
Even the murky green water smiles as I cross.
And now the sand and rocks and trees—the half-wild beach
    edging this dredged-up subordinate conjunction—
Say, come down here and hide out awhile.

William J. Moravec, University of South Florida. Written in response to this chapter in the first edition of *Explorations in the Teaching of English*. Reprinted by permission of the author.

BUT WHAT DO I WRITE ABOUT?

Young people bubble over with ideas and experiences they want to share with one another and with adults. Yet, when given a blank sheet of paper and a writing assignment, they often claim they have nothing to say. Part of the problem is that students remember past experiences: the teacher who treated them as if they were blockheads and said that everything they wrote was inadequate. But perhaps more important is that the assignments teachers offer are themselves frequently dull and uninviting. While I do not feel that every assignment given to the students must be wildly innovative, novel, or clever, it is evident that the assignments the teacher offers define the dimensions of composition for students. If assignments are of the 500-words-and-three-paragraphs variety, students are limited in the composition that they will do.

There is no single composition assignment appropriate for all students. I stumbled onto the idea of presenting multiple assignments—writing options—as a result of a bad time in a high school sophomore English class. At the time, I was interested in extending the journal concept to other situations, and I took the obvious route of establishing a free writing day for the class—one day each week when the students could write about anything they chose. The results were discouraging. The students sat around fussing and twitching, and most of the writing that they produced was mediocre. They kept claiming they had nothing to say, and I couldn't persuade them otherwise.

So I began developing lists of writing options for free writing day. Each week I sketched out a half-dozen writing possibilities—some dealing with current events and ideas, others suggesting starting points for personal narratives. I tried to build in choices for writing poems or plays, as well as activities that would lead to expository writing. I tried to find something that might appeal to everyone.

The tone of the class improved enormously. Interestingly enough, the change seemed to result less from the actual topics I designed than from the fact that I was helping the students see possibilities. Whether the students used my topics, modified them for their own purposes, or rejected them to strike off in new directions, being presented with options opened up new avenues of expression for them. By offering options, I was saying, "These are some of the things you can do with language."

To illustrate the wealth of options available on almost any topic, I want to play with one idea—chosen more or less at random. "Human Relationships" is relatively ageless as a school discussion and writing topic, since each new group of adolescents generates its own new set of human relationships problems.

What kinds of writing possibilities can grow from this topic? The most routine, perhaps, would involve informal essays:

> Why do you think people have so much trouble getting along in the world? Write an essay giving your views.

But far more imaginative possibilities exist:

Suppose you were the ruler of a country in which the inhabitants were constantly squabbling with one another. What kind of decree might you issue to force the people to get along better?

Write a science fiction story in which monkeys learn to get along with one another and as a result take over the earth from quarreling human beings.

The topic can lead to low key research projects:

Much has been written about communal living, a life style that involves some new and different patterns for human relationships. Read about some of these new family communities and write a report on the human relationships that are involved.

Read about some of the nineteenth-century experiments in communal living that were conducted in this country (the Oneida Community, for example) and look into some of the reasons why these experiments did or did not succeed.

The topic lends itself to creative writing assignments:

How do you feel when you are in deep conflict with another person? Try to express that feeling through a poem.

Write a short play showing a family that cannot solve its human relationships problems. What happens in the end? You might want to write an alternative ending in which things work out satisfactorily. Which seems more realistic?

The topic can generate speaking situations, including an old debate chestnut:

Resolved: Parents nowadays are too permissive toward their children.

The possibilities for improvisational activities are limitless, including at least one with a media orientation:

Videotape two episodes from a soap opera called "The Cozy Corner," the continuing story of a family in which all the members dislike one another.

One can go on almost without end considering possibilities for photo essays, cartoons, posters, letters, telegrams, satire—even though no teacher would ever want to list all of the possibilities on a given topic.

One problem that concerns teachers who are using a system of options is that of students getting stuck in ruts, choosing only one form of composition and failing to move beyond it. Of course this concern ignores the fact that in the past students *have* been stuck on one form—the expository essay. Exhausting the possibilities of other forms—say, drama or short story—can hardly be more harmful. However, given free choice, students' patterns of interest and skill change naturally with time. A choice example

SOME NEGLECTED FORMS OF COMPOSITION (Or, Must They *Always* Write Essays?)

Journals and diaries

Observation papers

Profiles and portraits (friends, enemies, adults, public figures)

Sketches (notebook jottings, gleanings)

Reminiscences and memoirs (high or low camp, serious or fun)

Autobiography

Confessions (real or fictional)

Dramatic monologues (written, improvised, or recorded)

Slide tape

Stream of consciousness

Editorial

Satire

Photo essay

Radio play

Children's stories and verse

Newspaper stories

Poetry, poetry, poetry (free forms and structured forms, rhymed and unrhymed, haiku, concrete poetry, light verse limericks, protest verse, song lyrics . . .)

Interviews

Cartoons

Policy Papers

Research (a record of something seen or learned)

Pamphlets

Fiction (short story or novel)

Light essays (Thurber, E. B. White, Jimmy Breslin)

Plays, plays, plays (short scenes, one acts, improvised, full-dress productions)

Advertisements

Commercials

Imitations of established writers

Riddles

Jokes

Posters

Flyers

Underground newspaper

Letters (real or fictional)

Telegrams

Aphorisms

Graffiti

Reviews (books, concerts, football games, dates)

Metaphors

Sound tapes

Monographs

Magazines

Propaganda

Petitions

Films

Television scripts

was presented by one of the girls in my sophomore class who was hooked on drama. For months she wrote scripts—10 or 15 pages each—about boy-girl romances. One day when I was on the edge of madness at the thought of reading another John-Marcia dialogue, she presented an acid attack on

America's involvement in the affairs of other countries. When I asked about her playwriting interests, she replied, "Eh! . . . plays are OK, but this stuff is a lot more important." People grow.

LEARNING TO WRITE BY WRITING

. . . children *learn* by writing. By learn I mean above all this process by which they shape their experience in order to make it available to themselves to learn from. Next it must be observed that, if they learn by writing, they also learn to write by writing. I know when it comes down to brass tacks, we have to qualify this assertion and make some exceptions, but we don't destroy the basic truth of it. They learn by writing and they learn to write by writing. In other words I am putting forward an operational point of view. There is a whole world of experience to be interpreted, and writing is a major means of interpreting it. Why therefore as teachers do we go around looking for practice jobs, dummy runs, rigged or stage-managed situations, when in fact the whole of what requires to be worked upon is there waiting to be worked upon? Everytime a child succeeds in writing about something that has happened to him or something he has been thinking, two things are likely to have happened. First, he has improved his chances of doing so the next time he tries; in other words, his piece of writing has given him practice. And secondly, he has interpreted, shaped, coped with, some bit of experience.

From James Britton, "Talking and Writing," in Eldonna Evertts, ed. *Explorations in Children's Writing.* Copyright © 1970 by the National Council of Teachers of English. Reprinted by permission of the publisher and the author.

That children learn to write by writing is another cliché, but it is a valid assertion, recognized as pedagogically sound for well over one hundred years. James Britton's comment that people "learn by writing and they learn to write by writing" is simply one of its most recent restatements.

Yet curiously, when it comes to actual practice, teachers seem to retreat from the wisdom of this learn-by-doing philosophy. In fact, they seem willing to go to great lengths to *avoid* actually assigning writing. Thus students engage in vocabulary study, spelling work, outlining practice, topic sentence composition, sentence combining, sentence uncombining, and error correction, but do not spend a great deal of time grappling with the task of composing. Part of this reaction on the part of teachers is self-defense. If you assign writing, you have to take time to comment upon it. (This is a problem that will be taken up in the next chapter in some detail.) But a more basic cause of teachers' not relying on actual practice is that they assume students will write badly unless given all kinds of preliminary instruction in writing form.

But James Britton's epigraph shows a very important linkage between learning and writing. He suggests that students need to learn about the world—their personal world or the public world—in order to write, and he implies that as students learn to structure their ideas, they will also learn to structure their language. This concept is a variation of the language/experience model I presented in Chapter 2.

The same sophomore class I described earlier helped me discover that teaching about writing was less important than helping students shape their ideas through language. While exploring the idea of writing options, I had encouraged the students to try different forms—TV reviews, poems, stories, satires, and the like. It dawned on me one day that although the students were composing in these forms, I had never given any lessons on how to write them. How had the students learned to do it?

There seemed to be two sources for these skills. First, for many of the activities, the students had an intuitive sense of form based on routine readings and TV viewing habits; they had all read or seen editorials, columns, plays, commercials. The second source was questioning. When students didn't know what something was, they naturally asked: "What's a broadside?" "What's satire?"

This discovery led to another from that same class, that questions about form are best answered in *operational,* not *definitional,* terms. When students ask, "What's satire?" they do not need to be told, "Satire is a poem or prose work holding up human vices, follies, etc., to ridicule or scorn." What proves helpful is advice on how to *make* a satire: "Well, suppose you wanted to make someone you disliked look foolish. One way might be . . ." Or better, "Who is somebody around here who you think needs to get taken down a notch or two? Now what could we say . . . ?" This kind of answer enables students to engage productively in writing without involved discussion of abstractions.

Such a philosophy also applies to one of the traditional mainstays of the English curriculum: teaching the paragraph. A great deal of time is spent in the schools teaching this rhetorical structure and its attendants: thesis and clincher sentences. Students are taught these forms as abstractions: "The paragraph contains one main idea." "The topic sentence presents the central concern." "The clincher sentence restates the topic sentence." Occasionally the abstractions are presented through metaphors: "Think of your paragraph as a sandwich with topic and clincher sentences as the bread and your supporting evidence as the meat."

This kind of teaching does little to improve student writing and much to damage it. In the first place, very few real life paragraphs follow the form very closely. In the second place, emphasizing paragraph structure makes students write by formula: "There are three things you should know about Abraham Lincoln and here are my reasons." "Abraham Lincoln was an honest man and here is how I know." While intended to help students learn structure (a worthy aim in itself), teaching form often makes their writing lifeless.[2]

Curiously enough, composition textbooks never said anything about the paragraph until well into the nineteenth century. Until that time, paragraphs were simply a natural division of discourse that followed no particular rules. And that historical oddity helps to clarify the relationship between form and substance. Writers form (shape, structure) papers to reach an audience, and they seek out forms that will accomplish what they want. Teaching structures before the fact of composition short-circuits the process by placing form ahead of content.

As students write, as they struggle with ideas, draft paragraphs, and form sentences, there are many opportunities for the teacher to suggest ways and means of structuring papers, always with the students' particular problems in mind.

The structuring of writing also is more easily learned and taught if students have a sense of purpose in writing.

In schoolroom practice, however, purpose has often been pleasing the teacher. "Think about your audience" has come to mean "Think about your teacher and the kind of writing he or she likes." Many student compositions done in schools are thus unreal—done as practice exercises.

But advice like "make writing real" is ambiguous. Does this mean that students should spend all their time filling out business forms and writing letters to real readers? I think not. Reality is something in the eye of the writer, and topics that interest and engage the student automatically become real. Part of the problem of reality is thus solved by engaging the students in writing that is truly personal and creative; and it is aided further by offering students a wide range of ways of expressing those ideas.

However, the students also need a *readership*, and a class should be alive with students reading to one another, reading one another's work, responding and reacting to the things that they have said and done. In the next chapter, I will be exploring some of the ways in which the teacher can supply a readership for students' work; for the moment, I simply want to note that the classroom needs to be a reading and publishing center, where students' work takes on reality by being given an audience. Providing readers can be done in many ways, ranging from the bulletin board to the manufacture of books, magazines, and monographs on an in-class press.

[2] In fact, knowing form often creates writing difficulties. A major problem teachers encounter with poetry is that other teachers have taught students about rhyme and meter, and the students struggle nobly to versify. Their speech rhythms are destroyed in the attempt, and this leads to peculiar inversions and falsely elevated language. One has to tell prospective poets constantly: "Don't rhyme. Write the way you feel." In essence, you must say: "Ignore the rules. Your intuition and experiences are more reliable as a guide."

THE WRITING WORKSHOP

Composing is not a neat, orderly process; it is highly idiosyncratic. Compositions can't be stamped out like lipstick cases or hubcaps, and writers must find their own style of working. I need to pace when writing; I can seldom write even a full paragraph without jumping up to do some foot-thinking, and I have the greatest admiration for people who can remain seated and work diligently at a composition task. Some writers produce a polished first draft; others—and I'm among these—pump out a crude "hack draft," something that is a cross between notes, rough draft, and a batch of odd sentences—all to be polished later. Students are no different in having a range of writing habits.

The teacher can accommodate individual writing styles by organizing the class as a writing workshop. Within the workshop, many diverse activities will be happening at once. On any given day, some students may be starting new projects while others are finishing. A few people will be at the stage of publication, while others may be displaying and distributing completed writing. A workshop environment encourages students to select new options, since it does not pressure them to complete a standard essay in a set time period. It also provides great freedom for the teacher, who can serve as a roving consultant—supplying help when and where needed—rather than as a monitor of 30 people writing in silence.

In the course of participating in a writing workshop, then, students may:

Talk with one another about writing assignments and possibilities.
Confer about writing ideas and sources for composition materials.
"Prewrite" papers in small groups, talking through assignments before actually committing pen to paper.
Write rough and polished drafts.
Work in small editorial groups.
Confer with the teacher about specific writing problems or about their growth in composition generally.
Read writing on the same topics: other students' or professional writers'.
Copyedit writing for publication.
Illustrate, print, and bind their work for distribution.

The workshop environment is one that must be built gradually. Only after a period of time will a workshop reach its peak of independent operation. I have found that providing writing options is especially useful in starting the workshop, since it invites individualized work from the beginning. Other teachers have had success with such diverse activities as free writing, contracts, independent study, or an idea box at the back of the room.

Perhaps the best way to summarize is to suggest that the students in a writing workshop will need to take a view of their work as *exploratory*. One way of obtaining this kind of attitude happened to me quite by accident in a college course. To encourage the students to try new ideas, I had asked them to write a series of what I called "experimental" papers. To relieve the fear of failure, I emphasized that we would regard these papers as experiments, as probings toward something rather than as failures to get there at the first attempt.

The student writing in the "experimentals" was excellent—good enough that I canceled plans for some longer, more sustained writing projects. I didn't realize the effect of this until the last week of the quarter when one of the students asked, "Say, when are we going to stop experimenting and do some real writing?" I don't know quite what he meant by "real" writing, but I like the idea that he disassociated "experimenting" from it. So I have assigned nothing but "experimentals" since then.

There is a finality to "real" writing. Since it is the end of the process, it has usually been associated with pain and penalties, corrections and revisions, polite and/or impolite notes pointing out that the writing isn't up to adult standards. I have tried to encourage students to consider everything they write as experimental, to treat it as if there was always time for a bit more work if they wanted to do it. This, in turn, makes the freedom of the writing workshop something felt inside the student as well as inside the class, ultimately helping to create students who can write freely and openly.

SEQUENCING WRITING ASSIGNMENTS

Many teachers are skilled at developing good writing assignments, yet their assignments stand alone, bearing no discernible relationship to one another. Frequently, this problem is a side effect of isolating composition from other parts of the curriculum. If writing is a Fridays-only activity, the assignments are likely to be gimmicky, one-shot affairs. The pervasiveness of this approach is testified to by the popularity of what-shall-I-do-on-Friday lists of writing ideas. While one learns to write by writing (and even isolated topics are better than no writing at all), writing ought to be assigned in ways that promote sustained student growth as well. To this end, it is important to sequence the kinds of writings one offers to students.

The Handbook Approach: A Bad Example

Of course, the typical composition/grammar handbook, widely used in the schools, offers one sequence for writing. The *handbook approach* begins with the smallest language particle it can find—the word—and teaches students how to describe it syntactically: through learning the parts of speech. The naming process then continues through larger and larger units—the sentence, the paragraph, the whole essay. Along the way, students are shown techniques of structuring such as writing the formal outline. The apex of the writing program is often the research or term paper.

While it is probably evident to the reader of this book why I think this approach is a bad one, it seems important to rehearse the weaknesses and disadvantages of the handbook approach one additional time:

1. It emphasizes mastery of terminology instead of offering actual writing experience.
2. It is divorced from the students' own experiences.
3. It is based on a false assumption that one must write or practice short discourse units before going on to longer ones.
4. It presents a simplistic view of structure by its emphasis on the formal outline and the form of the paragraph.

Alternative Sequences for Writing

Better writing sequences have a basic principle in common: They start with the students' linguistic skill and psychological maturity and guide them along natural patterns of growth. For example, in *Writing in Reality*, a college composition text, James Miller and I use what might be called an *experience-centered* sequence. We follow an "inner worlds to outer worlds" pattern, assuming that writers first need to explore their personal ideas and thoughts through private writing, before moving on to present ideas to a larger public.

We begin by explaining the differences between public and private writing (Chapters 1 and 2), but we emphasize that all good writing, public or private, must be deeply motivated, flowing from the students' own storehouse of experiences. Chapters 3–5 have the students examine their past and present experiences and capture their unique writing voice and style. The next two chapters (6 and 7) focus on the outer world and encourage observation of people, places, and things. Then the sequence moves fully into public writing of essays and persuasive papers (8 and 9) and ends (10) by reminding the students that all writing, public or private, comes from one's "ultimate self." Although this book is aimed at college students, the basic sequence—from private to public, from personal to objective experience—is one that works well with younger students as well. *The Creative Word* English program, which is outlined in this book in Chapter 3, shows how the same principles can be used in a grade 7–12 reading and writing curriculum.

Fred Morgan's writing textbook, *Here and Now*, shows another approach, one that emphasizes *perceptions* rather than experiences and produces a useful sequence of assignments. He argues (as does Patrick Creber,

THE HANDBOOK APPROACH

Parts of Speech
The Sentence
Sentence Variety and Style
The Topic Sentence
The Paragraph
The Outline
The Essay

THE EXPERIENCE-CENTERED SEQUENCE

1. Personal Writing
2. Public Writing
3. The Creation of the Self
4. Versions of the Self
5. How Deep Can One Go?
6. Encountering the World
7. Interweaving the World
8. Exploring / Probing / Researching
9. Causes and Commitments
10. Writing and the Ultimate Self

From James E. Miller and Stephen Judy, *Writing in Reality* (New York: Harper & Row, 1978).

also cited in Chapter 3) that bad writing often reflects poor perception. Students don't really look at their world and thus write badly about it. Morgan has his students begin by reveling in their senses, rediscovering the pleasures of perceiving, before moving through a sequence of assignments that has the students observe people, places, animals, emotions, themselves, finally pulling all these skills together in "seeing the whole picture." Like the Miller-Judy approach, Morgan's emphasizes informal and private writings at first, then moves on to more complex public writing.

A third approach is the *literary/thematic*. The editors of *The Scholastic American Literature Series* wanted to create a literature program that would encourage composition as well. They chose a series of major themes, "Who We Are," "What We Believe," and so on, then further divided these into subtopics, "The Young," "City and Country," and so forth. Each of these subtopics creates possible composition topics that draw on the students' personal experiences. The program shows clearly that one can use literature as a jumping-off point for writing without having to rely exclusively on that academic standby, the essay of literary analysis.

THE PERCEPTUAL APPROACH

1. Enjoying Your Senses
2. Employing Your Senses
3. Being Aware of Your Surroundings
4. Observing a Scene
5. Getting the Feel of Action
6. Observing a Person
7. Perceiving Emotional Attitudes
8. Estimating a Person
9. Identifying with a Person
10. Perceiving a Relationship
11. Identifying with a Person
12. Looking at Yourself
13. Examining a Desire
14. Seeing the Whole Picture

From Fred Morgan, *Here and Now III* (New York: Harcourt Brace Jovanovich, 1979).

LITERARY/THEMATIC APPROACH

WHO WE ARE

The Young
The Old
Men and Women

WHERE WE LIVE

City and Country
Journeys
A Sense of Place

HOW WE LIVE

At Work
At Play
At War

WHAT WE BELIEVE

Personal Values
American Myths and Dreams
Fantasy and Imagination

From The Scholastic American Literature Series (New York: Scholastic Magazines, 1977).

The sequences shown are generalized patterns, chosen by textbook writers in an attempt to reach as many students as possible. While these schema might be useful as models, teachers themselves must make the actual plans for a good sequence of assignments, and like any plan, the one chosen ought to be flexible, reflecting the needs and interests of the students and growing naturally from the course material. Under no circumstances should any sequence—be it the traditional handbook approach or something like the contemporary perceptual approach—be allowed to create a lockstep curriculum. The point, after all, is to take the students at their present developmental level and to help them move forward, not to ensure that they have followed a prescribed pattern created by either textbook writer or teacher.

A NOTE ON PREPARATION FOR COLLEGE

Obviously the kinds of assignments I recommend differ from the usual pattern prescribed in the schools, where work in the essay leads toward a culminating experience with the research paper. I would like to see students do less essay writing, not more, and more creative writing, not more college preparatory writing. At the same time, I want to emphasize that my recommendation is not neglectful of the college-bound. For supporting evidence I will present two excerpts from senior high school students' papers. Both were submitted to a youth talent contest as among the best essays in their school.

The first essay was part of a research paper discussing the movement toward minimum competency standards in the schools:

The concepts of American education are continually being reassessed. One of the questions presently being raised concerns the customary practice of granting a diploma after completion of a basic twelve year education. It has been determined that a standard high school education does not necessarily warrant the issuance of a diploma. This document, if dispensed to students with inferiour proficiency, ceases to signify that the possessor has gained the skills necessary to function as an acceptable adult in society. As each high school senior receives a diploma, whether or not they are fully competent, the standards of our country's educational system are decreased. Therefore, American high schools should not graduate students who do not pass minimum competency standards.

This paper, I hope the reader will agree, is very badly written. It is stuffy, filled with jargon, and awkward. I also believe the student is not entirely to blame that it turned out so poorly, for I suspect her teachers have encouraged this sort of writing for years, thinking it would help get her ready for college. It won't, I'm afraid, and the student will have to do a great deal of unlearning before she will find success in college writing courses.

By contrast, the second essay, part of a research paper on jazz, begins with an anecdote:

> I picked jazz because I play alto saxophone at school in the band, and I really like it. Another reason is that last summer I attended Blue Lake Fine Arts Camp and while there, heard the jazz band play. I loved the music and decided that was the kind of music I wanted to look into.

The language, of course, is fresher than the first example. Unfortunately, after this animated paragraph, the author plunged into essay prose of a very dull sort. Apparently she had gone to the library and looked up the facts about jazz, ignoring her personal experience and following the routine of research paper writing. As I read her paper, I searched in vain for any evidence that she had actually listened to some music or that she had actually followed up on her summer interest by playing some jazz. Unfortunately, the basics of the research paper—looking up books and writing down the facts—did not permit personal exploration and expression.

I believe that in the long run, a broadly based writing program, one that gives young people a sense of their own voice as writers and encourages them to trust their own perceptions is, in fact, the best preparation for college (and for writing demands outside school generally). The dummy run essays and term papers of the schools help very few students and actually stultify the writing growth of many others.

EXPLORATIONS AND RESOURCES

• Several years ago, Gilbert Tierney (who teaches at Harper College, Palatine, Illinois) and I began experimenting with an activity we call "The Assignment Makers"—an activity that helps teachers clarify what they see as the critical factors that go into the process of initiating student writing. The activity consists of nine hypothetical writing assignments. You are asked to select the three assignments that you think are "best" (using any criteria you think are appropriate) and the three that are "worst." As you study the assignments, make notes on what you see as the critical strong and weak points about each and compare your notes with those of others. As an interesting follow-up, you might give "The Assignment

Makers" to a group of students and compare their reactions to your own. (For those who would like to think over the choices as they read, I have included our notes and observations about the assignments.)

THE ASSIGNMENT MAKERS

(1) *Rosemary Clowan* brings in a dead crow to her tenth-grade English class. She explains that she found it along the side of the road and allows the students to look at it and talk about it. After a bit she asks if anybody has any writing ideas as a result of seeing the crow. She invites those who do to follow up their ideas while the rest of the class has a free reading period.

(2) *George Sears* brings in a 4′ x 5′ photo-poster showing a lonely old man feeding pigeons in the park. "Write about it," he tells his eleventh-grade class. "Use any form—prose, poetry, drama, or essay—that meets your needs. When you're through we'll see who has the best ideas."

(3) *Brad Merrimack* decides to take up the research paper with his college-bound senior English class. He tells the students to read James Roswell Lowell's practical text, *A Guide to Writing Academic and Research Papers* and has the class examine some marked-up freshman college papers that his former students have collected for him. After this, he tells each student to write a short paper on any serious topic in English or history, but limited to ten pages and five references.

(4) *Rob Wesley's* junior English students come in to class one day quite angry because one of their friends has been suspended—unfairly, in their opinion. One student suggests that they picket the principal's office in protest. Rob gives them the rest of the hour and all the paper they can use to plan the activity.

(5) *Jean Vernon* is teaching philosophy in her advanced world literature class. Following discussion of essays and fiction by Sartre and Camus, she makes the following assignment:

> Sartre and Camus are known as "existentialists." The word has such broad meaning, however, that few people have been able to write a precise, careful definition. Without consulting any other sources, write an essay that defines and explains your own view of existentialism, drawing on ideas and examples from Sartre and Camus where necessary. Pay particular attention to the concepts of *action, being,* and *death.*

(6) On the opening day of school, *Howard Upton* asks his eighth-grade class to "write about the most interesting thing you saw or did last summer." He says: "You probably have seen or done many interesting things during the past few months, either at home or on a trip. Pick one of these things and tell us about it. When you're through, we'll read them and find out what you've been up to.

(7) *Sharon LeBeau* has just led the class in a reading of Frost's "Mending Wall." "Write about your interpretation of the poem," Sharon says, "remembering that a poem can be interpreted in many ways. I'll accept any interpretation as long as you support your ideas."

(8) *Susan Schumacher* institutes a writing time in her sophomore class. Once or twice each week she says, "OK, stop what you're doing and write about anything you want for twenty minutes." At the end of that time she resumes the regular class work. She doesn't collect the papers, but the students can share them with each other if they want to.

(9) *Fred Houston* brings *Auschwitz,* a powerful, chilling documentary film, to show to his eighth-grade class. After the students have seen the film and asked a variety of questions about prison camps and the executions, Fred asks them to write a paper on "Man's Inhumanity to Man."

NOTES AND OBSERVATIONS

(1) ROSEMARY CLOWAN. Some of the people who have done the activity have argued that it is in poor taste for Rosemary to bring in a dead crow, that many of the students may be offended by it. We rather like the idea, since few kids have ever been able to look at a bird—particularly a large one—up close. However, to us, Rosemary seems a bit cavalier in simply asking "if anybody has any ideas." By suggesting a few starting points for stories, essays, poems, and perhaps even a fable or play, she might be able to involve more students.

(2) GEORGE SEARS. In the manner of Leavitt and Sohn's *Stop, Look and Write!,* the photo-poster seems like a good way of initiating writing activities. We like the way George avoids limiting his students to a single topic or even a single form by giving them unlimited ways of responding. We do think that like Rosemary Clowan, George could have supplied a few specific writing suggestions for those students who find it difficult to translate the bald instruction "Write!" into a concrete, workable writing-idea. The sharing of writing at the close of the hour builds in an audience, but why emphasize "the best" ideas in that situation?

(3) BRAD MERRIMACK. If one feels obligated to do the term paper with students, Brad's approach seems sensible. He does it with college-bound seniors; he limits the length and complexity of the project; and he bases his instruction "in reality" by bringing in actual freshman writing, complete with instructors' comments. We do question his reference to "serious" topics, which implies that all academic writing must be dull, boring, or pompous, and his failure to allow students to do work outside the area of the humanities.

(4) ROB WESLEY. This has many of the basic elements of the "ideal" writing assignment. The kids are ready to work without any pressure from the teacher. The activity is *real,* and the students will be able to move well beyond the limits of the classroom walls. However, quite aside from the fact that this will probably be Rob's *last* assignment once the principal finds out where the protest started, we wonder whether he couldn't have channeled the students' energies more productively. Rather than sending them off to what will probably prove to be a fruitless picket, Rob might help the students devise what Neil Postman and Charles Weingartner have called a "soft revolutionary" strategy, proposing and working for systematic changes in the school system.

(5) JEAN VERNON. This assignment strikes us as being "academic" in the worst sense of the word. It may help the students prepare for some of the horrors they will face in undergraduate seminars several years from now, but that doesn't seem to counteract the possible harm it can do now. It presents several serious problems. It pretends to be open-ended by inviting the student to present his "own view," but the general course of the essay is dictated by Jean's not-too-subtle reminder to include examples from Sartre and Camus, particularly concerning the concepts of *"action, being,* and *death."* It is also an *impossible* assignment; Jean acknowledges that experts can't define existentialism, yet she asks her students to do it anyway. She may unconsciously recognize this problem, since she carefully forbids "consulting outside sources" — a logical step for anyone faced with an impossible assignment. This kind of paper, because of its pseudointellectual nature, invites the cribbing, plagiarizing, and paraphrasing that sap so much of our energies.

(6) HOWARD UPTON. This assignment bothers many people because of its resemblance to the clichéd "My Summer Vacation." However, there are important differences. Howard makes the assignment open-ended but still asks the students to be fairly specific, thus avoiding the usual shotgun approach to vacation descriptions. Further, he does not favor kids who go away on trips, and he recognizes that things happen at home as well as in the Black Hills or the Poconos. He provides for sharing at the end of the hour and makes it clear to the students that they will be their own audience. However, as several teachers have pointed out to us, this might make a better *oral* than written assignment, particularly on the first day of school. Perhaps Howard should simply create a conversation circle or small groups and allow the students to share experiences informally.

(7) SHARON Le BEAU. In contrast to Jean Vernon's assignment about literature, this approach to academic writing seems quite humane. Sharon is not forcing an interpretation on the students. However, we still predict that the assignment will produce some rather dull, standardized writing that few people would voluntarily choose to read or write; e.g., "I think Robert Frost's 'Mending Wall' means . . ., and here are my reasons: . . . ." If a poem can be interpreted in many ways, Sharon might consider allowing the students to *respond* in many ways rather than forcing them into an exercise in *explication de texte.* Given freedom to respond, her students might write essays, poems, and stories about such ideas as barriers, human relationships, disagreeable people, making friends, the World Crisis . . . and a few might even choose to read more Frost and write about him.

(8) SUSAN SCHUMACHER. Most of the teachers we have talked with approve of the basic direction of this assignment. Many teachers have had great success with free writing activities like a journal, and the kind of atmosphere Susan has created lends itself to an open, honest style of writing. Most, however, object to the "fire drill" nature of the writing time. Few people can write on command—even when they are free to write about anything. Perhaps Susan could establish entire days when free writing is encouraged along with free reading, free talking, and free "listening." Several people have suggested that she might also set up an "idea box" or file of composition suggestions for kids who don't come up with instant ideas during the writing time.

(9) FRED HOUSTON. Although eighth-graders may be somewhat young for a showing of a film like *Auschwitz*, our greatest reservations about this assignment concern the topic "Man's Inhumanity to Man," which encourages abstract, possibly moralistic writing and seems to be several years beyond the eighth-graders. We like the way Houston goes from the film to discussion, and we imagine that the discussion would be quite lively after a film like *Auschwitz*. Perhaps he should simply end with discussion, or, like Susan Schumacher and Rosemary Clowan, invite the kids to do "free" writing—perhaps in a variety of forms—to express their responses to the film.

From Gilbert Tierney and Stephen Judy, "The Assignment Makers," *The English Journal,* February 1972. Copyright © 1972 by the National Council of Teachers of English. Reprinted by permission of the publisher.

- One of the best ways for teachers to prepare themselves to teach writing is to *do* some writing. Although teachers need not write every assignment along with their students, they certainly should have experience composing in many of the forms that they ask students to do. Try some writing. Do a poem (treat it as an experiment). Write an essay or a page of graffiti. Write a speech and an editorial commenting on the speech. Create a play, then make it into a story. Share your work with other people. Talk over what you learn about yourself and about composition in the process.
- Start a collection of writing ideas or assignments, preferably in collaboration with other people. It is enormously helpful to have a resource bank of good writing suggestions on hand for inspirationless moments. One good way to do this is to create a series of writing idea cards on heavy paper, posterboard, or blank file folders. Include a writing starter—a poem, a newspaper article, a photograph— then write some composition topics for the students. These cards can be used with individual students or serve as the starting point for class assignments.
- Choose a topic or theme or issue—love, war, identity, politics, pets—and develop an exhaustive list of composing ideas for it. How can your topic be developed as:

story	film	essay
drama	letter	sculpture
graffiti	satire	column

Use the list of "neglected forms of composition" provided in this chapter as a guide.
* Literature anthologies are notoriosly weak in providing good writing assignments. Choose an anthology that is widely adopted and create some writing activities to go with the readings.
* Choose a topic or theme and create a sequence of assignments for a group of young people with whom you would like to work. What kinds of assignments should come first? In what ways should the sequence (and the students) develop? How can you end the sequence?

Related Readings

Ken MacCrorie's *Uptaught* (Rochelle Park: Hayden, 1969) makes delightful reading. Although it is aimed at exploding some myths about teaching writing at the college level, most of what MacCrorie says can be applied at other school levels. Kenneth Koch's *Wishes, Lies, and Dreams* (New York: Chelsea House, 1970) is also a good, practical book, with many examples of student writing. Perhaps the best theoretical discussion of the teaching of writing is a set of four essays by James Britton in *Explorations in Children's Writing* (Urbana: National Council of Teachers of English, 1970); in 50 pages Britton sketches out a remarkably detailed theory of the teaching and learning of writing and how it relates to children's lives. Janet Emig's *The Composing Processes of Twelfth Graders* (NCTE, 1971), which presents case studies of how young people actually attack the problem of making things in language, helps to dispel a number of myths about good writing habits.

An excellent practical resource for teachers is *The Whole Word Catalogue II* (New York: McGraw-Hill, 1977), a book prepared by the New York Teachers and Writers Collaborative, packed with teaching ideas. Teachers interested in writing may also want to subscribe to the collaborative's magazine, *Teachers and Writers,* which discusses both theoretical and practical problems. Though intended principally as a book for college writing classes, Miller's and my *Writing in Reality* (New York: Harper & Row, 1978) contains discussion of current writing theory with an emphasis on the role of imagination in writing. It includes a number of writing options that can be used at a variety of grade levels. Morgan's *Here and Now III* (New York: Harcourt Brace Jovanovich, 1979), also mentioned in the chapter, makes a good reference for teachers because of its skillful use of art and literature as a way of launching writing assignments. Finally, James Moffett and Betty Jane Weaner's *A Student Centered Language Arts Curriculum, K–13* (Boston: Houghton Mifflin, 1976) and its companion volume, *Teaching the Universe of Discourse* (1968), present a detailed investigation of the oral and written composing processes, though at times the theoretical discussion becomes self-absorbed to the point of being unreadable.

10
Writing for Here and Now

PORTRAIT OF THE ENGLISH TEACHER AS A TIRED DOG

It is a November midnight, Johnny Carson has just ended, and throughout the block the last lights flick off—all but one that is. A single orange light blooms in the darkness. It is the English teacher, weary-eyed, cramped of leg, hand, and brain, sifting listlessly but doggedly through piles of themes, circling, marking, grading, commenting, guilt-ridden because the students were promised that the papers would be returned last week. The fifth cup of coffee grows cold and bitter. Just one more paper. And then one more. And then . . .

From Richard Behm, "Portrait of the English Teacher as a Tired Dog," *Exchange: A Newsletter for Teachers of Writing* 3, no. 1. Published by the Writing Laboratory of the University of Wisconsin, Stevens Point. Reprinted by permission of the author.

Assessing student compositions has been a problem for English teachers ever since writing became a regular part of the high school curriculum in the mid-nineteenth century. In his textbook, *Aids to English Composition*, published in 1845, Richard Green Parker was one of the first to comment on ways of evaluating writing: "Merits for composition should be predicated on their neatness, correctness, length, style, &c.; but the highest merits should be given for the production of ideas, and original sentiments, and forms of expression." Parker's approach to the problem seems quite contemporary, with its emphasis on rewarding "the production of ideas" and "original sentiments" rather than dealing exclusively with mechanical correctness and neatness.

Like many teachers, however, Parker also found it easier to correct mechanical errors than to wrestle with abstract and nebulous concepts like "content" and "originality." His text showed far more concern for pointing out "deficiencies" than for rewarding "merits." A theme-grading guide at the end of the text dealt almost exclusively with the kinds of errors that could be indicated in the margins of a paper with "shorthand" symbols, "arbitrary marks" of the kind "used by printers in the correction of proof sheets." Parker may have been one of the first teachers to recognize that it was impossible to write out detailed comments on every student's paper and thus turned to "shorthand" methods for relief. He may, in fact, have been one of the first to offer the rationalization that using symbols was pedagogically justifiable because it encouraged students to locate their own errors.

Many of the procedures used for evaluating student writing over the years have been created less out of intellectual commitment than from desperation on the part of teachers faced with enormous stacks of papers. Teachers have tried both pointing out errors and allowing students to discover their own errors. They have tried blanket red-penciling and selective gray-penciling of errors. Some have emphasized the positive with occasional comments about the negative. Others have experimented with grading systems: single grades, double grades, and multiple grades. There is even a market for a twentieth-century "improvement" on Parker's proofreading symbols: a rubber stamp showing a little duckie who says "AWK!," protecting the ego of the child on whose paper it is imprinted by adding a playful touch to the revelation of compositional awkwardness. Despite the energy and ingenuity invested in these devices and procedures, student writing has not seemed to improve in corresponding ways.

FUTURE-DIRECTED EVALUATION

Why haven't these approaches to evaluation worked? A major reason may be that from Parker's time to the present, approaches to evaluation have always been future directed rather than aimed at writing as something for the here and now. Evaluation has emphasized getting students ready for next time, instead of helping them find success in the present.

For instance, with his talk of "merits" and "deficiencies" Parker sounds rather like a preacher trying to prepare his flock for the hereafter. Although teachers have softened this kind of language to speak of "strengths" and "weaknesses," the attitude has remained much the same. Teachers have operated on the assumption that if students write enough themes and receive enough evaluation, they will, sometime in the near or distant future, write The Perfect Theme that will be their pass through the Golden Gates of composition.

However, few people write simply for the sake of learning to write better. When an evaluation procedure implies that all the work being done is merely preparation for more work in the future, the reality of the writing situation is destroyed. Future-directed evaluation, even when done humanely and sensitively, may actually inhibit growth in writing.

A friend who is in publishing once pointed out that magazine and book editors are not interested in teaching authors how to write better. When a manuscript arrives, an editor looks through it, makes comments, calls for some revisions, and submits changes. All this instruction is devoted solely to the aim of getting out a successful publication. The editor remains indifferent to whether or not the author's writing improves in the process. However, many authors acknowledge that the process does help them write better, and many writers depend quite heavily on their editors for advice. The moral here is that by concentrating on the present, editors help the writer find success, and when they do so, they become, almost incidentally, "teachers of writing."

A teacher can escape the trap of future-directed evaluation by adopting the general kind of attitude an editor takes—being concerned with the product at hand. An editor, of course, works with adults who are reasonably accomplished writers to begin with. Because the teacher works with young people who are in the process of growing, the concerns will be more complicated. At times the teacher should be an editor, dealing with strengths and weaknesses in papers—in particular, as "publication time" approaches. At other times he or she must serve in somewhat more sensitive roles: as respondent, interested human being, friend, or adviser. The roles will differ with the student, the circumstances, and the state of the composition that the teacher receives.

This does not mean that a teacher must abandon all standards and accept anything with praise. The teacher does need to have criteria for good and bad; however, these should be applied as a way of helping students find success now.

This means that a teacher cannot treat themes as a batch, giving every piece of work the same basic evaluative treatment. Rather, the teacher needs to find ways of individualizing the kind of response made to student papers, rejecting the narrow role of teacher-evaluator to become a "manuscript manager" who decides on an individual basis what needs to happen for a piece of writing to bring satisfaction to the student here and now. On the next few pages, I will discuss some of the key points that a teacher must consider when examining a student composition, whether essay, poem, or story.[1] There are a number of stages or checkpoints where the teacher can pause to consider alternative ways of helping students. A summary of these stages is presented in Figure 10.1.

[1] Obviously the response mechanism will differ for nonwritten or nonverbal composition; but most of the criteria I suggest can also be applied—with modification—to such forms as film, tape, photo essays, and the like.

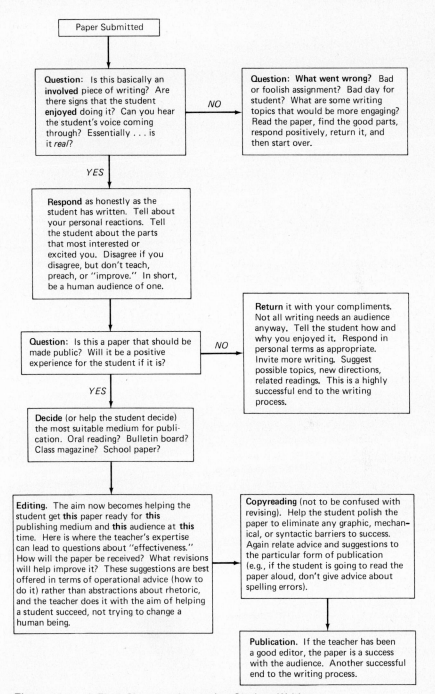

Figure 10.1   A Flow Chart for Assessing Student Writing.

LISTENING FOR THE STUDENT'S VOICE

When a paper first comes in, the teacher needs to begin the assessment by trying to discover whether or not the student was excited about the activity. The teacher needs to ask if this is *real* communication. Can you hear the student talking when you read it? Is it a lively piece of work that reveals the student's active participation? This quality in student writing is difficult to define but rather easy to detect. Many people call it "voice"— meaning that the paper sounds as if a unique person wrote it, not a computer or a bureaucrat. In *Children's Writing* (Cambridge, England: Cambridge University Press, 1967), David Holbrook describes this quality as "sincerity" and characterizes it as a feeling of openness, liveliness, and animation.

In approaching children's writing . . ., we need to seek beyond the problem of spelling, and the look of the writing, and get to the symbolic meaning. Once we have some sense of this, we judge it not in terms of its "psychological value" but as poetry. That is, from our experience of poetry of all kinds, we can ask ourselves, "In its symbolic exploration of inner and outer experience how sincere is this?" By "how sincere" here I think we mean how much real work is being done on problems of life: and the clue to this will be in the freshness, the energy, the rhythm and feel of the language. When anyone is really working on his inner world, he becomes excited—for he is making important discoveries and gains, as between his ego and the witches, princess, and threatening shadows within. He sees connections and relationships, and possibilities of structures, patterns, richness of content: and in these, joy and beauty. Expression will convey the bodily feelings of experience, and the "inscape" of an inward effort. So, if we are responsive, we can usually feel this excitement in the words (as we can usually feel this excitement in a piece of music: if we look at the score we are likely to find them marked *express*).

From David Holbrook, *Children's Writing.* Copyright © 1967 by Cambridge University Press. Reprinted by permission of the publisher.

In looking for excitement and the quality of sincerity in a student's writing, the teacher, in essence, asks, "Is there evidence that this has been a productive, reasonably enjoyable writing experience for the student?" If the answer is "yes," it will be revealed in the tone and vigor that one can sense in the language of the paper.

If the answer is negative, the teacher has reached an important decision point in the assessment process. Traditionally when teachers receive flat, dull, colorless writing, they blame it on the student: "You're not trying hard enough. Do it over!" I think this blame is often misplaced. No student deliberately creates a lifeless composition. Creating dull writing is boring, and few people outside the government would choose to do very much of it. In many cases the cause of dull writing can be traced indirectly to the assignment or to an unfavorable classroom climate. Perhaps the assignment was poor—too complicated, too easy, irrelevant, or just plain silly. Perhaps the student didn't trust the teacher or the class and was unwilling to share ideas. Whatever the cause, the teacher needs to find out what went wrong, looking as much to the assignment as to the student for an explanation. The teacher can then figure out something else for the student to do. What *will* work for him? What are her interests? What are his skills? What project will excite her? How can he or she be persuaded to trust others?

But what does the teacher do with the manuscript? It seems pointless to demand revision of something that was dead to begin with. I think the teacher should, therefore, respond as positively as possible to the paper, commenting on the good parts (without faking a response). Then the paper should be returned. Often the teacher can say quite directly, "Look, I had the feeling you didn't enjoy doing this. Am I right? Let's see if we can't come up with something else you would rather do."

Here is a paper that illustrates the problem of voice. It was written in a junior high school class in which the students were asked to write a letter of application for a job they might like to have sometime:

> Good morning Sir I would like to apply for a banking clerk. I think I am well qualified to fill the position. I have had three years of dealing with money I know how to handle money quite well. I am a very responsible man and also very dependable. I could be trusted to handle your money without your having any uncertainty about me. And as I said before since I have been handling money.
>
> My schooling is great, I have just graduated from college, and majoring in bookkeeping which deals with a lot of money.
>
> I can tell you how much money you are making or lossing. If you were to hire me you can be certain that I will do my job to the best of my ability. Yes! This is just the kind of bank that I would like to work at.
>
> I feel that it would be a privilege working for your bank.
>
> "(2C.) *allen Johnson*"
>
> (H.) Allen Johnson

Except for a few bright spots, this letter seems utterly lacking in voice, and I doubt that (H.) Allen Johnson profited much by doing it. Many of the phrases seem forced, unnatural, and excessively formal: "I could handle your money without your having any uncertainty about me." "I feel that it would be a privilege working for your bank." Occasionally Allen's real voice comes through. His exclamation, "Yes!," seems to be a victory over both The Business Letter and his own doubts about the banking business. His signature is done in playful parody of "official" looking signatures and adds an original touch. But the remainder is dull and repetitive, sounding much like a junior high school student trying to write what he imagines to be adult language.

The result is a letter that, by almost any criteria, is unsuccessful: Allen has not learned much about business letters; his letter wouldn't land him a job; and his teacher must be thoroughly frustrated by almost every aspect of his writing.

What went wrong? I suspect that despite an assignment that seemed reasonable and practical, the realities of job hunting are so far removed from the world of the junior high school student that the task became meaningless. Allen is simply not ready to worry about jobs, and there is no reason why he should be. So the assignment drove him into using a false, stuffy voice. In dealing positively with the paper, the teacher might compliment Allen on his enthusiasm and point out that he has done a good job of thinking about what a banker would want to know about a prospective employee (he *has* done a skillful job of surveying his audience, even though the topic and audience were not closely related to his current needs). The teacher should then turn Allen's attention to finding other projects that he will enjoy doing. It is conceivable that Allen might enjoy going to a bank to find out what actually happens there. I think it is more likely, however, that the teacher could find interesting writing ideas for Allen in less academic areas, topics more suitable for junior high, like writing sports stories or telling tales of the grotesque and macabre.

RESPONDING TO STUDENT WRITING

One hopes that the amount of voiceless writing teachers receive will be small, that early in the school year they can help each student find areas where writing is profitable and interesting. Once teachers recognize that a paper has voice, it is appropriate that they take time to respond (orally or in writing). Students have spent much time writing; they need response and reaction quickly.

To respond to student writing simply means to react to a paper openly and directly, as a person rather than as a teacher. It differs from evaluation in being a shared reaction rather than a set of future-directed instructions for improvement. In responding, teachers can tell how they reacted to the paper ("I really felt the fear you described when the storm hit"); they can share similar experiences ("I remember the fight I had with my parents over taking a job playing saxophone when I was a sophomore"); they can indicate their own beliefs and tell about the ways in which they agree or disagree ("I can see your point about the way newscasters operate, but I really don't agree that the networks control American thought").

Response can move beyond direct feedback to suggest new or related directions for the student to explore. ("You obviously enjoyed writing this; have you ever read any of Edgar Allan Poe's stories?" "Have you ever made a movie? I think it might be interesting for you to try to catch the same idea on film.") These more oblique comments express the honest reaction of an interested, informed adult, not just the pedagogically directed instruction of a theme grader.

In responding, however, teachers differ from the ordinary reader in a very significant way: Teachers should be willing to ignore all kinds of graphic, rhetorical, and syntactic problems that a regular reader might find frustrating or disagreeable. Teachers should fight to dig out the meaning of a page. They should puzzle over idiosyncratic spellings, ignore the 50-word run-on sentence, forget about the fact that statistics and supporting evidence are missing, and struggle to uncoil long strings of identical loops that pass for handwriting. This is not to suggest that such problems are blithely ignored. The key point is that response should not be confused with proofreading. To comment on mechanical problems before responding to content is fairly perverse. Such difficulties can be taken up later, after the teacher has responded fully and carefully. As David Holbrook has pointed out in *Children's Writing*, looking past problems to decipher, appreciate, and enjoy student writing without having one's reaction skewed by errors and blights is extremely difficult—possibly more difficult for English teachers than for most people, since we have earned advanced degrees in linguistic flaw detecting.

Perhaps the best model for this kind of response is the letter one would write in reply to a note received from a young relative—a son, daughter, nephew, or niece. For close relatives, most of us are willing to decipher and to respond directly to meaning, and few would grade or evaluate letters.

PUBLIC OR PRIVATE?

Another question that a teacher needs to ask concerns whether a paper should be made public: "Should it be given a wider audience than just the teacher?" Although we want to avoid writing that is merely written for the teacher, it is important to recall that not all writing is meant to be made public. The teacher should consider carefully whether providing an audience will create a positive experience for the student.

Here is a paper submitted by a high school sophomore girl:

One day me and this girl went to the store. The girl was from Chicago and she thought she was bad. She kept pointing her umbrella in my face. I told her stop but she kept pushing so I grabbed it out of her hand and stuck her with it. I felt sorry but I said no better for a person like that. Only fools fight. And when you fight you really lose whether you win or not. I believe that arguing is good because people have a way to say it without harming someone or hurting a live thing. But you can't always walk away. (You may not understand this because I haven't got the words to say it.)

—C.S.

It is possible that C.S. would find it helpful to have other students read and discuss this paper, and her classmates might be able to offer some useful or supportive advice. However, C.S. is obviously puzzled and concerned, and she may be less interested in communicating a message than exploring her own experience and seeking a response from someone else. She believes "only fools fight," and she is persuaded that people should settle disputes through argument rather than through "harming someone or hurting a live thing." Yet, as she says, "you can't always walk away," and in this situation she felt committed to action. As an adult being asked for help—a role that teachers should accept with pleasure, even if it puts them in the sometimes uncomfortable position of learning about students' problems—the teacher needs to respond directly to C.S., supporting her efforts to sort out her own beliefs and values.

If writing is judged to be private, little can be accomplished by offering instruction about writing skills. The teacher should respond—fully and helpfully—and return it to the student without any pedagogical comment. Although there may be some rhetorical problems with the writing, it becomes hollowly academic to do something about them in such a case. Here, C.S. openly expressed her feelings; the teacher read, understood, and responded. That seems to be enough.

ALTERNATIVE FORMS OF PUBLICATION

There are many different ways the teacher can provide students with a readership. Some papers are best "published" by having them read aloud to the class, either by the author or the teacher. Some writing should be read and tape-recorded to become part of a class library of recorded literature. Students' work can be posted on the board, submitted to a class newspaper or magazine, sent to the school paper or magazine, run off on ditto for the class, or circulated in manuscript form.

An excellent list of ways of publishing student writing, prepared by an Australian primary school teacher, is shown in the box.

It is important to note that every form of writing and each kind of publication make particular, specialized demands on the writer. Students should have an audience in mind while they are writing, but often the best form of publication will not be apparent until after the writing has been completed. A short, witty poem that might bring a good laugh to the class when read aloud may die if set in print. A play that has absorbed a student's time for several weeks surely deserves presentation, but it may work better as reader's theater or a radio play than as a stage production. As an expert on writing forms, media, and styles, the teacher can help the students find the most productive forms of publication.

Here, Roman Cirillo, an eighth grader, writes about "How Airplanes Flies," and his paper presents some interesting publication problems:

> Few people know why or how an airplane flies. The explanation is very simple. There no mysterious mechenism or machinery to study. You don't have to take a plane apart or crawl around inside to understand why it stays in the air. You just stand off and look at it. Airplanes flies because of the shapes of its wings. The engine and propellor have very little to do with it. The pilot has nothing to do with making the plane fly. He simply controls the flight. A glider without an engine will fly in the air for hours. The biggest airlines will fly for a certain length of time with all the engine shut off. A plane flies and stay in the air because its wings are supported by the air just as water supports a fellow. Toss a flat piece of tin on a boat. Toss a flat piece of tin on a pond and it will sink at once. If you bend it through the middle and fasten the end together so its is watertight it will float.

There are obviously many problems with this essay. It lacks clarity and it often leaves the reader confused. But if one looks past the errors and infelicities, "How Airplanes Flies" is a clever explanation of flight. The paper has a strong, clear voice; one can hear Roman's patient instruction to someone who is ignorant of the principles of flight: "You don't have to take a plane apart or crawl around inside to understand why it stays in the air. You just stand off and look at it." Roman is a good teacher, and his explanation of how shaping metal enables the plane to fly is skillful (even though incomplete). Roman would, no doubt, fail any test on writing analogies, similes, and metaphors; but he makes excellent use of analogy in relating how things float in an invisible substance—air—to an observable phenomenon—a boat floating on water.

In its present form, however, this paper will probably not find much success with an audience. It has too many problems of clarity, too much drifting and backtracking, for a reader (particularly one who doesn't understand flight) to stay with it for long.

Because Roman seems to have so much trouble handling the written word (one senses quite a struggle with the writing process behind this paper), I think the teacher might recommend that this project be completed as an oral "publication," particularly since Roman seems to be a good talker. Perhaps he can plan a demonstration for those members of the class who are interested. Drawing on his essay, he might bring in a dishpan and some aluminum foil to demonstrate the shaping of materials. Perhaps he can bring in some model planes or photographs or drawings to illustrate flight. An oral presentation should be a good experience for Roman, and quite significantly, it will be an experience that has its origins in writing. It might well pave the way for successful written composition in the future, but it would bring Roman success here and now.

100 WAYS TO PUBLISH CHILDREN'S WRITING

BOOKS OF ALL KINDS

1. A.B.C. Books
2. Story Books
3. Poetry Books
4. "My Best Writing"—Individual Scrapbook
5. "Introducing Our Class"
6. "Famous People" [The class as a set of VIPs]
7. Autograph Album
8. "I'd Like to Be . . . "
9. "What Do You Know About . . . ?" Series
10. Riddle and Joke Books
11. "How-to . . . " Books
12. Recipe Books
13. A Giant Book [Made from an appliance box and butcher paper]
14. "The Longest Story Ever!" [On rolls of butcher paper]
15. A "Group" Story
16. An All-School Story [With round-robin contributions]

NEWSPAPERS

17. School News
18. Family News
19. Good News
20. District News
21. "Crazy Paper" [Nursery rhymes retold]

SIMPLE NEWS SHEETS

22. News-Writing Competition
23. About Favourite Books
24. Natural Science Reports
25. Stop Press [School news flashes]

MAGAZINES

26. "Getting to Know You" [For a new class]
27. Specialist Magazines [From spear fishing to stamps]
28. "What Do You Want to Know about High School?" [or college]
29. Holiday Magazine
30. Class of 19__ [A class reminiscence]

LETTERS

31. Classroom Mailbox
32. Teacher Writes Too [Personal letters to students]
33. To Mum and/or Dad
34. To Gran and/or Grandad
35. To the Principal
36. To a Person in the News
37. To a Media Personality
38. To a Librarian
39. To the School Bus Driver
40. To a Favourite Author
41. To the Local Paper

PLAYS

42. Begin Without Dialogue [Written instructions for mime]
43. Proceed Through Simple Dialogue
44. Dramatise Stories
45. Dramatise Poems
46. Try Melodrama
47. An End-of-Term Drama Festival

NOTICE BOARDS—IDEAS FOR DISPLAYING DAY-TO-DAY WORK

48. Here's Good Work!
49. Have You Read This?
50. Food for the Mind [A "thoughts" bulletin board]
51. Mail Train [Each car carries a piece of writing]
52. Garden of Poems
53. Balloons or Kites [Each with some writing]
54. All Up in the Air! [A Full aeronautical display]

SPECIAL DISPLAYS TO SHARE WITH OTHERS

55. Information Charts
56. Posters
57. Conversations [Cartoon-fashion displays]
58. Patchwork Quilt [A "pastiche" of writing]
59. Sandwich Man [A walking display]
60. Advertisements

SPECIAL DISPLAYS AND EXHIBITIONS

61. Girl/Boy-of-the-Week Display
62. Rogue's Gallery [Student autobiographies or sketches of literary characters]
63. Corridor as Cemetery [In the manner of *Spoon River*]
64. Toy Exhibition [Of old or antique toys, with written histories]
65. Circus Exhibition [A history-social studies project]
66. Stamp Exhibition [Including postal history write-ups]
67. Photographic Exhibition
68. Photo Exhibition of a Field Trip

ASSEMBLY REPORTS

69. A Sampling of Good Writing
70. Reporting [Of newsworthy school events]
71. Celebrating Anniversaries [And national holidays]

USING ART AND CRAFT WORK

72. Mobiles of All Sorts
73. Group Production of Mobiles
74. Class Mobile
75. Enormous Posters
76. Window Craft
77. Birthday Cards
78. Congratulations Cards
79. Hand-out Cards
80. Portrait Gallery

81-85. Murals [Students write about and portray: passengers at a bus stop; performers at a concert; dancers at a discotheque; cats on a fence.]

USING TAPE RECORDERS

86. Write—Tape—Revise
87. Tape, then Write
88. Regular Recording by Struggling Writers

MISCELLANEOUS

89. Cartoon Show [Using overhead transparencies]
90. Run an Advertising Agency
91. Set Up a Writer's Centre
92. Form a Writer's Club
93. Hold a Writers' Barbecue [Picnic and writers' workshop]

A WIDER AUDIENCE

94. A Shop Display
95. Displays for Special Events
96. Municipal Library Display
97. A Hospital Visit
98. Children's Magazines
99. P & C Readings [PTA meetings]
100. End-of-year Report to a Local Newspaper

From Pat Edwards, "100 Ways to Publish Children's Writing," in R. D. Walshe, ed., *Better Reading/Writing Now!* The Primary English Association of New South Wales, Epping Public School, Epping, NSW, Australia 2121. Copyright © 1977 by the Primary English Teaching Association of New South Wales. Abridged by permission.

THE CLASSROOM PUBLISHING CENTER

Back in the middle of the nineteenth century, a farsighted high school principal, John S. Hart, of Philadelphia Central High School, had a policy that the school would support any student publication that showed it could attract a modest readership. Over the period of a decade, Central had at least a dozen different school newspapers and a wide range of magazines and other student publications. Hart's wisdom came in seeing that writers quite simply need audiences. When those audiences are provided through publication, student writing improves dramatically, both in content and correctness.

Reproducing Student Work

The mass reproduction of student work seems to me so important that a review of some in-class printing and duplicating techniques is appropriate.

• *Spirit Duplicating.* This is the old standby ditto machine. Although spirit printing produces an ordinary looking page, usually purple, the process can be used to produce interesting magazines and flyers if you exploit the possibility of color. Using different colored ditto carbons (they come in red, green, blue, purple, and black), one can produce five-color work on a single page. It looks good and is relatively cheap and easy to do.

If you are not able to requisition or steal a ditto machine for your own room, you might be interested in the poor person's ditto, a device called a hectograph. It uses a tray full of gelatin and some incomprehensible magic to produce spirit copies one sheet at a time, and Sears will sell you one for about $6. The hectograph is messy and slow, but it is also very satisfying for students to produce work on one.

• *Mimeograph.* This is the other old standby. It produces pages that are more professional looking than spirit-purple, but most inexpensive mimeographs are also rather messy. Multiple color work can be done on mimeographs, but it is a fairly complicated procedure. You can get some interesting accessories for a mimeograph, including a tracing board to reproduce student art; lettering sets for headlines, mastheads, and the like; and specially blocked stencils cut electronically. When run on your own machine, they will give quality that is close to printed.

• *Printing.* Hobbyist printing sets are available in many art and craft stores for $10 to $15. These enable the user to print with real type, one sheet of paper at a time. Setting the type is time consuming, and use of the press is probably best limited to short poems and magazine covers; but few things are more satisfying than a freshly printed page, especially if the students have set the type themselves.

• *Linoleum and Wood Blocks.* Here is a process that is useful chiefly for illustrations and covers. The art teacher can probably set you up with the basic tools and materials to do linoleum or wood block printing. Depending on the skill and energy of your students, rather intricate prints can be produced. By varying inks and papers, the student can produce a variety of finished prints from a single block, thus individualizing the appearance of the publication.

• *Silk Screen.* This process is more complex and more sophisticated than linoleum printing. Silk screen is especially useful for large work (posters, for example), printed covers, and finely detailed work. A beginner's silk screen kit can be purchased at a hobby store for $5, but the basic equipment can be built at home for less.

• *Potato Printing, String Printing, Finger Painting.* Anything that will pick up ink or paint and transfer it to another surface can be used to print designs, letters, and pictures.

• *Stencils.* These can be cut into all kinds of patterns and designs. Using spray paints, runs of one hundred can be completed quickly.

• *Offset Printing.* Offset is *not* a classroom process, but it deserves mention. Many instant printshops will run copies for about 3¢ to 4¢ per page, using the offset process. Copies look highly professional and are relatively inexpensive. Most offset houses will also "shrink" copy for you at no cost so you can squeeze lots of print onto a single page. Also explore the possibilities that *folding* offers. For example, an 11"x17" sheet (a standard two-page size) can be folded three times to make a 16-page magazine, 8½"x5½". Total cost, $10 per hundred copies. Sold at 10¢ per copy (to students, administrators, parents), the class magazine will just break even.

• *One-of-a-Kind Books.* The previous techniques are all concerned with producing multiple copies of students' work. There is also value in that one-of-a-kind books, done by hand, can be passed about the class or made a part of the permanent resource center. One-of-a-kind books can often be more elaborate than duplicated materials, and can include lavish use of colors and photographs, hand illumination, dry transfer printing, and special effects. Many different kinds of bindings are possible too, including cloth.

EDITING

Publishing is also important because it sets the stage for the final two parts of the response process: editing and copy reading. I have suggested that initially teachers should ignore surface errors to seek out the meaning of a page. But a concern for standards and correctess is appropriate in the context of revising and editing a paper.

Until the student and teacher have determined the audience for a paper, almost *any* instruction or advice in rhetoric or mechanics is irrelevant. However, when the form of publication has been determined, commentary about writing becomes appropriate; and the teacher and student can begin raising questions about effectiveness, clarity, organization, style, and structure. But it is critical that this commentary relate to the *particular form of publication* and the *particular audience* for the paper. Publications and readers have differing standards, and if editorial advice is to be helpful, it must be valid.

For instance, if a student writes, "*Space Outlaws* is the crummiest show on TV," the teacher's initial reaction may be to point out that "crummy" is not a standard critical term, that one cannot simply declare a show crummy without supplying reasons and supporting evidence. However, if the audience for the paper is a class of seventh graders who watch *Space Outlaws* regularly, "crummiest" may be *just* the word; the students know what the show is like and will either agree that it is crummy or argue that "it isn't all *that* crummy." In either case, the students don't need evidence or reasons; they already know the arguments. On the other hand, if the student is writing to the network president to demand that the show be removed from the air, the teacher can be genuinely helpful by pointing out that "crummiest" is inappropriate.

Advice of this kind should be operational, that is, couched in practical, "how to" terms. Abstractions about *unity, coherence, emphasis, narration, description, exposition, argumentation, topic sentences, grabber openings, clincher conclusions, brevity, antithesis, parallelism,* and *occlusion* are not likely to be of significant help to most young writers. Often, the best advice the teacher can give is simply helping the student see or discover alternatives: "Did you consider doing it this way?" or "Let me show you a couple of other ways to approach that." Although teachers may draw on their own knowledge of rhetorical principles for such advice, it isn't necessary for the student to memorize the abstraction while solving problems in the here and now.

COPYREADING

For too long, textbook writers and composition teachers have blurred the distinction between editing—changing content and form—and proofreading—polishing matters of spelling, mechanics, and usage. In their zeal to make students skillful writers of standard English, teachers have pounced on proofreading problems as early as the first draft, blithely pointing out errors in words and sentences that may well disappear entirely during the revision stage.

The discussion of mechanical and syntactic correctness should be delayed until the last possible moment in the writing process, leaving the students free to do the basic writing and revision of papers without any hesitation because of uncertainty over rules of correctness. Only after the students have edited their writing into a form that satisfies them should the teacher open the discussion of mechanics and usage. Even then, one should not charge in to red-pencil every error of mechanics, spelling, and punctuation. Rather, the teacher should concentrate on helping students put their papers into a form that will not confuse or irritate the readership. The teacher might point out to students that some audiences are offended by unclear handwriting or by language that doesn't conform to certain standards. The teacher can also note that failing to conform to some standards sometimes creates communication problems. Most students see this clearly, and if the quest for correctness has not dominated the entire writing process, they are willing to participate in a polishing session to get their paper into a form that will not cost them their readership.

Once again, however, it is important to note that the correctness demands of audiences differ widely. The teacher should not apply blanket standards of correctness or use the copyreading session as a way of slipping in standard English drill. The teacher should consider the proofreading changes that are necessary for *this* paper and *this* audience at *this* time. For instance, if the paper is simply to be read aloud or tape-recorded by the author, discussion of spelling, punctuation, or capitalization is largely a waste of time. Even if the paper is misspelled, illegibly written, and totally unpunctuated, the author can probably read it, and pointing out problems will contribute nothing to its success. If on the other hand, the paper is going to be duplicated, it is quite legitimate for the teacher to work with the student to help get the paper into audience acceptable form. Even here, however, the teacher needs to be cautious. If "it's me" is the standard form in the dialect of a class, the teacher should probably not try to insist on "it's I" as an appropriate form. What matters is success with the audience, not a textbook illustration of "standard."[2]

STUDENT SELF-ASSESSMENT

As I have described them, these considerations concerning assessment of student writing may seem too elaborate and time consuming for a teacher with five or six classes and 150 students. However, I have found that focusing assessment on the here-and-now actually speeds up the process of assessment and provides more time for the teacher to take up other classroom roles. For example, I find that it takes me less time to write a note of personal response on a paper than to mull through and write out detailed, pedagogically oriented evaluative comments. It is much faster to offer direct editorial advice keyed to specific publishing situations than it is to puzzle over the errors one will selectively attack this time.

In addition, as a class grows in the course of a quarter or semester, the students can take over more and more of the process. All this creates more time for the teacher to "float," working on a one-to-one basis with students who seek help.

There are also a number of specific steps that the teacher can take to engage the students directly in the process of assessing their own work:

Encourage the students to talk to you and to one another about problems while they are writing.

Make it a standing invitation that any student can propose an alternative topic at any time in the class, thus reducing the number of lifeless papers.

Let the students decide which of their writing is public and which is private. In practice, most teachers find that the students are more willing to share their personal concerns with one another after initial phases of "testing" one another.

Describe the publication forms that are available. As the writing program develops and students catch on to the idea of publication, they should more often write with a specific audience and form of publication in mind.

Encourage the students to serve as one another's editors. One doesn't need to be an expert in composition and rhetoric to make useful suggestions about the clarity and effectiveness of writing. Although students may not know terminology, they are certainly capable of spotting editorial problems and talking about them in their own

[2] The issue of standard English and its teaching will be taken up again in the next chapter.

language: "Hey, I don't know what you're talking about." (Translation for teachers: "Lacks clarity.") "That's crazy." (Translation: "Lacks logical structure.") "I don't believe it." (Translation: "Needs more supporting evidence.") Students are highly perceptive in these ways, and when their editing has real purpose, they can take over the process and make genuinely helpful suggestions to one another.

Leave proofreading to the students. In every class there are some students who have mastered most of the proofreading skills. Often such students are simply good spellers or intuitive punctuators. Acknowledge their skill by setting them up as proofreading consultants to the class.

Treat proofreading as something to be done quickly and efficiently, rather than as a climactic step in the process of composition. Only when proofreading is made a mysterious, complex part of the mastery of standard English does it become intimidating and therefore difficult for students.

Help the students learn to react to one another's work. Small- and large-group discussion of completed compositions should be a regular part of any English class. At first, you may find that students are a bit hard on one another, no doubt imitating previous teachers of their acquaintance. It may take some practice before the students can respond to the substance of one another's writing, but it will come with time and guidance.

Encourage students to develop criteria of excellence in advance for the work they are doing by putting themselves in the position of the audience and asking questions *it* would raise.

Encourage group and collaborative projects from time to time so that students can share both skills and critical knowledge.

Read some of your own writing to the class, and share your own satisfactions and dissatisfactions with it.

Encourage the students to develop lists of the problems and pleasures they associate with each project they do.

EXPLORATIONS AND RESOURCES

• Some unresolved issues and debatable questions:

What is an "error"?

Do people learn by having their errors pointed out to them? Under what conditions? Do people learn by having the errors of others pointed out?

How should assessment and evaluation procedures change as young people grow older?

Need a teacher respond to or evaluate every paper assigned?

Under what circumstances should a teacher say nothing about a bad paper? about a good one?

- The most difficult part of responding to student writing is getting over one's negative feelings about "blights" sufficiently to look at the real content of an essay. Collect some student writing and talk it over with another teacher. Share your ideas on the ways in which one could respond to it productively. Learn to look beyond mechanical and syntactic problems.
- Meet with a small group of students and engage them in a discussion of what makes good writing. To what extent do the students already have criteria of excellence of their own? How do these compare to yours?
- Develop a publishing center as recommended by Pat Edwards. Stock it with the necessary supplies to create a wide range of published books, magazines, and bulletin board displays. Then, create a series of posters or activity cards that show the students how to create various publications; for example, how to make a poem mobile, how to make a giant book.
- Learn the technical ins and outs of mass reproduction of student work, from ditto to offset. Collect well-done flyers, brochures, and ads to serve as graphic examples for students.
- Seek financial support for the publication of student writing. If the school cannot support a number of student publications, ask for contributions from local shops and industries for small and relatively inexpensive publications. Talk to the editor of your local newspaper about setting aside a page each month for student writing.

Related Readings

The single best source of ideas and techniques for responding to student writing is David Holbrook's *Children's Writing* (Cambridge, England: Cambridge University Press, 1967), quoted in this chapter. Holbrook includes chapters on seeing the "real" in students' work, deciphering their handwriting, and analyzing what students are saying. Haim Ginott's books *Between Parent and Child* (New York: Macmillan, 1965) and *Between Parent and Teenager* (Macmillan, 1969) are extremely helpful, stressing the need for parents and teachers to listen to, comprehend, and show empathy for young people's concerns before offering correction, instruction, or advice. Revision has been the focus of two issues of *The English Journal*, December 1975 and October 1978, with special emphasis on such alternative approaches as using conferences instead of red pencils and peer rather than teacher editing. Teachers who want to learn more about student self-assessment should also examine Peter Elbow's *Writing Without Teachers* (New York: Oxford/Galaxy, 1974), which has excellent, step-by-step procedures for teaching people to edit and respond to one another's work. Finally, teachers who are interested in expanding audiences and publication opportunities for student work might want to examine *Gifts of Writing*, by Susan and Stephen Judy (New York: Scribner's, 1980), which shows arts and crafts techniques plus writing ideas for over 50 different kinds of projects.

11
Exploring Language

Every few years politicians caught up in a difficult campaign reinvent "basics" and make their campaign theme "First Things First." They advocate "the elimination of frills" and promise a return to "old standards." Theirs is an appealing strategy that cuts to the heart of America's desire for efficiency, directness, and simplicity; and it often wins a good many votes.

English teachers also hear this cry from time to time. "Let's get back to the three Rs in school." "Why didn't someone teach my secretary to spell or punctuate?" "We here at the State U find our new students are abominably weak on fundamentals." "Of course I want my child to read literature, but after all, certain *other* things must come first." Often the demand for basics is phrased as a broad, unanswerable question: "Given all the money we spend on the schools, is it really too much to ask that the graduates be able to speak and write the Queen's English properly?"

In the past few years teachers have found themselves in the middle of a basics revival. More and more parents have become upset about what they take to be a neglect of basic skills, and have translated their concern into threats to limit school funding. This, in turn, has pressured administrators and led to the movement to hold teachers accountable for listing fundamental skills and showing student improvement on test scores.

Like the appeal of the politician, a proclaimed interest in basics is very satisfying for many parents and administrators. Blue-collar parents are given a kind of assurance that their children will be able to rise in life; white-collar and suburban parents are reassured that their supremacy will not be undercut by "progressivist" English teachers who encourage "sloppy" speech and act as if "anything goes."

It is ironic that English teachers themselves have helped to create this overemphasis on basic skills. Although teachers have never been entirely certain of how or why they were teaching literature or of what they were trying to do in writing classes, they have stressed grammar and correctness—faithfully, consistently, without hesitation or doubt, year after year. It is unlikely that the emphasis on grammar has actually taught very much to students, but it obviously has made the graduates of our schools intensely aware of correctness. Thus parents are delighted to join in the demand for a return to basics, *whether or not they ever learned anything from their own bout with grammar.*

It is ironic, too, that the movement toward basics is not a new one, though its proponents act as if they were the first to discover fundamentals.

Nearly a century of emphasis on the skills of English has brought almost universal literacy in our countries—a literacy dissipated, for the most part, on the impoverished literature of the popular press (which grew in answer to it). We should not be surprised. Whenever the so-called skill elements of language learning are divorced from the rest of English, the means becomes the end.

From John Dixon, *Growth Through English*, National Council of Teachers of English, 1968.

The direct focus on skill instruction proves fruitless because it fails to concentrate on language users and their needs. The net effect of skill-building programs is often to inhibit the skill users, crippling their natural ability and blunting their desire to do anything new with language.

"Putting first things first" has proven itself unsuccessful. Another possible approach—"Everything, *including basics,* in its place"—needs to be explored. Only by considering the total language program can one avoid the obvious problems created by teaching basic skills in isolation.

GRAMMAR, USAGE, MECHANICS

One area of study that clearly hasn't been kept in its proper place is the teaching of grammar. The hold of grammar over the curriculum has been strong. Beginning in the fifth or sixth grade, children usually receive five- or ten-week doses of grammar at annual intervals for six or seven years. Few children remember much grammar from year to year, and many students quite honestly tell the teacher in June that they don't recall having studied the noun in September, despite the fact that the entire month was devoted to it.

The development of new grammars—structural, transformational-generative, tagmemic, stratificational—has complicated the issue for teachers, for each offers a different system, an alternative approach, and makes new demands on the teacher's time.[1]

Much of the confusion can be traced to what people expect the teaching of "grammar" to accomplish. Indeed, part of the problem simply concerns terminology, and some preliminary definitions are thus in order. Teachers need to keep three terms and their relationships clearly separate in their minds.

Grammar

Grammar is most simply defined as "a description of how English works." Through a process of analysis, the grammarian discovers the various components or parts of the language system and how they fit together. Grammar is a description of the language conventions that a speaker of the language has mastered in order to be able to communicate with other people. Grammar is *not* a set of rules telling how one is supposed to speak, and it does not prescribe behavior. It simply makes note of the language behavior that native speakers have learned. Very few people actually speak "ungrammatically," because something that is ungrammatical does not follow the basic patterns of English and therefore cannot be understood by another person. This statement is ungrammatical:

> "Nobody ain't and got me ain't got nobody yet I."

It was produced by scrambling a sentence to break up English word order. This is the grammatical version of the sentence:

> "I ain't got nobody, and nobody ain't got me yet."

It follows normal English word patterns and it can therefore be understood by listeners, even though they might be somewhat offended or bothered by some of the word choices.

Usage

Usage is a range of socially significant choices available to a speaker *within* the grammar of a language. (Most people use the term grammar to refer to what is actually usage.) Usage is a sociological phenomenon, not principally linguistic. Either of the following can be understood:

> "I ain't got nobody and nobody ain't got me yet."
>
> or
>
> "I haven't anyone, and no one has gotten me yet."

[1] It is beyond the scope of this book to describe these new grammars. Almost any good introductory linguistics or English language text will discuss them. (See the readings suggested at the end of the chapter.)

The difference between the statements is that each speaker reveals himself or herself to be a member of a particular social class. Usage is relative, and it is neither correct nor incorrect. In fact, standard usage is generally little more than the usage habits of the people in a country who are either (1) envied because of their superior breeding, intelligence, charm, and wit or (2) envied because of their superior wealth. The latter is more often the case. To some, this seems a cynical view of the nature of the "pure" form of our mother tongue. But the history of English shows that standard usage is a matter of convention, custom, and prestige; it is not an inherently superior dialect.

Mechanics

iaintgotnobudyandnubudyaingotmeyethesaidafaintsmileplayinacrosthislips Straighten that out, and you've got[2] yourself an "A" for mechanics on your report card. *Mechanics* are[3] simply transcription conventions—spelling, capitalization, punctuation—that make it possible for one person to read the writing of another. Mechanical conventions[4] are standardized and do not vary the way usage does. Although usage variations seldom interfere with comprehension, it is important for writers to follow mechanical conventions if they are to get their message through. Like any code, mechanics need to be learned at one time or another by the language user.

TEACHING GRAMMAR

For generations, teachers of English have presented lessons in grammar (the description of how English works), thinking they were teaching standard usage (the conventions of language followed by the middle and upper classes) and mechanics (the standard code of transcription conventions). The motivation behind this has been to provide students with access to higher social levels. Thus students have been told such things as, "It's important for you to know grammar because you'll need it in life." It would be pleasant if life responded to laws like that, but not surprisingly, students have sensed that it doesn't and have gone on *not* learning the noun and the comma.

It seems apparent that teaching rules and laws does not significantly change performance, and most research attempts to prove otherwise have failed.

---

[2]Or should it be "gotten"?
[3]Or should it be "is"?
[4]I could have said "mechanics is-or-are" again, but rather than deal with the problem, I'll simply avoid it by choosing an alternative phrasing—the way most students do when faced with usage problems like this one.

A list of the most prominent claims made in behalf of the study of grammar over the years would include these: that it (1) disciplines the mind, (2) aids in the study of foreign languages, (3) helps one to use better English, (4) helps one to read better, and (5) aids in the interpretation of literature.

What does research tell us about these claims? . . . We believe the following excerpts from the *Encyclopedia of Educational Research* are worth reading:

(*On disciplining the mind*): Experimentation in this area failed to yield any significant evidence supporting the belief in grammar as a disciplinary subject.

(*On the interpretation of literature*): The results from tests in grammar, composition, and literary interpretation led to the conclusion that there was little or no relationship between grammar and composition and grammar and literary interpretation.

(*On improved writing and usage*): Further evidence supplementing the early studies indicated that training in formal grammar did not transfer to any significant extent to writing or to recognizing correct English. In general the experimental evidence revealed a discouraging lack of relationship between grammatical knowledge and the better utilization of expressional skills. Recently, grammar has been held to contribute to the better understanding of the sentence. Yet, even here, there is a discouraging lack of relationship between sentence sense and grammatical knowledge of subjects and predicates.

(*On the study of foreign languages*): In spite of the fact that the contribution of the knowledge of English grammar to achievement in foreign language has been its chief justification in the past, the experimental evidence does not support this conclusion.

(*On the improvement of reading*): The study of grammar has been justified because of its possible contribution to reading skills, but the evidence does not support this conclusion.

(*On improved language behavior in general*): No more relation exists between knowledge in a functional language situation than exists between any two totally different and unrelated subjects.

(*On diagraming sentences*): The use of sentence diagraming as a method of developing sentence mastery and control over certain mechanical skills closely related to the sentence has been subjected to a series of experimental investigations. In general the studies indicate that diagraming is a skill which, while responsive to instruction, has very slight value in itself. There is no point in training the pupil to diagram sentences except for the improvement it brings in his ability to create effective sentences. The evidence shows that this is insignificant.

If we accept these studies as valid, we must ask ourselves: What goes on here? For surely the meaning of these studies is that rarely have so many teachers spent so much time with so many children to accomplish so little.

That teaching rules does not change performance is a function of the relationship between rules and performance—not of the quality of grammar. That is, despite the obvious inadequacies of traditional grammar, the development of newer grammars is not likely to change student performance, because grammars are simply not capable of changing usage habits.

Teachers need to put the teaching of grammar in perspective for themselves and make their own set of judgments about what value, if any, grammar has in the schools. Without going into details or debating conflicting linguistic and sociolinguistic views, I will briefly present my own formula for putting grammar in its place by sketching out three areas where I think it is useful:

1. *As a source of information about language and language learning for teachers.* Grammar study, especially the study of transformational-generative grammar, provides numerous insights into the language learning process, and it is a vital part of a teacher's background. In fact, it is through the study of transformational grammar that one can most clearly see why the teaching of grammar does not promote language change. T-G grammar, in short, contains the seeds of destruction for grammar as the dominating component of English education. (Again see the recommended books for some introductory texts.)

2. *As a source of terms and tools for talking about language.* There are times when a knowledge of grammatical terminology provides a convenient way of talking about language. The discussion of language that will go on in the English class can sometimes be simplified through use of common terms. I advocate that in the junior high years the teacher offer a brief unit introducing most of the basic terms and definitions of grammar. However, this should be a *very* brief unit, and the teacher should watch closely to see whether it is producing any positive results. After all, there are many ways of talking about language and composition, and grammar is only one of them. In many cases, the time spent teaching grammar would be much more effectively given over to additional writing or speaking activities.

Several years ago when I was working on some composition materials for a language arts series, the publisher told me to delay choosing a grammatical system until the publisher and another writer could settle on which kind of grammar they wanted to use for a proposed grammar strand. While they were making up their minds I wrote, and I discovered that I never felt handicapped by the lack of terms. Most of what I wanted to say about writing could be phrased without any reference to grammar. Thus the argument that children and young people must understand grammar to analyze their writing properly is fallacious. However, some students can employ the abstract language of grammar to make changes in usage items. The brief introduction allows those who can to learn how, while not handicapping the others.

3. *As an elective course for high school students.* When divorced from concerns about usage and correctness, grammar courses—especially those involving the comparative examination of traditional, structural, and transformational grammar—can be an interesting study for some students. Offered as an elective, a course in grammar seems a perfectly legitimate option within a curriculum. It would however be important to define the aims of such a course clearly, to prevent students from thinking it would somehow improve their writing or get them ready for college.

TEACHING STANDARD ENGLISH

In *Teaching English Usage* Robert Pooley offered what has become a classic definition of "good English."

Good English is that form of speech which is appropriate to the purposes of the speaker, true to the language as it is, and comfortable to speaker and listener. It is the product of custom, neither cramped by rule nor freed from all restraint; it is never fixed, but changes with the organic life of the language.

From Robert Pooley, *Teaching English Usage* (Urbana: National Council of Teachers of English, 1946), p. 14.

It was an important statement in the history of English because it acknowledged the sociological nature of usage and dialects, and it helped to destroy the notion of a *single* standard form of the language. Pooley's definition allows for the linguistic fact that within specific language communities, people can be quite comfortable with language forms not generally found acceptable in broader circles, and it recognizes that it would be quite unnatural for speakers to change their style of speaking within that language community.

From those ideas has grown the concept of bi-dialectalism, which argues that the schools should not try to eradicate a natural home dialect but should encourage children to develop one or more additional dialects for use in other situations. The concept is an attempt to be humane and understanding about dialects, while at the same time allowing students to extend their linguistic capabilities.

Despite this enlightened attitude, bi-dialectalism has led to an enormous amount of debate, as these conflicting statements of James Sledd and Beryl Loftman Bailey suggest:

Predators can and do use dialect differences to exploit and oppress, because ordinary people can be made to doubt their own value and to accept subservience if they can be made to despise the speech of their fathers. Obligatory bi-dialectalism for minorities is only another mode of exploitation, another way of making blacks behave as whites would like them to. It is unnecessary for communication, since the ability to understand other dialects is easily attained. . . . In the immediate present, the time and money now wasted on bi-dialectalism should be spent on teaching the children of the minorities to read. . . . the direct attack on minority language, the attempt to compel bi-dialectalism, should be abandoned for an attempt to open the minds and enhance the lives of the poor and ignorant. At the same time, every attempt should be made to teach the majority to understand the life and language of the oppressed. Linguistic change is the effect and not the cause of social change. If the majority can rid itself of its prejudices, and if the minorities can get or be given an education, differences between dialects are unlikely to hurt anybody very much.

From James Sledd, "Bi-dialectalism: The Linguistics of White Supremacy," *The English Journal*, December 1969. Copyright © 1969 by the National Council of Teachers of English. Reprinted by permission of the publisher and the author.

Since speakers of social dialects do not seem to have any difficulty communicating with each other (whatever the difficulties may be in communicating with nonmembers of the group), we must recognize their linguistic system as a valid code and ascribe to them the same attitudes in the teaching of English that we would give to speakers with *patently* different language systems. That is, we must examine the code, make contrastive analyses with English, and on the basis of what we know about second language learning design programs for teaching the standard to social dialect speakers. . . . I think our raison d'être as English teachers is to produce good users of English, and no argument, no matter how feasible, should sway us from our task. Not all our pupils will achieve the standards we set for them, but this does not lessen our duty to them. English teachers must get themselves out of the corner into which the sociologists and psychologists have maneuvered them. We certainly have no right to police the youngsters' language outside the school, but we have a commitment to provide them with language which they can use to their personal advantage when their school days are over. Nor have we any right to denigrate the language of the community from which the child comes. But once he crosses the threshold of school and enters our classrooms, he has given us a contract to *change* him in many ways, one of which is his language behavior. *We cannot break that contract!*

From Beryl Loftman Bailey, "Social Dialects and the Teaching of English," in Stephen Dunning, ed., *English for the Junior High Years.* Copyright © 1969 by the National Council of Teachers of English. Reprinted by permission of the publisher and the author.

The dialect problem is also complicated by social and racial conditions in this country. Teachers find themselves in a dilemma: If they refuse to teach middle-class standard English, they will be accused by some of being racist, of denying black children access to a standard middle-class world. If they offer instruction in standard English, they may be attacked by more militant groups on the ground that they are forcing children to give up their cultural background along with their language. Some teachers have tried to solve the problem by requiring instruction in standard English, then letting the student decide whether or not to use it. This nonsolution seems rather like giving obligatory instruction in television repair, then giving children the choice of whether or not they wish to pursue it as a career.

No easy solution is forthcoming, but it does help one to draw back from the immediate problem to look at the question in broad terms. First, as Sledd has suggested, it seems apparent that teaching standard English, by whatever method, will not automatically open new doors to children. Often the lack of standard English is merely used as an excuse for rejecting people on racial, ethnic, or other grounds. Further, until society itself is better prepared to accept and integrate members of minority groups, there may be little value in providing minorities with standard English. Language is learned in response to needs felt by the language user. Unless students recognize a real opportunity to participate in a standard English community, they will not willingly learn its dialect.

Teachers might accomplish much more by approaching the problem indirectly. For instance, by helping students participate as fully as possible in the community of language through a variety of experiences—reading and writing, speaking and listening, role playing—teachers can ensure that students are comfortable users of language in many situations. When and if students are given a meaningful opportunity to participate in a standard English community—through school, employment, or housing—they will be better able to adapt their language use.

In addition, teachers ought to be concerned about destroying some of the old myths about good grammar, good usage, and upward mobility. If the schools spent as much time trying to end linguistic bias as they presently spend trying to enforce standard English, they might go a long way toward solving the problem. Certainly the teacher should concentrate on helping students—especially speakers of dialects other than standard English—understand what dialects are, where they come from, and what their effects on listeners are. Given such background understanding, students will be in a much better position to decide whether or not they want to change the way they talk or write.

OFFERING HELP WITH CORRECTNESS

I believe that the philosophy of writing (and, by implication, speaking) for the here and now, described in the previous chapter, offers the teacher a practical philosophy that can help resolve the dialects/correctness dilemma. The here-and-now approach strongly emphasizes the public use of language, recognizing that as students write and speak for audiences, they will realistically encounter situations where the use of a variant of standard English is appropriate.

What then? How do we provide the help students need to get their work into a form appropriate for their audience? One of my former students, Judy Kortright, a teacher in Lansing, Michigan, struggled with the problem and came up with the idea of providing a variety of approaches to editing and correctness in the classroom. In *Teaching Correctness: An Alternative to Grammar* (Detroit: Michigan Council of Teachers of English, 1977), she wrote:

> Every year (at least once or twice) a nagging thought enters my brain: "Why aren't you teaching grammar, parts of speech, diagramming? Sometimes the question comes from a comment by a well-meaning parent, "When my son got to high school, he had to diagram sentences. He didn't even know where to begin." Or I am reminded that some teachers "believe in grammar" when a colleague down the hall comes running into my room, "Do you have any extra copies of *Warriner's* for eighth grade?"
>
> . . . I know, however, that there is no documented evidence in the literature to prove that the teaching of grammar improves writing skills. . . . I know, too, from personal experience that hour after hour on nouns and verbs only produces boredom, not good writers. The only students who really benefit from grammar study are students who already read, write, and speak well, or those who are truly interested in how language is formed and works. For the average and especially for the marginal English student, grammar study is a waste of time.
>
> So what are the alternatives? What can I do to salve my conscience, to justify the lack of grammar drills in my classes? The answer for me, at least, is to find all the ways I can to teach *correctness*.

Ms. Kortright created what she called a "Correctness Corner" in her room: "this can be a table or cubicle in the corner, a designated desk, or even a book shelf." At this activity center she provides the following kinds of materials:

Usage handbooks (either commercial handbooks or materials created by the teacher).

Usage activities (teacher-made activity cards reviewing the basic usage shibboleths: *lay-lie, sit-set,* etc.).

Posters and charts (commercial and teacher-made materials that make help with correctness accessible).

Examples of good student writing.

Reference books (dictionaries, thesauruses, spelling demon lists).

Revision checklists (sequences of questions that guide students through the editing and copyreading of a paper).

Most important about the Correctness Corner, I think, is that it individualizes the process so that students can get the help they need at the time it is important. Further, the approach stresses independence, so that instead of the teacher constantly serving as proofreader, the students themselves become familiar with correctness aids and how to use them.

EXPLORING THE DIMENSIONS OF LANGUAGE

In all the debates over grammar and correctness, teachers often lose sight of the fact that language studies are complex and diverse, offering many classroom teaching possibilities. I am convinced that if students knew more of language beyond correctness—that is, if they better understood how language itself functions—they would be more effective writers and readers.

There are many alternative forms of language study that fall in the general area of "sociolinguistics"—the study of language, human beings, and their interactions—and it is an area that students find fascinating. Although knowledge of language and society will not automatically improve students' language skills, it often helps them deepen their feel for language and how it shapes their lives.

I propose that teachers explore language through "interludes," language mini-units of a day or a week. After students have finished a round of projects or a major project in reading and writing, pause to let them try some of the following language explorations.

1. *Body Talk.* In his book *Body Language* (New York: Bantam, 1971), Julius Fast presents a readable, informative introduction to "kinesics" the study of how people interact through physical mannerisms. The concept of body language is intriguing (and even a bit awesome), and young people of many ages enjoy talking about it and exploring its consequences. "Body Talk," a simulation game published by *Psychology Today* (P.O. Box 4758, Clinton, Iowa) teaches some basics of body language by having participants express emotions nonverbally. "Emotional Charades"—a game the teacher can develop—accomplishes the same thing by

having students mime basic emotions—love, hate, excitement, fear—using only facial expressions or physical movement. Some students may enjoy observing people at a distance and trying to record their nonverbal "conversations." Body talk also offers some interesting possibilities for film making and photography, both of which can supply visual data for class analysis and discussion.

2. *Artifacts*. The objects that people use and venerate tell a great deal about their value systems. Ask students to assume that your city has been covered by a giant lava flow, then unearthed by archaeologists from an alien culture hundreds of years later. Have each student choose one surviving object that the aliens might find and do an analysis of the unspoken "language" of that object. What would the strangers conclude if they dug up the Golden Arches of a McDonald's hamburger palace? What might they learn from a snowmobile? From the architecture of a city? From one of its automobiles or from parks or factories? As a variation, have each student bring in an object he or she prizes personally and turn it over to a partner for analysis.

3. *Baby Talk*. Psycholinguists who have examined the earliest stages of language acquisition have learned to write "baby grammars" that describe the young child's growing mastery of English. Ask students who have young brothers and sisters (ages one to three years) to bring in some tape recordings of their speech. Split your students into groups and have them discover the regularities—the "grammar"—of the child's speech. How does babbling seem to work? What kinds of words do children learn first? What patterns do they use for two-word strings? How do they seem to move from two- and three-word strings to whole sentences? While students should not try to duplicate the complex work of linguists in the field, studying baby talk brings about many insights into how human beings learn and use language. For helpful explanations and examples of the writing of baby grammars, see Roger Brown and Ursula Bellugi, "Three Processes in the Child's Acquisition of Syntax," in *Language and Learning*, edited by Janet Emig, James Fleming, and Helen Popp (New York: Harcourt Brace Jovanovich, 1966).

4. *Tutoring*. Find a class of younger students who have reading difficulties and arrange for interested students from your class to read with and to them. Hold frequent discussions with your team of tutors to discuss their observations and problems. For practical suggestions on organizing a tutoring program, see Leon Westbrock, "Input: A Communications Experience," *The English Journal*, October 1973.

5. *Greetings*. In *Relations in Public* (New York: Basic Books, 1972), Erving Goffman analyzed the ritualistic uses of language like greetings, farewells, inquiries into health and the weather. He tried to discover the real meanings behind these messages. (We say, "How are you?" for example, not to inquire about health, but to establish a communications setting

for further discussion.) Give your students the same task—observing and analyzing some of the secret communications that underlie greetings and farewells. Some questions that they might seek to answer:

How do greetings and farewells differ depending on whether people are friends, enemies, strangers, or rivals?
How do styles of ritual language differ with age? With culture or race?
What happens when people violate the unwritten rules of ritual talk (e.g., by *not* making a ritual greeting before speaking or by answering in detail when asked, "How 'ya doin'?")?

6. *Euphemism.* George Orwell's 1946 essay, "Politics and the English Language," remains a most effective attack on the use of euphemistic language to hide a person's true intent and purposes. After having them read the essay, send your students out to collect examples of euphemism at all levels of school and society. Simply analyzing and laughing at euphemism helps to make students more sensitive to it, but you can also encourage them to explore euphemism by such activities as translating clear prose into gobbledygook or writing instructions for a simple process—scrambling an egg—in euphemistic language. You might also want to explore the protective aspect of euphemism. Have the students role play some scenes in a society where everyone is blunt, direct, forthright, and to the point. Does this become the best of all possible worlds?

7. *Doublespeak.* Watergate made the nation acutely conscious of "doublespeak," political language that obscures and covers up rather than revealing the truth. In *Teaching About Doublespeak* (Urbana: National Council of Teachers of English, 1976), Daniel Diederich and his fellow contributors explore the investigation of political jargon and gobbledygook in the classroom. Why not have your students investigate the misuse of language through published statements in your area, then possibly present a set of Doublespeak Awards for the worst examples they find?

8. *Dialect Study.* Few people understand how or why dialects work, and too many adults are obsessed by dialect differences. To help bring enlightenment, engage the students in an informal examination of dialects. If you have speakers of different dialects, set up groups in which the students learn about alternative expressions. Have the two groups prepare bi-dialectal dictionaries of each other's dialects. Even if you don't have a rich mixture of dialects in a class, there are a number of investigations students can conduct around school and community to explore dialects. One example: Have students listen for the nefarious "ain't" and chart its occurrences in speech. For numerous other examples, see Jean Malmstrom's *Language in Society* (Rochelle Park: Hayden, 1973 and Roger Shuy's *Discovering American Dialects* (Urbana: National Council of Teachers of English, 1967).

9. *Inventing a New Language.* Many variations of this activity are possible. One is to "abolish" English and have the students design the theoretical model for a new, ideal language. What would be the most efficient way for this language to express relationships? What features of English would the students maintain? What aspects would they eliminate? How would the new language be written? The students might even try to develop samples of this language.

Alternatively, students can create a new lexicon based on English syntax—that is, they can invent a new vocabulary for the existing word order. "Nadsat," the teen language in Anthony Burgess's *A Clockwork Orange*, provides one example. Orwell's essay on "Newspeak" in *1984* provides another.

Students can also create pig Latin forms, systematically altering word structure so that only someone in possession of the code can translate. Developing sign languages offers additional possibilities.

10. *The Language of Personal Space.* Like body talk and the language of greetings and farewells, people have secret languages that involve the use of personal space. In *The Silent Language* (New York: Fawcett, 1962) and *The Hidden Dimension* (Garden City: Doubleday, 1966), Edward Hall investigated some of these cultural-linguistic uses of space. As a classroom activity students can duplicate some of Hall's experiments with face-to-face conversation. After pointing out that various cultures find different speaking distances comfortable, ask the students to discover what their own speaking conventions are. At what distance—two feet, one foot, eighteen inches—do students become uncomfortably close to one another? At what distance are they uncomfortably far away? How do we feel toward people who stand nose-to-nose with us in conversation?

In *The Hidden Dimension*, Hall goes into more complex areas of the language of space, including such problems as overcrowding, the design and layout of floor space, the theft of urban space by automobiles, and the human's need for privacy. As with other physical languages, students can deduce much of the structure of the language of space through simple experimentation and analysis. Again, photography and film making projects can easily evolve from the class study.

11. *Games and Puzzles.* Games involving language are as old as humankind, and such games often help to develop a sense of language. *Scrabble*, for instance, is a game that many students enjoy, and it serves incidentally as a vocabulary builder. Crossword puzzles, diacrostics, and anagrams are enjoyed by other students. Most bookstores carry dozens of paperback collections of word games, attesting to the popularity of this pastime. Purchase a half-dozen of these books, tear them into individual sheets, and file them away to produce a game collection of several hundred activities.

12. *The Recorded Rhetoric.* The formal study of rhetoric—rules and advice about writing—seldom changes students' writing. However, when

students raise questions about writing voluntarily, rhetorical advice may be welcomed. One of the obvious and best sources of rhetorical advice is the students themselves, after they have encountered the problems, pleasures, and technical strategies of composition. Toward the end of a school year, establish a library of tape-recorded rhetorical advice for use by next year's classes. Ask the participating students to choose a form they know well and to tape-record a five- to ten-minute informal talk of what they know about it. Often the speakers can also place some of their own writing on file to serve as illustrations and models. If teachers deliberately cultivate this practice, they will very quickly accumulate tapes on such diverse topics as, say, haiku, advertising, film making, and the essay.

13. *Analyzing Handwriting.* This activity won't necessarily improve penmanship but may produce a good deal more interest in it. Many handwriting analysis books are available in paperback stores and at supermarket check-out counters. Tell students about the basic principles of analysis, or let that be the topic for a small group presentation, and let them go. Students can analyze one another's writing, discuss signatures of famous personalities, experiment with disguising their own handwriting, or play guessing games about signatures.

14. *Propaganda.* An examination of World War II propaganda— German, Japanese, and Allied—makes a fascinating study. Examples are readily available—from tapes of Hitler's speeches to copies of leaflets dropped from planes on enemy troops. After a study of these materials and some discussion of how they work, turn the students loose to find examples of contemporary propaganda, often more subtle but seldom using new or different techniques. There is also a *Propaganda Game* as part of the Wiff 'n' Proof series of logic games. Though somewhat sophisticated, the game may appeal to many of your students and help them learn a number of propaganda terms and techniques.

15. *Learning a Language.* For years parents and teachers have rationalized the study of grammar on the ground that it was necessary for students engaged in the study of foreign languages. Not to miss a good bet, foreign language teachers have claimed utility for their discipline in helping students understand English. Both groups have little support for their positions. English teachers should not teach grammar simply because other teachers use a grammatical method. Teaching through grammar isn't any more successful in foreign languages than it is in English. Moreover, research has yet to show any direct correlation between skill in foreign languages and skill in English.

However, when divorced from utilitarian teaching schemes, knowing—or better, using—a foreign language may well help people become more comfortable, competent users of their native language. In classes that include both native speakers of English and speakers of another language, let the two groups teach each other. Drill and exercises are not necessary.

Often simply allowing the students to struggle with one another's languages over everyday concerns will be sufficient. If you don't have a mixed class of this sort, you might want to seek out tutoring opportunities for those students who are interested in foreign languages and acknowledge their work as part of their regular English studies.

16. *Study of Names.* The study of names can be an interesting class project. A common approach is for students to use a desk dictionary to find out the significance or meaning of their own name. Then the students move outward, first studying names around their city—names of streets, mountains, lakes—then names around the state and country. An excellent resource is Alan Wolk's *The Naming of America* (New York: Thomas Nelson, 1977).

17. *Logotypes.* A logotype or trademark is a self-contained message, a one-word visual language designed to identify a product or company and to project an image of it. Most industries spend a remarkable amount of time developing, testing, and marketing any new logo that they choose to use. Have students collect a number of logos (they can easily find hundreds in newspapers, magazines, and the yellow pages) and analyze the language. Afterward, invite the students to develop some trademarks of their own, perhaps a new insignia or logo for the school, for your class, for fictitious companies, or for themselves.

18. *Codes and Ciphers.* -•-•/--/-••/•/•••//•-/•-•/•//•-///--/-•--/•••/-/•/•-•/-•--/// (Codes are a mystery.) Codes and ciphers are as old as history, and literally thousands of ways of sending secret messages have been generated. John Laffin's *Codes and Ciphers* (New York: Abelard-Schuman, 1964) is an excellent short history of the subject, well illustrated, so that after reading it students can duplicate and use codes and devices like the Zodiac Alphabet, the Skytale, the Porta-Table, and the Pig-Pen Cipher. Another good book, more advanced but filled with how-to-do-it information, is James Raymond Wolfe's *Secret Writing: The Craft of the Cryptographer* (New York: McGraw-Hill, 1970).

19. *Inductive Definitions.* The great controversy over *Webster's New International Dictionary,* Third Edition, gave ample evidence of public ignorance about the nature of dictionaries and of the processes of lexicography. Assign the class a project of defining a word—just a single word. Students are not to consult dictionaries; rather, they should collect citations—examples of the word in use—and from that evidence, work inductively toward a definition. Words like "break" or "fast" (or "breakfast") are a good choice because of their functions as different parts of speech. From this activity, you can help students understand some of the ways in which words take on meaning, while helping them realize that meanings are flexible and evolutionary.

20. *Printing Processes.* The printing of books and magazines is interesting for many students, and modern printing processes are nothing short

of miraculous in their speed, quality, and accuracy. Let the students investigate printing processes, beginning with hand-set, single-sheet presses and working toward computer-set type and offset presses. A visit to a printing plant for whole class or just for interested students would be appropriate. When young people learn how books, magazines, and newspapers are made, their reading interest in those publications seems to increase considerably.

21. *Electronic Communications.* The effect of modern electronics on communications systems has been as miraculous as the effect of printing. Encourage your students who have interests in science and engineering to study electronics and the communications field. Many nontechnical volumes have been written about such devices as the transistor or diode chip and their effect on communications systems. Other topics of interest might be computer technology, miniaturization, laser beams as a form of communication, television and radio, and the electronics of the telephone.

22. *The Language of Advertising.* Although teachers often deprecate the "bad grammar" of ads, many advertisments show extremely clever use of language through wordplay and puns. In "Teaching English Through the Language of Advertising" (*The English Journal*, February 1976), Don Nilsen shows that the way advertisers break rules is highly creative. He uses ads to demonstrate everything from phonetics ("Emperor Lawnmowers: Built to Last a Lawn Time!") to ambiguities ("Salem refreshes naturally.")

23. *CB Languages.* The CB craze has died down a bit in this country, but millions of Americans have citizen's band units in their cars, vans, trucks, and campers. CB has a language of its own, almost incomprehensible to the novice, but one that demonstrates a number of regularities common to all language. For example, a person who speaks a nonstandard form of CB talk is frequently ostracized by other users. In "Breaker, Breaker, Broke" (*The English Journal*, December 1976), Harvey Daniels reviews a number of classroom teaching ideas and discusses ways of actually getting CB units into the school.

24. *The Language of Science.* Science books are filled with marvelous and curious terms. Where do they come from? What is the origin of such terms as *laser, biodegradable, black hole, quark, sea urchin, mollusk,* and *mesomorph*? Conduct an etymology unit on scientific words. As a variation, teach your students to read the ingredients labels on packages to learn what they are eating. Why must Disodium EDTA be added to "prevent spoilage" in something that is labeled, "Fresh, Hometown, Hearth-Baked Bread"?

25. *The Language of Law.* Collect samples of legal documents: insurance policies, contracts, warranties, rules of the road. Help the students learn to decode the language, both through examining technical or special-

ized words and through studying the very careful wording that compli-
cates legal writing. As a variation, have students study advertising and pro-
motional claims and disclaimers and the use of "waffle" or "weasel" words
that mean something other than what they seem to be saying. What does it
mean if 52 percent of people either preferred Brand A or had no preference between Brand A and Brand B?

These 25 activities barely begin to scratch the surface of possible language explorations for the English class. As interludes, they change the
pace of the class. As valid linguistic activities, they heighten students' critical awareness of something they consume and produce in prodigious quantities: language.

EXPLORATIONS AND RESOURCES

- If you want to be able to answer the questions of students about correctness matters, you need to have on hand a great deal of diverse material to satisfy different
learners. You need the usual handbooks plus games, visuals, and self-instructional
packets that present the material in many ways. Choose a skill that a student
might want to master (say, how to proofread a page or how to use quotation
marks) and develop a range of materials presenting it from several points of
view. Field-test your materials with students. If you are working with a group of
people, each person can choose a different skill and ditto or reproduce the materials to share.
- Some issues centering on bi-dialectalism:

    Can a teacher honestly preserve the home dialect while teaching an alternative
    school dialect?
    Is the bi-dialectal approach merely a way of disguising the teaching of a uniform
    standard?
    Does possession of a standard dialect in fact give members of a minority upward
    mobility?
    If the schools compel bi-dialectal studies for members of minority groups, should
    students from the "standard" community be compelled to learn the minority
    dialect so that they, too, are bi-dialectal?

- A white middle-class teacher is working in an inner city school where the students speak a nonstandard dialect that the teacher sometimes has difficulty understanding. If good English is that which is "appropriate to the purpose of the
speaker, true to the language as it is, and comfortable to speaker and listener,"
what should the teacher do about the students' speech forms?
- A broadly based skills program that puts grammar and correctness in their place
is likely to run into some opposition from parents and administrators who will cry
"Neglect!" Interview some basics enthusiasts to explore the reasons for their concern. Develop some explanations that allow a teacher to run a broadly based language program while still providing satisfactory evidence that basics are being
adequately covered.
- Create some materials for language interludes. These might be done as individual

resource or activity packets, or as handouts for use with an entire class. Start with those of my 25 that you found most interesting, then branch off into the recommended readings that follow and discover other possibilities.

Related Readings

For the teacher seeking more information on the various grammatical systems, I recommend two books by Suzette Hayden Elgin: *What Is Linguistics?* (Englewood Cliffs: Prentice-Hall, 1973) and *Transformational Grammar: A Primer for Rank Beginners* (Urbana: National Council of Teachers of English, 1975). Also useful is Constance Weaver's *Grammar for Teachers: Perspectives and Definitions* (NCTE, 1979), which explores the general nature of grammars and presents a grammar that combines aspects of traditional, structural, and transformational grammars.

On dialects and usage, see Robert Pooley's *Teaching English Usage* (available in an updated, revised edition from the National Council of Teachers of English) or Martin Joos's *The Five Clocks* (New York: Harcourt Brace Jovanovich, 1967), a lucid exploration of how language usage shifts with various situations. For an excellent discussion of black English and its origins, as well as consideration of implications for schooling, read Geneva Smitherman's *Talkin' and Testifyin'* (New York: Holt, Rinehart and Winston, 1977).

If you are looking for more language interludes, you should examine the classroom activities suggested in S. I. Hayakawa's *Language in Thought and Action* (New York: Harcourt Brace Jovanich, 1972). It is the most interesting basic source of ideas and information in this area, packed with ideas for language experiments. I also recommend that you obtain a copy of William Sparke and Clark McKowen's *Montage* (New York: Macmillan, 1970), a mind-blowing book done in supergraphics that contains hundreds of interesting investigations in language. *Montage* is aimed at the college market, but your students will enjoy selected investigations. James Miller's and my *Writing in Reality* (New York: Harper & Row, 1978) also includes these kinds of explorations and provides an example of how they can be woven directly into a writing program, rather than being treated simply as interludes in the flow of a course.

12
The Spoken Language

The development of the personality is inextricably bound up with the development of language. Language is the basic and essential instrument in the humanising of the species: without it thought above very primitive levels is impossible. Language and man are in continual interaction; change the man in some way and you change the language he uses; change the language he uses and you change the man. On the one hand the process of growth through education and experience causes him to reach out for new language in which to understand and communicate. On the other hand this language contains new thoughts and shades of thought, new feeling and shades of feeling, which help to determine such growth. His ability to direct rather than to be directed by experience, his ability to establish human relationships, are intimately related to his capacity for language; the frustrations of the inarticulate go deep. And it must be borne in mind that "language" in this context is overwhelmingly the *spoken* language; even in the (historically) rare literate societies such as our own this remains true. Without oracy human fulfillment is impossible; speech and personality are one.

From Andrew Wilkinson, *Spoken English.* Copyright © 1965 by the author and the *Educational Review*, University of Birmingham. Reprinted by permission of the author and publisher.

Whether its form is conversation, lecture, gossip, discussion, or monologue, the use of spoken English is one of the most critical operations that a member of the community of language learns. From birth, people acquire information, clarify their own thoughts and beliefs, and transmit ideas and information to others principally by means of talk and conversation. By far the greatest part of the languaging we do involves oral English, either receptive or productive. Even nonreaders and haters of writing have been known to enjoy talking—over Coke or telephone—for hours. As James

Britton has remarked, our lives are "afloat on a sea of talk."

Despite the pervasiveness of the spoken language in our lives, it has seldom been given much attention in the schools. Speech activities are often isolated in separate courses or brought into the English class only as enrichment units. Further, speech instruction seldom moves beyond a painful round of five-minute talks, followed by an evaluation of voice quality, enunciation, and eye contact. Even classes based on a seminar or discussion format are too often centered on the teacher. In many classes, "discuss" actually means "keep talking till you find out what the teacher wants." It is interesting to observe that the term *discuss* has even taken on a meaning in written English. A typical essay or examination question will ask the student to "discuss the effects of the French Revolution on. . . ." In this context, "discuss" in fact means "explicate," and in many classes, oral discussion is little more than an explication by the teacher, with occasional token questions tossed out for the students.

This neglect and abuse of oral English may well grow from a kind of blindness to our linguistic environment. As Marshall McLuhan has observed, "One thing about which a fish knows absolutely nothing is water." It can be said with equal accuracy, "One thing about which talkers know next to nothing is talk." It is clear that a large percentage of the population lack significant understanding of the way oral English affects their life.

TEACHING ORAL ENGLISH

At the heart of the problem is the point that teaching oral English is complicated. Linguists and sociologists are only beginning to understand the complexity of the oral communication process. By comparison, print literacy is simple: Everything is put down clearly on paper; there are 26 letters of the alphabet, no more, no less; the basic rules of punctuation and spelling are relatively fixed. Oral language, on the other hand, involves a complex interaction of speaker and listener, of voice, tone, style, intonation, nonverbal expression. For example, experts in Kinesis—body language—recognize that a person sends out hundreds of nonverbal signals—eyebrow twitches, frowns, leg crossings and uncrossings—every second while he or she is speaking and listening. When teachers try to contain, to teach oral English, they often present oversimplified advice, rather like that of the nineteenth-century elocutionary textbooks: "To emphasize a point, point the index finger directly upward, and moving the finger in a circular or spiral manner, extend the arm upward, to the point that the arm is fully extended above the shoulder." (Try it! Where did you last see that gesture practiced? What was your impression of the speaker?)

The spoken language cannot be "taught." People learn to speak and listen by doing it successfully. Conversely, they become inarticulate and inept when their oral language experiences are unsuccessful or constrained. Learning the skills of oral English is closely related to using them, and the teacher should thus focus attention on making the classroom a place where the use of spoken language is strongly supported. The student who is experienced in many speech areas—conversation, dialogue, discussion—is likely to be a fuller participant in the community of language than one who has spent the school years uttering one-sentence answers to recitation questions.

A wide range of spoken language activities are valuable in a classroom. These include speech that is principally expressive—done for the purposes and needs of the speaker—and productive, aimed at communicating with an audience or a listener. Some activities are spontaneous and occur without the teacher; others must be planned and structured.

THE USES OF CONVERSATION

It is especially important that the teacher consider the underlying motivation behind speech activities. It is through attempting to understand what happens when people talk that teachers are best able to structure a classroom setting that supports spoken language. For instance, conversation—chat, gossip, rappin', shooting the breeze—has been consistently misunderstood in the schools and regarded as something outside the educational process. I have often found myself cutting off student conversations at the beginning of a class: "Alright now, let's get down to *business*." The fact is, conversation is "business" of a very serious kind. Chat serves a great many different functions in a person's life, many of which are not obvious at a superficial level of examination.

For instance, sociologists and linguists have identified a number of uses of conversation by black youngsters, each style serving a different kind of psychological-sociological function. There are such variants as "rapping" (talking to express one's personality), "jiving" or "shucking" (putting somebody on, usually a white person), "running it down" (giving information or advice), "gripping" (acknowledging a superior without losing face), "copping a plea" (surrendering and pleading for mercy), and "sounding" (trying to arouse or release emotions through boasts, insults, and accusations).

Most of us recognize a similar range of languaging behavior in our own conversations. We use chat and gossip in many ways to establish our self-esteem, to make initial contact with others, to assess feelings, to form relationships, and seek information—in essence, to structure our world and to compare it to the world of others. Chat is the spoken equivalent of the writing journal, a language form that operates on the borderline between a person's inner and outer worlds.

This is not intended to glorify chitchat or to suggest that teachers are doing a good job helping students become orally literate if they merely let them exchange trivia. However, a teacher must recognize the critical role of conversation in people's lives and support it—welcome it—inside the classroom. In fact, one of the major ways in which people will become good conversationalists instead of gossipmongers is for the school to allow them to chat about matters of more than a trivial nature. People can discuss complex ideas as comfortably as they gossip about a new detergent. Through experiences in literature and composing, the teacher can provide students with a steadily expanding series of topics for conversation.

Students should feel free to discuss personal and academic problems, projects, books, television programs, films, one another, people, and world problems. When acknowledged as important, conversation will become the foundation for the entire spoken language program. Indeed, without students who are secure and competent conversationalists, other oral language activities will be dull, static, or ineffectual.

While conversation is not something easily structured, the teacher can demonstrate support for it by a device like the *question box*. Set up a container somewhere in your class in which students can deposit questions that they would like to have a chance to discuss. From time to time, open up the question box and let the students hash over one of the topics—as an entire class or in small groups. Even the room environment can contribute to the ease with which chat takes place, and the teacher might want to set up a conversation corner where students can go to talk.

STORYTELLING

John Rouse has suggested the intriguing idea that "we are all storytellers, and our lives are the fictions we have made."[1] As "fiction makers," he suggests, people abstract from their past experiences to create stories, and they use stories both to assess that experience and to sketch out scenarios for their future lives. Rouse's formula for teaching language use is simple and effective: Get people to tell you a good story and you will have released the real language power that they have inside themselves. Storytelling, like the less formal forms of conversing, serves many functions. It is often as important to the storyteller as to the listener.

Stories can be told in many ways—in speech and writing, in poetry, prose, and drama—but the most fundamental kind of storytelling is done face-to-face. Like conversation, storytelling is more easily promoted than taught, better encouraged than demanded. But there are a number of experiences one can provide to get it started.

One technique used by Rouse is to have students interview each other, with the listener/interviewer assigned the task of digging out the other person's "real" story. Eventually the *listener* retells the story

[1] "Fiction Making," *K-Eight* (September 1971).

to others, with the original storyteller having the option of correcting and amplifying.

Reminiscing is a natural starting point for storytelling. Without drifting to the summer vacation motif, the teacher can often lead off a class with a story about his or her own past that invites students to share some of their own experiences.

Literature—especially stories by and about adolescents—provides innumerable starting points. Following the reading of a good story, the teacher can simply ask, "Has anything like this ever happened to you?"

Tall tales, boasting, and exaggeration have an important storytelling function, since in creating an exaggerated tale, the students draw upon, expand, and develop their own view of the world.

Storytelling is a natural extension of conversation, and often the teacher can initiate it simply by saying "tell me more" when an incident or anecdote flashes by in informal conversation.

In many classes, once the storytelling concept is introduced, the students become hooked on the idea, and become habitual storytellers and story collectors.

DIALOGUES AND PARTNERSHIPS

The dialogue—a conversation between two people—is the fundamental unit of spoken English. Dialogue is simple and direct, an especially efficient form for productive work. Unfortunately, the dynamics of the two-member group has been neglected. Typically, students work together only to correct papers ("Exchange papers, class"), and *collaboration* is a term that to many teachers is synonymous with "cheating." While two-member groups have occasional problems with freeloading, inbreeding, or compounding of errors, they also avoid many of the problems that evolve in larger groups. Their use should be fully exploited in the classroom. Among the partnership projects that I have found valuable are the following:

1. *Collaborative writing (I).* Students work together as co-authors of a piece of writing—poem, play, story, or essay. This technique allows students to share writing skills with each other and to produce a stronger piece of writing than either could alone.

2. *Collaborative writing (II).* Students work on their own writing in partnership with another person, who serves as a writing coach in:

> *prewriting.* (The students share ideas and talk over what they plan to write.)
>
> *writing.* (The partners coach each other through rough spots and listen to readings of the drafts.)
>
> *postwriting.* (The collaborators serve as editors and proofreaders for

each other, each taking responsibility for getting the other's work in the best possible shape.)

3. *Minidebates*. Students take opposite sides of an issue and discuss it, either for themselves alone or before an audience.

4. *Response to Literature*. Partners read the same poem, story, or novel and work out their interpretation and response to it.

5. *Interviews (I)*. One student interviews another about an area of expertise.

6. *Interviews (II)*. As a team, students interview an outside expert: a parent, someone in business or industry, a community leader, a guest speaker.

7. *Dramatic Presentations*. The partners prepare a dramatic presentation of some of their work—say, a collection of poems or a two-character play.

In recent years, a number of writers have discussed the values of education in the conventional one-room schoolhouse, pointing out that in those schools, children gained a sense of community that may have been lost in large public schools. Much of that sense of community grew from collaborative learning and partnership projects. The teacher in the one-room schoolhouse was simply too busy to work with every child as often as necessary, and partnerships were set up, with older children teaching younger, the skilled teaching the unskilled. While few see a return to the one-room schoolhouse as a cure for our educational woes, the advantages of a strong collaborative learning program should not be ignored. The teacher can re-create the one-room schoolhouse, in spirit if not in fact, through the extensive use of partnership learning activities.

TEACHER-LED DISCUSSIONS

One of the most difficult skills for a teacher to master, and one that must be refined throughout a teaching career, is that of leading whole class discussions. The teacher faces a collection of 30 or more students and somehow must get them to talk. In its weakest form (which also happens to be a negative by-product of one-room schooling), teacher-led discussion is *recitation*, with students supplying answers to questions in order to demonstrate mastery of a text. At its best, class discussion takes on a momentum of its own under the gentle guidance of the teacher, with talk helping to generate new knowledge and understanding.

The heart of the teacher-led discussion is *the question*, and the quality and kinds of questions that teachers ask will make or break any class session.

Robert Nash and David Shiman have cited research that shows how unaware teachers are of the kinds and frequency of questions that they ask: "Summarizing the few research studies done on the questioning proc-ess, Seymour Sarason reports that while elementary teachers thought they averaged between *twelve* and *twenty* questions per half hour, actually the number ranged between *forty-five* and *one hundred and fifty*."[2] This is obviously a pattern of drill and recitation, not that of a sustained classroom discussion.

Like most teachers, English teachers spend far too little time learning to ask effective questions. In college programs, teacher educators rarely take the time to teach questioning skills; when they do, the questioning process is often treated either in a cursory manner or in such a highly technical way that it loses any practical value. Further, prospective and in-service teachers seldom have the opportunity to observe a good questioner at work. Yet, questioning is perhaps the central skill in the teaching-learning experience, because, whether we are aware of it or not, we bombard our students with all kinds of inquiries throughout the day.

From Robert J. Nash and David A. Shiman, "The English Teacher as Questioner," *The English Journal,* December 1974, p. 38. Copyright © 1974 by the National Council of Teachers of English. Reprinted by permission of the publisher and the authors.

Nash and Shiman describe three kinds of questioning categories and suggest that teachers become conscious of how often they use questions of each type:

1. *Factual.* Such questions call for rightwrong answers. While they may occasionally be useful to warm up a class or to check on comprehen-sion or understanding, factual questions are a conversational dead end, and sustained discussions seldom grow from them.

2. *Conceptual.* These ask students to move beyond mere facts to make generalizations. The key word in these questions is often *why*, since it asks the students to generalize and to draw on their own values. (The reader may have noted that in science fiction films and books, a common way to make a computer self-destruct is to ask it the simple question, "Why?" Computers, which are basically fact processors, do not like to an-swer what we in education call "thought questions.")

3. *Contextual.* These questions combine both factual and conceptual questions by having the students draw on their own perceptions to reach generalizations and to make conclusions of their own. Thus instead of sim-ply asking factual questions—"What is the rhyme scheme of this poem?" "What do adjectives modify?"—the teacher draws on facts as they are per-ceived by the student: "How does the rhyme of this poem affect *you*?"

[2]Robert J. Nash and David A. Shiman, "The English Teacher as Questioner," *The English Journal,* December 1974, p. 38.

"Why do you suppose the author used 'purple' to describe the girl's eyes?" The contextual question takes facts, perceived "in context," and encourages the student to create generalizations.

Subsuming all these categories is the *open-ended* question, a honest question to which the asker doesn't necessarily know the answer. The open-ended question encourages students to explore new territory, and the discussion that it generates is genuine. Factual questions—"What time is it?" "Where did you put the dustpan?" "How much is the British pound worth these days?"—are usually closed. They terminate discussion rather than opening it up.

Socrates is widely praised for his use of the questioning or inductive method, yet for all his skill, he seldom asked "open-ended" questions. Like a trial lawyer or a good many English teachers, Socrates simply kept on asking questions until he had elicited the single statement or concept he had in mind, at which point the discussion came to a close. A trial lawyer and many English teachers are able to create dialogues that appear to move toward an original conclusion. Yet if the answer is known beforehand—to the teacher/questioner if not to the students or the defendant—then this questioning is closed.

But can one always ask open-ended questions? Aren't there times when the teacher will know the answer or lead the students toward an accepted concept?

To some extent, this dilemma is resolved through Nash and Shiman's emphasis on *personal* interpretation of information through contextual questions. If teachers phrase questions in terms of the students' perceptions—"What did *you* think of the ending of the poem?" "What do *you* see as the key words in the passage?" "What do *you* think are the most important facts in the case?"—then discussion flows, even if teachers have in mind some basic ideas and concepts of their own.

Perhaps the most useful way for the teacher to avoid asking closed questions is to avoid taking sole responsibility for asking questions at all. As educators from John Dewey on have argued, learning how to ask a good question is even more difficult than learning how to answer one. The schools characteristically do very little to help students become good question askers. Perhaps the most useful role a teacher can play in leading group discussion is not that of setting the agenda of questions but of helping students channel and direct their own questions for investigation.

THE SMALL GROUP

Small group process is a relatively recent discovery in education, but one that offers enormous potential to the teacher. Such groups have all of the advantages of whole class talk activities, without the disadvantages of large size and unwieldiness. Further, small groups encourage a conversational tone that the large class does not. Groups allow the sharing of ideas and common learning. They are more effective than the large group in pooling knowledge, because the small group draws out the quiet people who do not contribute to the whole class.

Volumes have been written about small group dynamics and leadership, and any teacher who wants to use small groups effectively ought to study one of those books in detail. Several are listed at the end of the chapter. A few general considerations are appropriate for all small-group work.

Group Size and Composition

To work well, a group must have compatible membership and be of appropriate size, two factors that are at best unpredictable. Research is delightfully circuitous in identifying *five* as the "best" number of participants for a small group. More exactly, researchers have learned that people in groups of four never feel that the group is too large, while people in groups of six never feel the group is too small.

Many research workers have observed that groups with odd-numbered membership—three, five, and seven—seem to be more productive than even-numbered groups, simply because no tie votes or "hung juries" are possible. Unfortunately, most research cannot deal with the critical membership variable: what the group is trying to accomplish. A group of five may be too large for many tasks, while a group of nine may be too small for many others.

Group composition or make-up is equally reluctant to obey rules. Should students be allowed to choose group membership themselves or should the teacher make assignments? Should groups be permanent or rearranged regularly? Should one member of a group be selected as the leader, or can groups work their way to their own leadership patterns? My own experiences suggest that self-selected groups operate better than arbitrarily appointed or contrived groups, that leadership emerges without elections provided the need for leadership is made explicit by the teacher, that groups need to be rearranged from time to time. I have also had experiences that refuted each of these generalizations—assigned groups that worked well, groups that foundered until a chair was selected, groups that worked together successfully for long periods of time.

The Teacher Role

The teacher cannot use small groups as a way of manipulating people. The small group dynamic is a naturalistic one, and when the teacher interferes for pedagogical reasons, groups tend to collapse. Thus a tactic like assigning Bobby and Boris to different groups to break up their constant chattering won't work; the two simply talk across the room. Nor will gamesmanship work. Fake problems—"Let's split up into small groups and diagram these troublesome sentences"—are quickly spotted as such by the groups.

The most satisfactory teacher group-role that I have discovered is simply teacher-as-wanderer, drifting from group to group, joining in when there is something substantial to contribute. This role is a difficult one to manage. More than once I have joined a dynamic group only to see the conversation wither because of my interference.

The Group Task

Without a sense of task or purpose, any group will flounder. Thus many teachers have divided students into small groups with the assignment insufficiently described. Without sense of aim or purpose, the students talk aimlessly, often about events and personalities unconnected with English. Groups do not seem to do an especially good job of discussing issues, problems, or works of literature unless they can see a direction to it. Sometimes the task can be as simple as reporting back to the class. I have had greater success with such a task by having groups report on different questions or different aspects of the same problem. Best, perhaps, is a group that presents something other than notes of its own discussion, perhaps a demonstration, role play, or panel. On the whole, groups work better on tasks they devise themselves—that is, when the assignment is for the group to come up with and execute its own assignment.

Process Analysis

With the advent of small group discussion was created the process observer, someone who observes the interaction of a group and offers commentary and evaluation to the group about its performance. I am skeptical of the value of such people, in part because many of the process observers I have known took the job because they didn't know how to participate in a group and found the evaluative position an effective way of avoiding their own weaknesses. But some analysis of the group process—by the group or an outsider—can be helpful in facilitating group work and aiding people to become more effective participants. A good list of questions for such an analysis is Halbert E. Gulley's "Running Record of 'Groupness'."

RUNNING RECORD OF "GROUPNESS"

The questions to be answered concern such elements as these:
I. To what extent does the group climate promote free, permissive talk?
    A. Is the atmosphere informal rather than rigidly stiff?
    B. Does every member participate?

C. Do members react to contributions in ways that encourage the communicator to talk again later?

D. Do high-power members react to contributions in ways that encourage lower-power members to talk again later?

E. Are the physical surroundings pleasant and conducive to enthusiastic talk?

F. Do members seem enthusiastic about the importance of discussing the problem and do they consider participation worthwhile?

II. To what extent are members compatible?

  A. Are members friendly to each other?

  B. Do members seem to like each other?

  C. Do members seem to enjoy talking with each other?

  D. Do members smile occasionally as they talk to others?

  E. Do members behave in ways which generally minimize the threat to other's egos?

III. To what extent does the group operate as a cohesive unit?

  A. Is there mutual helpfulness among members?

  B. Do members seem to be dependent upon each other for support?

  C. Do members seem eager to hear the group's reactions rather than proceeding on their own?

  D. Is there effort to bring deviates back into agreement with this group?

  E. Do members seem more concerned with group interests than self-interests?

  F. Do members seem cooperative rather than competitive?

  G. Do members seem pleased when other members are congratulated for superior contribution?

IV. To what extent is there efficient communicative inter-action?

  A. Which members contribute most and which least?

  B. Which members' contributions are most helpful to the group?

  C. What kinds of information-opinion are contributed by each member?

  D. To which members are most communications directed?

  E. What proportion of communications are directed to the whole group?

  F. Are members attentive listeners?

  G. Do contributions relate to and build upon earlier contributions?

From Discussion, Conference and Group Process, second edition, by Herbert E. Gulley. Copyright © 1960, 1968 by Holt, Rinehart and Winston, Inc. Reprinted by permission of Holt, Rinehart and Winston.

VARIATIONS ON THE SMALL GROUP THEME

Group work rapidly grows dull if the tasks and the nature of the small group activity are not changed regularly. One can very quickly run a class to the point where students react to group work negatively, "Not groups *again!* C'mon, give us a break." As one of my students once said, *not* intending to compliment, "This is the groupinest class I've ever been in." A number of small group variations are possible. Some of many, ranging from informal to formal, are suggested below.

1. *Brainstorming.* The aim of a brainstorming session is to produce as many ideas as possible in a short period of time. A topic for inquiry is selected—"How can one build a better typewriter?"—and the participants suggest as many ideas as they can, building, borrowing, stealing one another's ideas freely. No criticism or evaluation is permitted; the aim of the group is idea production, not evaluation, and all ideas are recorded, since even silly ideas may prove to have a seed of a workable solution.

2. *Buzz Groups.* These are short discussions, limited to perhaps 10 or 15 minutes, based on a single, well-defined topic. Buzz groups move along quickly and actively, and break the routine of longer, sustained discussions.

3. *Committees.* The committee is the bane of American clubs and politics, not to mention school faculties, but perhaps this is because so few people have ever worked on productive committees. Appointing or asking for committees on all kinds of topics can add considerably to the class if the committee is engaged in a task that it finds important.

4. *Task Forces* or *Problem-Solving Groups.* These are committees-with-a-purpose, whose aim is to solve a particular problem or complete a project. Because of the emphasis on some kind of final product, a task force is often very strongly self-directed.

5. *Representative* or *Administrative Groups.* The school is filled with them: senior class officers, the prom site selection committee, the officers of the Latin Club. While representative groups are principally characteristic of extracurricular activities, there is no reason why they cannot be established within English classes, with tasks ranging from selecting books for an in-class library to assisting in the establishment of grading or evaluation standards.

6. *Seminars.* "Seminar" may conjure up images of stuffy gatherings of Ph.D candidates. But separated from some of its academicism, the seminar is a helpful device to use with many levels of students—as students engage in examination of an idea, a topic, or an issue—and deliberate to reach conclusions, propositions, or proposals.

FORMAL SPEECH SITUATIONS

Declamation, oratory, and forensics have declined in this country, and so has interest in their classroom use. The mainstream of oral English is informal talk, and few adults actually ever give a formal speech. Thus, most of the traditional speech-making practice supplied in the schools is unhelpful. But perhaps *practice* is the problem word here. As in writing, when speech activities are future-directed, aimed toward distant speaking engagements somewhere in the future, they tend to become trivial. This trivialization is illustrated by a remark one of my students once made while urging prospective teachers to give frequent impromptu speaking assignments: "This is really important because the student never knows when he will be at a dinner or banquet and be asked to say a few words."

All kinds of speech activities become appropriate and enjoyable when they are made a regular option within an English program. In fact, many students will select spoken English options in preference to writing and other forms if the speaking is not placed in a formal instructional setting. For instance, the "presentation"—a two-minute review of a book, a twenty-minute slide tape, a forty-minute talk on a subject of interest to the class—provides functional but not necessarily dull practice in public speaking. The panel discussion can be a lively small group equivalent of the presentation. Debates are a form of speaking that genuinely excites most students, especially if the teacher does not spend time belaboring debating terms and procedures. Minidebates, staged in a short period of time, without the formalities of judges and timekeepers, are almost a surefire teaching technique. Even parliamentary procedure, evolved through role playing or class decision-making activities, can be exciting. The spectrum of talk—chat to lecture—will emerge naturally if the teacher is successful in creating an environment that welcomes spoken English.

EXPLORATIONS AND RESOURCES

- Tune in on oral English by doing some eavesdropping. Listen to people engaged in an argument and think over their skill in speaking and listening to each other. Observe the oral English competencies of speakers at a town meeting or caucus. Listen to a politician talking over his program with reporters. What percentage of the people you listen to are, in fact, orally literate?
- Explore oral history and storytelling as a starting point for a spoken English unit. Have students recall and tell significant stories from their past. Then have them do the same through interviews with their parents and grandparents, either taping or transcribing the tales and anecdotes.
- Examine the implications of the questions you ask in class or plan to ask via your teaching notes. What percentage of your questions fall into Nash and Shiman's three categories: *factual, conceptual,* and *contextual?* What are the implications for the kinds of discussions you will promote? It might also be interesting to divide the questions along other lines; into questions that catalyze *divergent* thinking rather than *convergent* (leading to original conclusions rather than coming to a fixed point) or into *cognitive* versus *affective* (questions that emphasize knowledge versus those that are concerned with values and subjective responses). Again consider the implications of your division for the way student talk is likely to flow.
- Develop some conversation starters for a class—a list of, say, 20 or 30 topics. Or ask the students to propose a set of topics. Experiment with conversation sessions—five minutes to begin with—in which the students can talk over things informally.
- Experiment with small group dynamics, perhaps inviting students to join the investigation by proposing new techniques and patterns. Try groups of three, four,

five, and six. Test out leaderless groups, groups with appointed leaders, and groups that choose leaders. See what happens when groups do and do not have to report back. Try giving detailed assignments; broad, general assignments; and no assignments.

* Videotape a discussion, either small or large group. Then replay the tape and ask the students to analyze it in terms of Gulley's "Running Record of 'Groupness.'" This is a good activity to help students become aware of group process, but it is equally useful to teachers in helping them analyze their own role in the classroom oral English flow.

* Devise a set of oral English activities that call for a range of formal and informal speech forms on a single topic. For instance, how could you provide opportunities for chat, dialogue, small group discussion, brainstorming, debates, panels, and talks for a topic like "Religion in Today's Society"?

*

Related Readings

Three books by Andrew Wilkinson provide a comprehensive, pioneering examination of oral English (Wilkinson calls it "oracy") and ways of teaching it: *Some Aspects of Oracy* (Birmingham, England: Birmingham University Press, 1965); *The State of Language* (Birmingham: *Educational Review*, 1969); and *Spoken English* (Birmingham University, 1965). *Working in Groups*, by Ernest Stech and Sharon A. Ratliffe (National Textbook Company, 1976), is a manual designed for leaders and participants in small groups that provides an interesting description of communications theory along with practical classroom experiments. Kathleen Galvin and Cassandra Book's *Person to Person* (Skokie: National Textbook, 1978) is a textbook for classroom use that merits serious consideration; it is informative, entertaining, and practical. Gene Stanford has published two books, *Human Interaction in Education* (with Albert E. Roark, Boston: Allyn & Bacon, 1974) and *Learning Discussion Skills Through Games* (with Barbara Stanford, New York: Citation, 1969), that offer sound theory and practice in a wide range of speech situations.

Teachers interested in moving beyond the immediate concerns of the classroom might want to examine the related field of *conflict resolution*, which uses many group dynamics techniques as a way of helping disputants sort through and separate substantive and semantic differences. (See Fred E. Jandt and Mark Hare, *Instruction in Conflict Resolution* [Falls Church: Speech Communication Association, 1976].) Considerable work has also been done on *intercultural communication*, which might be of interest to teachers of nonnative speakers of English. (See Eileen Newmark and Molefi K. Asante, *Intercultural Communication* [Speech Communication Association, 1976].) Finally, Richard Budd and Brent D. Ruben's *Interdisciplinary Approaches to Human Communication* (Rochelle Park: Hayden, 1979) reviews communications and speech theory from the points of view of such diverse fields as zoology, anthropology, general semantics, systems theory, neurophysiology, and sociology.

13
Classroom Drama

Many people perceive drama as formal theater—something others present and we pay admission to see—or as something false or insincere: "Don't you think you're being a bit dramatic?" But as Peter Slade has observed, drama is tightly bound into human affairs. Whenever two people meet—to talk, to exchange ideas, to interact—drama results. Conversation and discussion are drama no less than is a formal stage presentation. Unless people live in utter isolation they cannot avoid daily participation in the human drama.

Drama is also intimately connected with personal growth and development. Young children engage in dramatic play spontaneously, using it to test out roles and identities, to explore facets of their personality. Although formal dramatic play diminishes as one enters adulthood, new forms of role playing develop, and mature adults skillfully manipulate dozens of different roles as they move through society and interact with others. As Slade has implied: without engaging in drama, people are literally in danger of losing their mental health.

Drama is larger than literacy—and earlier. It is mime and talk as well as script. It opens to the inarticulate and illiterate that engagement with experience on which literature rests. It permits them, and people in general, to discover their private human potentialities, to participate in and share the experience of the group, to make experience public. . . .

Drama liberates. It releases its practitioner from the inhibitions of self-consciousness. As it is play, make-believe rather than believe, it permits the individual to try on an attitude or to model an emotion without paying actuality's price. It releases its practitioner, too, from the explicit interpretive restraints more common in other forms of literature. The actor may and must find within himself what it is to be jealous, envious, distraught, ambitious. Finally, as the practitioner becomes creator, drama opens to him the discovery of something approaching the totality of himself. The many voices of his play and the many emotions—conflicting, harmonizing, commenting—are all his, spectroscopic fragmentations of a self which willy-nilly speaks in all he writes and which, discovered and released, can speak hereafter in his writing with new richness and vitality.

From Arthur Eastman, "Democracy in Education," in Douglas Barnes, ed., *Drama in the Classroom*. Copyright © 1968 by the National Council of Teachers of English. Reprinted by permission of the publisher and the authors.

The place of drama in the elementary grades and nursery schools is relatively secure; creative dramatics, children's theater, playacting, and dramatic play have been part of the lower schools' curriculum since the early part of this century. It is only in the past few years that secondary teachers have come to recognize the usefulness of drama for the values that Arthur Eastman describes. At the secondary level, it is especially helpful in allowing students to explore potential roles and aspects of their personality, as well as to establish their values and beliefs.

Further, drama is a ubiquitous teaching tool. Creative drama, for example, develops a host of spoken English skills. Writing plays draws on skills ranging from description to dialogue. Reader's theater and play production engage students in the study, analysis, and evaluation of literature. One could quite easily create a drama-centered curriculum that would encompass all areas that usually fall in the language arts. Finally, drama is the *lively* art, energizing the class where it is in use. Drama is *doing* and *struggling*—not sitting, listening, or note taking.

The urge to question, to invent, and to perform has been stifled in millions of schoolchildren now grown up, and their final cultural pattern can be seen all around us. But within this culture which in the past has tended toward rigidity, there are now definite needs for adaptability to rapid social change and a flexibility which will allow us to come with problems as yet to appear. Ours is a society which is finding habits, precedents, and traditions insufficient to guide and set courses for the future. For this reason alone we need, more than ever before, to place a higher priority upon the development of creative expression.

From Charles Duke, *Creative Dramatics and English Teaching* (Urbana: National Council of Teachers of English, 1974), p. 1.

IMPROVISATION, ROLE PLAYING, AND CREATIVE DRAMATICS

The three terms that head this section are used almost interchangeably in the schools. Although children's theater specialists have some fine distinctions to separate them, for our purposes, improvisation, role playing, and creative dramatics represent dramatic activities in which the actors and actresses create a play as they proceed, drawing on the drama inherent in a situation. In its simplest form, this drama might be an impromptu sketch or dialogue done to illustrate or extend a literary concept. Or it might be a full-blown play, carefully rehearsed (but still "scriptless"), with costumes and stage settings.

Although the research into this area is, by their description, "wobbly," Julie Massey and Stephen Koziol have shown that such drama develops a wide range of skills and abilities, including language development, cognitive development, and even creating attitude changes.[1] English teachers have been especially interested in role playing as useful in values clarification, where students explore through improvised scenes various decision-making processes and the implications of choices for the development of a value system. (See, for example, *Value Exploration Through Roleplaying*, by Robert C. Hawley [Amherst: ERA Press, 1974].)

Initial Experiences with Drama

Initiating drama is especially difficult. For the first few times, students— especially those of high school age—may be edgy, nervous, and frightened, and the teacher must be very careful to make the activities pleasant and nonthreatening.

Many experts in the field advocate opening classes with informal warm-up exercises designed to release tensions and get people into the mood for drama. Typical warm-ups include:

• *Rhythm and Movement.* The leader beats out a rhythm—slow, fast, in between—and the students respond, sometimes following instructions— "Walk in time to the beat." "Move your arms only"—other times creating

---

[1] Julie Massey and Stephen Koziol, Jr., "Research in Creative Dramatics," *The English Journal*, February 1978, pp. 92–94.

their own plan for movement. This activity can also be done with students responding to a musical composition.

• *Relaxation Exercises.* As in yoga, the students stretch and relax their bodies. Many yoga postures take their names from objects and animals in nature—the Lotus, the Lion, the Bridge—so students are already playacting and imitating as they relax.

• *Mime.* Wordlessly, the students imitate objects, actions, and feelings, for instance:

> *Pantomime.* Participants pantomime common actions—brushing teeth, talking on the phone, a person trying to keep from falling asleep at a lecture.
> *Objects and animals.* "Be a teacup." "Be a butterfly emerging from a cocoon." "Be a sunrise." "Be a melting snowman."
> *Moods.* Students pantomime joy, happiness, anger, sadness, or a kaleidoscope of moods.

My own experiences with warm-ups have been mixed. Often they succeed well, and drama proceeds successfully. But in some groups I have joined, the warm-ups have had the contrary effect of inhibiting people and raising tension. Most people feel somewhat inadequate when drama is first introduced, and something unfamiliar like "Be a butterfly" can intimidate them thoroughly. The people who thrive on these warm-ups are often the natural hams, and their successes can create further problems for those who are shy or cautious. Many people are so locked into themselves that even these simple warm-ups cause problems. The teacher must present them with great caution.

Structuring Creative Drama Experiences

Since drama pervades all areas of life, almost any issue, problem, or idea that concerns young people can work its way into a dramatic experience of one kind or another. Writing in *The English Journal*, Marianne and Sidney Simon describe three major sources of drama topics:[2]

> 1. *School.* Including "conflicts with peers, conflicts with teachers; conflicts with administration; problems within the classroom; boy-girl relationships in school; cliques and scapegoating; [and] events of urgent interest."
> 2. *Home.* Including family relationships; problems concerning the generations; and rules and regulations.

[2] Marianne and Sidney Simon, "Dramatic Improvisation: Path to Discovery," *The English Journal*, April 1965, pp. 323–327.

3. *Society*. Including issues of broad concern like "racial tensions; religious conflicts; social class barriers; and fears related to war and destruction."

Topics can grow from small group discussions, literature readings, current events, human relations problems (inside and outside the class), and other dramatic experiences. Most critical is that teachers must learn to integrate drama naturally into the classroom structure, so that it is not simply a thing done occasionally or only on set days.[3] Thus, the teacher should make it a point to offer a drama option—improvisation, say, or mime—as part of many assignments. Similarly, teachers should make it a point to draw on the dramatic possibilities in literature, moving as freely into dramatic interpretations as they would into direct discussion of a novel.

The principal aim of classroom drama is to help students understand, interpret, and talk about their world and themselves. It is *not* to train actors or produce theatrical experiences of professional quality. An audience at the theater does not especially care whether an actor grows through the acting experience; the teacher of classroom drama cares very much and ultimately bases evaluation of the drama on the extent to which it has helped the actor/student grow.

In planning the structure for improvisation, I have had good luck using a formula I call the "4 Cs": character, containment, conflict, and conclusion. These provide a useful way of seeing and organizing classroom drama.

1. *Character*. Obviously the drama will be made up of people—characters—and a central concern for the teacher is the extent to which it is necessary to predetermine the role of a character, rather than letting the actor work it out in process. As a general rule, the more familiar a character is to the students, the less direction and preplanning will be necessary to help them fit that role. Most students can role play young people, teachers, parents, and well-known public figures or celebrities with little preplanning. Other characters—older people, people from different generations or social classes—may require prior discussion. The teacher can conduct concentration sessions to help students feel the part:

> *Close your eyes. Think about the character you will be. Think about his appearance—how does he look? How does she feel? Is he satisfied with his life and himself? Who are her friends? Visualize what they look like.*

2. *Conflict*. The source of any dramatic action must be conflict of one sort or another. The conflict is essentially the topic of the drama. It may concern the characters—conflicts between young people and/or their

---

[3] This point is also stressed by Massey and Koziol in the research review cited previously. Creative drama cannot be expected to produce growth if it is not used systematically.

parents—or it may center on situations—say, conflicts of interest and ambition.

For drama to be integrated into the mainstream of a class, the conflicts should grow from the activities and feelings of the class. Drama ideas can thus be derived from:

human relations problems with the class.
struggles that emerge in stories and plays.
problems or themes that appear in poetry or essays.
the students' own writing.

3. *Containment.* Containment is the physical contrivance of putting all one's characters and conflict into one box so they have to bump into one another. It is the age-old setting with an emphasis on close fit. The containment of a drama can take place anywhere—it can be a room, the back seat of a car, a telephone booth, a dance floor. Containment can also cross over periods of time—2001, 1930, 1776—to provide focus. Once you contain characters and conflicts, the drama is spontaneous. It *must* happen.

4. *Conclusion.* The first three Cs provide the essential structure for a drama. If they are present, drama happens. The fourth C, conclusion, is the escape clause. A common happening in improvisation is for the actors to become so deeply involved in their roles that the drama becomes endless. The participants will not compromise, and the actors remain hopelessly deadlocked. Sometimes the actors simply forget to plan a conclusion. In any event, improvised theater pales very quickly when this happens. As a regular part of planning for drama, the teacher should stress the need for some sort of a conclusion that will help to resolve the conflict—not, however, by providing a *deus ex machina* or a contrived happy ending.

To visualize how the 4 Cs work (or as a starting point for a classroom drama), select several characters, give them a conflict, and provide containment from the suggestions in the box.

CHARACTERS

Baby	Sports hero(ine)	Butcher
Old man/woman	Movie star	Baker
Martian	Rock singer	Astronaut
Teenager	Literary character	Ship captain
Parent	Historical figure	Coach
Yourself	The president	Sitcom character
Principal	Spy	Brat
Taxpayer	Master criminal	Know-it-all
Police chief	Superhero(ine)	Engineer
Professor	Animal	God(dess)

CONFLICTS

Missing property	Faulty merchandise
Stolen property	Car troubles
Human rights	Curfew
New students	Homework
Friends and enemies	Parents
Race relations	International relations
Current events	Absurd happenings
Page one stories	Housecleaning
Election fraud	Homecoming queen
Broken things	Sports
Cheating	Love
Jealousy	Hero worship
Dirty clothes	

CONTAINMENT

2001	Mars	1920s
Hospital	Tree house	Old West
Department store	Jail	Rome
1812	Garage	Novel setting
Zoo	School	Prehistoric times
Car	Crowded bus	A test tube
Czarist Russia	Home	Your lungs
Movie theater	Fire station	Seaside
Classroom		

A variant of the whole class drama that I have used is the partially scripted drama. Upon entering the class, each student receives a card with a character's name and description. At the beginning of the drama, each student acts the assigned role. Here is a partially scripted drama for an improvisation at an airport:

PARTIALLY SCRIPTED AIRPORT IMPROVISATION

You are RON STRONG: member of the airport security guard. It's your job to keep trouble from springing up. In addition to helping out people in distress, look out for troublemakers, terrorists, loiterers, and stray dogs.

You are LANCE FARR, veteran pilot. It is your job to stroll around the airport chatting with customers in order to build the company's image (and, no doubt, to feed your king-sized ego).

You are little SHIRLY TREMBLE, traveling all by yourself for the first time. You're not lost; you're not hungry; you're not hurt or scared. But it sure would be nice if people would pay a lot of attention to you. Take turns being hopelessly cute or breaking down into hysterical weeping.

Your name is MILDRED GLEE, and you are the Chief Ticket Agent. Set up shop at the front of the room and make reservations for people. Take your time. Don't make any mistakes and don't let anybody be rude to you.

You are EUDORA PRY, ace reporter for WFLY, and you are here interviewing people who are at the airport. Get the portable tape recorder and do an on-the-scene broadcast. Talk to people who look interesting. Ask them what they're doing here. Afterward, play back your tape as an instant replay of the drama.

Other characters can include: a lost little boy, someone who has lost his baggage, someone who has lost her dog, a movie actress, an obnoxious old man, taxi drivers, baggage handlers, smugglers, etc. Simply make up enough characters (30 or so), divided by sex, to match your class distribution.

To initiate the drama, simply announce that the classroom has become the central terminal at _____Airport. If you have written a good cast of characters, the drama will begin spontaneously.

Other partially scripted dramas that I have used or seen my students use include *The Dog Show*, with participants miming dog owners showing off their animals; *Supermarket*, with actors and actresses finding imaginary goods in imaginary rows; and *Universal General International Incorporated*, with people role playing busy bureaucrats in a mad company that makes *nothing*.

By planning the characters of the drama carefully, the teacher can engineer some conflicts and confrontations. This variation of the whole class drama also saves the students the initial problem of having to think up an identity for themselves, something that is not easy under the stress of a drama experience.

Many variations of the whole class idea are possible. My students introduced me to *The Big Machine*, a group role playing in which everyone becomes a cog, gear, or lever in a giant Rube Goldbergian human machine devoted to some trivial task such as snapping open a peanut shell. Classes can become movie audiences, an orchestra, angels on the head of a pin, marooned victims of a shipwreck, or a group of parents worrying about what's wrong with the younger generation.

The Role of the Teacher in Creative Drama

The teacher's role is, above all, delicate. The role of organizer is reasonably clear, but there are also times—many times—when the teacher must contribute to an ongoing dramatic presentation to make it work. For instance, if a play seems to lack a conclusion, the teacher may need to intervene, suggesting that a character do something that will force a resolution. At other times, the teacher may need to nudge the participants into heightened conflict or say something that will keep a student from drifting out of a part. This intervention—or "side coaching" as it is sometimes called— must be done with caution lest the students sense it merely as a teacherly interruption. Perhaps the easiest way for it to happen is for the teacher to be prepared to assume a role and become a participant in the drama, acting as an additional character inserted into the play to help shape its direction.

The teacher should plainly not become a director. As Richard Crosscup has suggested, the teacher's role should be perceived as that of helping the students grow through drama, and the principal outcome is less the play than the growth of the students engaged in it.

The leader of children's dramatics activity . . ., will not be a "director." The "director" of a children's play tends to exploit children for his own ends, as a painter exploits pigment. The play director's creation is the play. But for the person concerned with the growth of children, it is not the play that is the end, but the child. Creative dramatics, creative activity of any kind, the educational process in general—these are the means by which the adult gives shape to a creature whose principal business is to shape itself.

From Richard Crosscup, *Children and Dramatics* (New York: Scribner's, 1966).

Whole Class Drama

Creative dramatics need not always involve small groups and small scenes. I enjoy organizing dramas that engage the entire class in a play for which there is no audience, or more accurately, in a drama in which the actors are also the audience. One form of the whole class drama involves asking the students to visualize themselves in a place where people gather—a department store, a jail, a rock concert, a football game—and to choose a role and act it out. The teacher or selected students can help to catalyze the drama by taking on a stimulating role—shoplifter, tough cop, angry guitarist, football coach's wife—and using that role to generate and focus the drama.

There are also many problems and pitfalls in creative drama, and in contrast to writing, where failures can easily be kept private, failures in drama are obvious and public. Douglas Barnes, a British teacher who has experimented extensively with drama in the classroom, reminds us of some of these problems.

DRAMA AS THREAT

We have all seen pupils blossom or shrink in dramatic activities. We must acknowledge our powerlessness in controlling the dramatic interplay. In the playground the pupils are finding their groups and subgroups—or their isolation—and taking up roles within them that provide some security and protection. But in the drama room we break down these temporary stabilities and safeties and make the children try other roles. Those who can will grow, but what of those who are not yet ready? In the playground they will escape from the intolerable situation, but not in our drama lesson. So we risk serious harm to them. . . .

The older student who has found a role in life may refuse to risk his hard-won security by joining in drama. For some pupils the impersonality of the scientific mode may be a life-style which, although inadequate by some standards of self-awareness, is essential to their stability. Even if they try to act, they will probably fail to enter the part. Do they not have the right to refuse? Should we ask them?

Clearly the drama teacher must always be ready to allow pupils to step aside and watch, though this, too, increases their isolation. At best he can find some administrative task which will involve the pupil in the group's activity until he feels ready to join in. Improvisation by creating a fluid social situation strengthens the self-assertive and weakens the insecure. The teacher must be vigilant to minimize this.

From Douglas Barnes, "The Final Word," in Douglas Barnes, ed., *Drama in the Classroom.* Copyright © 1968 by the National Council of Teachers of English. Reprinted by permission of the publisher and the author.

When people are deeply engaged in creative drama, feelings are released quickly and easily, and desirable through this may be, such openness needs to be handled carefully. Drama offers no hiding places and little opportunity for revision the way writing does. The teacher must be sufficiently in control—without "controlling"—to be able to anticipate and avoid problems. Although experimentalism is desirable in creative drama, as it is in all areas of teaching, the teacher needs to be especially cautious; unsuccessful experiments may be deeply harmful to students.

PUPPETRY

In one of my teacher education courses, a student did a project investigating puppetry as a way of introducing dramatic work. She constructed several simple glove puppets, wrote up some starter situations, and asked members of the class to put on the puppets and improvise. The two volunteers (draftees, actually) crouched down behind a table—a crude stage—and began improvising, a bit edgily at first but gaining enthusiasm as they entered into the play. I happened to be sitting to the side so I could see both puppets and puppeteers, and as the drama unfolded, an interesting thing happened: The puppeteers gradually became less conscious of the puppets and began to watch and speak to each other. A two-level drama emerged—one onstage, one behind stage.

This process intrigued me because these two students, seated on the floor, holding puppets in the air, shouting lines at each other, were among the shy members of the class; under no circumstances would it have been possible for me to get them this excited about an improvisation presented directly to the class. The puppets had released these students' dramatic talents.

Since then, I have used puppets with many groups at all age levels, and the results have been remarkably consistent. Puppets provide a mask—some basic protection—that allows people to open up to a high degree in dramatic work. Even older students, who I feared might see puppetry as juvenile, seem to enjoy it. I have even been forced to retire one set of classroom puppets that were demolished in a lively drama by two graduate students who had previously made a point of telling me what quiet, reserved people they were.

The equipment for puppetry is simple. The puppets themselves can be made from paper bags, paper plates, cloth remnants, clay, or paper-mache. They can be made in sizes ranging from finger puppets—simple tubes of cloth or paper—to the superpuppet, a variation on the pillowcase that the puppeteer wears. I like the idea of Sesame Street's "anything people"—faceless puppets that can be decorated with features fastened on with double-side transparent tape—and I keep on hand some blank mitten puppets that my students use to build a character they want.

The sources of puppet plays are endless. Improvisation is the obvious starting point, using the 4 Cs as a basic guideline. The students can also present puppet pantomimes, ballets, dramatic readings, plays, television programs, discussions, panels, debates, interviews, and conversations. Puppetry also makes a good road show, and students often enjoy taking a puppet repertory company to other classes, to other schools or to libraries.

ORAL INTERPRETATION

Literature is a performing art, and we often overlook the dramatic excitement that oral reading—by individuals or groups—can bring to a class. Teachers have traditionally acted as if silent reading is the only proper kind, intimating that somehow students are cheating if they listen to literature. It is shocking to observe that all but a few of the best student writers are almost totally incapable of doing an equally good oral reading of what they have written.

Students need not be polished readers or have theatrical experience in order to do successful dramatic reading. To the contrary, many students are put off or embarrassed by doing or listening to a formal theatrical reading. What is essential is a message—poem, story, play, essay—and a desire to communicate it to other people. In reading sincerely and naturally, most readers will be sufficiently dramatic to interest an audience.

The teacher can initiate an interest in oral interpretation simply by reading aloud regularly. Students of all levels seem to enjoy being read to, and it is unfortunate that oral experiences like story hour are abandoned after the early grades. A long novel, one that might be out of range for many students, can be read, a chapter at a time, over a period of several weeks or months. Literature to supplement a topical or thematic unit can be read to a class. Recordings of dramatic readings should be brought in as well, and all teachers should get a copy of the records catalog of Caedmon, a company that specializes in recordings of authors reading their own work.

The teacher should not be the only reader, of course, and students can be involved in oral interpretation. At first, the readings should be relatively short, and the student should have ample time to look over the material, though not necessarily to rehearse it, before reading aloud. By all means avoid "going around the class," having each student read a paragraph or two, in what often becomes a dull parade of uninvolved readings. If the teachers want to have students read aloud, they should organize it, prepare for it, and help the students do a polished job of it.

Having students read their own work is also a good oral interpretation project, since the reader begins by being familiar with the meaning of the work. Oral reading can also be encouraged by sponsoring activities like informal poetry readings or coffee house readings, in which writers come together to read and talk over their work. I like the idea of having a schoolwide festival involving the reading of student work on an annual or a semester basis. Good writing from all over the school is collected, and either the writers themselves or good oral readers read the work to the entire school or to groups of parents. This kind of festival not only honors student writers but gives your good readers a chance for public recognition as well.

GROUP THEATER

Group theater goes under a number of different names, described below, but moves beyond pure oral interpretation to involve several readers or actors.

Typically in *reader's theater* a literary work—short story, one-act play, television script—is read aloud by a group of readers, each of whom takes on a part. A narrator is included if necessary. No lines must be memorized; nor are any sets or stage props needed. Reader's theater can even be done as a mock radio play, complete with sound effects. It is also an effective way to present student writing.

In *chamber theater*, the literature (usually a short story) is acted out, so that students actually learn their lines. In effect, chamber theater simply converts a piece of fiction into something that can be presented as a work of drama.

In *improvisational theater*, the students start with a set text—a story or play or dramatic poem—and, having read and understood the work, they act it out, creating their own lines and actions. A popular variation of this approach is *story theater*, in which students pantomime the events of a story while a student or teacher reads it aloud.

None of these approaches, except possibly chamber theater, is as complex as launching a full stage play. Group theater allows students to read from scripts and thus avoid the time-consuming process of learning lines, or it allows the actors and actresses to make up their own lines. Using group theater frequently aids enormously in bringing literature to life, while helping students extend their own range of dramatic experience.

Play Presentation

Because of the many limitations that classroom preparation of a play imposes, few plays will reach the point of a full-dress production in an English class. However, there are many occasions when a play can and should be worked up into a full presentation, especially in the case of student-written works. One-act plays also make a good classroom presentation. Generally, the guidelines for preparing a classroom play are similar to those for any formal drama: The teacher needs to provide ample time for preparation and rehearsal and needs to participate in the process of shaping the play, helping the students see its full dramatic potential. The classroom presentation also provides opportunities for involvement by technically oriented students—technicians, stagehands, managers, effects people, prop people, and lighting experts. Once the work of a presentation has been done, the class play probably should be taken on the road to other classes or schools.

In general, I would like to see the schools place less emphasis on whole school dramatic productions and more on presentations by small groups and classes. While the senior class play or school musical is often an impressive show, the whole school drama involves relatively few students and is often quite expensive. In the interest of involving more students, I think administrators and secondary English departments might consider investing their funds in a number of small theater groups or providing money to support dramatic productions in individual classes.

GAMES AND SIMULATIONS

The value of games and simulations has only recently been recognized, and educational games are rapidly being developed in many fields. While not drama in a formal sense, games also draw students into new roles and identities by engaging them in simulated situations. The topics for games are endless; in *Serious Games* (New York: Viking Press, 1970), Clark C. Abt describes diverse games designed to teach color and shape, to engage students in a reenactment of colonial shipping problems, to simulate urban planning, and to develop an understanding of the political process. *Psychology Today* has developed such games as "Black and White" (simulating racial problems), "Society Today" (current issues), and "The Feel Wheel" (a starter for sensitivity training). Although many commercially prepared games are available, teachers and students can also enjoy creating their own. Indeed, as Clark Abt has pointed out in *Serious Games*, often the game designer learns more from the process than do the players.

My students and I have designed a number of games including "Newsprint" (which simulates the operation of a daily newspaper); "Tenure Track," a year in the life of a new teacher; "The Pollution Solution," a large group role playing people of a town faced with a pollution problem; and "Soap," involving the writing of a soap opera.

There are no hard-and-fast rules for designing simulations and games. Perhaps the best approach for interested teachers is to examine some commercial games like "Monopoly," "Clue," "Sorry," or "Bermuda Triangle" and to study how they work, then to apply the format of the game to the chosen topic.

However, I have also found that the following guidelines are helpful to people designing a game for the first time:

1. *Describe the learning objectives for the game.* Do you want students to read, write, speak, listen? What do you want them to gain from the game?

2. *Find a source of dramatic tension in the game.* In order for the game to progress, there must be a basic conflict or motivation. (In "Newsprint," for example, the drama is created by having rival newspapers competing for success.)

3. *Find a model for the game.* Using "Hollywood Squares" or "Authors" or "Wiff 'N Proof" or "Monopoly" or any other game that seems to fit your purposes as a model, draft a set of rules and procedures for your game.

4. *Create any needed materials.* These can include boards, spinners, decks of cards, and so on.

5. *Play the game experimentally.* (Do this some Friday or Saturday evening at a party with friends.) Find out what *doesn't* work in the game as you designed it.

6. *Play the game with your students.*

To my way of thinking, for a game to be a legitimate part of English, it should in one way or another directly engage students in examining or using language. While it might be fun to bring in a game simulating, say, life in the roaring twenties, or one that simulates male/female role problems, the game needs to have some connections with language use in order to be worth the time of the teacher and students.

Here is a list of games that have potential for use in an English class. To the best of my knowledge, none of these games exists, at least not in commercial or published form. I will simply present the titles and allow the reader to figure out what the game might be.

TOPICS FOR ENGLISH GAMES

The Debate Game
Censorship
Sitcom
Town Meeting
The Sexist Language Game
The Doublespeak Game
The Language of Advertising
Sign Language
Family Reunion
Discover a Dialect
Discover Your Dialect
The Lexicographer's Dilemma
The (Beat/Romantic/Victorian) Poetry Game
Name That Poem!
The Canterbury Tales Game
The Learn a New Language Game
Codes and Ciphers
The Library Game
The Hardy Boys/Nancy Drew Write Your Own Thriller Game
The Epistle Game
Esperanto in Action
Intergalactic Communication

EXPLORATIONS AND RESOURCES

• To draw on drama freely and easily, one needs to feel comfortable with it. Try some improvisations and a dramatic reading with some colleagues. Talk over the feelings you experience and consider ways of making drama pleasant for students. Be especially conscious of the initial feelings you have when improvising.

- Visit an actors' studio or class and observe the improvisational techniques employed by a skilled instructor. Consider applications for the English class.
- Talk over some of the problems that arise in a drama-oriented class. What should the teacher do about:

Students who are shy?
Students who probably would enjoy drama but seem reluctant to participate?
Students whose physical appearance—for example, overweight, tall, plain— might cause embarrassment if they were assigned to inappropriate roles?
A drama that becomes too serious, with the barrier between real life and drama dissolving?

- Design a series of creative dramatic activities for a unit of literacy work you are interested in teaching. Try to include some possibilities for wordless drama (pantomime), role playing, and full-fledged skits or playlets. Also consider the possibilities the unit offers for group theater presentations.
- Make some puppets and put on a play
- Practice your oral interpretation skills by reading aloud to some students. Don't try to become theatrical; simply relax and enjoy reading to others.
- Locate a good sound library close to where you live or teach and examine its holdings in dramatic readings and recorded theater.
- If you are interested in developing games and simulations, begin by conducting a one- or two-day "Tournament of Games" in which students bring in a range of games, play them, and share the results. From this discussion, evolve some ideas about game structure, including answers to some of the following questions:

How are winners and losers determined?
How does the game stimulate or imitate a real situation?
How is the flow of play directed and controlled by such devices as dice, cards, a game board, and other equipment?

- Design one of the games in the previous box and play it with friends or a group of students. (I'd like to see your results. Please send of copy of your rules to me, c/o Department of English, Michigan State University, East Lansing, Michigan 48864.)

Related Readings

Viola Spolin's *Improvisation for the Theater* (Evanston: Northwestern University Press, 1967) is a rich compendium of ideas for improvisational work, including a strong section on the art side of coaching. However, Spolin's book is actually intended for use in acting classes, and the activities thus need to be tempered appropriately. A good book for use with elementary children is Elizabeth Kelly's *The Magic If* (Baltimore: National Educational Press, 1973) as is *Children's Theatre and Creative Dramatics*, edited by Geraldine Brain Siks and Hazel Brain Dunnington (Seattle: University of Washington Press, 1961). *Drama in the Classroom*, edited by Douglas Barnes (Urbana: National Council of Teachers of English, 1968), provides a good theoretical background showing the interrelationship of drama and English studies. Charles Duke's *Creative Dramatics English Teaching* (NCTE, 1974) is conveniently divided into two parts: one presenting the basic theory of creative dramatic work, the other discussing classroom strategies. A good first article for the teacher new to drama is Catherine O'Shea and Margaret Egan's "A Primer of Drama Techniques for Teaching Literature" (*The English Journal*, February 1978, pp. 51–55.) Clark Abt's *Serious Games* (New York: The Viking Press, 1970) has already been mentioned as a resource on simulations. Teachers may also want to examine *Games in the Classroom*, edited by Ken Davis and John Hollowell (NCTE, 1978), which provides good advice on making and playing games and on their use in English classes. Finally, if you are interested in puppetry, check your library for a book on puppet making or see *A Puppetry Handbook*, by Mary Clare Yates, Patricia Lamb, and Stephen Judy (Detroit: Michigan Council of Teachers of English, 1979).

14

English: A Mass Medium

Electricity has made angels of us all—not angels in the Sunday school sense of being good or having wings, but spirits freed from flesh, capable of instant transportation anywhere.

The moment we pick up a phone, we're nowhere in space, everywhere in spirit. Nixon on TV is everywhere at once. That is the Neo-Platonic definition of God: a Being whose center is everywhere, whose borders are nowhere.

From Edmund Carpenter, *Oh, What a Blow That Phantom Gave Me!* (New York: Bantam Books, 1974), p. 3.

It's natural today to speak
of "audio and visual aids" to teaching,
for we still think of the book as norm,
of other media as incidental.
We also think of the new media
—press, radio, movies, TV—
as MASS MEDIA
& think of the book
as an individualistic form. . . .

Today in our cities,
most learning occurs outside the classroom.
The sheer quantity of information conveyed by
press-mags-film-TV-radio
far exceeds
the quantity of information conveyed by
school instruction & texts.
This challenge has destroyed

the monopoly of the book as a teaching aid
& cracked the very walls of the classroom,
so suddenly,
we're confused, baffled. . . .

In this violently upsetting social situation,
many teachers naturally view
the offerings of the new media
as entertainment,
rather than education.
But this view carries
no conviction to the student.
Find a classic
which wasn't first regarded
as light entertainment. . . .
The movie is to dramatic representation
what the book was to the manuscript.

It makes available
to many & at many times & places
what otherwise would be restricted
to a few at few times & places.
The movie, like the book,
is a ditto device.
TV shows to 50,000,000 simultaneously.
Some feel that the value
of experiencing a book
is diminished by being extended
to many minds.
This notion is always implicit
in the phrases "mass media," "mass entertainment"—
useless phrases obscuring the fact THAT
English itself
is a mass medium.

From Marshall McLuhan, "Explorations Number Seven," a broadcast of the Canadian Broadcasting Corporation, May 1957. Copyright © 1957 by the CBC. Reprinted by permission of Marshall McLuhan.

English Discovers the Media: A Play in Five Scenes

SCENE 1
A teacher leads a class discussing the merits of the film version of a novel the class has just completed reading. After carefully guided debate, the students reach the conclusion that the film maker took too many liberties with the novel and that reading is more interesting than film going anyway, since reading forces you to use your imagination. Later in the week, the students all go to the flicks instead of reading their English assignment.

SCENE 2
A class begins a newspaper unit. Each day the students bring in a paper and study its journalistic techniques. They discover biased and unbiased editorials, colorful sports writing, and a number of typographical errors. Some students read the want ads and the comics on the sly. After the newspaper unit, the class resumes its perusal of the history of British literature.

SCENE 3
The teachers in a school decide to purchase a number of attractive new slide-tape programs to back up the language arts classes. The kits, which cost $125 each, contain 80 slides, a cassette tape, and an instructor's manual. The titles purchased by the school include, "The Nature of the Noun," "Writing a Clear Topic Sentence," and "How to Write a Business Letter." Each of these topics was covered in the textbook series the faculty just decided not to readopt.

SCENE 4
An *au courant* teacher who has read Marshall McLuhan decides to teach film study. He opens his course by lecturing on the nature of visual symbolism and assigning a paper on the structural analysis of a film currently showing at the local cinema.

SCENE 5
The principal sets aside a portion of the school budget for film rental, something the teachers have long requested. Unfortunately, all films must be requisitioned the spring prior to the year in which the film will be used. Since teachers cannot possibly plan that far ahead, the film budget is never spent.

McLuhan is right when he says that the media confuse us. After years of either ignoring media or using them merely as audio-visual aids, teachers have discovered media, recognizing them as an important resource for teaching. But what to do with media remains a puzzle. Some teachers have simply put old content into new forms, as McLuhan predicts, gussying up the old curriculum with celluloid and acetate. Others have launched an extreme "visual literacy" campaign, portraying print as dead and putting film analysis at the center of the curriculum. Some teachers draw on television as a natural part of the curriculum; others declare it an abomination and stick exclusively to print.

It is questionable whether the debate over media superiority should take place at all, since it merely adds to the teacher's bafflement. While the advocates of visual literacy have done an important service in awakening teachers to the potential of media, it is appropriate to move beyond the question, "Which medium is best?" to the broader question, "How can we best use media?" The fully functioning members of the community of language can draw on many different media, print and nonprint alike. They can use telephone, telegraph, or letter depending on the demands of time, situation, and cost. They can see and become involved in a film, and perhaps not worry that it was or was not true to the book, appreciating it for what the experience *is*, not for what is *not*. "English"—the language—"is a mass medium," McLuhan suggests. To turn his phrase, we can also add "The media are English."

McLuhan suggests further:

> The educational task
> is not only
> to provide
> basic tools
> of perception,
> but to develop
> judgment & discrimination
> with ordinary social experience.

The form of McLuhan's statement provides a witty example of his point. In writing his essay in the visual shape of a poem, he traps us in a superficiality—judging content in terms of the medium. Often we lack the judgment and discrimination to look toward the language and content rather than superficial form.

Taking a clue from the previous passage, I want to suggest that what matters is the student, not the choice of media forms. Our aim as teachers must be to help the students develop powers of "perception . . . judgment & discrimination with ordinary social experience." (We ought to be concerned with discriminating among academic experiences as well.) Such discrimination is based in language, as young people observe their world and describe it in language.

Today's students are born in an electronic world, one that, as Edmund Carpenter suggests, has made "angels of us all," capable of instant flight to any place in the globe. With their horizons expanded, young people need to be able to respond to the media creatively and critically and to use them to communicate with others successfully. Those two aims—*responding to* and *using* the media—will be the focus of this chapter. I will not even begin to describe all of the possible media uses that are open to the elementary or secondary language arts teacher. But I will present a sampler of activities that can strengthen students' media skills by concentrating, first and foremost, on the student as a creator and consumer of language.

Although I have isolated the consideration of media in a single chapter in an obvious but structurally necessary violation of McLuhan's principle of integration, the teacher should be able to incorporate media in the class smoothly and comfortably, just as with practice and experimentation, drama becomes a regular part of the class, not something that is taken up on isolated days or in specialized units. The value of media comes in using them, either as sources of ideas and information or as forms of composition.

RESPONDING TO MEDIA: TELEVISION

What are we to make of television? Its worst critics blast it as being not only destructive but downright evil, creating a false set of standards and values for its watcher-victims. Others point to the informational and instructional value of many television programs, not just limited to public television and non-prime time hours, and argue for selective viewing. The networks present the themselves as brokers to public taste, offering whatever forms of instruction and entertainment the public will support.

It is perhaps most useful for a teacher *not* to take a two-value stand on television, but to help students become aware of the way it affects their lives. As McLuhan has argued, we tend to lose consciousness of familiar media, and television is the most familiar medium of all. Some of the following projects can help students rediscover the familiar on the tube and evaluate its effects on themselves.

TV-Watching Log

We've all read statistics on the number of hours students spend in front of the television set. Let your students analyze their own tube time by having them keep a complete log of their viewing for a single week. How many hours do they watch? How many hours on school days? On weekends? Have them discuss planned versus unplanned watching. How often do they turn on the set just to see what is happening? Encourage the students to break their watching into categories: news, adventure, comedy, cartoons, sports, movies and so on. Put your categories and figures on a large sheet of butcher paper and tack it on a bulletin board so that your students can see at a glance how the hours add up.

This activity will generate all kinds of follow-up discussion. Often young people will show a considerable savvy as they discuss their viewing. Students can also consider alternative ways of spending their time. I think I had some impact on a middle school class by pointing out if they cut their TV viewing in half until the time they graduated from high school, they would have time to jog 12,000 miles, to read the *Hardy Boys* or *Nancy Drew* books cover to cover 16 times, or to earn enough baby-sitting to pay cash for a new car!

TV Review Sheet

As a follow-up to the TV log, students can begin to critique the shows they watch. On a one-page ditto, students can review, say, the five best and the five worst shows for a given week. This is a good project to do with small groups, with a fresh group of critics being assigned each week. Students might also want to send their review sheets to the station managers of local television stations. "Criticism" in this case can be as informal or formal as the teacher and students wish. At first, it may be best simply to let students react informally, but as the term or year progresses, they ought to become more and more skilled at explaining just what triggered their reactions.

Study Television Conventions

Because of its domination by commercial interests, TV is highly repetitive and unimaginative. Once a new show succeeds, others follow the pattern. Have your students investigate a TV genre: police shows, situation comedies, cartoons, superhero shows, soap operas, westerns, made-for-TV movies. Encourage them to look for the stereotypes of character and plot that emerge. As a follow-up, let the students write satires of the genres they have been studying. These satires might even be presented for the class through improvised drama or recorded on video tape for showing around the school.

The Image of America on TV

Stereotypes are not limited to characters in the TV genre shows. Television also creates stereotypes of Americans. Have the students keep track of stereotypes for a week or more. Tell them to look at the roles of men and women, children, husbands and wives, singles, racial minorities, lawyers, doctors, blue-collar workers, and so on. It has been said that TV is a revolutionary medium because it shows the lower economic classes what the upper crust has and lives like. Do your students agree?

TV Commercials

TV ads are both better and worse than the programs: better, because they are developed with great skill to obtain high impact through brief exposure; worse, because they are highly exploitative, frequently verging on the dishonest. Conduct a TV commercials unit with your students, having them watch, analyze, and critique the the commercials they see. This too is a unit that can be followed up with a video or stage production, with students writing and taping their own satirical commercials.

TV Tie-ins

In a more positive vein, in recent years promoters have discovered the TV tie-in, in which a novel is made over for television, or a popular television is turned into a novel. While the quality of the by product—either TV show or new book—varies considerably, in general the tie-ins spur interest in literacy. Many paperback bookstores now have a "TV Novels" section with a hundred or more titles that have been or are being televised. Draw on the interest that the tie-ins produce by teaching some of the books or by assigning the show for discussion and analysis.

RESPONDING TO MEDIA: FILM

Film has come into its own in English and language arts classes in the past two decades. Where once films were used almost exclusively as visual aids, presenting instructional information rather than being used as entertainment or aesthetic experience, now they enter the class as a source of experience for reading/writing activities and as a communications medium in their own right. In addition, film forms a significant part of the common culture of young people, so that a teacher can safely refer to many feature films shown outside the school with a degree of certainty that students will have seen or heard about them.

At the same time, as film has become respectable, it has also suffered from "academization." That is, because teachers and professors feel a need to teach, rather than simply to let students view and respond, they often try to legitimize the film experience by engaging in formal analysis and criticism. In many film classes, much time is spent in detailed analysis of the technical properties of film and on the naming of film techniques and strategies. While some knowledge of how films are made is obviously useful, too much analysis simply has the effect of spoiling the viewer's pleasure. Sound familiar? English teachers have done the same thing with literature for years. Similarly, many teachers of English have drawn on their knowledge of literary criticism to lead their students in, say, a search for symbolism or the study of recurring motifs in films. As McLuhan would say, such analysis is a matter of viewing a new medium in terms of an old one.

There are a few exceptions, but in general it can be said that the public no longer discovers movies, the public no longer makes a picture a hit. If the advertising for a movie doesn't build up an overwhelming desire to be part of the event, people just don't go. They don't listen to their own instincts, they don't listen to the critics—they listen to the advertising. Or, to put it more precisely, they do listen to their instincts, but their instincts are now controlled by advertising. It seeps through everything—talk shows, game shows, magazine and newspaper stories. Museums organize retrospectives of a movie director's work to coordinate with the opening of his latest film, and publish monographs paid for by the movie companies. College editors travel at a movie company's expense to see its big new film and to meet the director, and directors preview their new pictures at colleges. The public-relations event becomes part of the national consciousness. You don't hear anybody say, "I saw the most wonderful movie you never heard of"; when you hear people talking it's about the same blasted movie that everybody's going to—the one that's flooding the media.

From Pauline Kael, "On the Future of Movies," *The New Yorker*, 1974. Reprinted in *Mass Media*, eds. Robert J. Glessing and William P. White (Chicago: Science Research Associates, 1976), p. 68.

One of the big problems with film viewing today is that the enormous public relations efforts of the film makers discourages independent judgment. Instead of seeing a movie and responding to it in personal terms, the viewer is predisposed to take a particular stance toward it. (These days, PR departments begin to "hype" a film as an Academy Award winner even before a single scene has been shot.) Students need opportunities to develop their own responses to "the language of film" and to form, in language, their own responses. Just as with television, we want to help them become independent judges of film, not just miniature critics.

The Short Film

A great boon to English/language arts teachers has been the evolution of the short film as an art form. Recent decades have seen the making of engaging, sophisticated films, some of which run just a few minutes, most which can be shown and discussed within a single class period. One thinks of such films as *Toys*, an eight-minute film about the "toys" of war; *Frank Film*, a nine-minute encapsulation of the filmmaker's life; *Doubletalk*, nine minutes on inept human communication; and *Blaze Glory*, a ten-minute satire on wild west movies. What teachers do with short films will naturally be dictated by the content of the film itself, though teachers should not fall into the trap of aimlessly showing films and letting the students do what comes naturally. These films are excellent sources of writing ideas, and many fit naturally into literature units, either following or leading into an exploration of a literary work. Many provide interesting examples of language in operation, and all can be studied in moderation as examples of the filmmaker's art.

Film Goers Polls

As a test of the responses and reactions of other young people and adults, have your students develop film goers polls. They might interview people going into and leaving a theater. (The theater owner's permission might be required.) Why are people going to the movie? What do they expect to see? Where did they first hear about the film? Do they already know how it ends? Are they pleased or disappointed afterward? Will they recommend the picture to their friends?

Such interviews can yield statistical data for tabulation or material for a student-written feature article about film. Both kinds of writing are a natural for a school paper. If actually traveling to the theater is not possible, students can conduct similar kinds of polls around school, asking fellow students what they watch and why.

Fads and Fancies in Film

Encourage your students to study film types or genres, particularly the more faddish sorts. For instance, the last decade saw a number of film fads: disaster films, subdivided into airplane disasters, deep sea calamities, and natural catastrophes—earthquakes, fires, comets; occult films; scare-the-daylights-out-of-you movies; and highway high jinks, with foolish looking police officers pursuing roguish heroes and heroines at high speed. Ask your students to search out the formulae of such films and try to explain the appeal these have for viewers.

Studying Response to Film

Teachers can help students become independent film viewers by encouraging them to be aware of how they respond to film and why. The questions following any film—including films shown on television—might run as follows.

1. *Response.* What is your response? How did you react? What did the film make you think or feel? Did you want to laugh? to cry? Where did the film touch your own life, you own experience? Did you relate to any of the characters in the film? Were any of the problems or characters just like life for you?

2. *Discussion.* Let's look at the film itself. Why did you react the way you did? What was it: the action? the characters? the pictures? (Without a lot of technical jargon, the teacher can help the students see how their responses were directed by the strip of acetate rolling through the projector.)

3. *Evaluation.* Did the film have an impact on you *skillfully?* Were the characters realistic? Did they need to be? Did the film hold together? (Again without introducing a great deal of sophisticated terminology, the teacher can help students engage in criticism that will help them clarify their own values and responses to cinema.)

RESPONDING TO MEDIA: STUDYING THE NEWSPAPER

Students usually enjoy a newspaper unit, and the materials are readily available. Often local newsstands carry both local and out-of-town papers, so the teacher can show a range of journalistic approaches. In addition, a great many papers have education programs that, among other things, will supply the class with newspapers for a period of time. Frequently these programs include guides for teachers, and sometimes guest speakers are available as well.

American newspapers began with bulletins hung on tavern walls or print-ed sheets from the local postmaster or printer. Anyone could start a newspaper, and this fact was most important in the development of a free press. Most schools have small newspapers that cover only events in school, but there is no legal reason why these papers could not be ex-panded to become neighborhood newspapers. On the other hand, a school radio or TV station cannot broadcast to the public without a gov-ernment license. New, inexpensive offset printing systems make it possi-ble for anyone with a few hundred dollars to produce a small newspaper with a circulation in the thousands.

From Jeffrey Shrank, *Understanding Mass Media* (Skokie: National Textbook Company, 1975).

However, analyzing the content of a paper does not teach as much as learning the ins and outs of journalism through actual experience. Instead of the conventional newspaper study unit, the teacher might consider a simulation game, "Newsprint."

"Newsprint"

The class is divided into teams of five or six students, each team forming the staff of a newspaper. Within the ground rules established by the teach-er, each team develops a paper that is run off in multiple copies. The newspapers are taken to another cooperating class whose students are asked one question: "If you were going to buy one newspaper, which of these would you purchase?" The resulting "circulation figures" determine the winner. The game is best played in several rounds, each group produc-ing a fresh paper for each round and adapting its style and format to at-tract more readers. The basic procedures for "Newsprint" are as follows:

TEACHER'S MANUAL FOR "NEWSPRINT"

ESTABLISHING GROUND RULES

Few limits need to be placed on the actual content or form of the newspapers since the aim of the game is for students to discover a form and content that will win them a readership. The teacher does need to ensure that the same production materials are available to each group and set common limits and ground rules. The teacher should establish:

Length Limits. Two-, three-, or four-page papers seem to work best, though sometimes longer papers can be produced.

Medium. Probably ditto or mimeograph. Ditto is generally more satisfactory since the students can do the layout themselves.

Special Limitations. The teacher may want to ban or encourage the use of typewriters, depending on availability, or set special limits on the shape or content of the newspapers. It may be necessary to limit the source of news—school only, city only, etc.—and to establish time limits—two days, four days, or whatever fits the schedule best.

PROCEDURES

Round I. Forming newspaper teams can be done by self-selection, teacher appointments, or choosing up sides by editors. After the students understand the ground rules, set them to work. You might want to bring in a supply of newspapers, preferably of many different styles and patterns, and leave them about the class for reference. You can serve as a consultant or not, depending on your interests and those of the students. When the papers are finished, rush them off to the cooperating class and wait for the results. (In addition to asking the cooperating students to indicate their first choice, you might want to have them rank the newspapers and/or fill out a simple feedback form telling what they saw as the strengths and weaknesses of each.)

Round II. Self-evaluation takes place. The winners bask in glory; the losers scramble about finding ways to increase circulation. The students study the feedback from their readership (or poll the other students in person), learn from one another's first editions, adapt ideas, beef up strong points, cut out losing ideas. The same evaluation procedure applies to winners as to losers, and it proves interesting to see what changes in circulation figures take place after the evaluation. Often the first-round winner will stay with the tried-and-true and be dethroned by an innovative former loser.

Additional Rounds. The game can continue as long as the newspapers evolve in new directions and as long as the students remain interested.

Like most simulation games, "Newsprint" does not require a great deal of analysis after the fact; competitors learn in the process. As a follow-up, however, the teacher can spend some time reviewing the events of the competition and helping the students relate their experiences to the problems of the daily paper in America. One way to focus the follow-up is to have the students evaluate a local newspaper and send their suggested changes to the editor. In fact, the editor might want to respond to your students' suggestions and could possibly be prevailed upon to analyze and critique the papers they produce.

If "Newsprint" works well, you might also try variations with other media and forms. Instead of newspapers, have the students develop a magazine on a topic of their choice—sports, home living, fashion, cars—and market their magazine in cooperating classes. Alternatively, conduct a literary magazine contest based on the students' own writing.

EXPLORING THE MEDIA OF PERSUASION

The analysis of persuasive language—advertising and propaganda—is a productive and intrinsically interesting study for English classes. Students enjoy sifting through newspapers and magazines and studying TV commercials to gain a sense of how mass media are used to market beliefs, ideas, values, personalities, and products. Rather than simply having students analyze, however, you might want to try engaging them in developing a persuasive campaign.

"The Campaign"

This activity can be done by a whole class or by small groups; it can be done as a simulation, with the students themselves serving as an audience or for real, with an audience selected from the school or community.

The students select an issue or a topic that they see as important in the school, community, or world; they identify a target audience that *dis*agrees with their point of view; and they develop a multimedia campaign to persuade that audience. Thus the students might campaign for more student privileges with the faculty as target; for better recreation areas with the town council as target; for a cleanup of a stream or river with landowners and industries as target. As a simulation, "The Campaign" might be aimed at passage of gun control legislation, with the class itself role playing Congress.

After helping the students find a topic and target, simply present a list of a few of the many possible means of persuasion:

Buttons	Television documentaries
Placards	Radio shows
Editorials	Guerrilla theater
Essays	Strikes
Laws	Propaganda
Petitions	Rumors
Sit-ins	Threats
Bumper stickers	Blackmail
Interviews	Films
Debates	Slide tapes
Letters	Media shows
Letters to editors	Appeals
Recall drives	Lobbying
Advertisements	

Some teachers are bothered by seeing unconventional and unethical persuasion forms like "threats" and "blackmail" on the list. The intent here is not to teach these forms but to help students recognize that both ethical and unethical means are not only considered, but used on them every day of their lives. Presumably the students will recognize that advertisements and editorials are, in the long run, more effective than the unethical means anyway. In doing so, they will naturally engage in a wide range of classical questions about persuasion:

What forms of persuasion are most effective with the various target audiences? Why?

Is it possible to be immoral or unfair when campaigning?

Is it wrong to make the worse appear the better cause?

The actual presentation of the campaign creates a spectacle. Students come to class armed with posters, placards, banners, and buttons. Their presentations—at least in my experience—are animated and involved.

When all the commotion has died down, it is important to include a follow-up discussion, so that the activity isn't just fun and games. Ask the students to evaluate the impact of the various campaigns: Which were most successful? Why? Which fell short of the mark? What went wrong?

At this time, too, the teacher might want to refer to models of professional persuasion in newspapers and magazines to enlarge the discussion.

COMMUNICATING THROUGH MEDIA

In the previous sections, I have outlined a few of the many ways teachers can use the mass media as a source of study in English classes. The task remains in this section to sketch some of the possibilities for media *composition*—using media to send a message or to create a work of art. Of course, responding to media and creating in them cannot be completely separated. In the previous section, both "Newsprint" and "The Campaign" involved students in preparing media materials as a way of understanding how they work. By analogy, as young people communicate through various mass media, they can be expected to understand more completely how the media work and to increase their ability to react critically.

Film Making

Film making has become one of the more popular media activities in English classes, frequently growing to the status of a separate elective course. Today's students are visually oriented as a result of the popularity of television and top-quality films, so that film is a language they find quite comfortable. Producing a film is also immensely satisfying; it is a tangible and visible accomplishment. Because of the high quality of contemporary camera equipment, film making often produces results that are apparently more professional than those of other modes of composition. What is a bit surprising is that today's "lazy" students who allegedly have "short attention spans" and need to be "entertained constantly" are delighted to spend the time necessary making a good film. The process is quite time consuming—a three-minute film can easily require 20 to 30 hours of work—and by comparison, writing is an easy medium.

Some teachers are reluctant to offer film making as an option in the class because of uncertainty about the nature of the equipment and its possible expense. In fact, it is neither complicated nor expensive, thanks in large measure to the home movie industry and its desire to put movie making within easy reach of Americans. A typical three-minute film made in Super-8-millimeter film costs less than $16, including film and processing charges. The camera used can be expensive, especially if it has elaborate features and special lenses, but it need not be; one can achieve quite interesting results with ordinary equipment. My own classes use a camera I picked up for $8 at a sidewalk sale (its original price was $16). Although this simple camera doesn't have the capability of producing zoom or wide angle shots of *War and Peace* scope, it produces quite satisfactory—frequently impressive—results, and more important, my students have never experienced a major failure with it.

If your budget will permit, the final results will be most satisfactory if your new film makers shoot one practice reel to learn about the camera and to learn about how their visualizations appear on film. Have them do everything imaginable with the camera—panning back and forth slowly and rapidly, running with the camera, shooting out of automobile windows, trick photography, shooting in dim or bright light. These exercises will help to diminish errors on the final copy and give your students some feel for the medium.

Topics for films are limitless. Almost any idea, feeling, poem, play, or song can lead to a short film. The best topics are those that lend themselves to montage effects, collections of thematically related shots. This kind of effect can be achieved for subjects such as people, animals, feet, moods and emotions, the seasons, poem interpretations, leaves, and songs. Least satisfactory are attempts to tell stories through film and films that involve actors. The problem is simply that narrative films involve complex sound-sight relationships that are beyond the capacity of 8-millimeter equipment, and the results are often rather sad, unconscious parodies of silent film melodramas. What 8-millimeter film does best is collect many images and many movements and fire them off in rapid succession. Among the better models for the 8-millimeter film maker are commercials and short art films, both of which exploit the capacity of film to create and sustain a mood, feeling, or theme over a short period of time.

Planning a film is critical. Films shot at random or solely on inspiration look it. In working out a formal or informal shooting script, the students should consider the scenes they want and how they will obtain them. To the fullest extent possible, students should try to edit in the camera—that is, to plan their sequence of shots so that, barring mistakes, little cutting and splicing of the film will be needed.

However, the editing process is one that many students enjoy and most films need, and you should encourage the students to think in terms of the necessary rearrangements, shifts, and deletions that would improve their film. A simple movie editor is inexpensive—$10 to $15—but usually someone's parents own one that has been sitting in a closet, unused for years.

A sound track of one kind or another may be important for an 8-millimeter film. In simplest form, this can simply be a record played while the film is shown. (One can achieve interesting results by playing different records with a film—each record contributing something new to sound-image relationship.) Other sophisticated sound tracks are more complicated to prepare and may require hours of work with a tape recorder. The central problem is synchronizing tape and film, and achieving a one-to-one correspondence between image and sound is virtually impossible. The best solution is for the student to visualize the film in sections or phases. After the length of each phase has been carefully timed, the students record appropriate music or speech, leaving a moment of silence or background music between phases. Though the correspondence will not be exact, the sound track and film phases will match closely enough to provide an integrated experience.

The Slide Tape

Somewhat less dramatic than film making is constructing a slide tape—a series of colored transparencies accompanied by a taped sound track. During presentation, the tape recording is played while the presenter/projectionist controls the showing of slides to match the tape. The medium offers some unique possibilities, and it is not simply a poor man's movie. Because the projectionist can control the pace of the slides, many of the problems of film sound tracks are eliminated, providing precise sound-image correspondence, even to the point of having images change in time to music or poetry. In addition, modern slide projection equipment makes changing slides easy, providing a rapid series of image changes and exposures of one second or less. Because the pace can be controlled, slide tapes are often longer and more complex in content than films. For students seriously interested in photography, the medium of the transparency provides a much more professional outlet. Good as student movies can be, they seldom have the visual quality of a good slide tape.

Most of the topics suitable for films can be explored through a slide tape in different but equally interesting ways. In addition, the slide tape opens up possibilities for such topics as:

Documentaries—substantial narrative discussions of problems and issues.

Literature presentations—with perhaps a dozen poems or poets represented in a sustained literary experience.

Readings of student works—with accompaniment of music and photography.

Reader's theater—a literary work read aloud with appropriate photographs shown on the screen.

As in film making, preplanning a slide tape is important. However, because of the ease of changing the order of a deck of slides, editing a slide tape is much easier. The movie maker usually begins with the film and shapes the sound track around it. The maker of a slide tape can work either way—beginning with an idea for a sound track and searching for pictures or developing the content of the tape around a set of visual images.

The final presentation of the slide tape is likely to be more spontaneous than a film show, for which the projectionist simply starts sound track and film and lets them both run. The slide tape projectionist must synchronize pictures and tape in process, and this requires a good deal of planning and rehearsal. It is possible to obtain a gadget that will automate the process, resulting in a perfectly synchronized show, time after time. This is easier, but in some ways it limits the spontaneity and adventure of the slide show.

Radio Play

It is unfortunate that the radio drama is almost dead, because radio plays developed an audience involvement that has never been and cannot be matched by film and or television. But the aural concepts behind radio

plays are alive and well in many English classes in the form of tape recorded simulations of radio programs.

Not all students will find live classroom drama to be their medium.
Not all students can perform comfortably in a dramatic reading. Radio
plays—done with a tape recorder—offer a productive outlet for such students, as well as being interesting for most other students in a class. Although radio dramas have all the advantages of improvisation, they leave
room for mistakes, which can be erased and retaped until the students are
satisfied. Tapes also provide a kind of anonymity for the student who wishes it.

Radio plays offer realism not available in other dramatic forms. No
matter how skilled an actor, a 17-year-old impersonating a 70-year-old onstage still *looks* 17, and putting on greasepaint doesn't help. But a 17-year-
old speaking into a tape recorder can be any age, so that with radio plays
students have available to them a wider range of roles that can be explored
realistically. The very boundaries of the drama can be extended through
the radio play—three students tape recording in a small room can become
a roaring party, the crew of a spaceship, or the entire cast of *Our Town*.

Radio also opens up the possibilities of using sound effects to create
impressions of mood and place. Many stores sell sound effects records that
contain a wide range of interesting noises—ping-pong games, marching
bands, leaky faucets, cavalry charges. But much of the fun comes in creating one's own sound effects, either by collecting real sounds on a tape recorder or developing in-class machinery that will duplicate the sound desired—say, an airplane, a truck, or an explosion.

Producing a radio drama is time consuming. The students can improvise or work from prepared scripts, using their own stories or adapting materials from other media. The basic studio tool is the tape recorder. Supplementary equipment can include additional microphones, linked together
through a mixing device, and various patch cords that allow the tape deck
to be wired directly to a record player, radio, or other tape recorder. Many
of the students in your class will understand the electronics even if you
don't. Also explore the possibility of using one of the newer stereo recorders that has the capability of layering "sound on sound," providing for
many interesting stereo effects and complex mixes of voice and music.

For examples of radio plays in case your students are not familiar with
the medium, bring an album on the history of radio, with such gems as
"The Shadow," "One Man's Family," and "The Lone Ranger."

In addition to the radio play, the tape recorder can be used to recreate
any number of other radio forms such as interviews and panels, documentaries, news and sports broadcasts. Survey the programs of a good FM station for samples, and investigate the AM filler broadcasts with shows like
"Ask the Doctor," "Dear Abby," "On the Road," "Perspectives," and
"Sports Shorts."

Finally, explore the use of the school's public address system for wider distribution of your students' radio work. Many schools have student-run radio stations that play through the PA into lounges, halls, and lunchrooms. Your students' creative radio programs might well fit into the schedule.

Video Tape

More and more schools have purchased small portable video tape units, and if you can break the monopoly that the athletic department generally has on the equipment, video tape has great possibilities for use in an English class. The equipment is easy to operate—only a bit more complicated than a tape recorder—and a trend toward video tape cassettes even solves the problem of threading the machine.

If you are in an area that has a cable TV the regulations of the Federal Communications Commission require that some cable channels be left free to public access. This means that your students can have their tapes shown—free—and sent into thousands of homes. Check with the local cable authority for details and procedures.

What can students do with video tape? Just about anything that appears on prime time—modestly, of course, and quite possibly in better taste. However, when students imitate commercial TV they tend to drift into satire. That may be good if you want to sharpen their critical viewing skills, but if you want them to enter into video seriously, you may have to propose some other projects. Some possibilities for school video:

Tape an improvised drama. Replay the tape for discussion. Then have the students do the improvisation a second time.

Prepare a documentary video tape. Have students investigate an issue or problem around town or school and report on it. This project will be easiest if your school has a "portapak" video outfit, one that can be carried from place to place easily.

Put on a puppet show for the cameras.

Stage a play, either chamber theater or a form where students learn lines. (Video makes memorizing easier, since it can be done a scene at a time.)

Tape instructional materials. Get some of your good writers to plan a tape showing how they write and revise a paper.

Tape a panel discussion.

Make a tape of a simulation game in progress.

Prepare a program on a favorite author, with a student dressing up as the writer.

TOWARD A MEDIA CURRICULUM

I have presented a sampler of media forms in this chapter. There are many more possibilities, many of them described in the references at the close of the chapter. It is important to stress, however, that media instruction will not succeed if it is simply treated as a novelty or gimmick. The various media should be used in English and language arts classes regularly, and the students should become very comfortable with them. James Morrow and Murray Suid have developed the outline for a K–12 media curriculum. (They include print and drama as well as electronic and visual media.) Whether or not a school system has such an elaborate curriculum, their program provides a model that can be used by teachers at any level and can serve as a conclusion to this chapter.

A MEDIA CURRICULUM

KINDERGARTEN AND GRADE 1

Stage: Playlets and skits improvised for live performance before other class members.

Design: Greeting cards, illustrations for original stories, one-panel cartoons.

Print: Simple dictated stories, poems, and picture captions.

Photography: Slide tapes made by teacher or older children with class members supplying drawings or body language for the camera and voices for the tape recorder.

Radio: Playlets and skits acted out for tape recorder operated by teacher or older children.

Movies: Movie stories acted out before equipment operated by teacher or older children.

Television: Playlets and skits acted out before equipment operated by teacher or older children.

GRADES 2 and 3

Stage: Magic shows, comedy routines, acts, speeches, and other prepared productions.

Design: Comic strips (not books), posters, ads, fun houses, and game boards.

Photography: Complete slide tape production, including creation of script, visual materials (drawings, collages, etc.), and sound track, but with older children or teacher holding the camera or tape recorder if necessary.

Radio: Complete radio production (including script, sound effects, and acting) can now include class members operating uncomplicated cassette recorders.

Movies: Complete movie production, with sets, costumes, props, and script devised by class members, but with teacher or older children running camera. Elementary cutout and object animation with teacher or older children setting up the camera and class members clicking off the frames.

Television: Studio production of plays and skits but with teacher or older children operating the equipment. Portable video production can now include kids aiming the camera.

GRADES 4, 5, AND 6

Stage: Preparation can now include formal rehearsal of a formal script (memorizing lines).

Design: Comic books running to several pages (not just strips), conscious use of propaganda in magazine ads and posters.

Print: Stories and plays running to several pages, poems of several verses, review of books read and movies seen.

Photography: Slide tape production can now include class members operating simple "Instamatic" cameras. Class members can also create photo exhibits and photo essays with Instamatic prints.

Radio: Complete radio production, with class members operating reel-to-reel tape recorders and taking battery-operated cassette recorders outside to make "sound essays."

Movies: Live action movie production can now include class members operating "Instamatic" cameras. Sophisticated cutout or object animation, with teacher or older children setting up the camera and class members clicking off the frames and checking out the shots.

Television: Portable video production, with class members using the camera with only casual supervision by teacher. Studio equipment still operated by teacher or older children with occasional placing of class members in the driver's seat.

GRADES 7, 8, AND 9

Stage: Complete play production, sustained improvisations, speeches before large groups.

Design: A wide range of design and art activities, including posters, magazine designing, advertising, etc.

Print: Stories, plays, and poems of greater sophistication, plus the beginnings of personal essays, newspaper and magazine forms, and the like.

Photography: Slide tape production can now include 35mm slide photography and sound track mixing (music under voice, etc.) by class members. Photo exhibits and books can include 35mm prints.

Radio: Radio plays running to 15 or 20 minutes in a full studio setup, with several microphone inputs mixed by class members onto one tape.

Movies: Live action and animation with class members running the camera and teacher checking out shots occasionally.

Television: Studio and portable production with class members running all the equipment under teacher supervision.

GRADES 10, 11, AND 12

A few students really take off. They write novels and plays, produce hour specials for television, and make feature length 8mm movies. More commonly, teachers work toward increaisng sophistication and higher standards in all the productions named thus far: skits, routines, acts, bits, comic books, posters, greeting cards, fun houses, game boards, magazine ads, stories, poems, plays, essays, reviews, scripts, captions, photo books, photo exhibits, slide tapes, radio plays, sound essays, live action films, animated films, portable television programs, and studio television programs.

EXPLORATIONS AND RESOURCES

- Using media effectively in a class depends in part on the extent to which the teacher feels comfortable with them. If you have never done so, make a film or a slide tape so you can learn the intricacies and problems of using cameras and tape. Find out where a video tape machine is kept and experiment.
- Still photography also offers some interesting media opprotunities. Explore and experiment with such forms as photo essay, photo journal, thematic photography, and sequence photos.
- Simulations, games, and real life experiences are possible for virtually all media and help one come to understand any medium better. Design and test out an activity that would engage students in considering the problems and quality of, say, television programs and films. One possibility for television: In a simulation mode, have small groups write (and ideally, videotape) 15-minute pilots for a new television series.
- Sponsor an 8-millimeter film festival. Get the neighborhood camera shop to donate prizes.
- Short films of five to twenty minutes in length are readily available for rental to teachers and can be used as an excellent media source for many different kinds of classroom activities. Find the names of several film distributors (addresses appear in the professional journals from time to time). Collect their catalogs. Systematically take advantage of short films as classroom resources.
- McLuhan said it: "The medium is the message." By that he meant that every medium—print, television, radio, film, telephone—places, shapes, and limits the message it carries and the effect of that message on a listener. Thus, you can do

things in some media that you can't in others, and each medium "messages" the audience in different ways.

Engage some students in an examination of medium messages. Have them select a favorite medium and analyze its potential and its message. Some questions that might be raised:

What does this medium do best (e.g., spread news, present literature, inform, amuse, entertain)?
What worst?
In what ways, if any, does it "bend" or "distort" reality in sending its message?
How is the reader/listener likely to be influenced or worked over by this medium?

An interesting variation of this activity is to have students examine the medium massages of various types of literature. A poem, like a television set, has certain ways of messaging people. Have students ask the same set of questions about poems, essays, stories, plays.
• Design the media component for a course you plan to teach someday. Include as rich a range of media forms—both for response and communication—as you can.

Related Readings

One could prepare an extremely long bibliography for this chapter, but I will simply describe 10 texts that might make up a basic library for a teacher interested in media exploration in English.

For an overview of the impact of media, see Edmund Carpenter's *Oh, What a Blow That Phantom Gave Me!* (New York: Bantam Books, 1974), which takes an anthropological view of the ways in which media shape our culture and values. The same theme is the topic of Marshall McLuhan's *City as Classroom* (with Kathryn Hutchon and Eric McLuhan [Agincourt, Ontario: Book Society of Canada, Ltd., 1977]), a textbook for students that leads them to investigate the impact of contemporary media from the television set to computers. Also directly useful in the classroom is Jeffrey Schrank's *Understanding Mass Media* (Skokie: National Textbook Company, 1975).

As a text for teachers, James Morrow and Murray Suid's *Media and Kids* (Rochelle Park: Hayden, 1977) provides a wealth of practical information on composing in various media forms. Hannah Elsas Miller's *Films in the Classroom* (Metuchen: Scarecrow Press, Inc., 1979) first reviews technical equipment, providing a primer for the teacher inexperienced with motion picture use, then gives guides for film selection and use. Film selection is also the focus of Jeffrey Shrank's *Guide to Short Films* (Rochelle Park: Hayden, 1979).

In recent years, a number of books analyzing television and its characteristics and effects have been written for both adults and young people. *Coping with Television*, edited by Joseph Littell (Evanston: McDougal,

Littell, 1973), is among the good books describing how television works and helping the reader gain a sense of the medium.

A single, comprehensive source of information for young film makers is *Simply Super 8: A Basic Guide to Moviemaking*, by Roger M. Sherman and Barry Schonhaut (Boston: Little, Brown, 1977), with sections on the camera, sound, editing, projectors, animation, and making films in natural settings. The camera companies are also a useful resource. Kodak, for example, has a number of free booklets on how to make interesting movies and sponsors a series of publications on various aspects of filmmaking that can be purchased at most camera stores. For information on video systems, see *The Videotape Book* by Michael Murray (New York: Bantam Book, 1975), with chapters on portable equipment, film versus video, hardware, shooting, organizing a video project, and reading to an audience. For information on radio study, see Howard Poteet's *Radio!* (Dayton: Pflaum Standard, 1975).

15
Evaluation, Grading, and Research

HOMEROOM TEACHER	STUDENT PROGRESS REPORT					SEMESTER	
STUDENT			YEAR 197___ - 197___ GRADE				

SUBJECT	TEACHER	1		2		SEM. EXAM	SEM. GRADE
		GRADE	COMMENTS	GRADE	COMMENTS		
DAYS ABSENT							
TIMES TARDY							

KEY TO MARKS

A—Excellent
B—Good
C—Average
D—Below Average
E—Failure
I—Incomplete

1. Excellent all-around student
2. Follows directions
3. Is able to give and accept constructive criticism
4. Volunteers for extras
5. Shows improvement
6. Consistently courteous and co-operative
7. Takes pride in work

KEY TO TEACHER'S COMMENTS (T. C.)

8. Attentive in class
9. Good attitude
10. Tests unsatisfactory
11. Capable of doing better
12. Talks too much
13. Disturbs others
14. Does not bring required materials to class
15. Wastes time

16. Careless with school property
17. Absent too much
18. Needs supervision of home study
19. Does not pay attention
20. Does not meet assignments
21. Careless work habits
22. Lack of respect for others

21-M—10-71—RIEGLE PRESS INC.—DR-9992

I sometimes think the educational system of this country is best characterized as a house of straw, bound together by the grading system. If Ph.D. candidates stopped hustling for grades in advanced seminars, if MA candidates didn't want good grades in order to gain entrance to a doctoral program, if undergraduates lost interest in high grade point averages, if high school students didn't grade-hunt to impress their way into colleges, if elementary school students were no longer threatened by the thought of failing to be passed along to high school, and if mommies and daddies stopped giving children quarters for every "A" on the report card, the entire structure might collapse in a tangle of arms, legs, minds, and intellectual fodder.

The metaphor is extreme, but it points out the principal objections that many of us have to the grading system. Grades often deal with trivial matters; students may be graded down as easily for their failure to "show respect for school property" as for their propensity of "talk too much" (especially ironic if this happens in a class dealing with language). Grades induce a false competitiveness in many children, producing students skilled at playing the grading game and unskilled at meeting the more substantial goals of education. Worst of all, grades are often used as mere binder for straw houses that *ought* to be blown away, supporting poor educational practice by threatening to fail those who do not acquiesce or perform.

Grades are also difficult to give. Sally Brown puts her finger on the problem very nicely in Figure 15.1: "How can anyone get a 'C' [or an 'A' or 'B'] in coat-hanger sculpture [or essay writing or novel reading]?" What does a "C" or an "A" or a "B" grade mean anyway? It is easy enough to grade automobile performance in acceleration or to rank the order of teams in a baseball league—one simply derives a scale of performance and tests it. It is much more difficult for teachers to derive accurate, consistent criteria of measurement and evaluation. Almost any system employed becomes either unworkable or unfair. Studies of theme grading, for instance, show that given a randomly selected group of evaluators, almost any composition will receive a range of grades from excellent to poor.[1]

Finally, grades have a negative effect on many students' self-esteem. Obviously any grade less than "A" means that failure of one kind or another is being perceived by the teacher. Thus in a class where, say, 25 percent of the students receive "A," the true failure rate is a painful 75 percent, despite the fact that the schools only acknowledge the "Fs" as failing.

THE GRADING SYNDROME

Given all this rather obvious evidence that grades are both harmful and ill-founded, why has grading survived so long? The answer, I think, is that grades have so permeated the school system that everyone has become addicted to their use. I chose the word "addicted" carefully, because I think it is appropriate. In the typical school, few people can live without grades. Despite the obvious harmful effects, students have become hooked on grades. When papers come back, the students immediately scan to the end to find out what the grade is, ignoring the teacher's comments. When assignments are given out, the students want to know more about how the grade will be given than how to approach the task. When teachers try to deemphasize the letter grade, they hear a howl of protest from the students. For the good students, grades are a prize and a goal, and they resent any attempt to devalue their "As" and "A-minuses." Somewhat surprising-

---

[1] See Richard Braddock, Richard Lloyd-Jones, and Lowell Schoer, *Research in Written Composition* (Urbana: National Council of Teachers of English, 1963), Chapter III, "The State of Knowledge about Composition." In a typical study examined, Paul Diederich and others found it "disturbing" to report that "94 percent of the papers [graded] received either seven, eight, or nine of the nine possible grades, that no paper received less than five grades, and that the median correlation between readers was .31" (p. 41). The Diederich study appeared in *Factors in Judgments of Writing Ability* (Princeton: Educational Testing Service, 1961).

Figure 15.1 Charles Schulz, "Peanuts," March 26, 1972. © 1972 United Feature Syndicate, Inc. Reprinted by permission.

ly, the average students are equally addicted, too, and unless they too receive their daily dose of "Cs" and "B-minuses," they start getting jumpy.

Teachers are often addicted, but in somewhat different ways. The teacher's habit comes from the use of grades to compel youngsters to do things. The teachers' lounge talk is infamous: "I always start them out with 'Ds' and 'Cs'; that scares them and they work harder." "Wait till they get a look at the test I've cooked up for them this time! It'll keep the grades down." Of course teachers faithfully disavow the addiction by offering rationalizations: "My students want to know where they stand." "People are evaluated all the time in life, so it's important for the students to be evaluated in school."

The addiction to grades is obviously highly destructive to the kind of English and language arts program described in this book. Students will learn language when they are using it for their own purposes, and it is doubtful that grading adds much to that reality. As often as not, grades are merely a distraction that interferes with the normal feedback and self-evaluation processes that will operate in a well-functioning English class.

KICKING THE GRADING HABIT

The National Council of Teachers of English has looked into the problem of grades through its Ad Hoc Committee on Grading. The committee made a number of recommendations about grading uses.

GRADING POLICY
National Council of Teachers of English

1. Reporting of a child's progress in the early years should be done through methods other than the assignment of a letter or numerical grade. Rather, the reporting of a child's progress should be through regular conferences based on anecdotal records, comparative samples of a child's own work, the teacher's estimates of the child's growth in skills, and his or her growth toward achieving other goals that the community and the school might have set.
2. After the early years, at all educational levels only passing grades (Pass, A-B-C, or any other symbols distinguishing levels of passing performance) should be recorded on a student's permanent records.
3. If a student has progressed in a course, but has not completed it when the calendar indicates the term is over, he or she may either withdraw without penalty or request a temporary mark of incomplete, subject to his or her later completing the work by a date agreed upon by the student and the instructor.

4. An instructor should not be required to record grades A-B-C or any other symbols distinguishing levels of passing performance if the course has been taken by the student on a Pass basis.
5. The institution will maintain no second set of books, no secret file in which instructors report the "actual" performance of the students in terms or symbols other than Pass or A-B-C or any other symbols distinguishing levels of passing performance.

The members of the committee were united in agreeing that the grading system ought to be eliminated, that English teachers should abolish grades as a method of evaluation. However, they were also aware of the depths to which grade addiction goes, and they sensibly called for some interim steps that schools can take to work toward kicking the habit. Quitting cold turkey, the committee reasoned, simply would not work.

Among the principal recommendations of the Grading Committee was that in the early years, roughly the primary grades, students should not be graded, and their work should be evaluated through conferences, discussions, written reports, and the like. Obviously this step would have substantial effects at the upper levels after a period of time. It is quite unlikely that students would succumb to the grading addiction quite so easily if their early years were freed from grades.

The committee's most controversial recommendation was that failing grades never be recorded on a transcript, that only records of *successful* course completions be kept. Thus if a student failed a course—even several times—only the final, successful grade would be recorded. The logic is simple—why punish a child for *not* having done something? Implementing such a plan is not easy, however, since most people—parents, administrators, even some students—seem to feel that some punishment for failing is vital; thus the need to record the failing grade for posterity.[2]

More realistically, the committee members observed that were grades to be abolished tomorrow, most teachers would flounder badly, since they have become so attuned to graded teaching. Thus the committee urged a period of experimentation in which teachers could discover alternative

---

[2] The degree to which this punishment syndrome permeates the schools is indicated by the policies of two universities toward failed courses. One allows students to take a failed course again, and the new grade is recorded on the transcript. However, this school also programs its computer to cross out, but not make illegible, the failing grade, so employers and graduate schools will still know of the student's evil ways. Another university has developed the humane notion of a "throwaway" term, and it allows students to drop out of school for one term without penalty. Thus students who have emotional or personal problems, overtax themselves, or become ill can bail out and start afresh. However, even this university claims it is impossible to "expunge" (note *that* cleansing word) the record of the dropout term from the student's transcript, thus undercutting the whole system.

ways of assessing student growth. In this way, by the time grades are totally discredited and the system is eroded, teachers will have found sensible ways of measuring progress that are useful to students, teacher, administrators, and parents without reliance on grades.

ALTERNATIVES IN EVALUATION AND ASSESSMENT

Experimentation leading toward the abolition of grades did not begin with the NCTE grading report, and many teachers have been exploring alternative forms of grading for years. For a person compelled by a school to give grades, this can be a frustrating task. No alternative grading system entirely satisfies students or teachers. Some unfairness or inadequacy always creeps in. Further, if one doesn't believe in the efficacy of grades in the first place, exploring alternatives is a frustrating diversion of energies.

As teachers examine alternatives, it is useful for them to keep in mind a distinction between *grading* and the broader concept of *evaluation*. Few English teachers would disagree that there is a need to evaluate students' work in one way or another. The difficulty enters in when a single symbol—the grade—is allowed or intended to stand for a wide range of students' performances in class. The following alternatives to traditional grading systems do not eliminate the concept of evaluation. Rather, they first attempt to evolve systems of letting the students know about the kind of progress they are making, and only second do they try to translate that performance into some sort of mark for a report card or transcript.

Self-Evaluation

I have experimented widely with a form of self-evaluation in both college and high school classes. I believe it is possibly more important for students to learn to judge their own work than for them to understand teacher's assessment. Thus I provide many opportunities for self-assessment. After they complete a paper, I ask students to describe their "pleasures and pains" in writing, in effect, describing what they think they did well and what they did badly. At the end of the term, I have them write an informal "intellectual history" of themselves in the course, summarizing what they have read, though about, talked over, and achieved.

I am convinced that this kind of self-assessment program is valuable for two reasons:

First, it gives students a true sense of their achievements in a course, so that no grade can substitute for their deeper understanding of what they have done.

Second, it provides a more solid basis for grading than any simple numerical system. If the only form of evaluation in a course is a series of numbers in the teacher's grade book, it is not surprising that students become grade conscious. In a self-evaluation system, the foundation is far more solid, so that the grade comes as a confirmation of what the student already knows through self-examination.

Students can even be involved in the grading process. At the end of the term, they can be asked to review the criteria that the teacher has established for the course and to suggest how they see themselves as measuring up. On that basis, students can recommend a grade and explain why the grade is appropriate. Note that the students *recommend* a grade (not "pick one"), and the teacher takes final responsibility for assigning a grade. When I use this system, I usually state that I will accept any recommendation that is written "in good faith"—that is, that makes an honest attempt at evaluation. Bad faith recommendations, described in advance for the class, include such problems as comparative grading ("All the rest of those people want 'A's' so why shouldn't I have one?"), task avoidance ("I really don't know what to say, so I'll ask for a 'B'."), or failure to discuss concrete accomplishments ("They say that you get out of a course what you put into it. Well, I must have put a lot into this course because I sure got a lot out of it!"). I also spend time discussing the range of grades that might be possible, given the basic expectations and requirements of the course. On the whole, the recommended-grade system works well. Occasionally students try to take it for a ride, recommending unreasonably high grades, but I have had more problems with students recommending a low grade out of false modesty.

Here are several other variations on the self-evaluation plan:

• *Matched Grades.* The student and teacher make up grade recommendations independently and compare notes. If the grades match (which they often do), all is well. For mismatches, a difference of opinion of one grade or more, a conference is called to settle the difference.

• *Conferences.* The student and teacher meet to work out the grade. The student brings along samples of the work for the term, and the two arrive at an evaluation.

• *Journal Evaluation.* The student keeps a detailed log of accomplishments in the class, a kind of running record in support of a grade recommendation.

Contract Grading

Contract grading provides a convenient alternative system that specifies two main components:

1. The amount of work a student must do to achieve a given grade, "C," "B," or "A."
2. The quality of acceptability for that work.

The student designs a program of work aiming toward a specific grade and discusses it with the teacher. When agreement has been reached, the student begins to execute his or her contract. Thus the method is appealing because of the way it provides for individual work.

The most obvious disadvantage of contracts was brought home to me when I experimented with the system in a high school English class. I passed out contract forms and the students and I hashed out agreements. All plans looked good on paper. One student planned to read seven novels and two magazines; another was going to write a collection of short stories; a third planned to do a film. About two weeks into the term, however, it became apparent that enthusiasm had decreased, or more accurately, that nobody was proceeding toward successful contract completion. I ask one of my student confidants about this, and he said with brutal directness, "Ah hell, Mr. Judy, we just filled those out to satisfy you." Had the students been truly free to choose their course of study, they would have chosen not to write contracts. In short, contract grading still keeps a high degree of control in the hands of the teacher.

Further, depending on how it is established, a contract system may also turn the students into what one teacher called "point grubbers." Knowing the number of "points" or books or stories required for a given grade, the students complete that work, and only that work, necessary to achieve the grade they want. In this situation, even though some negative aspects of the grading system have been eliminated, they have been replaced by others that may be just as bad in terms of increasing student dependence as learners. (That indictment also applies, by the way, to programs that use rewards—tokens, candy bars, toys, "kid cash" and prizes—as a way of inducing student motivation.)

NONGRADED SYSTEMS

A number of schools have experimented with nongraded systems. I hope that in coming years more and more schools will want to experiment with them.

Pass-Fail

Pass-Fail and the related Credit-No Credit plan are both examples of a workable nongraded system. Credit-No Credit has slight advantages because of its avoiding any mention of "passing" or "failing." Under these plans, the teacher can establish minimum levels of performance, allowing both for quantity and quality, without getting into the knotty and impossible situation of deciding on gradations of quality.

There are a few problems with the system. For instance "Pass" or "Credit" can cover a wide range of performances, lumping good students in with those whose performances are only satisfactory. However, if one is truly devoted to eliminating grade evaluations, such distinctions should not seem important.

The P-F/Cr-NCr system cannot be compromised, a practice that is rather common. Some schools, for instance, introduce a third level—"Pass *with Honor*" or "Credit *with Distinction*"—as a way of separating the good from the mediocre. Obviously such a distinction merely reintroduces grades; it matters little whether one uses letters of the alphabet, "A-B-C," or phrases: "cum laude," "magna cum laude," "super cum laude."

Another unworkable compromise is putting a school on two systems— one graded, the other P-F/Cr-NCr—and allowing students and teachers to choose which they prefer. This merely introduces gamesmanship and actually heightens rather than lessens concern for grades. The students try to take easy courses for grades, tough ones for Pass-Fail. Teachers who are inclined to see a P-F system as a watering down of standards tend to want their own courses to be on the grade system while other teachers use P-F.

Some people have argued that P-F and other nongraded systems are a bad idea because colleges "need grades to process admissions requests." While it is correct that secondary school grades are the single best predictor of college success, this is slim justification for maintaining a poor system in the schools. Convenient though grades may be, the colleges ought to be willing to look for better examples of student performance anyway.

The Portfolio

The most complex and perhaps the most valid alternative to grading is to give the children empty file folders when they enter school, and to have them fill the folders with documents describing and evaluating their experiences in school. This portfolio can be revised and updated from time to time, so that the students have a constant, manageable record of their school work. During the elementary grades, it can include the kinds of anecdotal records mentioned by the NCTE Grading Committee. Similar kinds of evaluation materials can be developed for the middle school, junior high, and high school years.

For instance, at the end of a course, term, or year, the teacher might file three items:

1. A description of the course, its goals, and the kinds of experiences it provides.
2. A self-assessment statement by the student.
3. An assessment of the student's work by the teacher.

The teacher and student might meet in conference to discuss their assessments, and appropriate appeals could be made by the student or teacher if wide differences of perception exist.

The portfolio would not be strictly limited to formal school experiences. The student might also request assessments from employers and include descriptions of out-of-school activities—from sports and camp to volunteer work.

The advantages of the portfolio system are many. It eliminates much of the concern for credits and grades. It also provides a comprehensive record of the student's work and it can be far more useful to colleges and employers than are the present grade-point averages.

Critics of the portfolio system raise many objections. What if teachers are unfair in their evaluations? Maintaining portfolios seems complicated—who wants to write or read all that stuff? Who would make decisions about which documents go in and which are left out?

But most of these objections simply can be reduced to one problem: Most schools and school systems are simply not ready for the portfolio yet. This does not invalidate the concept of a portfolio or similar system; it simply reemphasizes the point of the NCTE committee that time and experimentation will be required before the letter grade goes down for the last time.

GRADING PLANS AND PUBLIC RELATIONS

Teachers and students are not the only ones addicted to grades. Parents are often nearly fanatic about them, an especially dangerous situation because parents seldom understand the discrepancies and inconsistencies of grading systems. All too many parents, I fear, are most satisfied by what they see as a stern grading system with high standards (just like the one they seem to recall from their own school days), but one that tends to give their child high marks, thus reaffirming their sense of genetic superiority. Someone once offered the interesting thesis that standardized tests are nothing more than a compendium of what test makers' children know. This person argued that if the children of test makers were to slip to the lower percentiles, the tests would evolve until those children were on top again. Whether correct or not, that hypothesis does help to point out that the middle and upper classes put much stock in a grading system that has consistently helped to discriminate in favor of their children.

A teacher who wants to experiment with new grading systems or to abolish grades altogether must proceed cautiously, conquering public relations problems while solving the already knotty problem of developing a better evaluation scheme.

For the lone teacher, experimentation must be done with great care and a good deal of record keeping. If teachers move toward a recommended grade system, they should still keep detailed notes or charts describing what students are doing—preparing for the day when a parent asks the principal, "What's this I hear about kids getting any grade they ask for?" Even the students themselves may present some problems, since grade comparing is popular, and superficial discrepancies are bound to appear in any highly individualized teaching plan: "Jack only wrote two essays and three poems, and I wrote one essay and six poems. Why is his grade higher?" Again, record keeping, along with a prepared defense explaining that what Jack got is his own business, can help support the teacher's evaluation.

Much less risky, and ultimately far more valuable, are departmental or schoolwide discussions on grading, complete with public meetings with the parents. A major parental concern will be college entrance, and it might be useful to invite a college admissions officer to answer the critical question: "Will our students be at any disadvantage with our proposed new system?" Answers to that will vary, but in general a school will receive favorable replies *if* the new grading system is well founded and provides an adequate amount of information about the student. Many alternative systems—especially the portfolio plan—actually provide *more* information for the colleges than do grades (which only correlate about 50 percent with college performance anyway).

Above all, parents need to be told that the new system is experimental and exploratory, that the school is not irrevocably bound to it. Often, establishing pilot programs run on a comparative basis with the traditional grading plan proves useful. If the alternative is well designed and anticipates the concerns of parents, the results of comparisons will be satisfactory, even down to student evaluations of the new system.

ON SELF-ASSESSMENT AND EVALUATION

In a sense, this chapter has been a digression from the real purposes of *Explorations in the Teaching of English*. Grades are an impediment; they contribute little if anything to the schooling process, and they cause innumerable problems. Up to this point in the chapter I have simply been concerned with exploring ways of eliminating these negative effects as efficiently as possible so that the teacher can get on with the process of teaching.

As part of teaching, however, the teacher does need to consider the role of evaluation (not "grading"). In itself, evaluation is not a negative concept, and careful evaluation is a natural part of learning. For example, there are things a violinist cannot learn without being told, "That's not good; that's not the way to do it." However, in the schools we have traditionally neglected the end to which this feedback naturally aims, that is, to sharpen a person's ability to do self-assessment. What distinguishes the concert violinist from the hack is, in part, the ability to make discriminations, to recognize when things are and are not being done well. Ultimately, evaluation must become internal rather than external.

What the schools need to teach, McLuhan has suggested, is "social discrimination"—that is, the ability to judge experiences and activities independently, determining less whether things are good or bad than what they are good or bad *for*.

Specifically, in English, this introduces a whole new order of discriminations. The teacher must be more concerned about helping students learn to make their own personal assessments of novels than about judging enduring literary qualities. In writing, it means helping the students to the point where they have confidence that a way of saying things reflects well what they believe.

These refinements of judgment will also change with age. For the preschooler, value judgments are broad, fairly selfish, and unequivocal, as in the predictable response to "No, Henrietta, you may not have an ice cream cone." As students mature, their interests expand outward and their determinations of "good" and "bad" shift. A teacher needs to be especially concerned with observing the extent to which students are capable of involving outsiders in their considerations of value. Generally, for younger students, pleasing oneself is enough, so that attempts to make the student consider an audience are relatively pointless. Only for older students does satisfying the reader become a strong internalized part of a value system. Similarly, the judgmental criteria applied to reading will differ with age, and it may well be that only for the oldest are matters of style and form significant.

If teachers will keep that kind of developmental need in mind and plan appropriate self-evaluation activities for young people at all levels, much of the pain, confusion, and negative effects traditionally associated with grades will diminish. After all, if the students can truly learn to know "what they're worth," they won't be dependent upon teachers and other adults for formal evaluations. And that, in my judgment, is what good teaching is all about.

EVALUATING INSTRUCTION—THE ENGLISH TEACHER AND INFORMAL RESEARCH

"Research" does not have positive connotations for a good many teachers. Often, college level courses in research deal with abstractions only dimly related to classroom experiences. Many teachers—math haters all—have had to struggle through elementary research statistics courses, puzzling over and never quite comprehending the value of T-tests, Chi-squares, and Product-Moment Correlations.

But "research" in its general sense simply means "systematic inquiry into a subject in order to discover or revise facts, theories, etc." *(The Random House College Dictionary.)* Teachers ought to engage in that kind of research every day they walk into the classroom. It is a matter of exploring new options and possibilities and testing out their effectiveness. But a great many teachers lack an experimental attitude, tending to operate mainly on intuition, hunch, and gut level reaction rather than systematically reviewing their work. When that happens, administrators and parents rightfully complain that teachers "don't seem to know what they are doing" and look to accountability programs for a measure of protection or a guarantee of competence.

I believe that if teachers were to do systematic evaluation of and informal research into their own programs, they would not only be better teachers, they might well satisfy the outsiders as well.[3]

An informal research procedure that I have used in my own teaching follows a basic pattern for formal educational research but modifies it for classroom use (Figure 15.2). Using it, the teacher can systematically phrase questions about instructional effectiveness and seek out answers. I will take these five stages in order:

1. *Asking Research Questions.* A research scientist once remarked that a great deal of research seems to be a test of which is the worse of two bad ways of doing things. He implied that researchers often fail to ask *significant* questions. For example, "Which of these two grammars is better?" is a question often asked, but one that is limited in its value. A much better, more comprehensive question is, "Does grammar—any grammar—produce change in students' language use?"

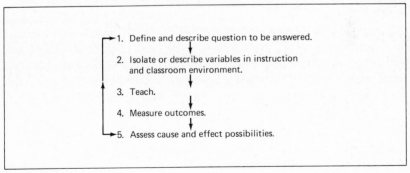

Figure 15.2

[3] I am equally convinced that teachers' negative responses to published research are quite valid, that because of the tendency of educational researchers to ape their colleagues in the physical sciences, many studies deal only in trivialities or abstractions, producing results that are interesting principally to other researchers, not to teachers. At the same time, some very good formal research is being conducted, and what I write here should not be taken as a reason for the teacher to ignore published research altogether. I think teachers should carefully scrutinize the research review columns in publications like *The English Journal* and possibly subscribe to a formal research journal, *Research on the Teaching of English*, as well.

I was guilty of this kind of sin in planning my MA research thesis. I compared two methods—lecture and small group discussion—for teaching a Shakespearean play. Unfortunately, the play was well beyond the range of all my students. Both experimental *and* control groups scored about 42 out of a possible 100 on the follow-up quiz. Instead of doing research into those two different methods, I should have been raising questions about the appropriateness of Shakespeare for my students.

What is a good research question? To me, it is a question that does not rely on unstated or unproven assumptions or unsubstantiated educational wisdom—for example, "All students 'need' this skill I want to teach." Most of the Explorations suggested at chapter end in this book imply what I take to be good practical research questions, exploring the domains of composition, literature, language, and so on. Ultimately, most research questions will center on student performance: "If I do X, will the students be better able to do Y?"

2. *Isolate Variables.* Educational research seems complicated to many teachers because of attempts to control variables. In seeking out controls to achieve what's called "validity" and "replicability" in the research jargon, researchers must take extreme steps to isolate the introduction technique under investigation. Often this results in making classroom settings contrived and unnatural, which in itself can produce false measurements.

Informal classroom researchers must be aware of variables but should not attempt to control them rigidly. The teacher can, however, try to describe all of the different factors that enter into the question under consideration. For example, if you are teaching a poem to several classes in different ways, your results may be influenced by the different performance levels of the classes: Your second hour class is bright and aggressive; your third hour kids are ready for lunch; the sixth people just want to go home. In conducting research you should try to describe all the different elements that are contributing to and shaping the class. A journal or teacher log is especially useful for this purpose, containing a running record of your observations.

3. *Teach.* A self-evident step. Less self-evident: Make certain you have kept accurate records of what you are teaching. Lesson plans, notes, and, once again, a journal are useful.

4. *Measure Outcomes.* Assessment here might be as simple as quizzing students at the end of the hour, or it might be a more complicated unit test. In an excellent article on classroom evaluation, Alan Purves describes three basic kinds of measurement:[4]

1. *Objective.* Results are measured as right/wrong or true/false.

2. *Formal Performance.* Students perform the task in a staged or con-

[4]"Evaluating Growth in English," in James R. Squire, editor, *The Teaching of English: The Seventy-Sixth Yearbook of the National Society for the Study of Education* (Chicago: University of Chicago Press, 1977).

trived setting, for example, an essay test. Presumably this performance also reflects their ability to execute the task in the real world.

3. *Naturalistic.* The teacher observes students performing in real-life settings. For example, if oral skills are being taught, the teacher watches the students work in small groups to determine if the skills are being learned.

Any of these forms of assessment may be used, alone or in combination, to determine your results. In addition, most assessment measures can be attached to grading procedures described earlier in the chapter, so that the evaluation of students and the evaluation of the new technique and method need not be done separately.

5. *Assess Cause and Effect.* Here informal research becomes tricky. The formal researcher uses statistical evidence and controls to eliminate variables and point the way toward analysis of cause and effect. Because informal researchers have no such controls, they must be cautious. So your fifth grade class responded well to your method—how do you know it was your teaching? Was there anything else that could have caused the response you observed? Here teachers must be downright cynical in looking for reasons *other* than their methods: "Of course they performed better— it's right after lunch!" "No wonder it didn't work—we had a fire drill right in the middle of the dramatic reading."

Attributing causality where none exists is a major sin in educational research.[5] You can never be altogether certain that your results show causality—a necessary connection between what you teach and what students know or can do—but if you are appropriately but not excessively suspicious, the odds are you'll draw good, sound conclusions from your informal research.

In the process of conducting informal research, I predict that you will not only become a better teacher, you will also find that matters of evaluation and assessment in your classes will go more smoothly as well. The previous topic sentence provides the basis for a good informal research question. I'll need to check it out.

EXPLORATIONS AND RESOURCES

- The grading plans described in this chapter—recommended grades, contracts, pass-fail—are only a few of many possible alternative grading systems, and even those can be used in many combinations. Work out plans for a grading arrangement that you find workable. Test it with students.

[5] I once sat in on a research seminar where a worker had found, quite accidentally, an inverse correlation between teacher attendance and the ratings students give teachers. The seminarians wasted the better part of an hour debating possible causes—"Do sick teachers teach better?" "Do kids like teachers who are absent a lot?" They finally decided that the connection was spurious and noncausal.

- Organize a schoolwide committee to review grading, whose principal function is to investigate the negative effects of evaluation systems and to arouse student and faculty interest in seeking alternatives. Such a committee might also initiate public meetings designed to elicit parental support for a changed system.
- As a class project, invite students to design evaluation plans that they see as fair and workable.
- Make an informal study of the ways in which students' abilities to make discriminations change with age and experience. What does a "good" book seem to mean for a fourth grader? What evaluative criteria does the eleventh grader apply? Do the same for writing.
- Few teachers believe that students are capable of fair and reasonable self-assessments. For your own edification, introduce an experiment of having the students take full responsibility for developing the criteria for evaluation and/or grading for all project work for a period of, say, a month or two. As teacher, you give assignments as usual. After hearing the topic or project assigned, the students should develop a set of evaluative criteria. Do their criteria change and mature?
- Create a list of good research questions: your own. Show the list to a colleague and compare notes on your views of the questions worth asking.
- Design an informal classroom research project using the pattern described in the chapter. Then conduct the project and evaluate results.

Related Readings

"Wad-Ja-Get?": The Grading Game in American Education, by Howard Kirschenbaum, Sidney B. Simon, and Rodney Napier (New York: Hart, 1971) is an outstanding exploration of the topic, including detailed discussions of the negative effects of grading, pointers on public relations, and an excellent survey of alternative grading and evaluation systems. Also excellent is William Glasser's *Schools Without Failure* (New York: Harper & Row, 1969), especially for its discussion of the ways in which failure distorts one's ability to perceive reality clearly. Two issues of *The English Journal* (March 1975 and October 1978) have focused exclusively on assessment and evaluation, including a variety of ways of responding to and grading student work. Although one can't really teach discrimination and judgment, one can help students think productively about their beliefs and value systems by using the value clarification activities described in *Values in Teaching*, by Louis Raths, Sidney Simon, and Merrill Harmin (Columbus: Merrill, 1966).

For the discussion of informal and formal assessment measures, see Alan Purves's essay, "Evaluating Growth in English," in James R. Squire, editor, *The Teaching of English: The Seventy-Sixth Yearbook of the National Society for the Study of Education* (Chicago: University of Chicago Press, 1977). The two issues of *EJ* previously cited also contain a good resource for teachers interested in conducting informal classroom research. In addition, the classroom researcher ought to have a look at two publications of the National Council of Teachers of English, *Measuring Growth in English*, by Paul B. Diederich (1974), and *Measures for Research and Evaluation in English and the Language Arts*, by William T. Fagan, Charles R. Cooper, and Julie M. Jensen (1975).

16
Professional Issues and Problems

Education as institution and English as subject are markedly sensitive to and influenced by the malaises, aspirations, and commitments of society at large. During the 1960s schools were temporarily closed by such diverse events as assassinations of national leaders, students' celebrations of "Earth Day," rioting in inner cities, failures of school tax elections, and students' protest against the continued fighting of American armed forces in Vietnam, Laos, and Cambodia. In recent years the subject of English has been forced to respond to the rightful desires of ethnic minorities and women that their contributions to literature be recognized and that their lives and values be represented accurately in textbooks; it has had to accommodate rapid and continuing growth in linguistic scholarship, particularly in psycholinguistics, sociolinguistics, and dialectology; and it has been compelled to broaden its curriculum to include study of film, mass media, and popular culture. Further, legislative demands for responsible justification of tax expenditures have shaped in part both education and English during the past decade, for "accountability" brought with it the writing of performance objectives, massive programs of testing, and new budgetary systems for the schools. At present both education and the profession of English teaching are being adversely affected by inflation and budgetary cutbacks; surpluses of teachers at all levels; declining enrollments of elementary-age students; growing violence in schools, which has necessitated the policing of school halls in many cities; and censorious groups of citizens who attempt to remove from classrooms materials they find objectionable.

In short, education as institution and English as subject exist in an environment which is simultaneously global, national, and local.

From Edmund J. Farrell, "Forces at Work: English Teaching in Context, Present to Perhaps," in James R. Squire, ed., *The Teaching of English: The Seventy-Sixth Yearbook of the National Society for the Study of Education,* Part I (Chicago: University of Chicago Press, 1977), pp. 310-311.

"No author of a single chapter of a book can do adequate justice to any one of a list of long- or short-range problems and concerns, let alone encompass them all," writes Edmund Farrell about the list of problems and influences on the teaching of English cited above. Professional problems come and go (or remain); difficult situations are resolved (or left unresolved); issues are raised and forgotten (or debated without conclusion); new methods surface and have their heyday (but instructional problems persist). In this chapter on "Professional Issues and Problems," then, I am neither going to list all the problems today's teachers are facing nor to offer solutions to them. As I stated in the Preface, teachers are in the best position to identify issues and problems and to seek solutions that fit their particular situations. ("The system is the solution," boasts a Bell Telephone commercial. How often is it that outsiders offer us their "systematic" solutions for problems we didn't know we had?)

Instead, I will address myself to three closely related issues of a general sort that seem to me crucial for English teachers in this decade of the 1980s, problems that move beyond the vagaries of topical concerns to focus on long-range priorities for the profession. These issues are, first, reintegrating English as a subject; second, extending English in new directions; and, third, coping with the historical tendency of society to restrict rather than support teachers. Then, in the Explorations section of this chapter, I will present a series of case studies dealing with contemporary issues that invite readers to propose their own solutions.

REINTEGRATING ENGLISH

The categories of the language arts are arbitrary and artificial; they do not refer to exclusive kinds of knowledge or activity in the human brain. Reading, writing, speaking, and understanding speech are not accomplished with four different parts of the brain, nor do three of them become irrelevant if a student spends a forty-minute period on the fourth. They are not separate stages in a child's development; children do not first learn to talk, then to understand speech, then learn to read, and then to write (or any variation of that order). And the four aspects of language do not require different "levels" of cognitive development. The labels are our way of looking at language from the outside, ignoring the fact that they involve the same processes within the brain.

From Frank Smith, "The Language Arts and the Learner's Mind," *Language Arts*, February 1979, p. 118. Copyright © 1979 by the National Council of Teacher of English. Reprinted by permission of the publisher and the author.

Frank Smith correctly objects to fragmenting English and the language arts into separate components. At both elementary and secondary levels, the components of English are too often taught separately from one another, and the separation increases as the students grow older. Thus, while elementary children may find themselves in a language arts block where spelling and reading are isolated and taught at different times, the high school student may be placed in a course labeled "literature" where written composition is totally ignored.

Of course, some fragmentation is necessary simply as a means of discussing and understanding the subject. English contains dozens and dozens of subfields and related subjects. Even in this book, committed as I am to something called "integrated" English, I found it important to write about composition separately from literature, to discuss the media in a chapter other than the one given over to language. Still, to borrow from the general semanticists, "the word is not the thing." The labels we use to discuss our subject should not be confused with the reality, stated by Frank Smith, that language processes are contiguous in the brain. We don't have separate faculties for reading, writing, listening, speaking, spelling, and media viewing.

I believe the need for integration can be kept in mind if I resurrect from an earlier chapter the sketch of a student (Figure 16.1) and remind the reader that the *student,* not the *subject matter,* is at the heart of what-

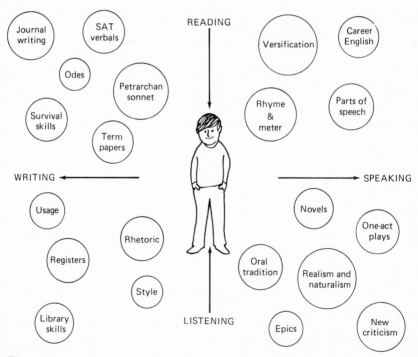

Figure 16.1

ever we label "English" or "language arts" or "communications skills." Further, it matters little whether the students themselves are conscious of the labels professionals use to describe the subject. What matters most is what children and young adults do with language—how they use it. (Perhaps I should alter the character in Figure 16.1 to show a young person immersed in language: watching TV while reading a book and talking on the telephone at the same time.)

Reintegrating English must be a conscious act for many teachers. If the curriculum guide dictates short stories, one must actively seek out other forms of literature—some plays, a poem or two—to avoid breaking the discipline into components. If a course is labeled "composition," the teacher will need to bring in literary selections and talk about writers as composers so that students see the connection between literature and their own experience with composition. If a unit involves media study, the teacher may take pains to include writing and books along with television and radio.

While many kinds of interconnections among the language arts are possible, the following seem to me most important for the teacher to keep in mind:

1. *From Reading into Writing.* Students' responses to what they read need not be limited to writing about books in pseudo-critical ways. Most important is that students be able to relate their own experiences to the ideas they find in literature, that they make a connection with the literary work. (See Chapter 7.) When this happens, students write about literature in many discourse modes, from poems and short fiction to letters and scripts. Reading provides a jumping-off point for the students to enter into the full dimensions of composing in English. (See also Chapter 9.)

2. *From Writing into Reading.* David Holbrook has reminded us (Chapter 10) that student writing may differ in quality but not intent from professional writing. This, in turn, suggests that we should treat student writing as literature and that students should read one another's work not just as critics or editors, but as real audiences who respond to classroom writing just as they would to a published work. Further, students can respond in writing to one another's literature, thus bringing the language arts class full circle.

3. *Language Study.* Most contemporary English educators argue against the study of language in the abstract as a means of changing students' usage. Still, as I have pointed out (Chapter 11), exploring language in its natural state outside of grammar texts can be quite exciting. Integrating language study and writing, then, means more than simply pointing out errors in student compositions; it means examining the intricacies of student writing as examples of language in use. Similarly, language study in literature becomes tedious if limited to the analysis of metaphor and simile or scansion of verse. A teacher can take what Jean Malmstrom calls a "linguistic attitude" toward literature by having students examine lan-

guage choices—words, syntactic structures—as they affect the reader's response.[1] Obviously, this technique helps to integrate reading and language study. It can also be used as a way of helping students respond to their own writing as well.

4. *Drama in the Classroom.* The interconnections between drama and the other language arts are too numerous to present in detail. It will suffice to note that drama has been described as the complete language art. It can involve oral composing through role playing; written composition through scriptwriting; reading, including script reading, reader's theater, and oral interpretation; media, through television and radio production; and language, including such matters as dialects and nonverbal cues. (See Chapters 13 and 14.) Scriptwriting alone is almost a complete composition course, involving everything from the expository writing of speeches to the narrative and description of stage directions.

5. *Media Study.* English is a mass medium; there is no need for a war between English teachers and media people, between print people and nonprint people. (See Chapter 14.) In media/English, students write and read scripts, see films and write or talk about them, evaluate television programs in speech or writing, and compose in various media languages, none of which, as Frank Smith would observe, is compartmentalized separately from reading and writing in the brain.

6. *Oral English.* If drama is the complete language art, oral English (Chapter 12) is the glue that cements the language arts together. No component of English—even silent reading—can be isolated from conversation or formal speech; and any lesson—whether in composition, literature, language, or media—offers opportunities for the teacher to help students develop their oral English skills.

EXTENDING ENGLISH AND THE LANGUAGE ARTS

Just as it seems unnatural to separate the components of English, it appears inappropriate to isolate English from other subjects and disciplines. From the very beginnings of our professional literature in the nineteenth century, English teachers have argued that language is an important part of every subject and should be taught by every teacher. But in an equally long history, teachers have tended to work by subjects or topics so that the elements of language are separated from, say, science, mathematics, history, and social studies.

In recent years, the cry for "English across the curriculum" has been heard again, this time in response to complaints from teachers in various disciplines that Johnny and Jane can't read and write. While English

[1] Jean Malmstrom, "Future Grammar," in Stephen Judy, ed., *Teaching English: Reflections of the State of the Art* (Rochelle Park: Hayden, 1979).

teachers have been willing to accept part of the responsibility for that problem, they have also pointed out that Johnny and Jane's subject area teachers have ignored teaching reading and writing skills in their areas, contributing to the problem. No English/language arts teacher, it is rightly pointed out, can possibly prepare students for all the reading, writing, and other language tasks they will face in other classrooms.

For the elementary school teacher in the self-contained classroom, the solution is relatively easy, for he or she takes responsibility for teaching all areas. If students are reading science or history books, the teacher can take time to show them how to read the text. If they are doing projects in geography or mathematics, the teacher can include writing projects that allow them to extend their literacy as well as their subject matter skills.

At the secondary level the problem is much more complicated, for typically in the junior high years and beyond, block, clustered, and team teaching diminish, so that more and more students are taught a single subject by a single teacher. In some schools where this is the case, the English faculty has taken steps to launch school-wide literacy programs. Faculty seminars on teaching reading and writing are established, so that interested subject teachers can learn how to include reading and writing work in their area. Ground rules are established for the grading of compositions, so that students know that writing quality as well as content will be under scrutiny in their subject classes. Reading beyond the textbook is encouraged in all classes, and free reading and paperback libraries become parts of every classroom, subject matter as well as English.

Encouraging as these kinds of programs may be, I do not believe they will be adopted on a massive scale. So long as subjects are isolated from one another, and so long as subject teachers have teaching loads and priorities of their own, full-scale cooperation in literacy across the curriculum programs does not seem likely.

An alternative possibility is for English teachers to extend the dimensions of their own teaching, making interdisciplinary concerns a part of their course. For too long, English has consisted of grammar, classic literature, and the writing of essays based on that literature. But why shouldn't students interested in science have an opportunity to read or write about that topic within the English class? Why should the student who wants to be an auto mechanic not be able to consume and create literacy materials on that subject? In my experience, interdisciplinary teaching opens up language arts classes, and teachers who are willing to cut across subject matter lines suddenly find all kinds of nonreaders and nonwriters actively engaging themselves in English work.

For convenience, I will divide the discussion of interdisciplinary English into three categories: mathematics and science, the humanities, and reading and writing in the real world.

Mathematics and Science

For many English teachers, the thought of teaching science is spooky, for they may well have chosen their college English major precisely to avoid college level work in science and math. But one does not have to be a scientist—or even be particularly knowledgeable about or interested in science—to include science in the curriculum. Neil Ellman, a former English/reading teacher who is now an assistant principal in New Jersey, has shown a few of the exciting possibilities for English-science work. Note that they draw on teachers' trained skill in language work rather than requiring them to learn a new discipline.

SCIENCE IN THE ENGLISH CLASSROOM

READING [The students read:]

Literary and scientific journals to compare them to each other for stylistic and organizational characteristics;

Biographies of scientists and literary creators to discover the similarities and differences between such individuals;

Literary works written by scientists themselves to determine their particular ways of looking at life, if indeed differences exist;

Newspaper accounts of scientific breakthroughs to determine how the press communicates difficult concepts to a mass audience;

Science fiction to compare it to science fact and futurism;

Science articles and texts to uncover their subtle biases of language and thought;

And literature about scientists to study how they are portrayed by their literary counterparts. . . .

LISTENING AND SPEAKING [The students engage in:]

Panel discussions and debates on contemporary scientific issues and problems, particularly concerning the moral and ethical dilemmas created by scientific advances;

Oral reports on recent discoveries and inventions;

Listening exercises involving tonal quality, decibel level, animal sounds, etc.;

Interviews with local scientists, science teachers, and ordinary people affected by scientific advances;

And role playing of hypothetical meetings between great scientists and politicians, religious leaders, or literary intellectuals. What would happen, for example, if Charles Darwin could debate with Plato or Pope Paul, or if Ptolemy could discuss the nature of the universe with Copernicus or Einstein? . . .

WRITING [The students write:]

Research reports on scientific and technological subjects;

Technical materials rewritten into language more suitable for the layperson, or more suitable for a child;

Imaginary conversations with and letters to scientific innovators;

Real letters to famous scientists, or letters-to-the-editor about current problems caused by technology;

Essays on the impact of science and technology;

Haiku capturing the precise moment of a scientific phenomenon, e.g., the moment of fertilization, binary fission, nuclear fusion, or osmosis;

Mystery stories in which the puzzle depends on a scientific principle;

"Found Poetry" from science textbooks and journals;

Futuristic scenarios in the manner of Herman Kahn and the Hudson Institute;

And jounalistic accounts of the activities in the school's own science program.

Excerpted from Neil Ellman, "Science in an English Classroom," *The English Journal,* April 1978, p. 64. Copyright © 1978 by the National Council of Teachers of English. Reprinted by permission of the publisher and the author.

Recognizing the centrality of language to all disciplines is the key to extending English successfully. As I suggested in Chapter 2, language is very much bound up with how we perceive, classify, and talk about our world. In entering the worlds of science and math, the teacher simply needs to let the student identify areas of interest and then pursue them through language.

Perhaps the best way to begin extending English is through individualized reading. The teacher can enlarge the paperback library by adding good fiction and nonfiction books on a science theme. Check the paperback bookstore science section for ideas, or if you don't feel confident, ask a science teacher to recommend some titles. Alternatively, ask the librarian to prepare a book cart with 50 to 100 science titles for your classroom use. Similarly, many good science magazines—*Scientific American, Science Digest, Popular Science*—can be brought into the classroom. Lest we ignore mathematics, you should know that there exist many good, readable, nontext books about mathematical ideas and concepts, including a great many books dealing with home computers and pocket calculators. Drawing on a modest library, the teacher can begin to invite individual science/ English projects, and the thrust toward interdisciplinary teaching has begun.

The Humanities

Most of us English types feel at home discussing interdisciplinary work involving the humanities: music, art, history, social studies. In recent years, there has been a move in both humanities and English toward so-called discovery learning, where, instead of merely mastering a textbook, students explore materials firsthand. This seems an ideal approach in English-humanities projects. For instance, *Experiments in History Teaching* (Cambridge: Danforth Center, 1977) is a collection of innovative programs currently being conducted by history teachers. But it takes little imagination to see how topics such as "American Experience" or "Women's History" could as easily be English as history units. "Mass Culture and Country Music" might not involve a great deal of reading other than song lyrics, but it certainly invites a range of writing projects. "Industrialization in America" is a topic that not only unites English and the humanities but also draws on science and technology as well, making it interdisciplinary in the fullest sense. "Simulating the Past" integrates dramatics and history, using role playing as a tool for teaching not only English, but history.

EXPERIMENTS IN HISTORY TEACHING

Artifacts in the Classroom [Studying historically important films, e.g., a 1934 German propaganda film.]

American Experience [Examining historical themes in the past one hundred years of American history through art, music, museum resources, and observation of historical artifacts.]

Landscape History [Using one's hometown or neighborhood.]

Afro-American Folk Culture [Through music, art, slave narratives, current street corner lore.]

Mass Culture and Country Music [Themes and concerns of Americans as expressed through their music.]

Historical Biography [Researching and writing a biography of a famous American.]

Simulating the Past [Role playing key events in history: the signing of the Treaty of Versailles, the trial of Galileo, Civil War diplomacy.]

The World of Work [Historical study of the work ethic.]

Industrialization in America [Investigating the evolution of technology in America with discussion of its side effects.]

Violence [Covert and overt violence in American history, with a discussion of implications about our values.]

Women's History [Examined through literature, film, journals, diaries.]

Baseball [A discovery unit on the history and evolution of the game.]

Topics from *Experiments in History Teaching* (Cambridge: Danforth Center, 1977). The annotations are mine, based on course descriptions in the book.

Reading and Writing in the "Real" World

Many English teachers are familiar with the *Foxfire* program of Eliot Wigginton, in which rural students met with and interviewed their elders to learn and ultimately write about folk arts and crafts. Other teachers have taken the Foxfire approach and applied it in the city, having students research a neighborhood and preserve its history in writing.

Community-based projects may include but go far beyond writing cultural history. In some school systems, upper-level students have been apprenticed to social service agencies, where they learn about the reading-writing requirements of a job through actual experience. In other schools, teachers use the community as a resource, encouraging students to learn about jobs and culture through interviews with community members. Elementary school teachers have long used the community for field trips and frequently draw community members into the school for presentations, two techniques that ought to be applied more frequently in the high schools as well. Literature teachers can draw on local writers and artists to speak to their classes both about their work and about literature. Newspapers can be visited and newspaper reporters can come to class to discuss their methods and techniques. Business executives can come to school to talk about clear writing and about the reading needs of business and industry. The list of school-community English projects is endless, and it would be pointless to list further possibilities here. The best bet for the teacher interested in this idea is to make a list of resources specific to his or her community: Alfred the Architect, Bernice the Baker, Cal the Carpenter, . . .

THE REAL WORLD OF TEACHING: RESTRICTIONS
ON THE TEACHER OF ENGLISH

It is important to place this discussion of the dimensions of English in the context of actual teaching situations. While it is all well and good to talk about school-wide and interdisciplinary programs that enlarge the range of English, the fact is that more and more forces are pushing the English teacher toward isolation and fragmentation. The back to basics people want more parts of speech and drill; parents want control over their children's reading matter and are objecting to new books; class loads are increasing despite a declining school enrollment, so that individualizing becomes increasingly difficult. Putting students at the center of the curriculum may seem important, but teachers have to think of themselves, too. For many teachers, the central consideration becomes just plain survival (Figure 16.2).

Survival

Survival is an unfortunate word to have to apply to activities in an educational institution. But it is something with which everyone involved with schools must be concerned, for the survival rate for both teachers and students is distressingly low.

The students who don't make it have been well described here and

Figure 16.2

elsewhere. Their failure to survive is reflected in dropout rates; disciplinary problems; public rejection of the schools; and above all, in a nation of adults who are marginal participants in the community of language.

Less well documented are the ways in which teachers fail to survive, perhaps because the tenure laws have a way of propping up devastated teachers and holding them in place. But it is clear that large numbers of teachers are not surviving in any real sense. One such teacher is a man I met during my first year of high school teaching, a history teacher who told me, "I really hate this place, and I'd rather be working on my flower gardens. I only have ten more years to go before retirement." Not much can be done about a sad case of that sort, except to urge the teachers' association to adopt a thirty-and-out policy that might force him into gardening a little sooner than expected.

I am more concerned about a second kind of teacher—represented by a group with which I worked for a year. In September, the teachers were bright and enthusiastic, ready to try anything. They plunged into their teaching with vigor, and this was reflected in the tone of excitement in our workshop sessions. As the year progressed, however, the meetings seemed to grow less interesting, and toward the end of the year, we realized that a negative pall had fallen over the group. Whenever one member proposed an idea, five others would instantly offer five reasons why "it'll never work." Their optimism was gone. Exploring deeper, we traced their discouragement to a range of mildly negative experiences that they were having on a day-to-day basis. Nothing traumatic like a student leaping out of a window or the principal chewing out the teacher in front of the students. Little things: no supplies; not enough ditto paper; too much red tape; too many students; too many absence reports, tardy slips, admits, and hall passes; no books; gloomy classrooms. Many of these teachers also felt very much alone in their schools because of little things like mild disapproval on the part of colleagues, occasional tut-tuts from the assistant principal about discipline or decorum, lack of support for new programs, and department meetings that failed to deal with substantive issues.

They realized that they were becoming victims of "teacher burnout." Once this problem was identified, the group was able to renew itself, and we managed to end up the year on as high a note as we began. But I feared for their survival the following year. "The schools," as someone once remarked, "are probably about the worst place for people to have to teach."

But some teachers *do* survive. Teaching next door to that history teacher who would rather garden than teach was a 62-year-old woman who could do Shakespeare in ways that deeply excited students. (She also enjoyed gardening—evenings and weekends.) One sees many other teachers who have learned not only to survive but, to borrow from Faulkner, to *prevail*. Such people seem to me to have two main characteristics:

First, they have a clear, stable sense of self and purpose. They are what John Gardner calls self-renewing persons, people who do not stagnate, whose interests and ideas are always at least two or three stages beyond their present accomplishments.

Second, they know how to function within an institution. In *The Vanishing Adolescent* (New York: Dell, 1960), Edgar Friedenberg talks about a student named Stanley, a self-directed learner who had learned to use the school for his own ends, while students all around him were being stifled by it. Stanley used the school like a railroad, Friedenberg said, checking out the scheduling possibilities until he found something that would take him where he wanted to go.

Too many teachers come to see the institution as a barrier rather than a form of transportation. In many cases, the train is not a luxury one. Often it is an ancient coach with sprung seats, torn upholstery, and dim lighting. This train often fails to run on time. While some of the passengers become depressed and spend their time fussing with the conductor, the survival-oriented traveler searches out the softest seat, and pulling out a supply of magazines, settles in to read, having informed friends at the end of the line not to expect the train to be on time. Surviving teachers just don't allow problems and pressures to place them on the defensive; they are alert to problems and aggressively work to take positive, even anticipatory, action. They are, in a very real sense, "idealistic."

Idealism is a badly understood concept. Most people take it to mean "naive optimism," the kind of thinking traditionally engaged in by liberals, free thinkers, and professors of education. In fact, idealism simply means having a set of ideas—a vision, if you will—of the way things can be and should be.

Advice to teachers wanting to survive: Keep your idealism. (Please note that I didn't say *youthful* idealism. Any teacher—20 or 65—needs to have ideals.) Don't change destinations simply because you don't like the conductor or the seating accommodations. Define your ideals carefully and don't let "them"—circumstances, clerks, administrators, and frustrations—force you to reject valid ideals.

Already I hear a voice muttering at the back of the lecture hall: "Who's he kidding? It's not *realistic* to be idealistic!" To the contrary, I submit it is actually not practical to be narrowly "realistic." If teachers do not have an idealized vision of what they want their teaching to be, and if they cannot see the remotest possibility of approximating that ideal by hook or by crook in the near or distant future, then the only "realistic" thing for them to do is to abandon teaching in favor of a "practical" profession like spot welding or steam fitting.

It would be naive to base one's vision on the assumption that next year unlimited funds will be available to every teacher for any teaching purpose, that in September all students will trot into classes eager to learn and capable of plunging into independent self-directed work. It would be equally naive to base a vision on the belief that a revolutionary storm is about to sweep across this country to dissolve the present system of education and to lead to something better. But it is both realistic *and* idealistic to visualize good, imaginative classes being taught under the present, less-than-ideal conditions.

Reality limits the ease and potential for accomplishing one's ideals overnight. Nevertheless, too few teachers are aggressive in fighting the limitations of their situation. They limit themselves by making false assumptions about their school. Too many teachers assume they will be fired if they don't teach *the noun*, but they never investigate whether or not the school actually checks up on teachers; they assume that the principal will not provide funds for a film festival, but no one has ever written such a proprosal; they assume that students aren't interested in books, but nobody has actually *tried* a full-scale free reading program.

Teachers often fail to exploit the available resources, even if minimal, losing sight of their ideal in the process: "My desks are bolted to the floor, so I guess I can't make an interesting environment for English." (Can't the walls be decorated?) "I'd like to let kids make film, but the school won't buy a projector." Has the teacher pounded on the door of the camera store to beg a donation?

Teachers can work toward their visions if they actively fight reality and refuse to take an all or nothing stance. The ideal can be approached only in stages, through successive approximations. Too many teachers quit after their first failure, or do not recognize a crude approximation as a first step rather than as a terminal plateau.

No chart or outline can conquer the limitations of one's situation, but I want to offer a three-step procedure for analyzing any situation, a procedure that should help to sort out the variables and lead you toward successive approximations of the ideal.

IDEALISM AND SUCCESSIVE APPROXIMATION

Step I

State the goal (the ideal) in detailed terms, without a thought for the limitations of reality. *Don't* compromise when thinking about your vision.

Example

I want a classroom library. An excellent one. I want 1000 brand-new paperback titles, subscriptions to 25 magazines and 5 newspapers, and a pamphlet file of 500 up-to-date monographs on every conceivable subject. And I want a comfortable display and lounge area where the students can browse and read.

Step II

List all the obstacles to that ideal. Don't leave any out. (This procedure, by the way, is an excellent way of releasing tensions.) But do not list any false or imagined obstacles; make certain that the barriers actually exist.

Example

1. There's practically no money in the book budget.
2. The department chairman has the book budget neatly tied up for his own classes.
3. The curriculum committee publishes a very limited list of approved books, and most of the ones I want aren't on it.
4. I have no place to store books, and I don't even have my own classroom.
5. There isn't any furniture for a reading center.

And so on. You can probably add ten more obstacles to the list, all of them valid.

Step III

Systematically design ways of approximating your goal, attacking the obstacles one by one, aggressively seeking ways to leap past them to approximate the ideal.

Solutions for obstacles 1 and 2 are relatively easy: You simply will have to look elsewhere for books. (You also have the option of demanding a greater share of the budget and wrestling with the department chairman for control of the English department, but let's assume for the moment that this is too dangerous to try.) First, of course, you can bring in titles from your own paperback collection, a hundred or more that have accumulated over the years and simply build up dust and moving expense. You can ask the students to do the same. Some of your friends may also be willing to contribute. You can accost the manager of the paperback bookstore for samples, damaged stock, and leftover magazines and newspapers. You can get the students to join a paperback book club, knowing that they always have 50 cents or so in loose change. You can start a paperback cooperative with other teachers in order to pool your meager resources. You can also help the student council set up a paperback bookstore. And so on. Any teacher can quickly build up resources of this sort in reasonable—though not ideal—quantities.

Obstacle 3—the curriculum committee—presents more of a challenge. First, you should do a little precensorship of the titles you have accumulated to pull out some harmless but censorially dangerous literature, like the well-thumbed copy of *The Amboy Dukes* that one student contributed and the U.S. Department of Agriculture Bulletin on sheep breeding. Having removed the most obvious sore spots, you can skim some professional book lists—*Books for You*, the Arbuthnot anthology, and *Reading Ladders for Human Relations*, for example—looking for references to the titles you have accumulated. It's unlikely that the curriculum committee will raise too many objections if books are recognized in nationally approved guides for reading. With this data in hand, you can approach the curriculum committee with this question:

> Is there any reason why I cannot supplement the curriculum selections with these titles, many of which have been approved by national book list committees as being suitable for reading by young people?

(Note that the question is *not* "Do I have to stick to your list?"—one that would bring a prompt, insulted, affirmative answer.)

It may be that the committee will reject the list in toto. If so, its judgment is suspect, and if you wanted to, you could make a mighty fuss about blanket censorship. More likely is that the committee will accept much of the list, rejecting a few titles to keep up its self-image. If they reject an unreasonable number, you can still try the old ploy of asking for reasons. Some sticky questions: "Why do you think the book is unsuitable?" "On what pages are the unsuitable passages?" and the clincher, "Have you read the entire book?"

Obstacles 4 and 5—concerning the facilities—are relatively easy ones to overcome. You can turn the problem of the reading center over to the students, explaining the idea and asking them to propose solutions. Some possibilities:

A cabinet on wheels that can be opened during class time, rolled aside or to other classes, built by the shop class.

The same thing, supplied by the local paperback distributor.

Rug remnants for seating.

Inflatable furniture that can be deflated and stored in the cabinet.

Seating cushions made by the home economics class.

I do not mean to imply that these solutions are complete. Perhaps they won't work at all. But if they don't, the process is simply begun anew, with the newer obstacles listed.

I am convinced, then, that the ideal of integrated, experience-based English can be realized (or approximated) even in these difficult times for English teachers. I am equally convinced that interdisciplinary English is not only possible, but practical, and something of which we will see more and more as we move toward century twenty-one.

Science fiction, it has been explained, is not so much a vision of a different future as it is an extension of our current view of the possible. Thus at the turn of the century, H. G. Wells correctly prophesied that the new "aeroplane" would be used for warfare, but because one part of his vision was cramped, he failed to realize the speed and sophisticated weaponry of air combat and visualized planes filled with armed sharpshooters, plugging away at one another with small arms. As often as not, the real limits placed on English teachers are their own imaginations. Once they have visualized something as possible, they can find ways to make it practical.

At this point, the text of *Explorations in the Teaching of English* draws to a close. If we were having a final examination, this would be it:

1. Be an education-fiction writer and describe a best-of-all-possible worlds school for the year 2001, including the role of English language work prominently in your description.
2. Realistically describe the barriers that stand in the way of bringing that vision into reality.
3. Describe what you as a teacher can expect to do during your teaching career (whether you plan to teach two years or forty) to start your classes on the way toward realizing that vision.

EXPLORATIONS AND RESOURCES

- The explorations in this section involve a series of case studies centering on some of the problems discussed in the chapter. In several instances, the descriptions may remind you of situations you have encountered or heard about. If so, substitute your real life case studies for mine.

GETTING BACK TO BASICS

Sandra Farmer is teaching in a relatively conservative urban school, one run by a principal who used to be a Latin teacher. The school prides itself on giving good courses in fundamentals, and one of the things that the principal likes to do is quiz teachers (informally, of course) about how they are getting along with "basics." "We don't need poets," he says, "we need plumbers, and the guy who fixes my pipes better know how to read and write. When I taught Latin . . . ."

Here are a few excerpts from the school's tenth grade curriculum:

Grammar and Word Forms

Noun forms: Plurals, possessives.
Pronoun forms: Subject and object, possessives, using pronouns to refer to indefinites, using pronouns with gerunds.
Modifiers: Forms, adjective or adverb, position of adverbs, comparison.
Verb forms: Tenses, confusing pairs of verbs, tenses of verbals, agreement with the subject.

Writing Your Paragraphs

Writing narrative paragraphs
Writing descriptive paragraphs
Writing expository paragraphs
Topic sentences
Supplying details
Adequate development
Unity
Continuity
Orderly arrangement
Tying sentences together
Emphasis through proportion

Sandra doesn't really have much use for all this, but she does feel under pressure. Devise a composition program for average tenth graders that will allow her to teach her ideal of personal, experience-oriented writing while still being able to tell the principal, in some detail, how she is covering basics.

THE PURSUIT OF LITERATURE

Materials needed: Some conventional literature anthologies

Jack Hawkins discovers, to his dismay, that the school to which he has transferred has a very traditional view of literary study, with sophomore year stressing literary types: junior year, American literature; senior year, British. The department chairman makes it clear that he wants the basic materials in the text covered, and he distributes a model syllabus that blocks out the main aims of each year's work. (He does not, however, specify whether or how he will check up on how materials are covered.)

Jack searches for alternatives. But when he goes to the book room, he finds mostly dusty anthologies and a few old copies of *Julius Caesar.* He can't depart from the text even if he wants to.

Look through a conventional literature anthology and figure out how one could use the materials inside—less the critical apparatus and discussion questions—to teach in a response-centered, issue-oriented way. In short, re-design the book the way you might teach the materials. Suggestion: First look through the book and identify every piece you would genuinely like to teach. Then think about themes, issues, and problems of interest to students that will relate to the selections you've chosen.

MAKING IT!

Samuel Gordon has had what he regards as a successful first year of teaching. The students seemed to like him and they did some interesting and creative things in class. He stressed free and individualized reading programs, lots of journal writing, and did units on science fiction, women in literature, and minorities. He did not do grammar; he did not assign book reports; he did not pay much attention to the required literature anthology. He let the students grade themselves, and the grades were higher than usual for general English classes.

Now, at the end of the year, trouble is emerging. Aside from just giving him disapproving looks, the department chairman is becoming actively hostile. The principal has, on two occasions, been seen shaking his head in concern at the noise level coming from Sam's classes. As part of the school policy, Sam must face the principal and chairman in the annual "conference," a meeting that will lead directly to a hiring (or firing) recommendation.

Role-play the tenure hearing, showing how Sam presents his case.

As an alternative assignment, devise a strategy whereby Sam could have avoided the confrontation altogether.

CENSORSHIP

Jean Miller teaches Richard Wright's *Black Boy* in an eleventh grade general English class in a conservative school district. One day the roof falls in. A minister and a mother show up to complain to the principal about the book's contents—in particular the "damns" and "hells" and the intercourse scene when Richard was six. Shortly after that, the president of the PTA calls to complain that the book whitewashes [sic] bad boys and makes all parents look dumb and tyrannical. Finally, a member of a racist political group calls to claim that the book is "black racist," giving a false picture of white people and ignoring all they have done for the Negro.

Role-play the public hearing at which *Black Boy* is discussed, with members of your group taking on the various roles. Assign two or three people to counsel Jean, helping her work out an anti-censorship case and self-defense.

INTERDISCIPLINARY ENGLISH (I)

Marcia Collins teaches third grade at Pawnee Trail Elementary School. The school curriculum guide lists "insects" as the central science topic for the spring months. No bug fan herself, Marcia decides to make the project truly interdisciplinary.

How could she link her topic to the other subjects she teaches: mathematics (basic addition, subtraction, and multiplication), music, art, social studies (featuring "America"), geography (also American), and biology (the functions of the human body)?

What kinds of reading, writing, listening, and speaking projects should be introduced?

INTERDISCIPLINARY ENGLISH (II)

The English department at Whitman High is being besieged with complaints from other departments about the reading and writing skills of students. "They can't read the text," complains a physics teacher. "They can barely write a complete sentence," observes the business education teacher.

Design an interdisciplinary English plan for Whitman High that might help to satisfy other departments without turning English into a mere service department, with its own interests absorbed by prepping students for other classes.

INTERDISCIPLINARY ENGLISH (III)

Jane Vincenzo has been assigned to the junior American literature survey second semester—from Ralph Waldo Emerson to Kurt Vonnegut, Jr. The test she has been given treats literature chronologically and conventionally, but the school's library is a good one.

Brainstorm for ways in which Jane could make her course truly interdisciplinary, including science, history, art, music, etc. Consider, too, the kinds of community based projects she might design for her course.

Related Readings

There are many good books on surviving as a teacher. The best one I have ever read is James Herndon's *How to Survive in Your Native Land* (New York: Simon & Schuster, 1971); it is an honest account of what happens when a teacher tries new methods and ideas with less-than-ideal students. Also useful is Gray Cavanagh and Ken Styles's essay, "Stress in Teaching and How to Handle It," which appeared in *The English Journal* (January 1977), pp. 76–79. Also of interest from *EJ* is Charles Bonnici's "The Two

Personalities of Teaching" (September 1978, pp. 48–50), which includes a self-test that allows the teacher to better understand his or her own personal style.

For refuge in times of stress, I suggest that every English language arts teacher ought to join and, if possible, attend the conferences of the National Council of Teachers of English (1111 Kenyon Road, Urbana, Illinois 61801) or your state or local affiliate professional organization. (A list of local groups is available from the NCTE at the address above.) The NCTE, it should be added, maintains an excellent list of professional books on topics ranging from censorship to teaching Shakespeare and thus is a good source for up-to-date readings on problem areas.

For a discussion of future directions and priorities for the profession, see *Teaching English: Reflections on the State of the Art,* a collection of essays by distinguished teachers which I compiled on behalf of the Michigan Council of Teachers of English (Rochelle Park: Hayden, 1979). For an in-depth discussion of the interdisciplinary, integrated curriculum, see my *The ABCs of Literacy* (Oxford University Press, 1980).

Selected Bibliography

Alschuler, Alfred, and Tabor, Diane. *Teaching Achievement Motivation.* Middletown, Conn.: Educational Ventures, 1970.

Applebee, Arthur. *A Survey of Teaching Conditions, 1977.* Urbana, Ill.: National Council of Teachers of English, 1978.

Bogojavlensky, Anna Rahnasto, and others. *The Great Learning Book.* Reading, Mass.: Addison-Wesley, 1977.

Botein, Stephen, and others. *Experiments in History Teaching.* Cambridge, Mass.: Danforth Center, 1977.

Braddock, Richard, and others. *Research in Written Composition.* Urbana, Ill.: NCTE, 1963.

Budd, Richard, and Ruben, Brent D. *Interdisciplinary Approaches to Human Communication.* Rochelle Park, N.J.: Hayden, 1979.

Carpenter, Edmund. *Oh, What a Blow That Phantom Gave Me!* New York: Bantam Books, 1974.

Chukovsky, Kornei. *From Two to Five.* Berkeley, Cal.: University of California, 1962.

Creber, J. W. Patrick. *Sense and Sensitivity.* London: University of London Press, 1965.

Crosscup, Richard. *Children and Dramatics.* New York: Scribner's, 1964.

Davis, Kenneth, and Hollowel, John, eds. *Games in the Classroom.* Urbana, Ill.: NCTE, 1978.

Dewey, John. *School and Society.* Chicago: University of Chicago Press, 1956.

Diederich, Daniel, ed. *Teaching About Doublespeak.* Urbana, Ill.: NCTE, 1976.

Dixon, John. *Growth Through English.* Urbana, Ill.: NCTE, 1975.

Donelson, Kenneth, ed. *The Student's Right to Read.* Urbana, Ill.: NCTE, 1972.

Duke, Charles. *Creative Dramatics and English Teaching.* Urbana, Ill.: NCTE, 1974.

Dunning, Stephen, ed. *English for the Junior High Years.* Urbana, Ill.: NCTE, 1969.

Elbow, Peter. *Writing Without Teachers.* New York: Oxford/Galaxy, 1974.

Elgin, Suzette Hayden. *What Is Linguistics?* Englewood Cliffs, N.J.: Prentice-Hall, 1973.

Erickson, Erik. *Childhood and Society.* New York: Berkley, 1976.

Farallones Srapbook. New York: Random House, 1971.

Friedenberg, Edgar. *Coming of Age in America.* New York: Random House, 1963.

Galvin, Kathleen, and Book, Cassandra. *Person to Person.* Skokie, Ill.: National Textbook Company, 1978.

Gardner, John. *Self-Renewal.* New York: Harper & Row, 1964.

Glasser, William. *Schools Without Failure.* New York: Harper & Row, 1969.

Goodman, Paul. *Growing Up Absurd.* New York: Random House, 1960.

Gulley, Halbert E. *Discussion, Conference, and Group Process.* New York: Holt, Rinehart and Winston, 1968.

Hall, Edward. *The Hidden Dimension.* Garden City, N.Y.: Doubleday, 1966.

Hatfield, W. Wilbur, ed. *An Experience Curriculum in English.* Chicago: National Council of Teachers of English, 1935.

Hawley, Robert C. *Value Exploration Through Roleplaying.* Amherst, Mass.: ERA Press, 1974.

Hayakawa, S. I. *Language in Thought and Action.* New York: Harcourt Brace Jovanovich, 1972.

Henry, Mabel Wright. *Creative Experiences in Oral Language.* Urbana, Ill.: NCTE, 1967.

Herndon, James. *How to Survive in Your Native Land.* New York: Simon & Schuster, 1971.

Holt, John. *How Children Learn.* New York: Pitman, 1967.

Illich, Ivan. *DeSchooling Society.* New York: Harper & Row, 1972.

Judy, Stephen. *The ABCs of Literacy.* New York: Oxford University Press, 1980.

Judy, Stephen, and others. *The Creative Word.* New York: Random House, 1973, 1974.

Judy, Stephen, ed. *Teaching English: Reflections on the State of the Art.* Rochelle Park, N.J.: Hayden, 1979.

Judy, Stephen, and Judy, Susan. *The English Teacher's Handbook.* Cambridge, Mass.: Winthrop Publishers, 1979.

Judy, Susan, and Judy, Stephen. *Gifts of Writing.* New York: Scribner's, 1980.

Kirschenbaum, Howard; Simon, Sidney B.; and Napier, Rodney. *"Wad-Ja-Get?" The Grading Game in American Education.* New York: Hart, 1971.

Kortright, Judy. *Teaching Correctness: An Alternative to Grammar.* Detroit, Mich.: Michigan Council of Teachers of English, 1977.

Labov, William. *The Study of Nonstandard English.* Urbana, Ill.: NCTE, 1970.

Macrorie, Ken. *Uptaught.* Rochelle Park, N.J.: Hayden, 1969.

Mager, Robert F. *Preparing Instructional Objectives.* Belmont, Calif.: Fearon-Pitman Publishers, Inc., 1962.

Malmstrom, Jean. *Language in Society.* Rochelle Park, N.J.: Hayden, 1973.

Marshall, Sybil. *An Experiment in Education.* Cambridge, England: Cambridge University Press, 1963.

Martin, Nancy, and others. *Writing and Learning Across the Curriculum.* London: Ward Lock Educational, 1976.

Maxwell, John, and Tovatt, Anthony, eds. *On Writing Behavioral Objectives for English.* Urbana, Ill.: NCTE, 1970.

Miller, James E., Jr., and Judy, Stephen. *Writing in Reality.* New York: Harper & Row, 1978.

Moffett, James, and Wagner, Betty Jane. *Student-Centered Language Arts Cur-*

riculum, K-13. Boston: Houghton Mifflin, 1976.

Morgan, Fred. *Here and Now III.* New York: Harcourt Brace Jovanovich, 1979.

Morrow, James, and Suid, Murray. *Media and Kids.* Rochelle Park, N.J.: Hayden, 1977.

Oliver, Albert. *Maximizing Minicourses.* New York: Teachers College Press, 1978.

Piaget, Jean. *The Language and Thought of the Child.* New York: Humanities Press, 1956.

Pincus, Edward. *A Guide to Filmmaking.* New York: New American Library (Signet), 1971.

Pooley, Robert. *Teaching English Usage.* Champaign, Ill.: National Council of Teachers of English, 1945.

Posner, George, and Rudnitsky, Alan. *Course Design.* New York: Longman, 1978.

Postman, Neil, and Weingartner, Charles. *Linguistics: A Revolution in Teaching.* New York: Dell, 1966.

Postman, Neil, and Weingartner, Charles. *The Soft Revolution.* New York: Dell, 1971.

Postman, Neil, and Weingartner, Charles. *Teaching as a Subversive Activity.* New York: Dell (Delacorte Press), 1969.

Purves, Alan, ed. *How Porcupines Make Love.* Lexington, Mass.: Ginn/Xerox, 1972.

Purves, Alan, and Beach, Richard, eds. *Literature and the Reader.* Urbana, Ill.: NCTE, 1972.

Raths, Louis; Harmin, Merrill; and Simon, Sidney. *Values in Teaching.* Columbus, Ohio: Merrill, 1966.

Rosenblatt, Louise. *Literature as Exploration.* New York: Noble and Noble, 1968.

Rosenblatt, Louise. *The Reader, the Text, and the Poem.* Carbondale, Ill.: Southern Illinois University Press, 1978.

Schrank, Jeffery. *Understanding Mass Media.* Skokie, Ill.: National Textbook Company, 1975.

Sherwin, Stephen. *Four Problems in Teaching English.* Urbana, Ill.: NCTE, 1969.

Shuy, Roger. *Discovering American Dialects.* Urbana, Ill.: NCTE, 1967.

Siks, Geraldine Brain, and Dunnington, Mabel, eds. *Children's Theater and Creative Dramatics.* Seattle, Wash.: University of Washington Press, 1961.

Slade, Peter. *Child Drama.* London: University of London Press, 1957.

Slatoff, Walter. *With Respect to Readers.* Ithaca, N.Y.: Cornell University Press, 1970.

Smith, Frank. *Understanding Reading: A Psycholinguistic Analysis of Reading and Learning to Read.* New York: Holt, Rinehart, and Winston, 1971.

Smitherman, Geneva. *Talkin' and Testifyin'.* New York: Holt, Rinehart, and Winston, 1977.

Spolin, Viola. *Improvisation for the Theater.* Evanston, Ill.: Northwestern University Press, 1964.

Squire, James R., ed. *Response to Literature.* Urbana, Ill.: NCTE, 1968.

Squire, James R., ed. *The Teaching of English: The Seventy-Sixth Yearbook of the National Society for the Study of Education.* Chicago: University of Chicago Press, 1977.

Squire, James R. and Applebee, Roger. *High School English Instruction Today.* Englewood Cliffs, N.J.: Prentice-Hall, 1968.

Stanford, Gene, and Roark, Albert E. *Human Interaction in Education*. Boston: Allyn & Bacon, 1974.

Stratta, Leslie, ed. *Writing*. London: National Association for the Teaching of English, 1966.

Summerfield, Geoffrey. *Topics in English*. London: Batsford, 1965.

Taba, Hilda. *With Perspective on Human Relations*. Washington: American Council on Education, 1955.

The Whole Word Catalogue II. New York: McGraw-Hill, 1975.

Tway, Eileen, ed. *Reading Ladders for Human Relations*. 6th ed. Washington, D.C.: Council on Basic Education, 1980.

Van Allen, R., and Lee, Dorris M. *Learning to Read Through Experience*. Englewood Cliffs, N.J.: Prentice-Hall, 1966.

Way, Brian. *Development Through Drama*. New York: Longman, 1967.

White, Mary Lou. *Adventuring with Books*. Urbana, Ill.: NCTE, 1980.

Wilkinson, Andrew. *Some Aspects of Oracy*. Birmingham, England: Birmingham University Press, 1968.

Wilkinson, Andrew. *The State of Language*. Birmingham, England: Educational Review, 1965.

Yates, Mary Clare; Lamb, Patricia; and Judy, Stephen. *A Puppetry Handbook*. Detroit, Mich.: Michigan Council of Teachers of English, 1979.

Index